A Thousand Years of Persian Rubáiyát

D1603649

Also by Reza Saberi:

The Poems of Hafez (Maryland, 1995)
An English translation of all the ghazals of Hafez.
Impressions and Expressions (Fargo, 1992)
A journal of feelings and thoughts.
Splendor of the Light (Nashville, 1991)
A book about the unity of existence.
The Labyrinth (New York, 1982)
A novel about the adventures of a young Iranian man.
The Pentagon of Wisdom (New York, 1980)
A guide for young adults.
Shabi dar Ruz (Tehran, 1970)
A Persian language novel about an Iranian marriage.

A Thousand Years
of
Persian Rubáiyát

An Anthology of Quatrains from the
Tenth to the Twentieth Century
Along with the Original Persian

Translated into English
by
Reza Saberi

IBEX Publishers
Bethesda, Maryland

One Thousand Years of Persian Rubáiyát
An Anthology of Quatrains from the Tenth to the Twentieth Century
Along with the Original Persian
Translated into English by Reza Saberi
Cover miniature by Hossein Behzad

Manufactured in the United States of America

The paper used in this book meets the minimum requirements of the
American National Standard for Information Services - Permanence of
Paper for Printed Library Materials, ANSI Z39.48-1984

IBEX Publishers, Inc.
Post Office Box 30087
Bethesda, Maryland 20824
Telephone: 301-718-8188
Facsimile: 301-907-8707
www.ibexpub.com

Library of Congress Cataloging-in-Publication Information

A thousand years of Persian rubáiyát : a selection of quatrains from the
tenth to the twentieth century along with the original Persian / translated
into English by Reza Saberi.
p. cm.
Includes bibliographical references and index.
ISBN 1-58814-002-4
1. Persian poetry — Translations into English. 2. Persian poetry.
I. Saberi, Reza, 1941-
PK6449.E5 S2213 2000
891'.55008 — dc21
00-58164

Table of Contents

Introduction

Rubáiyát is the plural of *rubái*, meaning quatrain. A *rubái* is a poem consisting of four lines, the first, second, and fourth (and sometimes also the third) of which rhyme together. According to the method used in this book for the transliteration of Persian words, the word should have been spelt *robâiyyât* (*o* as in "go," *â* as in "father," *i* as in "inn") the plural of *robâi*. However, since the form *Rubáiyát* is better known in the West, an exception is made to the rule.

Most Persian language poets have tried their hands at the *rubái* form, but the bulk of Persian poetry is in other verse forms, such as *qasida, ghazal,* and *masnavi.* Some poets wrote only a few *rubáis*, which are often listed at the end of their divans. Some never did. Even so, a comprehensive collection of Persian rubáiyát can add to several volumes. I have selected quatrains from 106 poets covering more than one thousand years of Persian poetry. Almost all the quatrains composed in Persian are beautiful and meaningful and worth translating, which means the reader should expect more translated rubáiyát in future.

In order to appreciate and enjoy any poetry completely, one must read it in its original version. Even in the original, the reader must have a good command of that language, because poetry is the most sophisticated and refined form of expression in every language. It is possible to master one or two or perhaps a few languages, but no more. Therefore, those readers who are interested in the poetry of different languages must settle for less than complete enjoyment which comes only from the original language.

The above is especially true about the Persian poetry, which has been refined and perfected through its long history of development. Persian poems, except some which were composed in recent decades, have rhythm, rhyme, meter, and many metaphorical and figurative terms, which are often hard to duplicate in translation. However, readers can still obtain enough enjoyment from the translation of Persian poetry provided that they do not concretize the figurative language and that they understand the philosophy behind the poetry.

Many of the Persian poets are mystical poets. They are known as Sufis and their mysticism is known as Sufism. Although the words Sufi and Sufism are better known in the West, some Persian scholars prefer the words *âref* and *erfân* in describing the mystical poets and poetry of Iran. An *âref* is a person who has obtained *erfân*, gnosis, mystical or divine knowledge, knowledge of mysteries or spiritual truths.

Sufism is an Irano-Islamic mysticism with some elements of India's Advaita Vedanta monism, and its basic tenets are not so different from the mysticism of other cultures. Sufism, and in fact any form of mysticism, is based upon the perennial philosophy of the oneness and wholeness of being, the philosophy of the unity of existence. All that exist are One, and this One in Sufism is God who transcends all forms and images and concepts, who is the Ultimate Reality, free from all the limitations of space and time, and who is the origin and destination of the whole existence.

The Sufi's approach to this Transcendent Ultimate Reality is by way of love. Love, which is the central theme of Sufism and Persian poetry, is closely related to the notion of beauty. In the eye of a Sufi, this whole universe is the manifestation of God, who is the source of all beauty and love. Although every beautiful object can inspire love to a Sufi, nothing is worthy of being loved for its own sake, because everything is but an ephemeral image of one eternal beloved. In Sufism, all forms of love lead to the love of God. It is the love of God that inspires the love of nature and humans. God is the Ultimate Beloved and the Sufi the lover, and the only goal of the lover is union with the beloved.

Union in love means disappearance of all kinds of distinctions and separateness between the lover and the beloved. The two become one. This happens when the finite self of the Sufi merges with the infinite Self of his beloved. Then all that remains is the beloved.

To express this divine love, the mystical poets of Iran often use the figurative terms of fire, light, and wine. Love is a fire that consumes and annihilates the lover. It is a light that radiates from the face of God and illuminates the soul of man and the whole world. It is a light that eliminates the darkness of ignorance and suffering. Love is a wine that intoxicates and enraptures the lover to a point where he is unconscious of everything except his beloved.

Iranian poets have expressed this mystical love by means of many symbols, paradigms, images, and metaphors. Among their most favorite imagery are the attraction of a moth to the candle, a nightingale to the rose, a drinker to the sâqi, and everyone's love of youth's beauty. Every form of being — a child, a boy, a girl, a man, a woman, a flower, a tree, a mountain, a lake, a forest, the moon, the sun, the planets and stars, in a word, everything that exists upon the Earth and in heavens — is beautiful. If man sees ugliness in some forms of nature, it is because his prejudices, biases, ignorance, bad education, or insensitivity paints an ugly picture for him and blinds him to the beauty which is all-pervading. If he opens his eyes, changes his attitude, rises above his ordinary consciousness to God-consciousness or superconsciousness, he will surely see beauty everywhere.

The poetical expressions of Sufi poets often transcend the limits of physical, material, earthly and ordinary loves and lead the reader to an ethereal, heavenly, mystical and divine love. To miss this point is to miss the meaning of the greatest part of Persian poetry. Without an appreciation of the mystical dimension of Persian poetry, the reader is left with some poetical exaggerations of a passion for an unknown and unavailable beautiful beloved who may be either male or female, or with some unreal and deceptive statements about wine and drunkenness.

Fortunately most admirers of Persian poetry know that the love expressed in the majority of poems is not limited to physical desire nor is wine to the intoxicating drink made from grapes. Most mystic poets of Iran have had families and normal sexual lives, and their apparent exaggerations of love are not indicative of their sexual privation or their excessive carnal desire but of their deeper appreciation of love and beauty. Some poets have expressly stated in their poetry that by love they do not mean physical and emotional love nor by wine the drink made from grapes. For example, Nezâmi, who often used the terms "wine" and "drunkenness" in his poetry, states in one of his poems that never in his life did his lips touch wine. In short, the reader is warned against concretizing the symbols and metaphors of Persian poetry, which have far broader and deeper meanings than their physical references.

The mystic poets of Iran, some of whom are represented in this selection, exalt beauty and love to the highest degree. Their masterly use of imagery, their expressions of profound feelings and sentiments, and their very skilful use of rhythm and meter have resulted in the creation of one of the richest and sweetest literatures of the world.

With this brief introduction, the reader is now invited to enter the rose garden of Persian poetry, listen to the rapturous songs of the nightingales of this paradise of beauty, and become intoxicated with the wine of love.

—Reza Saberi,
Fargo, North Dakota

Sources

Divân-e Anvari, ed. M.T. Modarres Razavi, Sherkat-e Enteshârât-e Elmi va Farhangi, Tehran, 1944.

Divân-e Hâtef-e Isfahâni, ed. Vahid Dastgerdi, Nashriyyât-e Majalle-ye Armaghân, Tehran, 1967.

Divân-e Kâmel-e Shams-e Tabrizi, ed. B. Fruzânfar, Enteshârât-e Javidân, Tehran, 1990.

Divân-e Sanâi-ye Ghaznavi, ed. Modarres Razavi, Third Printing, Ketâbkhâne-ye Sanâi, Tehran, 1984.

Divân-e Shâh Ne'matullâh Vali, (Introduction by Said Nafisi, Notes by M. Darvish), Seventh Printing, Ketâbfrushi Mohammad Elmi, Tehran, 1994.

Hâfez, ed. Qazvini-Ghani, Second Printing, Enteshârât-e Asâtir, Tehran, 1990.

Kolliyyât-e Sa'di, ed. Mohammad Ali Frughi, Ketâbfrushi Musa Elmi, Tehran.

Rubâi Nâme, ed. Sayyed Ahmad Beheshti Shirâzi, First Edition, Enteshârât-e Rozane, Tehran, 1994. (Note: This book has been my main source in the present selection of quatrains and I am very grateful to its editor for adding this valuable book to the treasury of Persian poetry.)

Rubâiyyât-e Khayyam, ed. Mohammad Ali Frughi, Enteshârât-e Amir Kabir, Tehran, 1966.

Shâere Âyenahâ, Dr. M. R. Shafii Kadkani, Enteshârât-e Âgâh, Tehran.

Transliteration of Persian Words:

a	fat	**g**	get
â	father	**h**	hat
e	ten	**j**	jet
i	inn	**k**	kit
o	go	**s**	sea
u	do	**ch**	church
ay	say	**sh**	she
c	cat	**kh**	as *ch* in German Nacht
gh	like a soft g	**q**	like a guttural g.

The sounds of **kh**, **gh**, and **q** do not exist in English.

Any letter written twice is pronounced twice. For example, Mohammad is pronounced Moham-mad; Allâh, Al-lâh.

In any vowel combination, each vowel is pronounced separately. For example, Moezzi is pronounced Mo-ez-zi (o as in go, e as in ten); Abusaid, Abu-sa-id (a as in at, i as in ring).

H is always pronounced as in "hat," except in gh, ch, sh, kh. For example, Ahmad is pronounced Ah-mad (A as in at, h as in hat), Mahasti as Ma-hasti.

' indicates a pause after pronouncing the preceding letter, as in Sa'di, which is pronounced Sa-di.

The only exception made to the above system in this book is for the word *rubáiyát*, which was too popular to change.

Chapter One
10th Century C.E.
4th Century Hejri

جعفر رودکی
(۳۲۹ هجری قمری)

۱

بر هر رگ جان صد آرزو ماند گره
چون کار دلم ز زلف او ماند گره
امید ز گریه بود افسوس افسوس
کان هم شب وصل در گلو ماند گره

Ja'far Rudaki
(d. 941 C.E.)

1

Since my heart's affair with her tress remained knotted,
A hundred desires in each vein of mine remained knotted.
My hope for relief was in crying. Alas, alas! That, too,
The night of union, in my throat remained knotted.

٢

ای از گل سرخ رنگ ربوده و بو

رنگ از پی رخ رخ ربوده بو از پی مو

گلرنگ شود چو روی شویی همه جو

مشگین گردد چو مو فشانی همه کو

2

O you, who have stolen the color and scent of the rose,
The color for your face and the scent for your hair,
You wash your face, and the whole stream becomes rosy,
You let your hair down and the whole lane becomes musky.

٣

دل سیر نگرددت ز بیدادگری

چشم آب نگرددت چو در من نگری

این طرفه که دوستتر ز جانت دارم

با آنکه ز صد هزار دشمن بتری

3

Never does your heart have enough of cruelty.
Never do your eyes water when you look at me.
Though you are worse than a hundred thousand enemies,
How strange that I love you more than my own soul!

۴

هان تشنه جگر مجوی زین باغ ثمر

بیدستانیست این ریاض به دو در

بیهوده ممان که باغبانت به قفاست

چون خاک نشسته گیر و چون باد گذر

4

O desirous one, seek not any fruit in this orchard!
This two-portalled garden is a willow-grove.
Linger not in vain, for the gardener is after you.
Regard it like the settled dust and the blowing wind.

۵

با داده قناعت کن و آزاد بزی

در بند تکلف مشو آزاد بزی

در به ز خودی نظر مکن غصه مخور

در کم ز خودی نظر کن و شاد بزی

5

Be content with what is given and freely live.
Be not fettered by formalities and freely live.
Do not look at those better off than you and grieve.
Look at those worse off than you and happily live.

۶

با آنکه دلم از غم هجرت خون است

شادی به غم توام ز غم افزون است

اندیشه کنم هر دم و گویم به خیال

هجرانش چنین است وصالش چون است

6

Though my heart bleeds in the grief of separation,
My joy exceeds my suffering in this grief.
I ponder every moment and wonder in my imagination:
If his separation is like this, how will his union be?

۷

بی روی تو خورشید جهانسوز مباد

هم بی تو چراغ عالم افروز مباد

با وصل تو کس چو من بد آموز مباد

روزی که ترا نبینم آن روز مباد

7

Besides your face, let there be no world-blazing sun.
Besides you, let there be no world-illumining light.
May no one be spoiled like me with your presence.
May the day I should not see you never be a day!

٨

جز حادثه هرگز طلبم کس نکند
یک پرسش گرم جز تبم کس نکند
ور جان بلب آیدم بجز مردم چشم
یک قطره آب بر لبم کس نکند

8

None seeks me out except misfortune.
None makes a warm inquiry of me except fever.
And if my soul rises to my lips,
None offers a drop of water to me except my eyes.

٩

زلفش بکشی شب دراز اندازد
ور بگشایی چنگل باز اندازد
ور پیچ و خمش ز یکدگر بگشایند
دامن دامن مشک طرار اندازد

9

If you let her hair down, a long night spreads out.
And if you open it, an eagle's claws spread out.
If you untangle its curls and its twists,
Lapful after lapful of musk spread out.

١٠

نامت شنوم دل ز فرح زنده شود
حال من از از اقبال تو فرخنده شود
وز غیر تو هر جا سخن آید به میان
خاطر بهزار غم پراکنده شود

10

I hear your name, my heart is revived with delight.
You turn your face to me, I am overfilled with joy.
If any word about other than you is utterred anywhere,
My mind becomes agitated by a thousand sorrows

۱۱

چون کشته بینی ام دو لب گشته فراز
از جان تهی این قالب فرسوده به آز
بر بالینم نشین و می گوی به ناز
کی کشته ترا من و پشیمان شده باز

11

When you find me dead with gaping lips,
My body emptied of spirit and wearied of craving,
Sit down at my bedside and say with all your charm,
"O you whom I killed, I am full of regret and repentance."

۱۲

در جستن آن نگار پر کینه و جنگ
گشتیم سراپای جهان با دل تنگ
شد دست ز کار و رفت پا از رفتار
این بسکه بسر زدیم و آن بسکه بسنگ

12

In search of that warlike and rancorous sweetheart,
I roamed the whole world with a doleful heart.
So many times my foot hit the rocks it stopped walking!
So many times my hand beat my head it stopped working.

شهید بلخی
(۳۲۵ هجری قمری)

۱
دوشم گذر افتاد به ویرانه طوس
دیدم جغدی نشسته جای طاووس
گفتم چه خبر داری از این ویرانه
گفتا خبر اینست که افسوس افسوس

Shahid Balkhi
(d. 937 C.E.)

1
Last night I happened to pass by the ruins of Tus
And saw an owl sitting in place of a peacock.
I asked, "What news do you have about these ruins?"
It answered, "The news is: Alas! Alas!"

ابونصر فارابی
(۳۳۹-۲۳۵ هجری قمری)

۱

اسرار وجود خام و ناپخته بماند
و آن گوهر بس شریف ناسفته بماند
هر کس بدلیل عقل چیزی گفتند
آن نکته که اصل بود ناگفته بماند

Abunasr Fârâbi
(869-951 C.E.)

1
Vague and unrefined did the secrets of existence remain.
Unpierced did that highly-revered pearl remain.
Each person said something according to his reason.
Yet untold did the point which was of essence remain.

ابولقاسم فردوسی

(۳۲۹-۴۱۱ هجری قمری)

۱

دوش از سر لطف بنده پروردن خویش

بنمود طریق مردمی کردن خویش

جرمم همه عفو کرد و دستم بگرفت

خندان خندان فکند در گردن خویش

Abulqâsem Ferdowsi
(941-1021 C.E.)

1

Last night, favoring his servants with kindness,
He showed the way of humaneness:
He forgave all my faults, took my arm, and,
Blossoming with laughter, placed it around his neck.

۲

تا چند نهی بر دل خود غصه و درد

تا جمع کنی سیم سپید و زر زرد

زان پیش که گردد نفس گرم تو سرد

با دوست بخور که دشمنت خواهد خورد

2

How much pain and grief to your heart will you deliver,
So that you gather yellow gold and white silver?
Before your warm breath becomes cold,
Spend them with your friend, else your enemy will.

۳

غم در دل من در آمد و شاد برفت
باز آمد و رخت خویش بنهاد و برفت
گفتم به تکلف که زمانی بنشین
بنشست و کنون رفتنش از یاد برفت

3

Sorrow came into my heart and joyfully out it went.
It came back, dropped its chattels, and again went.
I said, as a formality, "Sit down for a minute."
It sat down, and then departure out of its mind went.

دقیقی طوسی
(۳۶۸ هجری قمری)

۱

چشم تو که فتنه در جهان خیزد از او
لعل تو که آب خضر می ریزد از او
کردند تن مرا چنان خوار که باد
می آید و گرد و خاک می بیزد از او

Daqiqi Tusi
(d. 979 C.E.)

1

Your eyes, from which the riots of the world arise,
Your ruby lips, from which the water of life pours,
Made my body so degraded that
The wind comes and sifts dust from it.

فرخی سیستانی
(۴۲۹ هجری قمری)

١

یا ما سر خصم را بکوبیم بسنگ
یا او سر ما به دار سازد آونگ
القصه در این زمانه پر نیرنگ
یک کشته بنام به که صد زنده به ننگ

Farrokhi Sistâni
(d. 1038 C.E.)

1

Either I will knock the enemy's head on the rock
Or he will make my head dangle from the gallows.
In short, in this treacherous world, one dead with honor
Is better than a hundred living with shame.

٢

تا در طلب دوست همی بشتابم
عمرم بکران رسید و من در خوابم
گیرم که وصال دوست در خواهم یافت
این عمر گذشته را کجا در یابم

2

While I dashed about in search of the friend,
My life came to an end unawares.
Where shall I find the life which is lost,
Even if I be united with the friend?

٣

زاغان به چمن فتنه برانگیخته اند
خوش دستانان زباغ بگریخته اند
بر ماتم بلبلان درختان رزان
دستار سپید برف بر پیخته اند

3

Kites have raised riot in the meadow
And nightingales have escaped from the garden.
Vine trees, mourning for the nightingales,
Have wrapped [their heads with] white turbans of snow.

عنصری
(۴۳۱ هجری قمری)

۱

گفتم صنما دلم ترا جویان است
گفتا که لبم درد ترا درمان است
گفتم که همیشه از منت هجران است
گفتا که پری ز آدمیان پنهان است

Hasan Onsori
(d. 1040 C.E.)

1

I said, "O my idol, my heart aspires for you."
She said, "My lip is the remedy of your pain."
I said, "But you are always far from me."
She said, "Fairies hide from humans."

٢

گفتم که چرا چو ابر خون بارانم
گفت از پی آنکه من گل خندانم
گفتم که چرا بی تو چنین پژمانم
گفت از پی آنکه تو تنی من جانم

2

I asked, "Why do I rain blood like a cloud?"
She replied, "Because I am a blooming rose."
I asked, "Why am I so dejected without you?"
She answered, "Because you are the body, I am the soul."

٣

چون مهره بروی تخت نردیم همه
گاهی جمعیم و گاه فردیم همه
سرگشته چرخ لاجوردیم همه
تا در نگرید درنوردیم همه

3

Like pawns on a backgammon board we all are.
Sometimes together sometimes separate we all are.
Bewildered by the blue wheel we all are.
Before we notice, huddled together we all are.

Chapter Two
11th Century C.E.
5th Century Hejri

ابن سینا

(۴۲۸-۳۷۰ هجری قمری)

۱

پرسید یکی ز من که بیچون چون است

بیچون ز گمان و وصف ما بیرون است

ما را سخن از چون و چرایش نرسد

بیچون داند که حال بیچون چون است

Ibn Sinâ
(981-1037 C.E.)

1

Someone asked me, "What is the Absolute?"

Beyond our imagination and description is the Absolute.

We cannot speak of its *what* and *why*.

Only the Absolute knows the description of the Absolute.

۲

کفر چو منی گزاف و آسان نبود

محکمتر از ایمان من ایمان نبود

در دهر چو من یکی و او هم کافر

پس در همه دهر یک مسلمان نبود

2

The blasphemy of a person like me is not an easy matter.
No faith can be stronger than mine.
There is only one like me in the world, and he is an infidel.
So there is not even one Muslim in the whole world.

۳

با این دو سه نادان که چنین میدانند

از جهل که دانای جهان ایشانند

خر باش که این طایفه از فرط خری

هر کو نه خر است کافرش می خوانند

3

With these two or three ignorant ones, who think,
In their ignorance they are the learned of the world,
Be an ass. For these people are so asinine that
Whoever is not an ass, they call him an infidel.

۴

دل گرچه در این بادیه بسیار شتافت

یک موی ندانست ولی موی شکافت

اندر دل من هزار خورشید بتافت

و آخر بکمال ذره ای راه نیافت

4

Though my heart dashed about in this desert far and wide,
And learned to split hair, it could not understand a hair.
A thousand suns illuminated my heart,
Yet I could not comprehend the perfection of a particle.

۵

می حاصل عمر جاودانیست بده
سرمایهٔ عمر جاودانیست بده
سوزنده چو آتش است لیکن غم را
سازنده چو آب زندگانیست بده

5

Wine is the fruit of immortal life, give it!
It is the capital of eternal life, give it!
It burns like fire, but to sorrow,
It is like the water of life, give it!

۶

ایکاش بدانمی که من کیستمی
سرگشته به عالم از پی چیستمی
گر مقبلم آسوده و خوش زیستمی
ورنه به هزار دیده بگریستمی

6

I wish I knew who I am,
Bewildered in this world, in pursuit of what I am.
If blessed, I will live happily and comfortably.
If not, weeping with a thousand eyes I am.

۷

ای در دو نفس عمر تو افزاینده
بادی است نفس شونده و آینده
بر باد نهاده‌ای بنای همه عمر
بر باد کجا بود بنا پاینده

7

O you, whose life by two breaths is enduring,
A breath is a wind, by coming and going enduring.
Upon the wind is laid the foundation of your life.
How can a building upon the wind be enduring?

٨

عشاق برآمدند پیرامن گل

یکباره زدند دست در دامن گل

وز بس که همی کشند پیراهن گل

آنگه به هزار شاخ شد بر تن گل

8

Lovers came out and surrounded the rose,
And suddenly took hold of the skirt of the rose.
So much they pulled on the garment of the rose
It tore into a thousand shreds on the body of the rose.

٩

آتش چو فکند باد در خرمن گل

بر خاک چکید آب پیراهن گل

ای ساقی می دست تو و دامن گل

وی دختر رز خون تو در گردن گل

9

When the wind set fire to the harvest of the rose,
Water dripped down from the garment of the rose.
O Sâqi of wine, take hold of the skirt of the rose.
O daughter of vine, your blood is on the head of the rose.

١٠

ماییم نهفته گریه در خنده چو گل

مرده به دمی و از دمی زنده چو گل

خود را بهمه میان در افکنده چو گل

واندر همه مجمعی پراکنده چو گل

10

We have concealed weeping in laughter like the rose.
We are dead and revived by a breath like the rose.
We have cast ourselves in the center of all like the rose.
And in all gathering, we are scattered like the rose.

١١

بگسست فلک چو عقد در دانه صبح
پر در خوشاب کردپیمانه صبح
او نیز چو من اسیر و شیدا گشته
کای عاشق شامگاه و دیوانه صبح

11

When the sky broke the pearl-necklace of the morning,
With lustrous pearls it filled the bowl of the morning.
Even the sky has become captured and frenzied like me,
O lover of the night and mad after the morning.

ابوالحسن خرقانی
(۴۲۱ هجری قمری)

١

مست توام از باده و جام آزادم
صید توام از دانه و دام آزادم
مقصود من از کعبه و بتخانه تویی
ورنه من از این هر دو مقام آزادم

Abulhasan Kharqâni
(d. 1034 C.E.)

1

Drunk by you, from the goblet and wine I am free.
Captured by you, from the seed and snare I am free.
You are my goal in the Kaaba and the idol-temple,
Otherwise, from both of these places I am free.

۲

اسرار ازل را نه تو دانی و نه من
این حرف معما نه تو خوانی و نه من
هست از پس پرده گفتگوی من و تو
چون پرده بیفتد نه تو مانی و نه من

2

The primordial secrets neither you know nor I.
The words of the puzzle neither you can read nor I.
Your discourse and mine are behind the curtain.
When the curtain falls, neither you remain nor I.

ابوالفرج رونی
(۵۰۵ هجری قمری)

۱

تا یک نفس از حیات باقیست مرا
در سر هوس شراب و ساقیست مرا
کاری که من اختیار کردم این بود
باقی همه کار اتفاقی است مرا

Abulfaraj Runi
(d. 1112 C.E.)

1

As long as one breath of life remains for me,
Desire for wine and Sâqi will endure for me.
The work I myself chose was this.
All other works were fortuitous for me.

۲

چون است که عشق اول از تن خیزد

زو بر دل و جان هزار شیون خیزد

آری بخورد زنگ همی آهن را

هر چند که زنگ هم ز آهن خیزد

2

How is it that love first from the body arises,
Then much lamentation from it to the heart arises?
It is true that the rust eats the iron,
But from the iron itself the rust arises.

۳

در عشق کسی که از زیان اندیشد

به زان نبود که ترک آن اندیشد

در عالم عاشقی کسی را نرسد

کز عشق زند لاف و ز جان اندیشد

3

If you ever think of loss in love,
It is best you never think about love.
In the world of love, it is not right
To think of one's life and brag about love.

ابوسعید ابوالخیر
(۳۵۷-۴۴۰ هجری قمری)

١

جسمم همه اشک گشت و چشمم بگریست
در عشق تو بی جسم همی باید زیست
از من اثری نماند این عشق ز چیست
چون من همه معشوق شدم عاشق کیست

Abusaid Abulkhayr
(968-1049 C.E.)

1

My body turned to tears and my eyes shed them.
One must live without body in your love.
No trace remained of me. Of what is this love?
Since I became the beloved completely, who is the lover?

٢

در دیده بجای خواب آب است مرا
زیرا که بدیدنت شتاب است مرا
گویند بخواب تا به خوابش بینی
ای بیخبران چه جای خواب است مرا

2

There is water in place of sleep in my eyes.
So impatient that I am for seeing you.
They tell me to sleep so that I see you in my dream,
Unaware that there is no room to sleep for me?

٣

دل جز رهٔ عشق تو نپوید هرگز
جان جز سخن عشق نگوید هرگز
صحرای دلم عشق تو شورستان کرد
تا مهر کسی در او نروید هرگز

3

My heart never walks except the road of your love.
My soul never speaks except the word of your love.
Your love changed the plain of my heart into a salt-marsh
So that no other person's love may ever grow in it.

۴

دل جای تو شد وگرنه پر خون کنمش
در دیده تویی وگرنه جیحون کنمش
امید وصال تست جانرا ورنه
از تن به هزار حیله بیرون کنمش

4

My heart became your place, else I would fill it with blood.
You are in my eye, else I would make it like the Oxus.
My soul has hope for your union, or else
I would drive it out of my body with a thousand tricks.

۵

اندر طلب یار چو مردانه شدم
اول قدم از وجود بیگانه شدم
او علم نمی شنید لب بر بستم
او عقل نمی خرید دیوانه شدم

5

When I ventured into the search of the beloved,
I became a stranger to existence at the first step.
He would not care for knowledge. I closed my lips.
He would not buy reason. I became mad.

۶

از بیم رقیب طوف کویت نکنم
وز طعنهٔ خلق گفت و گویت نکنم
لب بستم و از پای نشستم اما
این نتوانم که آرزویت نکنم

6

Afraid of the rival, I do not go around your street.
Afraid of people's taunt, I do not speak with you.
I close my lips and sit down,
But I cannot help desiring you.

۷

از واقعه ای ترا خبر خواهم کرد
و آنرا به دو حرف مختصر خواهم کرد
با عشق تو در خاک نهان خواهم شد
با مهر تو سر ز خاک بر خواهم کرد

7

Let me inform you of a certain event,
And summarize it in two lines:
I will hide in the earth with your love
And rise from the earth with your love.

۸

ما را بجز این زبان زبانی دگر است
جز دوزخ و فردوس مکانی دگر است
قلاشی و عاشقی سرمایهٔ ماست
قرایی و زاهدی جهانی دگر است

8

I have a language other than this.
I have a place other than heaven and hell.
Being in love and drunkenness are my possessions.
Reading the Koran and asceticism are other than this.

۹

بر دارم دل گر از جهان فرمایی
بر هم زنم ار سود و زیان فرمایی
بنشینم اگر بر سر آتش گویی
بر خیزم اگر از سر جان فرمایی

9

I will take my heart off the world if you command.
I will mix up profit and loss if you command.
I will sit on fire if you say so.
I will surrender my soul if you command.

۱۰

راهٔ تو به هر قدم که پویند خوش است
وصل تو به هر سبب که جویند خوش است
روی تو به هر دیده که بینند نکوست
نام تو به هر زبان که گویند خوش است

10

With any gait they walk your path, it is good.
By any means they seek your union, it is good.
With any eye they see your face, it is good.
In any language they utter your name, it is good.

۱۱

ای روی تو مهر عالم آرای همه
وصل تو شب و روز تمنای همه
گر با دگران به ز منی وای بمن
ور با همه کس مثل منی وای همه

11

O you, whose face is the world-decorating sun of all,
Day and night your union is the desire of all.
If you are better with others than with me, woe is me.
And if you are with all as you are with me, woe is all.

۱۲

در کوی تو می دهند جانی به جوی

جانی چه بود که کاروانی به جوی

از وصل تو یک جو به جهانی ارزد

زین جنس که ماییم جهانی به جوی

12

In your street, one life is sold for a barley-corn.
Nay, there a caravan of lives is worth a barley-corn.
With your union, a barley-corn is worth a world.
The way we are, a world is worth a barley-corn.

۱۳

دل داغ تو دارد ارنه بفروختمی

در دیده تویی و گرنه می دوختمی

دل منزل تست ورنه روزی صد بار

در پیش تو چون سپند می سوختمی

13

My heart has your brand, otherwise I would sell it.
You are present in my eye, or else I would sew it.
My heart is your abode, or else, like rue,
I would burn it before you a hundred times a day.

۱۴

دل کرد بسی نگاه در دفتر عشق

جز روت ندید هیچ رو در خور عشق

چندان که رخت حسن نهد بر سر حسن

شوریده دلم عشق نهد بر سر عشق

14

For long did my heart gaze at the book of love.
And saw no face but yours worthy of love.
Just as your face lays beauty over beauty,
So does my frenzied heart lay love over love.

۱۵

از باد صبا دلم چو بوی تو گرفت

بگذاشت مرا و جستجوی تو گرفت

اکنون ز من خسته نمی آرد یاد

بوی تو گرفته بود خوی تو گرفت

15

When my heart caught your scent from the zephyr,
It left me and went looking for you.
Now it no longer recalls the weary me.
First it caught your scent, and now your habit.

۱۶

پرسید یکی ز من که معشوق تو کیست

گفتم که فلانی است مقصود تو چیست

بنشست و به های های بر من بگریست

کز دست چنین کسی تو چون خواهی زیست

16

Someone asked me who my beloved was.
I named a certain person and asked the reason.
He sat down and cried loudly for me, saying,
"How are you going to save your life from such a person?"

بابا کوهی
(۴۴۲ هجری قمری)

۱

بی آتش عشق کار خام است ای دل

هر دل که نسوخت ناتمام است ای دل

می سوز شب و روز چو پروانه و شمع

زلف و رخ یار صبح و شام است ای دل

Bâbâ Kuhi
(d. 1051 C.E.)

1

Without love's fire, the work is undone, my dear.
Any heart not consumed [by love] is imperfect, my dear.
Burn like the moth and candle day and night.
The beloved's face and tress are day and night, my dear.

۲

جامی ز شراب ارغوان می طلبم

وین باده ز ساقیان جان می طلبم

تا با می و نقل باشم از لطف شما

یک بوسه از آن لب و دهان می طلبم

2

A goblet of purple wine, I desire.
And this wine from the Sâqis of life, I desire.
If you wish to favor me with wine and comfit,
One kiss from those lips and mouth, I desire.

٣

ما روز ازل عاشق و مست آمده ایم
تا دور ابد جام بدست آمده ایم
گر عاشق و مست و می پرستم بینی
عیبم مکن از روز الست آمده ایم

3

Since the Primordial Day, lover and drunk I have come.
With a goblet in hand till eternity I have come.
If you find me a lover, a drunkard, and a wine-worshipper;
Blame me not, for from the beginning thus I have come.

۴

هر جا که دلی است خونفشان می بینم
دیوانهٔ زلف مهوشان می بینم
آن ذات یقین که در دو عالم فرد است
در دیدهٔ پاک مهوشان می بینم

4

Wherever there is a heart, spewing blood I see it.
Crazed for the tress of the moon-faced ones, I see it.
That certain Essence which is one in both worlds,
In the innocent look of the moon-faced ones, I see it.

خواجه عبدالله انصاری

(۳۹۶-۴۸۱ هجری قمری)

۱

گر از پی شهوت و هوا خواهی رفت

از من خبرت که بینوا خواهی رفت

بنگر که که ای و از کجا آمده ای

می دان که چه میکنی کجا خواهی رفت

Khâja Abdullâh Ansâri
(1006-1089 C.E.)

1

If after lust and carnal desire you are going,
Let me warn you, after misery you are going.
See where you are and where you have come from!
Know what you are doing and where you are going!

۲

در عشق تو من بیدل و بیجان شده ام

وز بهر تو چون زلف تو پیچان شده ام

نی نی غلطم کنون که از قوت عشق

بگذشته ام از دو کون جانان شده ام

2

In your love, without heart and soul I have become.
For your sake, twisted like your hair I have become.
No, no. I am wrong. Now that by the power of love
I have surpassed both worlds, the beloved I have become.

۳

هر دل که طواف کرد گرد گرد در عشق
هم خسته شود در آخر از خنجر عشق
این نکته نوشته ایم بر دفتر عشق
سر دوست ندارد آنکه دارد سر عشق

3

Any heart that goes around the door of love
Will finally be wounded by the sword of love.
This subtlety has been written in the book of love:
He who has love in his head does not love his head.

۴

دی آمدم و نیامد از من کاری
و امروز ز من گرم نشد بازاری
فردا بروم بی خبر از اسراری
نا آمده به بودی از این بسیاری

4

I came yesterday and did nothing,
And today no market grew brisk by me.
I will go tomorrow, unaware of any mysteries.
Had I not come, it would have been better than all these.

۴

در عشق تو گه مست و گهی پست شوم
وز یاد تو گه نیست گهی هست شوم
در پستی و مستی ار نگیری دستم
یکبارگی ای نگار از دست شوم

5

In your love, sometimes I am high, sometimes low.
In your remembrance, now I exist, now I do not.
If you did not hold my hand in agony and ecstasy,
I would suddenly go out of existence, my love.

۶

خون شد جگرم ز غصهٔ خویش مرا
از بیم رهی که هست در پیش مرا
هرگز نرسد به نوش توحید دلم
تا کژدم نفس می زند نیش مرا

6

My grief made my heart bleed,
Fearing the road that is ahead of me.
My heart will never attain the honey of unity
As long as the scorpion of concupiscence stings me.

۷

من بندهٔ عاصیم رضای تو کجاست
تاریک دلم نور و ضیای تو کجاست
ما را تو بهشت اگر به طاعت بخشی
آن بیع بود لطف و عطای تو کجاست

7

I am a disobedient slave, where is your acquiescence?
I am dark in the heart, where is your light and radiance?
If you grant me the paradise for obedience,
That is a trade. Where is your grace and munificence?

۸

مقصود دل و مراد جانی عشق است
سرمایهٔ عمر جاودانی عشق است
آن عشق بود کزو بقا یافته خضر
یعنی که حیات جاودانی عشق است

8

My heart's goal and my soul's aim is love.
The capital of immortal life is love.
It was love that gave immortality to Khezr.
That is to say, the eternal life is love.

٩

جز عشق تو در ملک دلم شاه مباد

وز راز من و تو خلق آگاه مباد

کوته نشود عشق توام زین دل ریش

دستم ز سر زلف تو کوتاه مباد

9

May there be no king in my heart's country but your love.
May the people never know the secret between you and me.
Your love never fails to reach my wounded heart.
May that my hand never fail to reach your tress.

١٠

با شمع رخت دمی چو دمساز شوم

پروانه مستمند جانباز شوم

وآن روز کزین قفس بباید پرداخت

چون شهبازی بدست شه باز شوم

10

If I see the candle of your face for a moment,
I will be like a needy and self-sacrificing moth.
And the day I have to leave this cage,
I shall go back, like a royal falcon, to the king's hand.

امیر معزی
(۵۱۸ هجری قمری)

۱

با لشگر عشق تو مباهات خوش است
با حلقهٔ زلف تو مناجات خوش است
شطرنج که در عشق تو بازیم همی
ما برد نخواهیم که شهمات خوش است

Amir Moezzi
(d. 1124 C.E.)

1

To take pride in the army of your love is good.
To pray before the ringlet of your tress is good.
In the chess-game I play with your love,
I do not wish to win. There to be checkmated is good.

۲

گر نور مه و روشنی شمع تراست
پس سوزش و کاهش من از بهر چراست
گر شمع تویی مرا چرا باید سوخت
ور ماه تویی مرا چرا باید کاست

2

If the moon's light and the candle's are yours,
Why then are the burning and the waning mine?
If *you* are the candle, why should *I* burn?
If *you* are the moon, why should *I* wane?

۳

شاها اثر صبوح کاری عجب است
نازد به صبوح هر که شادی طلب است
باده بهمه وقت طرب را سبب است
لیکن به صبوح کیمیای طرب است

3

O king, the morning wine has a wonderful effect.
Anyone who seeks pleasure endears the morning wine.
Wine is always the cause of pleasure.
However, in the morning, it is the elixir of pleasure.

۴

دلها همه در زلف تو آویخته باد
جانها همه از طبع تو آمیخته باد
هر شور که در جهان برانگیزد چرخ
آن شور ز جعد زلفت انگیخته باد

4

Let all the hearts hang from your tress.
Let all the souls blend with your nature.
Any frenzy that the world incites,
Let it be incited by the curls of your tress.

۵

هر شب که وصال یار دلبر باشد
شب زورق و ماه باد صرصر باشد
وآن شب که فراق آن سمنبر باشد
شب کشتی و آفتاب لنگر باشد

5

Any night there is union with that heart-ravishing beloved,
The night is a boat and the moon a hurricane.
Any night there is separation from that fragrant bosom,
The night is a ship and the sun an anchor.

۶

ای عشق تو عمرم بکران آوردی
ای هجر تنم را بفغان آوردی
ای دل تو مرا کار بجان آوردی
ای دیده دلم را بزبان آوردی

6

O love, you brought my life to the shore.
O separation, you made my body lament.
O heart, you brought my work to an end.
O eye, you brought my heart to my tongue.

۷

ای ماه چو ابروان یاری گویی
یا نی چو کمان شهریاری گویی
نعلی زده از زر عیاری گویی
در گوش سپهر گوشواری گویی

7

O moon, you are like the beloved's eyebrows, as it were.
Nay, you are like a king's bow, as it were.
You are like a horseshoe made of gold, as it were.
You are like a ring in the ear of the sky, as it were.

۸

خورشید رخی که عشق او شد دینم
گفت امشبی آیم بر تو بنشینم
نومید شد و گفت دل مسکینم
خورشید بشب که دید تا من بینم

8

A sun-faced one, whose love became my faith,
Told me she was coming to stay with me tonight.
My poor heart became disappointed and said,
"Who has seen the sun at night that I see, too?"

٩

ای دیده و دل هر دو پسندیده ترا
دارم ز عزیزی چو دل و دیده ترا
از دیدن دیده گر شود دل عاشق
دل عاشق گشت و دیده نادیده ترا

9

O you whom the eye and heart have both chosen,
You are dear to me like the eye and heart.
If the heart would fall in love because of the eye's seeing,
Without the eye's seeing of you, the heart fell in love.

١٠

در هجر تو با دو چشم پر خون باشم
در رنج ز هر چه گویی افزون باشم
یک بار بدیدمت بدین حال شدم
گر بار دگر ببینمت چون باشم

10

In your separation, I am with two blood-filled eyes.
I am suffering more than any word can describe.
I saw you only one time and this is how I am!
If I see you another time, how am I going to be?

محمد غزالی
(۵۰۵-۴۵۰ هجری قمری)

۱

دل گر ره وصل تو نپوید چه کند
جان وصل ترا بجان نجوید چه کند
آن لحظه که بر آینه تابد خورشید
آیینه انا‌الشمس نگوید چه کند

Mohammad Ghazzâli
(1058-1112 C.E.)

1

If the heart take not your road, what shall it do?
If the soul seek not your union eagerly, what shall it do?
The moment the sun shines upon it,
If the mirror say not, "I am the sun," what shall it do?

۲

کس را پس پرده قضا راه نشد
وز سر قدر هیچ کس آگاه نشد
هر کس ز سر قیاس چیزی گفتند
معلوم نگشت و قصه کوتاه نشد

2

Behind the screen of destiny was seen by no one.
The secret of fate was made known to no one.
Everyone said something by way of analogy.
The secret remained and the story was finished by no one.

٣

ما جامه نمازی به سر خم کردیم

وز خاک خرابات تیمم کردیم

شاید که در این میکده ها دریابیم

آن عمر که در مدرسه ها گم کردیم

3

I lost my prayer-mat over the wine-vat,
And performed my ablutions with the dust of the taverns.
Perhaps I shall find in the taverns,
The life which I lost in the schools.

۴

ای عین بقا در چه بقایی که نیی

در جای نیی کدام جایی که نیی

ای ذات تو از جا و جهت مستغنی

آخر تو کجایی و کجایی که نیی

4

O Essence of Being, what being are you not in?
You are in no place, what place are you not in?
O' you whose nature is needless of places and directions,
What place are you anyway, and what place are you not in?

شیخ احمد غزالی
(۵۱۷ هجری قمری)

۱

از دی که گذشت اگر خوری غم نرسی
فردا چه عجب اگر در این دم نرسی
خوش باش در این نفس که هستی تو در او
دادش بدهی که اندرین هم نرسی

Shaykh Ahmad Ghazzâli
(d. 1123 C.E.)

1

Your regret will not bring back yesterday, which is past.
What wonder if you do not find this moment tomorrow?
Be happy at this moment in which you exist.
Do justice to it, for even this you will not find again.

۲

زان باده که جان عقل از او یافت کمال
پیش آور جانا قدحی مالامال
مستم کن و گو حرام باشد نه حلال
تا نیست شوم که هستی ام هست وبال

2

From the wine that gave perfection to the life of reason,
Bring me a cup, full to the brim, my darling!
Make me drunk, and never mind if it is forbidden or not.
Let me cease to exist, for my existence is a torture.

۳

در وصف توام دو صد زبان می باید
یا پیشکشم هزار جان می باید
آنجا که تویی دست سخن می نرسد
فی الجمله چنانی که چنان می باید

3

To describe you, I need two hundred tongues.
Else, a thousand lives I must devote.
Where you are, words do not reach.
In short, you are the way you must be.

۴

گر تو به شکرخنده دهن بگشایی
بند غمم از سینهٔ جان بگشایی
خاموشی تو همه ز گفتار من است
من لب بستم تا تو زبان بگشایی

4

If you open your lips with a sweet smile,
You will untie the chain of sorrow from my life.
Your silence is all because of my speaking.
Now I close my lips, so that you may speak.

۵

تا جام جهان نمای در دست من است
از روی خرد چرخ برین پست من است
تا کعبهٔ نیست قبلهٔ هست من است
هشیارترین خلق جهان مست من است

5

As long as the world-viewing cup is in my hand,
The highest heaven is under my feet.
As long as the Kaaba of nonbeing is the kebla of my being,
The soberest men of the world are drunk by me.

۶

چون آب و گل مرا مصور کردند

جانم عرض و عشق تو جوهر کردند

تقدیر و قضا قلم چو بر میکردند

عشق تو و عمر من برابر کردند

6

When they designed me from earth and water,
They made my soul the form and your love the essence.
And when they began to write my destiny and fate,
They made my life equal to your love.

قطران تبریزی
(۴۶۵ هجری قمری)

۱

تا فتنه دلم بر آن لب میگون است

صبرم کم و عشق هر زمان افزون است

گویند برون فتاد رازت چون است

چون راز درون بود که دل بیرون است

Qatrân Tabrizi
(d. 1073 C.E.)

1

As long as my heart is charmed by those wine-colored lips,
Every hour my patience decreases and my love increases.
They ask me how my secret fell out.
How can a secret be in while the heart is out?

۲

ای زلف تو از رخان من پر چین تر

وز خون دو چشم من رخت رنگین تر

هر روز تو نیکوتر و من زارترم

هر روز تو دلبرتر و من بی دین تر

2

O you, whose hair is more wrinkled than my cheeks
And whose face is rosier than my eyes' blood,
Everyday you are more beautiful and I more miserable.
Everyday you are more charming and I more infidel.

۳

ای دوست بیا تا رهٔ دیگر گیریم

و آزار و جفاها ز میان بر گیریم

مر یکدیگر را خود به بر اندر گیریم

کینه بنهیم و صحبت از سر گیریم

3

O friend, come, let us take a different road.
Let us put an end to unkindness and cruelty.
Let us embrace and cease rancor.
Let us resume our companionship.

۴

تا همبر من نشسته ای خاموشم

چون یاد آرم فراق تو بخروشم

از من نرهی که هست چندان هوشم

کانرا که به دل خرم بجان نفروشم

4

When you are sitting next to me, I am silent.
When I recall your separation, I am boisterous.
You will not be rid of me. For I have this much intelligence
Not to sell for my soul what I have bought with my heart.

۵

پیوسته چو شمع در گدازم بی تو
شب تا به سحر به سوز و سازم بی تو
نه سوی شراب دست یازم بی تو
نه سوی نشاط قد فرازم بی تو

5

I am ever ablaze, like a candle, without you.
I am in agony and pain all night without you.
I neither extend my hand toward wine without you,
Nor take any step toward pleasure without you.

عنصرالمعالی
(۵۰۰ هجری قمری)

۱

هر آدمیی که حی و ناطق باشد
باید که چو عذرا و چو وامق باشد
هر کو نه چنین بود منافق باشد
مؤمن نبود که او نه عاشق باشد

Onsorulmaâli
(d. 1107 C.E.)

1

Any human being who is alive and vocal
Must be like Azrâ and Vâmaq.
Whoever is not like them is a hypocrite.
Whoever is not a lover is not a believer.

٢

گر مرگ بر آورد ز بدخواه تو دود

زان دود چنین شاد چرا گشتی زود

چون مرگ ترا نیز بخواهد فرسود

بر مرگ کسی چه شادمان باید بود

2

If death raised the smoke of your enemy,
Why should you soon become so happy with that smoke?
Since death will also weary you out,
Why should you rejoice in another person's death?

٣

ای در دل من فکنده عشق تو فروغ

بر گردن من نهاده تیمار تو یوغ

عشق تو بجان و دل خریدستم من

دانی به خریده بر نگویند دروغ

3

O you, whose love has thrown light into my heart
And whose sorrow has put a yoke on my neck,
I have bought your love with my heart and soul.
You know what is bought cannot be lied about.

۴

بر دست نهاد لاله در صحرا مل

بر قبهٔ سرو ها و هو زد بلبل

رعد آمد و در هوا فروکوفت دهل

کامد پسری بهار را یعنی گل

4

The tulip took wine in its hand in the plain.
The nightingale cried at the top of the cypress.
The thunder came and beat its drum in the air.
For a son named Rose was born to the spring.

۵

از دل صنما مهر تو بیرون کردم
وآن کوهٔ غم ترا به هامون کردم
امروز نگویمت که چون خواهم کرد
فردا دانی که گویمت چون کردم

5
I put your love out of my heart, darling.
I put that mount of grief out in the desert.
Today I am not going to tell you what I will do.
Tomorrow you will know when I tell you what I did

۶

تا دور شدی شدستم ای روی چو ماه
اندیشه فزون و صبر کم حال تباه
تن چون نی و بر چو نیل و رخساره چو کاه
انگشت به لب گوش به در دیده به راه

6
Since you went away, O beautiful one,
I have had more anguish, more misery, and less patience.
My body like a reed, my face like straw, my side the Nile,
My finger to my lip, ear to the door, and eye on the road.

عمر خیام

(۵۱۷ هجری قمری)

۱

بر خیز بتا بیا ز بهر دل ما

حل کن بجمال خویشتن مشکل ما

یک کوزه شراب تا بهم نوش کنیم

زان پیش که کوزه ها کنند از گل ما

Omar Khayyâm
(d. 1123 C.E.)

1

Arise, O idol. Come for our hearts' sake,
And resolve our difficulty with your beauty.
Let us drink wine together from a jug,
Before they make our clay into a jug.

۲

چون عهده نمی شود کسی فردا را

حالی خوش دار این دل پر سودا را

می نوش بماهتاب ای ماه که ماه

بسیار بتابد و نیابد ما را

2

Since tomorrow is not guaranteed for anyone,
Keep your melancholic heart happy now.
O Beauty, drink wine in the light of the moon.
For many a night will the moon shine but not find us.

٣

گر می نخوری طعنه مزن مستانرا

بنیاد مکن تو حیله و دستانرا

تو غره بدان مشو که می می نخوری

صد لقمه خوری که می غلام است آنرا

3

If you drink not wine, taunt not the wine-drinkers.

Lay not the foundation of deception and lie.

Boast not that you take no wine!

You take a hundred things worse than wine.

۴

هر چند که رنگ و بوی زیباست مرا

چون لاله رخ و چو سرو بالاست مرا

معلوم نشد که در طربخانه خاک

نقاش ازل بهر چه آراست مرا

4

Although I am beautiful in color and scent,

My face like a tulip and my stature like a cypress,

It never became known to me why the Primordial Painter

Designed me in the earth's house of mirth!

۵

ما ئیم و می و مطرب و این کنج خراب

جان و دل و جام و جامه پر درد شراب

فارغ ز امید رحمت و بیم عذاب

آزاد ز خاک و باد و از آتش و آب

5

With wine and the minstrel in this ruined corner,

My heart and soul, my cup and garment full of dregs,

Released from the hope of mercy and fear of retribution,

I am free from earth, air, fire, and water.

۶

آن قصر که جمشید در او جام گرفت
آهو بچه کرد و روبه آرام گرفت
بهرام که گور میگرفتی همه عمر
دیدی که چگونه گور بهرام گرفت

6

Where Jamshid used to hold the Cup,
Now the deer reproduces and the fox lies calm.
Bahrâm, who hunted the *gur* (onager) all his life,
Did you see how he was hunted by the *gur* (grave)?

۷

اکنون که گل سعادتت پر بار است
دست تو ز جام می چرا بیکار است
می خور که زمانه دشمنی غدار است
در یافتن روز چنین دشوار است

7

Now that the rose of your happiness is blooming,
Why is your hand idle from holding the cup of wine?
Drink wine, for time is a treacherous enemy.
It is hard to find another day like this.

۸

امروز ترا دسترس فردا نیست
واندیشه فردات بجز سودا نیست
ضایع مکن ایندم ار دلت شیدا نیست
کاین باقی عمر را بها پیدا نیست

8

Today you have no access to tomorrow.
And your fear of tomorrow is but an illusion.
Waste not this moment with a heart that is not in love.
This remainder of life is priceless.

٩

ای آمده از عالم روحانی تفت
حیران شده در پنج و چهار و شش و هفت
می خور چو ندانی از کجا آمده ای
خوش باش ندانی بکجا خواهی رفت

9

O you — who have come brisk from the world of spirit,
Bewildered by four, five, six, and seven — drink wine!
For you do not know where you have come from.
And be happy, for you do not know where you shall go.

١٠

ای چرخ فلک خرابی از کینه تست
بیدادگری شیوه دیرینه تست
ای خاک اگر سینه تو بشکافند
بس گوهر قیمتی که در سینه تست

10

O heaven, this devastation is from your rancor .
Cruelty is your ancient habit.
O Earth, if they split your chest open,
Many precious jewels are buried there.

١١

ای دل چو زمانه میکند غمناکت
ناگه برود ز تن روان پاکت
بر سبزه نشین و خوش بزی روزی چند
زان پیش که سبزه بر دمد از خاکت

11

While you are grieving in this world, my dear,
Your pure soul may suddenly leave your body!
Before the grass grows from your dust,
Sit on the grass and live happily for a few days,

۱۲

این بحر وجود آمده بیرون ز نهفت

کس نیست که این گوهر تحقیق بسفت

هر کس سخنی از سر سودا گفتند

زان روی که هست کس نمیداند گفت

12

This ocean of being has come out of the invisible.
No one was ever able to pierce this pearl of truth.
Each person said something from imagination.
No one can describe existence as it really is.

۱۳

این کوزه چو من عاشق زاری بوده است

در بند سر زلف نگاری بوده است

این دسته که بر گردن او می بینی

دستی است که بر گردن یاری بوده است

13

The jug was a desperate lover like me,
Chained by the tress-tip of a beloved.
This handle that you see on its neck
Used to be an arm around a beloved's neck.

۱۴

این کوزه که آبخواره مزدوریست

از دیده شاهیست و دل دستوریست

هر کاسه می که بر کف مخموریست

از عارض مستی و لب مستوریست

14

This jug, which is the drinking-vessel of a hireling,
Is from a king's eyes and a vizier's heart.
Any bowl of wine you see in a drinker's hand
Is from a drunkard's face and a chaste woman's lips.

۱۵

این کهنه رباط را که عالم نامست

وارامگه ابلق صبح و شامست

بزمیست که واماندهٔ صد جمشید است

قصریست که تکیه گاه صد بهرامست

15

This old caravanserai, called the world,
Where days follow nights, and nights days,
Is a place where a hundred Jamshids have feasted,
A palace where a hundred Bahrâms have rested.

۱۶

این یک دو سه روزه نوبت عمر گذشت

چون آب بجویبار و چون باد بدشت

هر گز غم دو روز مرا یاد نگشت

روزی که نیامده است و روزی که گذشت

16

The few days of this short life passed quickly,
Like the water in a brook and the wind in a desert.
Yet my heart never sorrowed for two days:
The day which has not come and the day which has passed.

۱۷

بر چهره گل نسیم نوروز خوشست

در صحن چمن روی دل افروز خوشست

از دی که گذشت هر چه گوئی خوش نیست

خوش باش و ز دی مگو که امروز خوشست

17

On the cheek of the rose, the breeze of *Noruz* is good.
On the stage of the meadow, a heart-cheering face is good.
Of yesterday which passed whatever you say is not good.
Be happy, say nothing of yesterday, for today is good.

١٨

بیش از من و تو لیل و نهاری بوده است

گردنده فلک نیز بکاری بوده است

هر جا که قدم نهی تو بر روی زمین

آن مردمک چشم نگاری بوده است

18

Before you and me, days and nights have been.
The turning heaven at its work has been.
Any place on earth whereon you plant your step,
There the pupil of a beloved's eye has been.

١٩

ترکیب پیاله ای که درهم پیوست

بشکستن آن روا نمیدارد مست

چندین سر و پای نازنین از سر دست

بر مهر که پیوست و بکین که شکست

19

To break a bowl after it is completed,
Even a drunkard will not deem it right.
So many perfect bodies, beautiful from head to feet,
Whose love does create and whose hatred does destroy?

٢٠

ترکیب طبایع چو بکام تو دمی است

رو شاد بزی اگرچه بر تو ستمی است

با اهل خرد باش که اصل تن تو

گردی و نسیمی و غباری و دمی است

20

If nature has favored you with good health,
Be happy, even though life is hard on you.
Be among the wise, for the substance of your body is:
Dust and wind, ashes and a blow.

۲۱

چون ابر بنوروز رخ لاله بشست

بر خیز و بجام باده کن عزم درست

کاین سبزه که امروز تماشاگه تست

فردا همه از خاک تو بر خواهد رست

21

When the cloud washes the tulip's cheek in Noruz,
Get up and walk straight to the goblet of wine.
For this verdure, which is your spectacle today,
Will grow all from your ashes tomorrow.

۲۲

چون بلبل مست راه در بستان یافت

روی گل و جام باده را خندان یافت

آمد بزبان حال در گوشم گفت

در یاب که عمر رفته را نتوان یافت

22

When the drunk nightingale found his way to the garden,
And saw the smiling faces of the rose and wine,
It came over and whispered in my ear in its own tongue:
Find the present, for the life past can not be found.

۲۳

چون چرخ بکام یک خردمند نگشت

تو خواه فلک هفت شمر خواهی هشت

چون باید مرد و آرزوها همه هشت

چه مور خورد بگور و چه گرگ بدشت

23

Since heavens never turn to any wise man's wish,
What matters if you count them seven or eight?
Since we all must die and leave all our desires behind,
What difference if eaten by desert wolves or grave ants?

۲۴

چون لاله بنوروز قدح گیر بدست
با لاله رخی اگر ترا فرصت هست
می نوش بخرمی که این چرخ کهن
ناگاه ترا چو خاک گرداند پست

24

Like the tulip in *Noruz*, take the bowl of wine in your hand,
With a tulip-cheeked one, if you get a chance.
Drink wine joyfully, for this ancient wheel of the sky
Will suddenly make you low, like the dust.

۲۵

چون نیست حقیقت و یقین اندر دست
نتوان بامید شک همه عمر نشست
هان تا ننهیم جام می از کف دست
در بیخبری مرد چه هشیار چه مست

25

Since truth and certainty are beyond our reach,
We cannot spend our whole life in doubt.
Oh, we should never let down the wine-cup off our hands!
In the absence of knowledge, what matters drunk or sober?

۲۶

چون نیست ز هر چه هست جز باد بدست
چون هست بهر چه هست نقصان و شکست
انگار که هر چه هست در عالم نیست
پندار که هر چه نیست در عالم هست

26

Since of all that exists nothing remains but wind in the hand,
And since anything that exists decays and breaks down,
Suppose all that exists in the world does not!
Imagine all that exists not in the world does!

۲۷

خاکی که بزیر پای هر نادانی است
کف صنمی و چهره جانانی است
هر خشت که بر کنگره ایوانی است
انگشت وزیر یا سر سلطانی است

27

The dust under the feet of every ignorant person
Is an idol's hand or a beloved's face.
Every brick in the battlement of a palace
Is a vizier's finger or a sultan's head.

۲۸

دارنده چو ترکیب طبایع آراست
از بهر چه افکندش اندر کم و کاست
گر نیک آمد شکستن از بهر چه بود
ور نیک نیامد این صور عیب کراست

28

When the Creator put the elements of nature in order,
Why did he put defect and imperfection in them?
If the product was good, why did he destroy it?
If it was not good, whose fault was it?

۲۹

در پردهٔ اسرار کسی را ره نیست
زین تعبیه جان هیچکس آگه نیست
جز در دل خاک هیچ منزلگه نیست
می خور که چنین فسانه ها کوته نیست

29

No one is allowed behind the screen of secrets.
Not a single soul is aware of this mystery of existence.
Since there is no destination except in the heart of dust,
Drink wine, for such fables are not short.

٣٠

در خواب بدم مرا خردمندی گفت
کز خواب کسی را گل شادی نشکفت
کاری چه کنی که با اجل باشد جفت
می خور که بزیر خاک می باید خفت

30

When I was asleep, a wise man told me:
The flower of joy has not bloomed for anyone by sleeping.
Why should you do something that is like death?
Drink wine, for under the earth sleeping shall be.

٣١

در دایره ای که آمد و رفتن ماست
او را نه بدایت نه نهایت پیداست
کس می نزند دمی در این معنی راست
کاین آمدن از کجا و رفتن بکجاست

31

This circle, wherein our going and coming takes place,
Has neither its beginning nor its end in sight.
No one tells the truth about this matter for a moment:
Where is this coming from and where is this going to?

٣٢

در فصل بهار اگر بتی حور سرشت
یک ساغر می دهد مرا بر لب کشت
هر چند بنزد عامه این باشد زشت
سگ به ز من است اگر برم نام بهشت

32

In the season of spring, beside a field of crops,
Would a houri-natured idol give me a goblet of wine,
Although common people may deem it wrong,
A dog is better than me if I ever mention the paradise.

۳۳

در یاب که از روح جدا خواهی رفت
در پردهٔ اسرار فنا خواهی رفت
می نوش ندانی از کجا آمده ای
خوش باش ندانی بکجا خواهی رفت

33

Capture the moment: for apart from your soul you will go.
Behind the veil of the secrets of non-existence you will go.
Drink wine, for you do not know where you came from.
Be happy, for you do not know where you will go.

۳۴

ساقی گل و سبزه بس طربناک شده است
در یاب که هفته دگر خاک شده است
می نوش و گلی بچین که تا در نگری
گل خاک شده است و سبزه خاشاک شده است

34

Sâqi, the grass and the rose have found a pleasant turn.
Capture this moment, for next week to dust they will turn.
Drink wine and pick a rose! For before you notice,
The rose to dust and the grass to straw will turn.

۳۵

عمریست مرا تیره و کاریست نه راست
محنت همه افزوده و راحت کم و کاست
شکر ایزد را که آنچه اسباب بلاست
ما را از کس دگر نمی باید خواست

35

My life is dark and my affairs are in distress,
My troubles are more and my comforts less.
Thank God there is no means of calamity
Which I need to ask of someone else.

۳۶

فصل گل و طرف جویبار و لب کشت

با یک دو سه اهل و لعبتی حور سرشت

پیش آر قدح که باده نوشان صبوح

آسوده ز مسجدند و فارغ ز کنشت

36

In the season of the rose, beside a stream in a plantation,
With a houri-natured sweetheart and a few bosom friends,
Bring the cup of wine! For drinkers of the morning wine
Are free from the mosque and clear from the synagogue.

۳۷

گر شاخ بقا ز پنج بختت رست است

ور بر تن تو عمر لباسی چست است

در خیمهٔ تن که سایبانی است ترا

هان تکیه مکن که چار میخش سست است

37

If your affairs are going as you would have wished,
And if life is like a suitable garment on you,
Beware of leaning against the tent of your body,
Which is a canopy with all its supporting nails loose.

۳۸

گویند کسان بهشت با حور خوش است

من میگویم که آب انگور خوش است

این نقد بگیر و دست از آن نسیه بدار

کاواز دهل شنیدن از دور خوش است

38

People say, paradise with houris is good.
I say, the juice of the grape is good.
Grab this cash and relinquish that credit.
For the sound of a drum from far is good.

٣٩

گویند مرا که دوزخی باشد مست
قولی است خلاف دل در آن نتوان بست
گر عاشق و میخواره بدوزخ باشند
فردا بینی بهشت همچون کف دست

39

They tell me drunkards will dwell in hell.
This statement is false. One cannot believe it.
If lovers and drunkards dwell in hell,
Tomorrow you see heaven [empty] like the palm of a hand.

۴۰

من هیچ ندانم که مرا آنکه سرشت
از اهل بهشت کرد یا دوزخ زشت
جامی و بتی و بربطی بر لب کشت
این هر سه مرا نقد و ترا نسیه بهشت

40

I do not know at all whether the one who molded me
Made me one of the people of heaven or the ugly hell.
A cup of wine, a sweetheart, and a harp beside a plantation,
Let these in cash be mine and the heaven on credit yours.

۴۱

مهتاب بنور دامن شب بشکافت
می نوش و می بهتر از این نتوان یافت
خوش باش و میندیش که مهتاب بسی
اندر سر خاک یک بیک خواهد تافت

41

Moonlight cleft the night's skirt with its radiance.
Drink wine, for wine better than this cannot be found.
Rejoice and do not worry! For the light of the moon
Will long shine over the dust of one and all.

۴۲

می خوردن و شاد بودن آیین من است

فارغ بودن ز کفر و دین دین من است

گفتم بعروس دهر کابین تو چیست

گفتا دل خرم تو کابین من است

42

To drink wine and be joyful is my creed.
To be free from belief and disbelief is my religion.
I asked the bride of time, "What is your dower?"
She replied, "Your happy heart is my dower."

۴۳

می لعل مذاب است و صراحی کان است

جسم است پیاله و شرابش جان است

آن جام بلورین که ز می خندان است

اشکی است که خون دل در او پنهان است

43

Wine is a molten ruby whose mine is the decanter.
The body is a bowl whose wine is the soul.
That crystal chalice wherein the wine is smiling
Is a teardrop wherein the heart's blood is hiding.

۴۴

می نوش که عمر جاودانی این است

خود حاصلت از دور جوانی این است

هنگام گل و باده و یاران سرمست

خوش باش دمی که زندگانی این است

44

Drink wine, for the life eternal is this.
The very fruit of your youth is this.
Your friends are drunk at this time of roses and wine.
Rejoice for a moment, for [real] life is this.

۴۵

نیکی و بدی که در نهاد بشر است
شادی و غمی که در قضا و قدر است
با چرخ مکن حواله کاندر ره عقل
چرخ از تو هزار بار بیچاره تر است

45

Good and evil, which are in human nature;
Joy and woe, which are in fate and destiny —
Do not attribute to the wheel of the universe.
Indeed the universe is far more helpless than you are.

۴۶

در هر دشتی که لاله زاری بوده است
از سرخی خون شهریاری بوده است
هر شاخ بنفشه کز زمین میروید
خالی است که بر رخ نگاری بوده است

46

Any plain whereon tulips have grown,
Has its redness from a king's blood.
Any violet-bush that grows from the ground
Used to be a mole on a sweetheart's cheek.

۴۷

هر ذره که در خاک زمینی بوده است
پیش از من و تو تاج و نگینی بوده است
گرد از رخ نازنین بآزرم فشان
کانهم رخ خوب نازنینی بوده است

47

Any particle in the dust of the ground
Was a crown or a signet before you and me.
Wipe the dust from your charming cheek gently.
For that, too, used to be the fair cheek of a lovely one.

۴۸

هر سبزه که بر کنار جوئی رسته است
گوئی ز لب فرشته خوئی رسته است
پا بر سر سبزه تا بخواری ننهی
کان سبزه ز خاک لاله روئی رسته است

48

Any grass which on the bank of a brook has grown,
It is as if from the lips of an angelic person has grown.
Watch out, lest you should step on the grass with contempt!
For that green from the dust of a tulip-cheeked has grown.

۴۹

یک جرعهٔ می ز ملک کاوس بهست
از تخت قباد و ملکت طوس بهست
هر ناله که رندی بسحرگاه زند
از طاعت زاهدان سالوس بهست

49

A gulp of wine than the kingdom of Kâwus is better,
Than the throne of Qobâd and the realm of Tus is better.
Any lament that a *rend* makes at dawn
Than the prayers of pretentious ascetics is better.

۵۰

چون عمر بسر رسد چه شیرین و چه تلخ
پیمانه چو پر شود چه بغداد و چه بلخ
می نوش که بعد از من و تو ماه بسی
از سلخ بغره آید از غره بسلخ

50

When life reaches the end, sweet or bitter, what difference?
When the cup fills up, Baghdâd or Balkh, what difference?
Drink wine. For after you and me, how many times
The moon waxes and wanes, what difference?

۵۱

آنانکه محیط فضل و آداب شدند

در جمع کمال شمع اصحاب شدند

ره زین شب تاریک نبردند برون

گفتند فسانه ای و در خواب شدند

51

Those who mastered arts and sciences,
And became the light of the assemblies of the learned,
Never found their way out of this dark night.
They spun a yarn and fell asleep in silence.

۵۲

آنرا که بصحرای علل تاخته اند

بی او همه کارها بپرداخته اند

امروز بهانه ای در انداخته اند

فردا همه آن بود که در ساخته اند

52

Before a person is forced into this plain of pains,
Everything about him has been decided without his consent.
Today they have offered an excuse for what
They have already determined for tomorrow.

۵۳

آنها که کهن شدند و اینها که نوند

هر کس بمراد خویش یک تک بدوند

این کهنه جهان بکس نماند باقی

رفتند و رویم دیگر آیند و روند

53

Those who are old and those who are young,
Are all dashing after their desires.
This ancient world will not remain for anyone.
They are gone, we are going, and others will come and go.

۵۴

آنکس که زمین و چرخ و افلاک نهاد
بس داغ که او بر دل غمناک نهاد
بسیار لب چو لعل و زلفین چو مشک
در طبل زمین و حقه خاک نهاد

54

He who built the Earth and the skies
Laid many a brand on the doleful heart.
Many a lip like ruby and many a tress like musk
Placed he on the tray of the Earth and the box of dust.

۵۵

آرند یکی و دیگری برﺑایند
بر هیچکسی راز همی نگشایند
ما را ز قضا جز این قدر ننمایند
پیمانه عمر ماست می پیمایند

55

One is brought forth and another is taken away,
And the secret is revealed to none.
This is all we are shown of our destiny.
This is how the measure of our life is measured.

۵۶

اجرام که ساکنان این ایوانند
اسباب تردد خردمندانند
هان تا سر رشته خرد گم نکنی
کانان که مدبرند سر گردانند

56

Those celestial bodies that fill the sky
Are the vehicles of confusion for the wise.
Beware, lest you should lose the thread of reason!
Those who seek to understand are bewildered.

۵۷

از آمدنم نبود گردون را سود

وز رفتن من جلال و جاهش نفرود

وز هیچ کسی نیز دو گوشم نشنود

کاین آمدن و رفتنم از بهر چه بود

57

The world gained no benefit from my coming,
Nor will it add to its glory and pomp from my going.
Yet never my two ears heard from anyone
The purpose of this coming and going.

۵۸

از رنج کشیدن آدمی حر گردد

قطره چو کشد حبس صدف در گردد

گر مال نماند سر بماناد بجای

پیمانه چو شد تهی دگر پر گردد

58

Through suffering, humans gain their freedom.
The waterdrop becomes a pearl in the prison of the shell.
If your possessions did not remain, let your spirits do.
When the measuring-cup is emptied, it is filled again.

۵۹

افسوس که سرمایه ز کف بیرون شد

وز دست اجل بسی جگرها خون شد

کس نامد از آن جهان که پرسم از اوی

کاحوال مسافران دنیا چون شد

59

Alas, the capital of life went out of my hand.
Many a heart bled by the hand of death.
No one came from the next world so that I ask him:
What happened to those travellers from this world?

۶.

افسوس که نامهٔ جوانی طی شد
وان تازه بهار زندگانی دی شد
آن مرغ طرب که نام او بود شباب
فریاد ندانم که کی آمد کی شد

60

Alas, the book of youth came to an end!
And that fresh spring of life became winter.
That bird of joy whose name was youth,
Alas, I did not notice when it came and when it went!

۶۱

ای بس که نباشیم و جهان خواهد بود
نی نام ز ما و نی نشان خواهد بود
زین پیش نبودیم و نبود هیچ خلل
زین پس چو نباشیم همان خواهد بود

61

Long, long without us the world will be.
Neither a name nor a sign from us there will be.
Before now without us nothing was amiss.
After now if we are not, the same will be.

۶۲

این عقل که در ره سعادت پوید
روزی صد بار خود ترا میگوید
در یاب تو این یک دم وقتت که نه ای
آن تره که بدروند و دیگر روید

62

This reason that walks on the road of happiness,
Tells you a hundred times a day:
Capture this one moment of your life!
For you are not that chive which grows after it is reaped.

۶۳

این قافلهٔ عمر عجب میگذرد

در یاب دمی که با طرب میگذرد

ساقی غم فردای حریفان چه خوری

پیش آر پیاله را که شب میگذرد

63

Behold how this caravan of life is passing!
Capture the moment that is pleasantly passing.
Sâqi, why worry about the drinkers' tomorrow?
Bring forth the cup, for the night is passing.

۶۴

بر پشت من از زمانه تو می آید

وز من همه کار نانکو می آید

جان عزم رحیل کرد و گفتم بمرو

گفتا چکنم خانه فرو می آید

64

Time is folding my back over.
No longer can I do anything right.
My soul decided to depart. I said, "Don't go!"
It said, "What shall I do? The house is falling down."

۶۵

بر چرخ فلک هیچ کسی چیر نشد

وز خوردن آدمی زمین سیر نشد

مغرور بدانی که نخوردست ترا

تعجیل مکن هم بخورد دیر نشد

65

Never did anyone conquer the wheel of the sky.
Nor did the Earth consume enough humans.
You are proud it has not consumed you yet.
No rush! It is not too late. It will consume you, too.

۶۶

بر چشم تو عالم ارچه می آرایند

نگر ای بدان که عاقلان نگرایند

بسیار چو تو روند و بسیار آیند

بربای نصیب خویش کت بربایند

66

However they adorn the world before your eyes,
Attach not yourself to it, for the wise avoid attachment.
Many like you will go, and many will come.
Grab your share before it is snatched from you!

۶۷

بر من قلم قضا چو بی من رانند

پس نیک و بدش ز من چرا میدانند

دی بی من و امروز چو دی بی من و تو

فردا بچه حجتم بداور خوانند

67

Since my destiny was determined without me,
Why am I held accountable for its good and bad?
Yesterday without my consent, and today like yesterday.
For what reason should I be called to justice tomorrow?

۶۸

تا چند اسیر رنگ و بو خواهی شد

چند از پی هر زشت و نکو خواهی شد

گر چشمه زمزمی و گر آب حیات

آخر بدل خاک فرو خواهی شد

68

How long shall you be the captive of colors and scents?
How long shall you chase every beauty and ugly?
Whether you are the Spring of *Zamzam* or the water of life,
You will sink into the heart of dust in the end.

۶۹

تا راه قلندری نپویی نشود

رخساره بخون دل نشویی نشود

سودا چه پزی تا که چو دلسوختگان

آزاد بترک خود نگویی نشود

69

Unless you walk the road of the calenders, it won't do.
Until you wash your face with the heart's blood, it won't do.
Why entertain a fancy? Unless you renounce yourself freely,
Like the heart-consumed ones, it won't do.

۷۰

تا زهره و مه در آسمان گشت پدید

بهتر ز می ناب کسی هیچ ندید

من در عجبم ز میفروشان کایشان

به زانکه فروشند چه خواهند خرید

70

Since Jupiter and the moon appeared in the sky,
Better than pure wine no one has seen anything.
I am surprised at the dealers of wine.
What will they buy better than what they sell?

۷۱

چون روزی و عمر بیش و کم نتوان کرد

دل را به کم و بیش دژم نتوان کرد

کار من و تو چنانکه رای من و تست

از موم بدست خویش هم نتوان کرد

71

Since the span of life and the *ruzi* cannot be more or less,
One should not worry about what is more and less.
Your affair or mine, even if it were like wax in our hands,
Could not be made according to your wish or mine.

۷۲

در دهر چو آواز گل تازه دهند
فرمای بتا که می باندازه دهند
از حور و قصور وز بهشت و دوزخ
فارغ بنشین که آن هر آوازه دهند

72

When they announce the arrival of fresh roses in the world,
Order, my dear, that wine be given in right measure.
Forget about the houris, palaces, heaven and hell.
People always talk about things like these.

۷۳

در دهر هر آنکه نیم نانی دارد
از بهر نشست آشیانی دارد
نه خادم کس بود نه مخدوم کسی
گو شاد بزی که خوش جهانی دارد

73

Whoever has a loaf of bread for his food,
A place of living for his shelter,
And is no one's servant or master,
Oh, what a happy world he has!

۷۴

دهقان قضا بسی چو ما کشت و درود
غم خوردن بیهوده نمیدارد سود
پر کن قدح می بکفم ورنه زود
تا باز خورم که بودنیها همه بود

74

The farmer of destiny sowed and reaped many like us.
There is no use grieving in vain.
Fill the cup of wine and hand me, lest before the next drink,
All things should become things of the past.

۷۵

روزی است خوش و هوا نه گرم است و نه سرد
ابر از رخ گلزار همی شوید گرد
بلبل بزبان حال خود با گل زرد
فریاد همی کند که می باید خورد

75

It is a pleasant day, neither hot nor cold.
Clouds are washing the dust from the garden's face.
And the nightingale, in its own language,
Is shouting at the yellow rose: "It is time to drink wine!"

۷۶

زان پیش که بر سرت شبیخون آرند
فرمای که تا بادهٔ گلگون آرند
تو زر نه ای ای غافل نادان که ترا
در خاک نهند و باز بیرون آرند

76

Before you are attacked by surprise at night,
Order some rosy wine to be brought forth.
You are not gold, O negligent ignoramus,
That could be buried under the earth and brought out again.

۷۷

عمرت تا کی بخود پرستی گذرد
یا در پی نیستی و هستی گذرد
می نوش که عمری که اجل در پی اوست
آن به که بخواب یا بمستی گذرد

77

How long would you let your life in selfishness pass?
Or in the pursuit of haves and have-nots pass?
Drink wine! For a life which is chased by death,
Better in sleep or drunkenness pass.

۷۸

کس مشکل اسرار اجل را نگشاد

کس یک قدم از نهاد بیرون ننهاد

من مینگرم ز مبتدی تا استاد

عجز است بدست هر که از مادر زاد

78

Not one person did reveal the secrets of death.
Not one step did anyone take beyond nature.
As I see it, from the novice to the master,
Anyone born from a mother has but helplessness with him.

۷۹

کم کن طمع از جهان و میزی خرسند

وز نیک و بد زمانه بگسل پیوند

می در کف و زلف دلبری گیر که زود

هم بگذرد و نماند این روزی چند

79

Lessen your greed for the world and live contentedly.
Sever your attachment from any good and bad of the world.
Take wine in one hand and a sweetheart's tress in another.
For soon these few days also will pass and vanish.

۸۰

گر چه غم و رنج من درازی دارد

عیش و طرب تو سرفرازی دارد

بر هر دو مکن تکیه که دوران فلک

در پرده هزار گونه بازی دارد

80

Although the story of my grief and suffering is long
And your joy and happiness make you proud,
One cannot rely on either one. For the heaven has
A thousand kinds of games behind the screen.

٨١

گردون ز زمین هیچ گلی بر نارد
کش نشکند و هم بزمین نسپارد
گر ابر چو آب خاک را بر دارد
تا حشر همه خون عزیزان بارد

81

Heaven never brings forth a rose from the earth,
Which it does not wither and return to the earth.
If clouds picked up dust as they do water,
They would be raining the loved ones' blood till doomsday.

٨٢

گر یک نفست ز زندگانی گذرد
مگذار که جز بشادمانی گذرد
هشدار که سرمایهٔ سودای جهان
عمر است چنان کش گذرانی گذرد

82

If only one breath of life is there to pass,
Allow not but happily for it to pass.
Remember, the capital of the world's trade is life,
Which passes anyway you make it pass.

٨٣

گویند بهشت و حور عین خواهد بود
آنجا می و شیر و انگبین خواهد بود
گر ما می و معشوق گزیدیم چه باک
چون عاقبت کار چنین خواهد بود

83

They say a paradise with dark-eyed houris there will be.
Plenty of wine, milk, and honey there will be.
If I chose wine and a sweetheart, why fear?
For this is how the end of the work will be.

۸۴

گویند بهشت و حور و کوثر باشد
جوی می و شیر و شهد و شکر باشد
پر کن قدح باده و بر دستم نه
نقدی ز هزار نسیه خوشتر باشد

84

They say a paradise with houris and *Kosar* there will be.
Streams of wine, milk, honey, and sugar there will be.
Fill the cup of wine and put it in my hand.
For one *is* is better than a thousand *will be.*

۸۵

گویند هر آنکسان که با پرهیزند
زان سان که بمیرند چنان بر خیزند
ما با می و معشوقه از آنیم مدام
باشد که بحشرمان چنان انگیزند

85

They say those who are virtuous will be resurrected
In the same manner as they die.
That is why I am always with my sweetheart and wine,
So that I be resurrected in this manner.

۸۶

می خور که ز دل کثرت و قلت ببرد
و اندیشهٔ هفتاد و دو ملت ببرد
پرهیز مکن ز کیمیایی که از او
یک جرعه خوری هزار علت ببرد

86

Drink wine to wash excess and shortage from your heart,
And take away the worries of the seventy-two nations.
Do not abstain from the elixir, one gulp of which
Would remove a thousand maladies from you.

٨٧

هر راز که اندر دل دانا باشد

باید که نهفته تر ز عنقا باشد

کاندر صدف از نهفتگی گردد در

آن قطره که راز دل دریا باشد

87

Every secret in a wise man's heart
Must be more concealed than *Anqa*.
For a waterdrop, which is the secret of the heart of the sea,
Becomes a pearl because of its concealment inside a shell.

٨٨

هر صبح که روی لاله شبنم گیرد

بالای بنفشه در چمن خم گیرد

انصاف مرا ز غنچه خوش میآید

کو دامن خویشتن فراهم گیرد

88

Every morning, when dewdrops appear on the tulip's cheek,
The stature of the violet bends in the meadow.
I really like the way the rosebud
Holds her skirt gathered up around her.

٨٩

هر گز دل من ز علم محروم نشد

کم ماند ز اسرار که معلوم نشد

هفتاد و دو سال فکر کردم شب و روز

معلومم شد که هیچ معلوم نشد

89

My heart was never deprived of knowledge.
Not many secrets remained unknown to me.
I spent seventy-two years thinking day and night.
It became known to me that nothing was known.

۹۰

هم دانهٔ امید بخرمن ماند

هم باغ و سرای بی تو و من ماند

سیم و زر خویش از درمی تا بجوی

با دوست بخور گرنه بدشمن ماند

90

The seed of hope till the harvest will remain.
The house and garden without you and me will remain.
Your silver and gold, whether much or little,
Spend with your friend, or else for the enemy will remain.

۹۱

یاران موافق همه از دست شدند

در پای اجل یکان یکان پست شدند

خوردیم ز یک شراب در مجلس عمر

دوری دو سه پیشتر ز ما مست شدند

91

All our sincere friends have passed away.
Crushed under the feet of death one after another.
We drank from the same wine in the assembly of life.
They became drunk a few rounds before us.

۹۲

یک جام شراب صد دل و دین ارزد

یک جرعهٔ می مملکت چین ارزد

جز بادهٔ لعل نیست در روی زمین

تلخی که هزار جان شیرین ارزد

92

One bowl of wine is worth a hundred hearts and faiths.
One gulp of wine is worth the Kingdom of China.
Except the ruby wine, there is no bitter one on earth,
Which is worth a thousand sweet lives.

۹۳

یک قطرهٔ آب بود با دریا شد
یک ذرهٔ خاک با زمین یکتا شد
آمد شدن تو اندرین عالم چیست
آمد مگسی پدید و ناپیدا شد

93

A drop of water merged with the sea.
A particle of dust united with the earth.
What is your coming and going in this world?
A fly that appeared and then disappeared.

۹۴

یک نان بدو روز اگر بود حاصل مرد
وز کوزه شکسته ای دمی آبی سرد
مامور کم از خودی چرا باید بود
یا خدمت چون خودی چرا باید کرد

94

If a loaf of bread is available for a couple of days,
And a gulp of cold water from a broken jug;
Why should a man obey the one lower than himself?
Or serve the one who is like himself?

۹۵

آن لعل در آبگینهٔ ساده بیار
وان محرم و مونس هر آزاده بیار
چون میدانی که مدت عالم خاک
باد است که زود بگذرد باده بیار

95

Inside a clear glass, bring that ruby wine!
Bring that confidante and intimate of every free person!
Bring wine, for you know that the span of this earthly life
Is like that of the wind which moves quickly.

۹۶

از بودنی ایدوست چه داری تیمار

وز فکرت بیهوده دل و جان افگار

خرم بزی و جهان بشادی گذران

تدبیر نه با تو کرده اند اول کار

96

Why do you grieve over existence, my friend?
Why do you afflict your heart and soul with futile thoughts?
Live joyfully and spend your life happily in the world.
They did not consult you in the beginning anyway.

۹۷

افلاک که جز غم نفزایند دگر

ننهند بجا تا نربایند دگر

ناآمدگان اگر بدانند که ما

از دهر چه میکشیم نایند دگر

97

The heavens, which increase nothing but grief,
Never give anything without snatching it back.
If those who have not come knew
How we suffer in this world, they would never come.

۹۸

ای دل غم این جهان فرسوده مخور

بیهوده نه ای غمان بیهوده مخور

چون بوده گذشت و نیست نابوده پدید

خوش باش غم بوده و نابوده مخور

98

O heart, grieve not over this wearied world.
You are not useless; suffer not useless griefs.
Since what was has passed and what is not is invisible,
Be happy, grieve not over what was and what is not.

۹۹

ایدل همه اسباب جهان خواسته گیر
باغ طربت بسبزه آراسته گیر
وانگاه بر آن سبزه شبی چون شبنم
بنشسته و بامداد بر خاسته گیر

99

O heart, suppose all your wishes in the world are obeyed,
Suppose your garden of pleasure is adorned with verdure,
And suppose one night, like a dewdrop,
You sat on that verdure and got up the next morning!

۱۰۰

این اهل قبور خاک گشتند و غبار
هر ذره ز هر ذره گرفتند کنار
آه این چه شراب است که تا روز شمار
بیخود شده و بیخبرند از همه کار

100

These dwellers of graves turned into ashes and dust.
Every particle took distance from every other.
Oh, what wine was it that made them so drunk
And unaware of everything till the Day of Reckoning?

۱۰۱

خشت سر خم ز ملکت جم خوشتر
بوی قدح از غذای مریم خوشتر
آه سحری ز سینهٔ خماری
از نالهٔ بو سعید و ادهم خوشتر

101

The wine-vat's brick-lid is better than Jamshid's kingdom.
The wine-cup's scent is more pleasant than Mary's repast.
The morning sigh from a drunkard's chest is
More amiable than the laments of Bu Said and Adham.

۱۰۲

در دایرهٔ سپهر ناپیدا غور

جامی است که جمله را چشانند بدور

نوبت چو بدور تو رسد آه مکن

می نوش بخوشدلی که دور است بخور

102

In the sphere of the sky, whose depth is invisible,
There is a cup from which everyone must drink in turn.
When your turn comes, do not sigh.
Drink it happily, for it is your turn to drink.

۱۰۳

دی کوزه گری بدیدم اندر بازار

بر پاره گلی لگد همی زد بسیار

و آن گل بزبان حال با او میگفت

من همچو تو بوده ام مرا نیکو دار

103

Yesterday I saw a jug-maker in the bazaar,
Who was treading a lump of clay repeatedly,
While that clay told him in its own language:
"I used to be like you. Treat me kindly!"

۱۰۴

زان می که حیات جاودانی است بخور

سرمایهٔ لذت جوانی است بخور

سوزنده چو آتش است لیکن غم را

سازنده چو آب زندگانی است بخور

104

From that wine which is eternal life, drink!
It is the substance of the joy of youth, drink!
From that wine which burns like fire,
But washes grief like the water of life, drink!

۱۰۵

گر باده خوری تو با خردمندان خور

یا با صنمی لاله رخی خندان خور

بسیار مخور ورد مکن فاش مساز

اندک خور و گه گاه خور و پنهان خور

105

If you drink wine, drink with the wise.
Or drink with a smiling, tulip-cheeked idol.
Neither drink too much, nor shout, nor make a display.
Drink a little, once in a while, and in private.

۱۰۶

وقت سحر است خیز ای طرفه پسر

پر باده لعل کن بلورین ساغر

کاین یکدم عاریت در این کنج فنا

بسیار بجوئی و نیابی دیگر

106

It is dawn. Rise, O pleasant youth!
Fill the crystal goblet with the ruby wine.
This one borrowed breath in this corner of nonexistence
You will seek much but never find again.

۱۰۷

از جملهٔ رفتگان این راه دراز

باز آمده کیست تا بما گوید راز

پس بر سر این دو راههٔ آز و نیاز

تا هیچ نمانی که نمی آیی باز

107

Of all those who have traveled this long road,
Who has returned to tell us the secret?
Therefore, in this junction of greed and need,
Leave nothing behind, for you will never return.

۱۰۸

ای پیر خردمند پگه تر بر خیز

وان کودک خاک بیز را بنگر تیز

پندش ده و گو که نرم نرمک می بیز

مغز سر کیقباد و چشم پرویز

108

O wise old man, rise early in the morning,
And take a sharp look at that dirt-sifting child.
Give him an advice and tell him to sift gently
The brain of Kay Qobâd and the eyes of Parviz.

۱۰۹

وقت سحر است خیز ای مایهٔ ناز

نرمک نرمک باده خور و چنگ نواز

کانها که بجایند نپایند بسی

وانها که شدند کس نمی آید باز

109

It is morning. Rise, O my charming one!
Sip your wine slowly and play the harp!
For those who are here will not stay long,
And those who have gone will never return.

۱۱۰

مرغی دیدم نشسته بر بارهٔ طوس

در پیش نهاده کلهٔ کیکاوس

با کله همی گفت که افسوس افسوس

کو بانگ جرسها و کجا ناله کوس

110

I saw a bird perched on the rampart of Tus,
In front of her the skull of Kay Kâwus.
She was saying to the skull: *Alas! Alas!*
What happened to that toll of bells and sound of drums?

١١١

جامی است که عقل آفرین میزندش
صد بوسه ز مهر بر جبین میزندش
این کوزه گر دهر چنین جام لطیف
میسازد و باز بر زمین میزندش

111

Here is a bowl that reason praises with bravos
And kisses a hundred times its brow with love.
This potter of the world makes such a delicate bowl
And then smashes on the ground!

١١٢

خیام اگر ز باده مستی خوش باش
با ماه رخی اگر نشستی خوش باش
چون عاقبت کار جهان نیستی است
انگار که نیستی چو هستی خوش باش

112

Khayyâm, if you are drunk with wine, be happy.
If you are together with a moon-faced one, be happy.
Since the end of the affair of the world is nonexistence,
Suppose you did not exist, now that you do, be happy.

١١٣

در کارگهٔ کوزه گری رفتم دوش
دیدم دو هزار کوزه گویا و خموش
ناگاه یکی کوزه بر آورد خروش
کو کوزه گر و کوزه خر و کوزه فروش

113

Last night I went to a potter's workshop
And saw two thousand jugs silent and vocal.
Suddenly one jug roared out:
Where is the jugmaker, the jugseller, and the jugbuyer?

۱۱۴

ایام زمانه از کسی دارد ننگ
کو در غم ایام نشیند دلتنگ
می خور تو در آبگینه با نالهٔ چنگ
زان پیش که آبگینه آید بر سنگ

114

Time is ashamed of that person
Who sits lonely and grieves over the past days.
Drink wine from a glass to the sound of a harp
Before the glass smashes into a rock.

۱۱۵

از جرم گل سیاه تا اوج زحل
کردم همه مشکلات کلی را حل
بگشادم بندهای مشکل بحیل
هر بند گشاده شد بجز بند اجل

115

From the nadir of the black mud to the zenith of Saturn,
I solved all the major problems [of being].
I untied many difficult knots, using many tricks.
Every knot became opened, except the knot of death.

۱۱۶

با سرو قدی تازه تر از خرمن گل
از دست منه جام می و دامن گل
زان پیش که ناگه شود از باد اجل
پیراهن عمر ما چو پیراهن گل

116

With a cypress-statured one, lovelier than a rose,
Avoid not the cup of wine and the skirt of the rose,
Before the wind of death suddenly make
The garment of your life like the shirt of the rose.

۱۱۷

ای دوست بیا تا غم فردا نخوریم

وین یکدم عمر را غنیمت شمریم

فردا که از این دیر فنا در گذریم

با هفت هزار سالگان سر بسریم

117

O friend, let us not worry about tomorrow.
Let us appreciate the value of this moment of life.
Tomorrow when we pass from this house of nonexistence,
We will be the same as those long deprived of life.

۱۱۸

این چرخ فلک که ما در او حیرانیم

فانوس خیال از و مثالی دانیم

خورشید چراغدان و عالم فانوس

ما چون صوریم کاندر او حیرانیم

118

This wheel of the sky at which we are bewildered,
Can be likened to a magic lantern.
Think of the sun as a candle, and of the world as a lantern.
We are like images wandering about in this lantern.

۱۱۹

بر خیز ز خواب تا شرابی بخوریم

زان پیش که از زمانه تابی بخوریم

کاین چرخ ستیزه روی ناگه روزی

چندان ندهد زمان که آبی بخوریم

119

Rise from your sleep, so that we can have a drink
Before the hand of time pushes us to a brink.
For suddenly one day, this violent wheel of the sky
Will not give us enough time to swallow a sip of water.

۱۲۰

بر خیزم و عزم بادهٔ ناب کنم

رنگ رخ خود برنگ عناب کنم

این عقل فضول پیشه را مشتی می

بر روی زنم چنانکه در خواب کنم

120

I shall rise and go toward the pure wine,
And make my face the color of jujube.
I shall splash a handful of wine on the face of
This meddling reason so that I may put her to sleep.

۱۲۱

بر مفرش خاک خفتگان می بینم

در زیر زمین نهفتگان می بینم

چندانکه بصحرای عدم می نگرم

نا آمدگان و رفتگان می بینم

121

On the spread of dust, many sleepers I can see.
And beneath the earth, many hidden ones I can see.
In this plain of annihilation, as far as I look,
Many have-not-comes and have-gones I can see.

۱۲۲

تا چند اسیر عقل هر روزه شویم

در دهر چه صد ساله چه یک روزه شویم

در ده تو بکاسه می از آن پیش که ما

در کارگهٔ کوزه گران کوزه شویم

122

How long shall we be captive to common sense?
What difference if we live one day or a hundred years here?
Give me some wine in a bowl
Before I become a jug in a potter's workshop.

۱۲۳

چون نیست مقام ما در این دهر مقیم

پس بی می و معشوق خطائی است عظیم

تا کی ز قدیم و محدث امیدم و بیم

چون من رفتم جهان چه محدث چه قدیم

123

Since our position in this world is not stable,
It is a big mistake to be without wine and a beloved.
How long shall I hope for the eternal and fear the transient?
When I am gone, let the wolrd be eternal or transient.

۱۲۴

خورشید بگل نهفت می نتوانم

و اسرار زمانه گفت می نتوانم

از بحر تفکرم بر آورد خرد

دری که ز بیم سفت می نتوانم

124

I cannot cover the sun with mud,
Nor can I utter the secrets of the world.
From the sea of meditation, intellect brought me
A pearl which I cannot pierce because of fear.

۱۲۵

دشمن بغلط گفت که من فلسفیم

ایزد داند که آنچه او گفت نیم

لیکن چو در این غم آشیان آمده ام

آخر کم از آنکه من بدانم که کیم

125

Wrongly did the enemy call me a philosopher.
God knows I am not what he said.
But since I have come to this nest of suffering,
Should I not, at least, know who I am?

۱۲۶

مائیم که اصل شادی و کان غمیم
سرمایهٔ دادیم و نهاد ستمیم
پستیم و بلندیم و کمالیم و کمیم
آیینهٔ زنگ خورده و جام جمیم

126

It is we who are the source of joy and the mine of sorrow,
The building of justice and the founding of injustice.
It is we who are perfect and imperfect, low and high,
A rusted mirror or the cup of Jamshid.

۱۲۷

من می نه ز بهر تنگدستی نخورم
یا از غم رسوائی و مستی نخورم
من می ز برای خوشدلی میخوردم
اکنون که تو بر دلم نشستی نخورم

127

Not because of poverty am I not drinking.
Not from fear of disgrace or drunkenness am I not drinking.
I used to drink in order to cheer my heart.
Now that you settled in my heart, I am not drinking.

۱۲۸

من بی می ناب زیستن نتوانم
بی باده کشید بار تن نتوانم
من بنده آن دمم که ساقی گوید
یک جام دگر بگیر و من نتوانم

128

Without pure wine, I cannot live.
Without wine, I cannot carry the burden of the body.
I am the slave of that moment when the Sâqi says,
"Have another glass!" but I cannot.

۱۲۹

هر یک چندی یکی بر آید که منم
با نعمت و با سیم و زر آید که منم
چون کارک او نظام گیرد روزی
ناگه اجل از کمین در آید که منم

129

Every now and then someone comes along and says, *I am.*
With wealth, silver, and gold comes along and says, *I am.*
When his little affair finds some order, suddenly one day,
Death leaps out of its ambush and says, *I am.*

۱۳۰

یک چند بکودکی باستاد شدیم
یک چند باستادی خود شاد شدیم
پایان سخن شنو که ما را چه رسید
از خاک در آمدیم و بر باد شدیم

130

For some time, I went to the master in my childhood.
Then for some time I was happy to be a master.
Listen to the end of the story what came to me:
I came out of the earth and was gone with the wind.

۱۳۱

یک روز زبند عالم آزاد نیم
یک دم زدن از وجود خود شاد نیم
شاگردی روزگار کردم بسیار
در کار جهان هنوز استاد نیم

131

Not one day free from the chain of the world am I.
Not one instant happy with my existence am I.
I did a long apprenticeship to the world.
Still unskilled in the affair of the world am I.

۱۳۲

از دی که گذشت هیچ از و یاد مکن

فردا که نیامده است فریاد مکن

بر نامده و گذشته بنیاد مکن

حالی خوش باش و عمر بر باد مکن

132

Of yesterday which has passed, recall nothing!

Of tomorrow which has not come, complain nothing!

Rely not on what has passed and what has not come.

Be happy now. Cast not your life to the wind for nothing!

۱۳۳

ای دیده اگر کور نه ای گور ببین

وین عالم پر فتنه و پر شور ببین

شاهان و سران و سروران زیر گلند

روهای چو مه در دهن مور ببین

133

O my eyes, if you are not blind, see the grave!

See this riotous and tumultuous world!

Kings, nobles, and notables are under the mud.

See the moon-like faces in the mouths of ants!

۱۳۴

بر خیز و مخور غم جهان گذران

بنشین و دمی بشادمانی گذران

در طبع جهان اگر وفائی بودی

نوبت بتو خود نیامدی از دگران

134

Rise, and suffer not for the transient world.

Sit, and spend a moment with joy.

If there had been any fidelity in the nature of the world,

It would have never reached you from others.

۱۳۵

چون حاصل آدمی در این شورستان

جز خوردن غصه نیست تا کندن جان

خرم دل آنکه زین جهان زود برفت

و آسوده کسیکه خود نیامد بجهان

135

Since the human share in this salt-marsh
Is nothing but suffering until death,
Blissful is the one who departed from this world soon.
Peaceful is the one who never arrived in this world.

۱۳۶

رفتم که در این منزل بیداد بدن

در دست نخواهد بجز از باد بدن

آنرا باید بمرگ من شاد بدن

کز دست اجل تواند آزاد بدن

136

I am going. For in this cruel dwelling of the body,
There will be nothing but wind in the hand.
Only that person should be glad for my death
Who himself can be free from the hand of death.

۱۳۷

رندی دیدم نشسته بر خنگ زمین

نه کفر و نه اسلام و نه دنیا و نه دین

نه حق نه حقیقت نه شریعت نه یقین

اندر دو جهان کرا بود زهره این

137

I saw a *rend* sitting on the horse of the earth.
Neither a Moslem, nor an infidel, nor worldly, nor religious.
He did not believe in God, Truth, religion, or certitude.
How can anyone dare to be like that?

۱۳۸

قانع بیک استخوان چو کرکس بودن
به زانکه طفیل خوان ناکس بودن
با نان جوین خویش حقا که به است
کالوده بپالودهٔ هر خس بودن

138

To be content with a bone, like a vulture, is better than
To be an unwelcome guest at the table of an ignoble person.
To be content with one's own barley bread is better than
To be tainted by the *pâluda* of a mean person.

۱۳۹

قومی متفکرند اندر رهٔ دین
قومی بگمان فتاده در راهٔ یقین
میترسم از آنکه بانگ آید روزی
کای بیخبران راه نه آنست و نه این

139

Some people are thoughtful about religion.
Others are suspicious of any conviction.
I am afraid one day a voice may call out:
O ignorant ones, the way is neither this nor that.

۱۴۰

گاویست در آسمان و نامش پروین
یک گاو دگر نهفته در زیر زمین
چشم خردت باز کن از راه یقین
زیر و زبر دو گاو مشتی خر بین

140

There is a cow in the sky, whose name is Pleaides,
And another hidden under the Earth.
Open your eye of wisdom with certainty and see
A drove of asses between two cows.

۱۴۱

گر بر فلکم دست بدی چون یزدان

بر داشتمی من از این فلک را ز میان

وز نو فلک دگر چنان ساختمی

کازاده بکام دل رسیدی آسان

141

If I had power over the universe like God,
I would wipe it out of existence.
Then I would build a new universe where
A freeman could easily attain to his heart's wish.

۱۴۲

مشنو سخن از زمانه ساز آمدگان

می خواه مروق بطراز آمدگان

رفتند یکان یکان فراز آمدگان

کس می ندهد نشان ز باز آمدگان

142

Listen not to those who are pleased with the world.
Drink limpid wine with those your eyes are pleased with.
Those who came before us went away one after another.
And there is no sign of anyone who came back.

۱۴۳

می خوردن و گرد نیکوان گردیدن

به زانکه بزرق زاهدی ورزیدن

گر عاشق و مست دوزخی خواهد بود

پس روی بهشت کس نخواهد دیدن

143

To drink wine and to hover around the lovely ones
Is better than practicing pretentious asceticism.
If the lover and the drunkard were to dwell in hell,
No one would want to see the face of the paradise.

۱۴۴

نتوان دل شاد را بغم فرسودن
وقت خوش خود بسنگ محنت سودن
کس غیب چه داند که چه خواهد بودن
می باید و معشوق و بکام آسودن

144

One should not depress one's happy heart with grief,
Nor let the millstone of suffering grind one's happiness.
Who knows what will happen in the future?
There must be wine, the beloved, and fulfilment of desires.

۱۴۵

آن قصر که بر چرخ همی زد پهلو
بر درگهٔ او شهان نهادندی رو
دیدیم که بر کنگره اش فاخته ای
بنشسته همی گفت که کوکو کوکو

145

That palace which used to reach the sky,
At whose threshold kings lowered their faces,
We saw a ringdove perched on its turret,
Singing, *Where? Where? Where?*

۱۴۶

از آمدن و رفتن ما سودی کو
وز تار امید عمر ما پودی کو
چندین سر و پای نازنینان جهان
میسوزد و خاک میشود دودی کو

146

What is gained from our coming and going?
Where is a woof for the warp of our life's hope?
So many heads and feet of the lovely ones of the world
Burn to ashes, but where is the smoke?

۱۴۷

از تن چو برفت جان پاک من و تو

خشتی دو نهند بر مغاک من و تو

وانگاه برای خشت گور دگران

در کالبدی کشند خاک من و تو

147

When our pure souls leave your body and mine,
They put a few bricks on your grave and mine.
Later, to make bricks for other people's graves,
They pour into molds your ashes and mine.

۱۴۸

می خور که فلک بهر هلاک من و تو

قصدی دارد بجان پاک من و تو

در سبزه نشین و می روشن میخور

کاین سبزه بسی دمد ز خاک من و تو

148

Drink wine! For heaven, to destroy your life and mine,
Is going to make an attempt at your life and mine.
Sit on the grass and drink some clear wine.
For long this grass will grow from your ashes and mine.

۱۴۹

از هر چه بجز می است کوتاهی به

می هم ز کف بتان خرگاهی به

مستی و قلندری و گمراهی به

یک جرعهٔ می ز ماه تا ماهی به

149

From anything except wine negligence is best.
And wine from the hands of the intimate idols is best.
Drunkenness, being a calender, and being lost are best.
In the whole world, a sip of wine is best.

۱۵۰

بنگر ز صبا دامن گل چاک شده
بلبل ز جمال گل طربناک شده
در سایهٔ گل نشین که بسیار این گل
در خاک فرو ریزد و ما خاک شده

150

Behold how the rose's skirt is split by the zephyr!
And how the nightingale delights in the rose's beauty!
Take your seat near the rose. Many times this flower
Will scatter on the dust while we have turned into dust.

۱۵۱

تا کی غم آن خورم که دارم یا نه
وین عمر بخوشدلی گذارم یا نه
پر کن قدح باده که معلومم نیست
کایندم که فرو برم بر آرم یا نه

151

How long shall I worry whether I have or not?
Or whether I spend my life happily or not?
Fill the bowl of wine! For I do not know whether
This breath which I inhale I will exhale or not?

۱۵۲

یک جرعه می کهن ز ملکی نو به
و ز هرچه نه می طریق بیرون شو به
دردست به از تخت فریدون صد بار
خشت سر خم ز ملک کیخسرو به

152

One gulp of old wine is better than a new kingdom.
It is better to stay away from anything except wine.
The brick on top of the wine-vat is a hundred times
Better than Feridun's throne and Key Khosrow's kingdom.

۱۵۳

آن مایه ز دنیا که خوری یا پوشی

معذوری اگر در طلبش میکوشی

باقی همه رایگان نیرزد هشدار

تا عمر گرانبها بدان نفروشی

153

You are excused if you strive to obtain from this world
As much as you need for your food and clothing.
Anything extra is not worth the trouble.
Beware, lest you should sell your precious life for nothing.

۱۵۴

از آمدن بهار و از رفتن دی

اوراق وجود ما همی گردد طی

می خور مخور اندوه که فرمود حکیم

غمهای جهان چو زهر و تریاقش می

154

The comings of springs and the goings of winters
Turn over the pages of our existence.
Have wine, not sorrow! For the doctor says,
Sorrow is like poison whose antidote is wine.

۱۵۵

از کوزه گری کوزه خریدم باری

آن کوزه سخن گفت ز هر اسراری

شاهی بودم که جام زرینم بود

اکنون شده ام کوزه هر خماری

155

One day I bought a jug from a potter.
The jug spoke about all kinds of secrets:
"Once I was a king with a golden cup in my hand.
"Now I am a jug in every drunkard's hand."

۱۵۶

ای آنکه نتیجهٔ چهار و هفتی

وز هفت و چهار دائم اندر تفتی

می خور که هزار بار بیشت گفتم

باز آمدنت نیست چو رفتی رفتی

156

O you, who are the sum of four and seven,
And always in bondage of the four and seven,
Drink wine! A thousand times and more I have told you:
You will not come back. When you're gone, you are gone.

۱۵۷

ایدل تو باسرار معما نرسی

در نکته زیرکان دانا نرسی

اینجا بمی لعل بهشتی میساز

کانجا که بهشت است رسی یا نرسی

157

O heart, to the secrets of this puzzle, you will not reach.
To the subtlety of the astute savants, you will not reach.
Here, be content with the heavenly ruby wine.
For there where heaven is, you may or may not reach.

۱۵۸

ایدوست حقیقت شنو از من سخنی

با بادهٔ لعل باش و با سیم تنی

کانکس که جهان کرد فراغت دارد

از سبلت چون توئی و ریش چو منی

158

My friend, hear a word of truth from me:
Be with ruby wine and someone with a fair body.
For the one who made this world cares
Neither for your moustache nor for my beard.

۱۵۹

ای کاش که جای آرمیدن بودی
یا این ره دور را رسیدن بودی
کاش از پی صد هزار سال از دل خاک
چون سبزه امید بردمیدن بودی

159

I wish there were a place to rest,
Or a destination to arrive at the end of this long road!
I wish there were a hope of rising, like the grass,
From the heart of dust after a hundred thousand years!

۱۶۰

بر سنگ زدم دوش سبوی کاشی
سرمست بدم چو کردم این اوباشی
با من بزبان حال میگفت سبو
من چون تو بدم تو نیز چون من باشی

160

Last night, I smashed an earthen jug on the rock.
I was drunk when I committed this asperity.
The jug told me in a mute language,
I used to be like you. You, too, will be like me.

۱۶۱

بر شاخ امید اگر بری یافتمی
هم رشتهٔ خویش را سری یافتمی
تا چند ز تنگنای زندان وجود
ایکاش سوی عدم دری یافتمی

161

If I could see a fruit on the branch of hope,
I would find the end of my rope.
How long should I wish for a door to open
From the prison of existence into nonexistence?

۱۶۲

بر گیر پیاله و سبوی ای دلجوی
فارغ بنشین بکشته زار و لب جوی
بس شخص عزیز را که چرخ بد خوی
صد بار پیاله کرد و صد بار سبوی

162

O dear of my heart, pick up the bowl and the jug,
And sit peacefully on the bank of a brook in a field of crops.
This ill-tempered wheel has turned many a dear person
A hundred times to a bowl and a hundred times to a jug.

۱۶۳

پیری دیدم بخانهٔ خماری
گفتم نکنی ز رفتگان اخباری
گفتا می خور که همچو ما بسیاری
رفتند و خبر باز نیامد باری

163

I asked an old man in a wine-dealer's house
"Have you no news of those who passed away?"
"Drink wine!" said he. "For never any news came
"From so many like us who passed away."

۱۶۴

تا چند حدیث پنج و چار ای ساقی
مشکل چه یکی چه صد هزار ای ساقی
خاکیم همه چنگ بساز ای ساقی
بادیم همه باده بیار ای ساقی

164

How long the story of the four and five, O Sâqi?
What matters if the problem be one or a thousand, O Sâqi?
We all are from dust. Play the harp, O Sâqi!
We all shall go with the wind. Bring the wine, O Sâqi!

۱۶۵

چندانکه نگاه میکنم هر سوئی

در باغ روانست ز کوثر جوئی

صحرا چو بهشت است ز کوثر کم گوی

بنشین به بهشت با بهشتی روئی

165

As far as I can see in every direction,
There is a stream of *Kosar* flowing in the garden.
The plain is like the paradise, say nothing of Kosar.
Sit in this paradise beside someone with a heavenly face.

۱۶۶

خوش باش که پخته اند سودای تو دی

فارغ شده اند از تمنای تو دی

قصه چه کنم که بی تقاضای تو دی

دادند قرار کار فردای تو دی

166

Cheer up! For they finished your business yesterday.
They did away with your desire yesterday.
How should I tell this story that, without your request,
They decided your tomorrow's work yesterday?

۱۶۷

در کارگهٔ کوزه گری کردم رای

در پایهٔ چرخ دیدم استاد بپای

میکرد دلیر کوزه را دسته و سر

از کلهٔ پادشاه و از دست گدای

167

I went to a potter's workshop
And saw the master at the foot of the wheel,
Shaping boldly the handle and head of a jug
From the hand of a beggar and the head of a king.

۱۶۸

در گوش دلم گفت فلک پنهانی
حکمی که قضا بود ز من می‌دانی
در گردش خویش اگر مرا دست بدی
خود را برهاندمی ز سرگردانی

168

The firmament whispered in my heart's ear secretly:
"You think I am responsible for the rule of destiny!
"If I had a choice in my own revolution,
"I would free myself from this wandering."

۱۶۹

زان کوزهٔ می که نیست در وی ضرری
پر کن قدحی بخور بمن ده دگری
زان پیشتر ای صنم که در رهگذری
خاک من و تو کوزه کند کوزه گری

169

From that jug of wine, in which there is no harm,
Fill a cup for yourself, and one for me, too;
Before a potter along a road, my darling,
Makes jugs of your dust, and mine, too.

۱۷۰

گر دست دهد ز مغز گندم نانی
وز می دو منی ز گوسفندی رانی
با لاله رخی و گوشهٔ بستانی
عیشی بود آن نه حد هر سلطانی

170

If a loaf of wheat bread be available,
Two gallons of wine and a thigh of mutton,
A rosy-cheeked one, in a corner of an orchard,
That would be a pleasure not every king could reach.

۱۷۱

گر کار فلک بعدل سنجیده بدی

احوال فلک جمله پسندیده بدی

ور عدل بدی بکارها در گردون

کی خاطر اهل فضل رنجیده بدی

171

If the heaven's work had been based on justice,
Its conditions would have been all agreeable.
And if there was justice in the world,
Would the hearts of the learned be distressed?

۱۷۲

هان کوزه گرا بپای اگر هشیاری

تا چند کنی بر گل مردم خواری

انگشت فریدون و کف کیخسرو

بر چرخ نهاده ای چه می پنداری

172

O Potter, mind what you are doing, if your are intelligent!
How long shall you debase the clay [made]of people?
What do you think it is you have laid on the wheel?
The fingers of Fridun and the palm of Kay Khosrow!

۱۷۳

هنگام صبوح ای صنم فرخ پی

بر ساز ترانه ای و پیش آور می

کافکند بخاک صد هزاران جم و کی

این آمدن تیر مه و رفتن دی

173

Morningtide, O elegant sweetheart,
Compose a song and bring wine!
For this going of the winter and coming of the summer,
Lowered to dust a hundred thousand Jamshids and Kays!

Chapter Three
12th Century C.E.
6th Century Hejri

سنائی غزنوی
(۵۲۵ هجری قمری)

۱

ما عقل بدست عشق دادیم گرو

بی عقل خوشیم اگر نباشد به دو جو

مر عاشق را عقل چه محرم باشد

ای عقل حدیث عشق بی توست برو

Sanâi Ghaznavi
(d. 1131 C.E.)

1
I pawned reason in the hand of love.
I am happy without reason. Let it go.
How can reason be a lover's confidante?
It has no part in the story of love, let it go!

٢

عاشق شوی ای دل و ز جان اندیشی

دزدی کنی و ز پاسبان اندیشی

دعوی محبت کنی و لاف زنی

وانگه ز زبان این و آن اندیشی

2

O heart, you fall in love and about your life you worry.
You commit theft and about the policeman you worry.
You claim to be a lover and brag about it,
Then about what people may say you worry.

٣

بی روی تو بر نیاید از دل دم عشق

در فتنه تست سربسر عالم عشق

ما را گویی چرا نگیری کم عشق

عاشق باشی تو تا بدانی غم عشق

3

Without your face, my heart will not breathe out love.
The world of love, from end to end, is under your charm.
You ask me why I do not give up love.
You must become a lover to know the longing of love.

۴

با دل گفتم چرا نگیری کم عشق

گفتا نه به اختیار باشد غم عشق

گفتم نرسی بوصل گفتا شاید

آواره چو من بسی است در عالم عشق

4

I asked my heart, "Why do you not give up love?"
It answered, "Love is not a matter of choice."
I said, "You may not attain union." It said, "Perhaps.
"There are many wanderers like me in the world of love."

۵

ای دل چو همی حل نشود مشکل عشق
بر خیره چه جویی ره بی حاصل عشق
بس کس که چو تو بتیغ غم بسمل عشق
کاخر نشناخت هیچ کس منزل عشق

5

O heart, since none could solve the problem of love,
Why do you follow the futile way of love?
Many like you fell victim to the sword of love.
Yet none could attain to the goal of love in the end.

۶

ای دل پس از این مگرد گرد در عشق
تو خاک بگردی و نداری سر عشق
بس کس چو تو جان بداد بر بستر عشق
ناکرده درست حرفی از دفتر عشق

6

O heart, from now on do not go near the door of love.
You may turn into dust and not know the meaning of love.
Many like you surrendered their souls in the bed of love,
Without having figured a single letter from the book of love.

۷

بیهوده مزن تو ای سنایی دم عشق
زیرا نشود چو تو کسی محرم عشق
پندی بپذیر و گیر یک ره کم عشق
کز آب روان گرد بر آرد غم عشق

7

O Sanâi, do not brag about love in vain!
For a person like you will not be a confidant to love.
Take this advice and get off the road of love.
For the sorrow of love can turn the running water into dust.

٨

جز دست بلا نیست جنیبت کش عشق
جز تیر نیاز نیست در ترکش عشق
هر چند معطرم ز بوی خوش عِشق
شد ریخته آبرویم از آتش عشق

8

Nothing but the hand of calamity leads the steed of love.
Nothing but the arrow of need exists in the quiver of love.
Although I am perfumed by the pleasant scent of love,
My honor was consumed in the fire of love.

٩

پیوسته دل من است فرمانبر عشق
همواره تن من است خدمتگر عشق
همچون سپر ایستاده ام در بر عشق
دارم سر آنکه سر کنم در سر عشق

9

My heart is always obedient to love.
My body is always the servant of love.
I am standing like a shield beside love.
I have in mind to lose my head over love.

١٠

تا دید زمانه در دلم غایت عشق
در پیش دلم همی کشد رایت عشق
گر وحی ز آسمان گسسته نشدی
در شان دل من آمدی آیت عشق

10

As soon as the world saw my heart's goal was love,
It began to wave the banner of love before my heart.
If revelations from the heaven had not stopped,
In regard to my heart would have come the verse of love.

۱۱

گویند که کردهای دلت برده عشق
وین رنج دل تو هست آورده عشق
گر بر دارم ز پیش دل پرده عشق
بینند دلی به ناز پرورده عشق

11

They tell me I have made my heart the slave of love,
And this suffering of my heart is the result of love.
If I remove the veil of love from the face of my heart,
They will see how my heart is tenderly nurtured by love.

۱۲

با دل گفتم مگرد پیرامن عشق
بر کش ز سر وجود پیراهن عشق
دل سر ز گریبان هوس بر زد و گفت
تا من بزیم دست من و دامن عشق

12

I told my heart, "Stay away from love,
"And remove the garment of love from your body."
My heart, nurturing a fancy, said:
"As long as I live, I will hold on to the skirt of love."

۱۳

کی بسته کند عقل سراپرده عشق
کی باز آرد خرد ز ره برده عشق
بسیار ز زنده به بود مرده عشق
ای خواجه چه واقفی تو از خرده عشق

13

How can reason close the chamber of love?
How can intellect bring back the one stolen by love?
Far better than the living is the one killed by love.
O *khâja*, what do you know about the subtlety of love?

۱۴

هر روز به نو بر آید آن زرگر عشق
در گردن محنت افکند زیور عشق
احداد از آن نهاده اند بر در عشق
تا بگریزد هر که ندارد سر عشق

14

Everyday in a new way comes that goldsmith of love
And puts around the neck of suffering the ornament of love.
Obstacles are placed at the door of love
So that escape those who lack the determination of love.

۱۵

هر دل که شود سوار بر مرکب عشق
شاید که شکار گیرد از مخلب عشق
وان دل که کند بدو نظر کوکب عشق
گر جان بدهد رواست در مذهب عشق

15

Any heart that rides on the horse of love,
May catch a prey from the claws of love.
And the heart upon which shines the star of love,
If it dies, it is allowed in the religion of love.

۱۶

آنها که اسیر عشق دلدارانند
از دیده سرشک خون دل بارانند
هر گز نشود بخت بد از عشق جدا
بخت بد و عاشقی بهم یارانند

16

Those who are captured by the heart-ravishers' love,
Rain from their eyes the blood of their hearts.
Never does bad luck separate from love.
Bad luck and love are bosom friends.

۱۷

با سوز تو چون گل همه لب خنده شدم

در پای تو مردم و دگر زنده شدم

آزادی مادر آورم سود نداشت

آزاد کنونم که ترا بنده شدم

17

With your fire I became all laughter like a rose.
I died at your feet and came to life again.
My inborn freedom did not benefit me.
Now that I am bound to you I am free.

۱۸

در دل ز طرب شکفته باغیست مرا

بر جان ز عدم نهاده داغیست مرا

خالی ز خیالها دماغیست مرا

از هستی و نیستی فراغیست مرا

18

There is a garden in my heart blooming with joy.
Yet, my soul is branded by nonexistence.
I have a mind devoid of illusions.
I am free from both existence and nonexistence.

۱۹

قصاب چنانک عادت اوست مرا

بفکند و بکشت و گفت این خوست مرا

سر باز بعذر می نهد در پایم

دم میدمدم تا بکند پوست مرا

19

The butcher, as is his custom, knocked me down,
Killed me, and said this is my nature.
Then, apologizing, he brought his head to my foot
And breathed in me, so that he could peel my skin.

۲۰

چون پوست کشد کارد بدندان گیرد

آهن ز لبش قیمت مرجان گیرد

او کارد بدست خویش میزان گیرد

تا جان گیرد هر آنچه با جان گیرد

20

After he peeled me, he held the knife with his teeth.
The touch if his lips made the iron precious like a pearl.
Then he held the knife balanced in his hand,
So that life may return to the one whose life he had taken.

۲۱

بیرون جهان همه درون دل ماست

این هر دو سرا یگان یگان منزل ماست

زحمت همه در نهاد آب و گل ماست

پیش از دل و گل چه بود آن منزل ماست

21

The world outside is all inside our hearts.
These two houses are both our dwellings, one after another.
The trouble is with the nature of our physical body only.
Whatever existed before this physical body is our home.

۲۲

لشگرگه عشق عارض خرم توست

زنجیر بلا زلف خم اندر خم توست

آسایش صد هزار جان یک دم توست

ای شادی آن دل که در آن دل غم توست

22

Your cheerful face is the camp of love.
Your twisted and curled hair is the chain of calamity.
O you, who are the joy of the heart which has your sorrow,
A single breath of you comforts a hundred thousand souls.

۲۳

مهراب جهان جمال رخساره توست
سلطان فلک اسیر و بیچاره توست
شور و شر و شرک و زهد و توحید و یقین
در گوشه چشمهای خونخواره توست

23

The beauty of your face is the altar of the world.
The king of the sky (the sun) is your helpless captive.
Passion, piety, faith, duality, and unity are
All in the corners of your blood-thirsty eyes.

۲۴

خواهم که به اندیشه و با رای درست
خود را بدر اندازم از این واقعه چست
کز مذهب این قوم ملالم بگرفت
هر یک زده دست عجز در شاخی سست

24

With right thinking and right intention,
I want to get out of this situation nimbly.
I grew tired of these people's creed.
Everyone has helplessly clutched at a feeble twig.

۲۵

غم خوردن این جهان فانی هوس است
از هستی ما به نیستی یک نفس است
نیکویی کن اگر ترا دسترس است
کاین عالم یادگار بسیار کس است

25

To grieve for this transient world is futile.
A single breath separates being from nonbeing for us.
Do good deeds if you can.
For this world is the memorial of many people.

۲۶

گر گویم جان فدا کنم جان نفس است

گر گویم دل فدا کنم دل هوس است

گر ملک فدا کنم همان ملک خس است

کی بر تر از این سه بنده را دسترس است

26
If I were to sacrifice my soul, the soul is a breath.
If I were to sacrifice my heart, the heart is a desire.
If I sacrifice my property, the property is straw.
What better things than these three do I have access to?

۲۷

شبها ز فراق تو دلم پر خون است

وز بی خوابی دو دیده بر گردون است

چون روز آید زبان حالم گوید

کای بر در بامداد حالت چون است

27
Every night my heart bleeds in separation;
And my eyes, unable to sleep, gaze at the sky.
When the day breaks, my inner voice calls:
"How do you feel at the threshold of the morning?"

۲۸

آنکس که سرت برید غمخوار تو اوست

وان کت کلهی نهاد طرار تو اوست

آن کس که ترا بار دهد بار تو اوست

وان کس که ترا بی تو کند یار تو اوست

28
He who cuts your head (ego) is your sympathetic friend.
He who puts a hat on your head is your robber.
He who gives you a feast is your burden.
He who makes you without you is your friend.

۲۹

ما را بجز از تو عالم افروز مباد
بر ما سپه هجر تو پیروز مباد
اندر دل ما ز هجر تو سوز مباد
چون با تو شدم بی تو مرا روز مباد

29

May there be no world-illuminer except you for me.
May the host of your separation not triumph over me.
May there be no blaze of your separation in my heart.
After our union, may there be no day without you for me.

۳۰

سودای توام بی سر و بی سامان کرد
عشق تو مرا زنده جاویدان کرد
لطف و کرمت جسم مرا چون جان کرد
در خاک عمل بهتر از این نتوان کرد

30

Desire for you made me a vagabond.
Love for you made me immortal.
Your grace and generosity made my body like a soul.
In the field of action, better than this could not be done.

۳۱

در آینه رخ تو آه نتوان کرد
آیینه به یک آه تبه نتوان کرد
روی تو ز نازکی بحدی که در او
از غایت نیکویی نگه نتوان کرد

31

In the mirror of your face one can not sigh.
One can not corrode a mirror with a sigh.
So delicate is your face and so intense its beauty
It is impossible to gaze at it.

۳۲

روزی که سر از پرده برون خواهی کرد
آن روز زمانه را زبون خواهی کرد
گر حسن و جمال ازین فزون خواهی کرد
یا رب چه جگرهاست که خون خواهی کرد

32

The day you put your head out of the veil,
You will humble the world.
If your beauty and charm grow more than this,
O what hearts that you will cause to bleed!

۳۳

تا از تو بتا بناگهی گشتم فرد
یکباره برآورد فراق از من گرد
گر باز رسم به پیش تو با غم و درد
آنگاه بگویم که فراق تو چه کرد

33

My sweetheart, since you suddenly left me alone,
Your separation made me quite miserable.
If pain and grief allow me to reach you again,
I will tell you what your separation did to me.

۳۴

روزی که دلت بود ز جانان پر درد
شکرانه هزار جان فدا باید کرد
اندر سر کوی عاشقی ای سره مرد
بی شکر قفای نیکوان نتوان خورد

34

The day your beloved fills your heart with pain,
You should sacrifice a thousand lives in gratitude.
In the path of love, O sincere man, a slap on the neck
From the lovely ones should not go without thanks.

۳۵

گر خاک شوم چو باد بر من گذرد

ور باد شوم چو آب بر من سپرد

جایش خواهم بچشم من در نگرد

از دست چنین جان جهان جان که برد

35

If I become dust, he passes by me like wind.
If I become wind, he flows by me like water.
If I ask for his place, he looks at me in the eye.
Who can save his life from such a soul of the world?

۳۶

چون چهره تو ز گریه باشد پر درد

زنهار به هیچ آبی آلوده مگرد

کاندر ره عاشقی چنان باید مرد

کز دریا خشک آید از دوزخ سرد

36

If your face be full of pain with tears,
Beware, lest you should contaminate it with any water.
For in the path of love, man must be so as
To emerge dry from the sea and cold from the hell.

۳۷

گفتا که به گرد کوی ما خیره مگرد

تا خصم من از جان تو بر نارد گرد

گفتم که نبایدت غم جانم خورد

در کوی تو کشته به که از روی تو فرد

37

He said, "Do not wander in my street in vain,
"Lest my enemy should reduce your life to dust."
I said, "Do not worry about my life.
"Better to die in your street than to be separate from you."

۳۸

منگر تو بدان که ذوفنون آید مرد
در عهد و وفا نگر که چون آید مرد
از عهده عهد اگر برون آید مرد
از هر چه گمان بری فزون آید مرد

38

Regard not how skilful a man is.
Regard how loyal and faithful he is.
If a man be able to carry out his promise,
He is higher than anything you can imagine.

۳۹

این اسب قلندری نه هر کس تازد
وین مهره نیستی نه هر کس بازد
مردی باید که جان برون اندازد
چون جان بشود عشق ترا جان سازد

39

Not every man can gallop this horse of calendership.
Not every man can play with this die of nonexistence.
Man must needs courage to cast away his life,
And when it is done, to make your love his life.

۴۰

نقاش که بر نقش تو پرگار افکند
فرمود که تا سجده برندت یکچند
چون نقش تمام گشت ای سرو بلند
می خواند «وان یکاد» و میسوخت سپند

40

When the Painter was painting your portrait,
He ordered [angels] to prostrate before you for a while.
When the portrait was completed, O tall cypress,
He was reciting *Va in yakâd* and burning wild rue.

۴۱

خورشید ز اوج خویش نظاره تست
گلزار غلام رنگ رخساره تست
یک شهر همه تشنه و آواره تست
دلشاد بود کسی که غمخواره تست

41

The sun watches you from its climax.
The rose-bower is humbled by your face's color.
The whole city is bewildered by you and thirsty for you.
Blissful is the one who suffers for you.

۴۲

مردی که براه عشق جان فرساید
باید که بدون یار خود نگراید
عاشق به ره عشق چنان می باید
کز دوزخ و از بهشت یادش ناید

42

He who lays his life on the path of love
Must not tend toward any other than his love.
A lover must be so as the thought of heaven and hell
Never occurs to his mind on the path of love.

۴۳

آسیمه سران بینواییم هنوز
با شهوتها و با هواییم هنوز
زین هر دو پی هم بگراییم هنوز
از دوست بدین سبب جداییم هنوز

43

We are still provoked and miserable,
Victims of our sensuality and passion.
Because of these two, we are still chasing each other.
Hence, we are still separate from the Friend.

۴۴

با سینه این و آن چه گویی غم خویش

از دیده این و آن چه جویی غم خویش

بر ساز تو عالم ز بیش و کم خویش

آنگاه بزی بناز در عالم خویش

44

Why do you tell your suffering to this person or that?
Or seek sympathy from the eye of this person or that?
Create your own world with whatever you have,
Little or much, and live graciously in your own world.

۴۵

هر نیم شبی خاطر دوراندیشم

یاد آورد از گوهر و اصل خویشم

بنشیند شادی بقا در جانم

برخیزد اندوه فنا از پیشم

45

Every midnight my far-sighted mind
Reminds me of my origin and essence.
Then the joy of being fills my heart,
And the sorrow of nonbeing quits me.

۴۶

پر شد ز شراب عشق جانا جانم

چون زلف تو در هم زده شد ایامم

از عشق تو این نه بس مراد و کامم

کز جمله بندگان نویسی نامم

46

The wine of love filled my cup, my darling.
And my life became disheveled like your hair.
Is this not enough for me from your love
That you write my name as one of your bondmen?

۴۷

زان یک نظر نهان که ما دزدیدیم

دور از تو هزار درد و محنت دیدیم

اندر هوست پرده خود بدریدیم

تو عشوه فروختی و ما بخریدیم

47

From that one secret glance I stole,
I suffered many troubles away from you.
I tore my veil while desiring for you.
You sold coquetry, and I bought it.

۴۸

اندر دریا نهنگ باید بودن

واندر صحرا پلنگ باید بودن

مردانه و مرد رنگ باید بودن

ورنه بهزار ننگ باید بودن

48

In the sea, a whale one must be.
In the desert, a leopard one must be.
Manly and courageous one must be,
Else with a world of shame one must be.

۴۹

تا با خودی ار چه همنشینی با من

ای بس دوری که از تو باشد تا من

در من نرسی تا نشوی از خود گم

کاندر ره عشق یا تو کنجی یا من

49

As long as you are with yourself, though sitting beside me,
O what a long distance there is between you and me!
Unless you lose yourself, you can not find me.
For in the path of love, there is room for either you or me.

۵۰

طبعی نه که با دوست بر آمیزم من
عقلی نه که از عشق بپرهیزم من
دستی نه که با قضا در آویزم من
پایی نه که از میانه بگریزم من

50

I have neither the nature to mix with my beloved
Nor the wisdom to avoid love.
I have neither the strength to wrestle with my destiny
Nor the ability to escape from the field of battle.

۵۱

دلها همه آب گشت و جانها همه خون
تا چیست حقیقت از پس پرده و چون
ای بر علمت خرد رد و گردون دون
از تو دو جهان پر و تو از هر دو برون

51

Many hearts bled and many lives dissolved in order to know
What and how the truth behind the veil is.
In knowing you, reason is helpless and the sky is low.
Both worlds are full of you, yet you are outside both.

۵۲

ما ذات نهاده بر صفاتیم همه
موصوف صفت سخره ذاتیم همه
تا در صفتیم در مماتیم همه
چون رفت صفت عین حیاتیم همه

52

We have all left the essence and stuck to attributes.
We are praised by attributes and humiliated by the essence.
As long as we are stuck with attributes, we are all dead.
When attributes are gone, we are all the water of life.

۵۳

غم کی خورد آنکه شادمانیش تویی
یا کی مرد آنکه زندگانیش تویی
در نسیه آن جهان کجا بندد دل
آنرا که بنقد این جهانیش تویی

53

When does the one whose joy is you suffer?
When does the one whose life is you perish?
When does the one whose cash in this world is you
Attach his heart to the credit of the next world?

۵۴

بیزار شو از خود که زیان تو تویی
کم گو ز ستاره کاسمان تو تویی
پیدا دگران راست نهان تو تویی
خوش باش که در جمله جهان تو تویی

54

Hate your ego! For your loss is you.
Speak less of the stars! For your sky is you.
The visible is for others, the invisible is you.
Be happy! For all said, your world is you.

۵۵

صد چشمه ز چشم من براندی و شدی
بر آتش فرقتم نشاندی و شدی
چون باد جهنده آمدی تنگ برم
خاکم به دو دیده بر فشاندی و شدی

55

You drew many streams from my eyes and went away.
You made me sit in the fire of separation and went away.
Like a salient wind, you came up against me,
Threw dust in my eyes, and went away.

۵۶

ای دل منیوش از آن صنم دلداری

بیهوده مفرسای تن اندر خواری

کان ماه ستمکاره ز درد و غم تو

فارغتر از آنست که می پنداری

56

O heart, do not listen to that idol's sympathy.
Do not in vain wear yourself out with humility.
For that tyrant beauty is more inattentive
To your sorrow and suffering than you think.

۵۷

تا هشیاری به طعم مستی نرسی

تا تن ندهی به جان پرستی نرسی

تا در ره عشق دوست چون آتش و آب

از خود نشوی نیست به هستی نرسی

57

As long as you are sober, you will not taste drunkenness.
Unless you give up the body, you will not love the spirit.
Unless you become naught in the path of love,
Like fire and water, you will not reach to existence.

۵۸

تا چند ز جان مستمند اندیشی

تا کی ز جهان پر گزند اندیشی

آنچه از تو توان شدن همین کالبد است

یک مزبله گو مباش چند اندیشی

58

How long are you going to worry about your wretched life?
How long are you going to worry about this perilous world?
What can be lost from you is this body only.
Suppose a dump does not exist. Why do you worry?

۵۹

گر آمدنم ز من بدی نامدمی

ور نیز شدن ز من بدی کی شدمی

به زان نبدی که اندرین دیر خراب

نه آمدمی نه شدمی نه بدمی

59

If my coming was up to me, I would not have come.
If my going was up to me, when would I go?
It would have been best if in this ruinous world,
I had never come, never gone, and never been.

۶۰

جز راه قلندر و خرابات مپوی

جز باده و جز سماع و جز یار مجوی

پر کن قدح شراب و در پیش سبوی

می نوش کن ای نگار و بیهوده مگوی

60

Take the way of calendership and the tavern only.
Ask for wine, music, and the beloved only.
Fill the goblet and, in front of the jug of wine,
Drink happily, my dear, and speak sense only.

۶۱

از خلق ز راه تیز گوشی نرهی

وز خود ز سر سخن فروشی نرهی

زین هر دو بدین دو گر بکوشی نرهی

از خلق و ز خود جز به خموشی نرهی

61

From people by listening keenly, you will not be free.
From yourself by speaking eloquently, you will not be free.
From these two, however hard you try, you will not be free.
From people and self, but by silence, you will not be free.

عطار نیشابوری
(۶۲۷ هجری قمری)

۱

گه تحفه بناله سحرگاه دهی
گه تشریفم برای یک آه دهی
زان میخواهم بیخودی خویش که تو
بیخود کنی آنگاه بخود راه دهی

Attâr Nishâburi
(d. 1230 C.E.)

1

Sometimes you reward me for my laments at dawn.
Other times you honor me because of one sigh.
I desire my selflessness because when you make me selfless
You admit me into your own self.

۲

چیزی که دمی نه تو در آنی و نه من
کیفیت آن نه تو بدانی و نه من
گر برخیزد پرده پندار از پیش
او ماند و او نه تو بمانی و نه من

2

That in which neither you exist nor I,
Its quality neither you know nor I.
If the veil of illusion is lifted from before us,
Only He will remain, He. Neither you nor I.

٣

در بند گره گشای می باید بود

گمره شده رهنمای می باید بود

یک لحظه هزار سال می باید زیست

یک لحظه هزار جای می باید بود

3

When in chain, a chain breaker one must be.

Having lost the way, a road-guide one must be.

In one moment, a thousand years one must live.

In one instant, a thousand places one must be.

۴

ای دل دیدی که هر چه دیدی هیچ است

هر قصه دوران که شنیدی هیچ است

چندین که ز هر سوی دویدی هیچ است

و امروز که گوشه ای گزیدی هیچ است

4

O heart, did you see whatever you saw was naught?

Any story of time you heard was naught?

So much dashing in all directions was naught.

And today sitting in one corner is also naught.

۵

گفتم ز فنای خود چنانم که مپرس

گفتا به بقاییت رسانم که مپرس

یعنی چو به نیستی بدیدی خود را

چندان هستی بر تو فشانم که مپرس

5

I said, "In my mortality, I am so as I cannot explain."

He said, "I will take you to an immortality you cannot explain.

"That is to say, when you see yourself as nonexistent,

"I will give you so much existence you cannot explain."

۶

ای مرغ عجب ستارگان چینه تست

از روز الست عهد دیرینه تست

گر جام جهان نمای می جویی تو

در صندوقی نهاده در سینه تست

6

O wonder bird, stars are your seeds to pick.
Your ancient covenant is from the Day of *Alast*.
If you are searching for the world-viewing cup,
It is laid in a safe in your breast.

۷

سری که بتو رسد ز خود پنهان دار

امید همه بدرد بی درمان دار

وانگاه ز جان آینه ای ساز مدام

و آن آینه در برابر جانان دار

7

If a secret is revealed to you, keep it hidden.
Hope only for a pain without remedy.
Then make a permanent mirror of your spirit,
And hold it in front of the Beloved.

۸

تیری که ز شست حکم جانان گذرد

از جان هدفش ساز که از جان گذرد

زان تیر سپر مجوی کز هر دو جهان

آن تیر ز خویش نیز پنهان گذرد

8

The arrow that passes the Beloved's commanding hand,
Make your soul its target and let it pass through.
Shield not yourself from the arrow that
Pierces both worlds hidden even from itself.

٩

گر جان گویم عاشق آن دیدار است
ور دل گویم واله آن گفتار است
جان و دل من پر گهر اسرار است
لیکن چه کنم که بر زبان مسمار است

9

My soul is in love with that countenance.
My heart is enamored of that speech.
My soul and heart are replete with precious mysteries.
But what shall I do since my tongue is locked?

١٠

یک عاشق پاک و یک دل زنده کجاست
یک سوخته بی فکر پراکنده کجاست
چون بنده اندیشه خویشند همه
پس در دو جهان خدای را بنده کجاست

10

Where is a sincere lover and a spirited heart?
Where is a burned-in-love without scattered thoughts?
Since everyone is the slave of his thoughts,
Who in both worlds is the slave of God?

١١

ای در طلب گره گشایی مرده
در وصل بزاده در جدایی مرده
ای بر لب بحر تشنه با خاک شده
وی بر سر گنج در گدایی مرده

11

O you who have died in search of a savior,
You who were born in union and died in disunion,
You are buried thirsty on the seashore,
You have died of poverty on top of a treasure!

١٢

هر روز ره عشق تو از سر گیرم
هر شب ز غم تو ماتمی در گیرم
نه زهره آنکه دل نهم بر چو تویی
نه طاقت آنکه دل ز تو بر گیرم

12

Every day I start walking the road of your love anew.
Every night I mourn, longing for you.
I have neither courage to give my heart to the one like you
Nor the strength to take my heart off from you.

١٣

ای دل چو شراب معرفت کردی نوش
لب بر هم نه بر سر الهی مفروش
در هر سختی چو چشمه کوه مجوش
دریا گردی گر بنشینی خاموش

13

O heart, since you drank the wine of gnosis,
Close your lips. Do not sell the secret of God.
Do not boil, like a mountain spring, in every hardship!
You become an ocean if you sit silent.

١۴

دل در پی راز عشق پویان میدار
جان میکن و راز عشق در جان میدار
سری که سر اندر سر آن باخته ای
چون پیدا شد ز خویش پنهان میدار

14

Let your heart keep searching the secret of love.
Strive to keep the secret of love in your soul.
A secret over which you have lost your head,
When it is found, keep it hidden even from yourself.

۱۵

اجزای تو جمله گوش می باید و بس

جان تو سخن نیوش می باید و بس

گفتی تو که مرد راه چون می باید

نظارگی و خموش می باید و بس

15

Each organ in your body an ear must be.
Your soul only a listener must be.
You asked how the man of the Path must be?
Observing and silent he must be.

۱۶

ای مرد رونده مرد بیچاره مباش

از خویش مرو برون و آواره مباش

در باطن خویش کن سفر چون مردان

اهل نظری تو اهل نظاره مباش

16

O walker of the Path, do not be a wretched man.
Do not go out of yourself and become astray.
Journey within yourself, like [real] men.
You are a man of perception, do not be a spectator!

۱۷

گر مرد رهی میان خون باید رفت

وز پای فتاده سرنگون باید رفت

تو پای براه در نه و هیچ مپرس

خود راه بگویدت که چون باید رفت

17

If you are a man of the Path, through blood you must walk.
And if your feet collapse, on your head you must walk.
Plant your step on the road and ask nothing.
For the road itself will tell you how you must walk.

۱۸

گه پیشرو نبرد میباید بود
گه پسرو اهل درد میباید بود
این کار بسرسری بسر می نشود
کاریست عظیم مرد میباید بود

18

Sometimes in the front row of the battle one must be.
Sometimes behind the sufferers [of love] one must be.
This work will not come to an end perfunctorily.
It is a tremendous work. A [real] man one must be.

۱۹

چون نیست کسی را سر مویی غم تو
چون تو که کند در دو جهان ماتم تو
ای مانده ز راه یکدم آگاه نه ای
تا فوت چه میشود ز تو هر دم تو

19

Since no one cares for you even as little as the tip of a hair,
Who on earth would feel your grief like yourself?
O you, who are left behind on the road,
You are not aware what is lost from you with every breath!

۲۰

گر میخواهی که وقت خود داری گوش
رنجی که بتو رسد مرنج و مخروش
گر هر دو جهان چو بحر آید در جوش
جمعیت خود بهر دو عالم مفروش

20

If you want to be in control of your time,
Be not offended and shout not when you are suffering.
If both worlds become turbulent like a sea,
Remain calm, and trade not your peace for both worlds.

۲۱

خواهی که ز اضطرار و خواری برهی
و ز بی ادبی و بی قراری برهی
تا چند بخود کنی تصرف در خویش
گر کار بدو باز گذاری برهی

21

If you want to be free from anxiety and misery,
And be rid of impudence and restlessness,
Stop taking so much possession of yourself.
Put your affairs in His trust and be free.

۲۲

گفتم دل و جان در سر کارت کردم
هر چیز که داشتم نثارت کردم
گفتا تو که باشی که کنی یا نکنی
کان من بودم که بیقرارت کردم

22

I said, "I gave my heart and soul over your affair,
"And sacrificed whatever I had for you."
He said, "Who are you to do or not to do?
"It was *I* who made you restless."

۲۳

در هر چیزی ترا جمالی دگر است
در هر ورق حسن تو حالی دگر است
هر ناقص را از تو کمالی دگر است
هر عاشق را ز تو وصالی دگر است

23

In each object, you manifest a different beauty.
In each facet of your beauty, there is a different state.
Each imperfect one has a different perfection from you.
Each lover has a different union with you.

۲۴

سرگشته تست نه فلک میدانی
گرد در تو گشته بسرگردانی
تو خورشیدی ولی میان جانی
خورشید که دیدست بدین پنهانی

24

The nine heavens are wandering for you, you know it.
Bewildered, they are turning around your threshold.
You are the sun, yet hidden in the center of the spirit.
Who has seen such a hidden sun?

۲۵

دیر است که سودای تو در سر دارم
وز عشق دلی خون شده در بر دارم
در راه تو یک مذهب و یک شیوه نیم
هر لحظه بتو مذهب دیگر دارم

25

For long I have had your thought in my head,
And a heart bleeding from love in my breast.
In your way, I have not just one faith and one method.
Every moment I have a different faith in you.

۲۶

دوش آمد و گفت ای شب و روزت غم من
هرگز نشوی تا تو تویی همدم من
من خورشیدم تو سایه ای بر سر خاک
تا محو نگردی نشوی محرم من

26

Last night he said, "O you who suffer for me day and night,
"You will never be my companion as long as you are you.
"I am the sun, and you are a shadow on earth.
"Unless you are annihilated, you will not be my confidant."

۲۷

دوش آمد و گفت گرد اعزاز مگرد

خواری طلب و دگر سر افراز مگرد

میدان که تو سایه منی خوش میباش

هر جا که روم از پی من باز مگرد

27

Last night he came up and said, " Do not go after honor.

"Seek humility, and do not walk proudly any longer.

"Know that you are my shadow and rejoice.

"Wherever I go, do not stop following me."

۲۸

دی گفت کجا شدی چنین می باید

از دوست جدا شدی چنین می باید

روزی دو ز بهر آنکه دور افتادی

بیگانه ز ما شدی چنین می باید

28

Yesterday he said, "Where did you go? Must it be so?

"You separated yourself from your friend. Must it be so?

"Just because you fell away from me for a couple of days,

"You became a stranger to me. Must it be so?"

۲۹

عشقت بهزار پادشاهی ارزد

وصل تو ز ماه تا به ماهی ارزد

آنرا که رخی بود بدین زیبایی

انصاف بده که هر چه خواهی ارزد

29

A thousand monarchies your love is worth.

From the earth to the sky your union is worth.

With a face so beautiful as yours,

In all fairness, whatever you want is worth.

۳۰

گر کشته شوم کشته بنام تو شوم
ور بنده کس شوم غلام تو شوم
چون دست بدام زلف تو می نرسد
هم آن بهتر که صید دام تو شوم

30

If I am to be killed, I shall be killed in your name.
If I am to be anyone's slave, I shall be your slave.
Since I cannot reach the snare of your tress,
It is better that you capture me in your snare.

۳۱

از بس که تو خود به خویشتن مینازی
یک لحظه به عاشقی نمی پردازی
با پشت خمیده همچو چنگی شده‌ام
تا بوک چو چنگ یک دمم بنوازی

31

You are so enamored of yourself that
You do not pay attention to your lover for an moment.
I have become like a harp with my bent back,
Hoping that you play me, like a harp, for a moment.

۳۲

عاشق ز همه کار جهان فرد بود
از هر دو جهان بگذرد و مرد بود
پیوسته دلش گرم و دمش سرد بود
از ناخن پای تا بسر درد بود

32

A lover is detached from all the work of the world.
Having given up both worlds, he is a real man.
His heart is always warm and his breath cold.
He is full of pain [of love] from head to foot.

٣٣

معشوقه نه سر نه سروری میخواهد

حیرانی و زیر و زبری میخواهد

من زاهد فوطه پوش چون دانم بود

چون یار مرا قلندری میخواهد

33

The Beloved does not want any eminence from you.
He wants amazement and astonishment from you.
How can I be an ascetic wearing a lion cloth
If the Friend wants me to be a calender?

٣۴

خون شد جگرم بیار جام ای ساقی

کاین کار جهان دم است و دام ای ساقی

می ده که گذشت عمر و بگذاشته گیر

روزی دو سه نیز والسلام ای ساقی

34

My heart is bleeding, bring wine, O Sâqi.
For the affair of this world is brief and a trap, O Sâqi.
Bring wine, for my life passed!
A few more days, and all is over, O Sâqi.

٣۵

بر چهره گل شبنم نوروز خوش است

در باغ و چمن روی دل افروز خوش است

از دی که گذشت هر چه گویی خوش نیست

خوش باش و ز دی مگو که امروز خوش است

35

On the cheek of the rose, the Noruz dew is pleasant.
In the garden and grove, a mirthful countenance is pleasant.
Of yesterday that passed whatever you say is not pleasant.
Be happy. Speak not of yesterday, for today is pleasant.

۳۶

ساقی به صبوحی می ناب اندر ده

مستان شبانه را شراب اندر ده

مستیم و خراب در خرابات فنا

آوازه بعالم خراب اندر ده

36

Sâqi, bring pure morning wine,
And give it to the drunkards of the night.
We are drunk and ruined in the tavern of annihilation.
Announce this news to the ruined world.

۳۷

هر روز بر آنم که کنم شب توبه

وز جام پیاپی لبالب توبه

واکنون که شکفت برگ گل برگم نیست

در موسم گل ز توبه یارب توبه

37

Everyday I intend to repent at night,
To repent of drinking successive brimful cups.
Now that the rose-petals began to bloom, I cannot.
O Lord, I repent of repentance in the season of the rose.

۳۸

مهتاب فتاده در گلستان امشب

گل روی نموده سوی بستان امشب

در ده می گلرنگ که می نتوان خفت

از مشغله هزاردستان امشب

38

Moonlight has fallen in the rose-garden tonight.
The rose has turned its face toward the orchard tonight.
Give the rosy wine, for sleep is not possible
With the nightingale's busyness tonight.

۳۹

ماییم بمیخانه شده جمع امشب
داده به سماع مطربان سمع امشب
بر خاسته از دو کون و خوش بنشسته
با شاهد و با شراب و با شمع امشب

39

We have gathered in the tavern tonight,
Listening to the minstrels' music.
Detached from both worlds, we are now happily sitting
With our beloved, wine, and candle tonight.

۴۰

ای رفته به آسمان نفیرم بی تو
یک لحظه قرار می نگیرم بی تو
تو شمع منی بیا و می سوز مرا
کان دم که نسوزیام بمیرم بی تو

40

O you, without whom my lament has gone to the sky,
Not a moment can I rest away from you.
You are my candle. Come and burn me.
For the moment you do not burn me, I die without you.

۴۱

از بس که ز غم سوختم ای شمع طراز
چون شمع ز تو سوخته می مانم باز
کوتاه کنم سخن که می نتوان گفت
غمهای دلم مگر به شبهای دراز

41

So much did I burn from longing, O elegant candle,
That I am still aflame by you, like a candle.
To make a long story short, I cannot describe
The longings of my heart except during long nights.

۴۲

درویشی را به هر چه خواهی ندهم

وین ملک به ماه تا به ماهی ندهم

چون صحت و امن و لذت علمم هست

تنهایی را به پادشاهی ندهم

42

I will not trade dervishhood for anything.

I will not trade this kingdom for the whole universe.

Since I have health, security, and joy of knowledge,

I will not trade my solitude for monarchy.

۴۳

گاهی سخنم بصد جنون بنویسند

گاه از عقل ذوفنون بنویسند

گر از فضلایند به زر نقش کنند

ور عاشق زارند بخون بنویسند

43

My words are sometimes written with a lot of madness,

And sometimes with complete rationality.

If the writers are scholars, they inscribe them with gold;

And if desperate lovers, they write them with blood.

۴۴

عقلی که کمال در جنون می بیند

بنیاد وجود خاک و خون می بیند

چشمی که دو کون در درون می بیند

مشتی رگ و استخوان برون می بیند

44

The wisdom that perfection in madness sees

The foundation of being dust and blood sees.

The eye that both worlds within sees

A handful of veins and bones without sees.

۴۵

مرغی بودم پریده از عالم راز

تا بو که برم ز شیب صیدی به فراز

چون هیچ کسی نیافتم محرم راز

زان در که درآمدم برون رفتم باز

45

I was a bird, flown in from the world of mystery,
Hoping to carry a prey from nadir to zenith.
Because I did not find anyone to confide my secret,
I went out from the same door I came in.

۴۶

تا جان دارم همچو فلک می پویم

وز درد وصال او سخن می گویم

آن چیز که کس نیافت آن می طلبم

وان چیز که گم نکرده‌ام می جویم

46

As long as I live, I shall move like the sky
And speak of longing for his union.
I seek that which no one has found.
And I search that which I have not lost.

۴۷

نه چاره این عاشق بیچاره کنی

نه غمخوری این دل غمخواره کنی

گیرم که ز پرده می نیایی بیرون

این پرده عاشقان چرا پاره کنی

47

You neither help this helpless lover
Nor sympathize with this sympathetic heart.
Supposing that you do not come out of the veil,
Why should you tear this veil of lovers?

مهستی گنجه ای
(قرن ششم هجری قمری)

۱

آنها که هوای عشق موزون زده‌اند

هر نیم شبی سجاده در خون زده‌اند

نشنیدستی که عاشقان خیمه عشق

از گردش هفت چرخ بیرون زده‌اند

Mahasati Ganjei
(12th century C.E.)

1

Those who have desired the elegant love
Have soaked their prayer-rugs in blood every midnight.
Have you not heard that lovers have pitched
The tent of love beyond the seven turning heavens?

۲

شب را چه خبر که عاشقان می چه کشند

وز جام بلا چگونه می زهر چشند

ار راز نهان کنند غمشان بکشد

ور فاش کنند مردمانشان بکشند

2

What does the night know how lovers suffer
And how they sip poison from the cup of calamity?
If they conceal their secret, grief will kill them.
And if they reveal it, people will kill them.

۲

جان در ره غمهاش خطر باید کرد

آسوده دلی زیر و زبر باید کرد

وآنگه ز رضای یار نادیده اثر

با درد دل از جهان گذر باید کرد

3

In the way of love, one must risk one's life
And turn the peace of the heart upside down.
And then, having seen no sign of the beloved's satisfaction,
One must pass from this world with a suffering heart.

۳

از بسکه کند زلف تو با روی تو راز

بیم است که از رشک کنم کفر آغاز

من بنده بادی شدم ای شمع طراز

کاو زلف تو از روی تو بر دارد باز

4

So much that your tress coos with your face,
I fear I may start blasphemy from envy.
O elegant one, I shall bow to that wind
Which can remove your tress from your face.

۵

شخصی دارم دلی خراب اندر وی

جانی دارم هزار تاب اندر وی

وز آرزوی روی تو دارم شب و روز

چشمی و هزار چشمه آب اندر وی

5

I have a body with an ecstatic heart inside,
And a soul with a thousand flames inside.
And in longing for your face day and night,
I have an eye with a thousand streams inside.

۶

شبها که بناز با تو خفتم همه رفت
رفتی و هر آنچه با تو گفتم همه رفت
آرام دل و مونس جانم بودی
رفتی و هر آنچه با تو گفتم همه رفت

6

The nights I lovingly slept with you are all gone.
You went away and whatever I told you is all gone.
You were the peace of my heart and companion of my soul.
You went away and whatever I spoke to you is all gone.

۷

کار از لب خشک و دیده تر بگذشت
تیر ستمت ز جان و دل بر بگذشت
آبیم نمود بس تنک آتش عشق
چون پای بر آن نهادم از سر بگذشت

7

Beyond dry lips and wet eyes my affair passed.
Through my heart and soul your arrow of cruelty passed.
The fire of love seemed like a shallow water to me;
But when I stepped in, over my head it passed.

۸

این اشک عقیق رنگ من چون بچکد
آب از دل سنگ و چشم گردون بچکد
چشمم چو ز تو برید ازو خون بچکید
شک نیست که از بریدگی خون بچکد

8

When these ruby-color tears drip from my eyes,
From the stone's heart and the sky's eye water drips.
When my eyes cut off from you, they bled.
Obviously from what is cut blood drips.

۹

هر کارد که از کشته خود بر گیرد

واندر لب و دندان چو شکر گیرد

گر بار دگر بر گلوی کشته نهد

از ذوق لبش زندگی از سر گیرد

9

Any knife he takes off his victim,
He puts between his sweet lips and teeth.
And if he puts back the knife on his victim's throat,
The joy of his lips gives another life to his victim.

۱۰

در بستان دوش از غم و شیون خویش

می گشتم و می گریستم بر تن خویش

آمد گل سرخ و چاک زد دامن خویش

و آلود به اشکم همه پیراهن خویش

10

Last night in the orchard, grieving and moaning,
I was walking and shedding tears on my body.
The red rose came up and tore her skirt,
And tainted her whole shirt with my tears.

۱۱

گر باد پریر خود نرگس بفراخت

دی درع بنفشه نیز بر خاک انداخت

امروز کشید خنجر سوسن از آب

فردا سپر از آتش گل خواهد ساخت

11

If the day before yesterday the wind raised the helmet
Of the narcissus, yesterday it threw down the violet's armor.
Today it drew the lily-of-the-valley's sword out of water.
Tomorrow it will make a shield from the fire of the rose.

۱۲

هر لحظه غمی به مستمندی رسدت
تیری ز جفا به دردمندی رسدت
در کشتن عاشقان ازین بیش مکوش
زنهار مبادا که گزندی رسدت

12

Every moment a sorrow from you to a needy one comes.
An arrow of cruelty from you to a sufferer comes.
Make no more effort in killing your lovers.
Beware, lest a harm [from them] to you comes.

۱۳

در میکده پیش بت تحیات خوش است
با ساغر یکمنی مناجات خوش است
تسبیح مصلای ریائی خوش نیست
زنار مغانه در خرابات خوش است

13

In the tavern, salutations before an idol is good.
Incantation with a heavy goblet is good.
The rosary of the pretentious worshipper is not good.
In the tavern, a Magian girdle is good.

۱۴

دریای سرشک دیده پر غم ماست
و آن بار که کوه بر نتابد غم ماست
در حسرت همدمی بشد عمر عزیز
ما در غم همدمیم و غم همدم ماست

14

The sea of tears is my eyes full of sorrow
The burden a mountain cannot bear is my sorrow.
Life precious passed in desire for a companion.
I desire for a companion, and my companion is sorrow.

۱۵

دل جای غم تست چنان تنگ که هست
گل چاکر روی تو بهر رنگ که هست
از آب دو چشم من بگردد هر شب
جز سنگ دلت هر آسیا سنگ که هست

15

My heart is the place of your sorrow, lonely as it is.
The rose is the servant of your face, any color it is.
The water that flows from my eyes every night turns,
Except the stone of your heart, every millstone there is.

۱۶

در عالم عشق تا دلم سلطان گشت
آزاد ز کفر و فارغ از ایمان گشت
اندر ره خود مشکل خود خود دیدم
از خود چو برون شدم رهم آسان گشت

16

Since my heart became a king in the world of love,
It was liberated from disbelief and released from belief.
I saw my *self* as an obstacle in my way.
When I came out of my *self*, the way opened for me.

۱۷

سودا زده جمال تو باز آمد
تشنه شده وصال تو باز آمد
نو کن قفس و دانه لطفی تو بپاش
کان مرغ شکسته بال تو باز آمد

17

The one stricken by your beauty has come back.
The one thirsty for your union has come back.
Renew the cage and strew some seed of kindness.
For the wing-broken bird of yours has come back.

۱۸

چشم ترکت چو مست بر می خیزد
شور از می و می پرست بر می خیزد
زلفت چو برقص در میان می آید
صد فتنه بیک نشست بر می خیزد

18

As your Turkish eyes awake drunkenly,
Frenzy from wine and wine-worshipers arises.
And as you sit up and let your hair dance in the air;
By one sitting, a hundred riots arise.

۱۹

پیوسته خرابات ز رندان خوش باد
در دامن زهد و زاهدی آتش باد
آن درعه صد پاره و آن صوف کبود
افتاده بزیر پای دردی کش باد

19

May the cheers of the *rends* fill the taverns all the time!
May that fire catch on the skirts of austerity and asceticism!
May that patched frock and that blue woolen cloak
Fall under the feet of a dreg-drainer!

۲۰

تا سنبل تو غالیه سائی نکند
باد سحری نافه گشائی نکند
گر زاهد صد ساله ببیند دستت
بر گردن من که پارسائی نکند

20

Unless your hyacinth spread ambergris,
The morning wind will not open its musk-bag.
If the hundred-year-old ascetic sees your hand,
Blame me if he ever practices asceticism again.

٢١

در دل همه شرک روی بر خاک چه سود
زهری که بجان رسید تریاک چه سود
خود را بمیان خلق زاهد کردن
با نفس پلید جامه پاک چه سود

21

Prostration with many gods in the heart, what good is it?
Antidote after the poison reaches the heart, what good is it?
To appear virtuous among the people
And have a clean garment on a dirty self, what good is it?

٢٢

اشکم ز دو دیده متصل می آید
از بهر تو ای مهر گسل می آید
زنهار بدار حرمت اشک مرا
کاین قافله از کعبه دل می آید

22

Ceaselessly from both eyes, my tears are coming.
For you, who have ceased to love, they are coming.
Beware that you have respect for my tears.
For from the Ka'ba of my heart, this caravan is coming.

٢٣

چشمم چو بچشم خویش چشم تو بدید
بی چشم تو خواب چشمم از چشم پرید
ای چشم همه چشم به چشمت روشن
چون چشم تو چشم من دگر چشم ندید

23

Since I saw your eyes by my own eyes,
Far from your eyes, sleep escaped from my eyes.
O you, whose eyes brighten the sight of everyone's eyes,
Never again did my eyes see other eyes like your eyes.

۲۴

جانا تو ز دیده اشک بیهوده مبار
دلتنگی من بس است دل تنگ مدار
تو معشوقی گریستن کار تو نیست
کار من بیچاره بمن باز گذار

24

My dear, you should not rain tears from your eyes in vain.
My grief is enough, you should not grieve your heart.
You are a beloved. Weeping is not your work.
I am a desperate lover. Leave my work to me.

۲۵

بازار دلم با سر سودات خوش است
شطرنج غمم با رخ زیبات خوش است
دائم داری مرا تو در خانه مات
ای جان جهان مگر که با مات خوش است

25

The bazaar of my heart is happy with your trade.
The chess of my longing is happy with your beautiful rook.
You always put me in the square of the checkmate.
O Soul of the World, who is happy with a checkmate?

۲۶

آن دیده که دیدن تو بودی کارش
از گریه تباه میشود مگذارش
وان دل که بتو بود همه بازارش
در حلقه زلف تست نیکو دارش

26

The eye, whose work was seeing you,
Is now perishing in tears. Let it not!
And the heart, whose business was only with you,
Is now in the loop of your tress. Be good to her!

۲۷

برخیز و بیا که حجره پرداخته ام
وز بهر تو پرده خوش انداخته ام
با من به شرابی و کبابی در ساز
کاین هر دو ز دیده و ز دل ساخته ام

27

Get up and come! I have decorated my chamber
And have spread a beautiful mat for you.
Join me for wine and kebâb, both of which
I have made from the eye and the heart for you.

۲۸

در کوی خرابات یکی درویشم
زان خم زکات بیاور پیشم
صوفی بچه ام ولی نه کافر کیشم
مولای کسی نیم غلام خویشم

28

I am a dervish in the street of the tavern.
Give me charity from that vat of wine.
I am a Sufi's child, but not an infidel.
I am my own servant and no one's master.

۲۹

قلاش و قلندری و عاشق بودن
در مجمع رندان موافق بودن
انگشت نمای خلق و خالق بودن
به زانکه به خرقه منافق بودن

29

To be a frequenter of taverns, a calender, and a lover,
To be in the assembly of amiable *rends*,
And to be notorious before the creation and the creator
Is better than to be in the cloak of a hypocrite.

۳۰

ای گشته خجل پری و حور از رویت
خورشید گرفته وام نور از رویت
در آرزوی روی تو داریم امروز
روئی و هزار اشک دور از رویت

30
O you, whose face has shamed the fairy and the houri,
And from which the sun has borrowed light,
In desire for your face and far from it,
I have a thousand teardrops on my face today.

۳۱

ابریست که خون دیده بارد غم تو
زهریست که تریاک ندارد غم تو
در هر نفسی هزار محنت زده را
بیدل کند و ز جان بر آرد غم تو

31
The cloud that rains blood is your sorrow.
The poison that has no antidote is your sorrow.
That which deprives a thousand grief-stricken ones
Of their hearts and souls every moment is your sorrow.

۳۲

ابریست که قطره نم فشاند غم تو
در بوالعجبی هم بتو ماند غم تو
هر چند به آتشم نشاند غم تو
غمناک شوم گرم نماند غم تو

32
The cloud which sprinkles raindrops is your sorrow.
In its wonderwork, like you is your sorrow.
Although your sorrow puts me on fire,
I would be sad if I were left without your sorrow.

۳۳

دل از ازل آمد آشیان غم تو

جان تا به ابد بود مکان غم تو

من جان و دل خویش از آن دارم دوست

کاین داغ تو دارد آن نشان غم تو

33

Since preexistence my heart has been the nest of your love.
For all eternity my soul has been the dwelling of your love.
I love my soul and my heart, for my heart has your brand
And my soul the sign of your love.

۳۴

گر من بمثل هزار جان داشتمی

در پیش تو جمله بر میان داشتمی

گفتی دل هجر هیچ داری گفتم

گر داشتمی دل دل آن داشتمی

34

If I had a thousand lives, so to speak,
I would place them all before you.
You asked me if I had the heart for separation.
If I had a heart, I would have the heart for it.

۳۵

از دیده اگر نه خون روان داشتمی

رازت ز دل خسته نهان داشتمی

ور زانکه نبودی دم سرد و رخ زرد

رازت نه ز دل نهان ز جان داشتمی

35

If blood did not flow from my eyes,
I could hide your secret from my weary heart.
And if my breath was not cold and my face sallow,
I would hide your secret from my heart and even my soul.

۳۶

بس خون که بدان دو چشم خونخواره کنی
بس دل که بدان دو زلف آواره کنی
ایزد به دل تو رحمتی در فکناد
تا چاره عاشقان بیچاره کنی

36

So much blood that you shed with those bloodthirsty eyes,
And so many hearts that you lead astray by those tresses,
May God cast some mercy in your heart,
So that perhaps you redress your wretched lovers.

ابوالفضل رشیدالدین میبدی
(قرن ششم هجری قمری)

۱

یک تیر بنام من ز ترکش برکش
وانگه به کمان عشق سخت اندر کش
گر هیچ نشانه خواهی اینک دل و جان
از تو زدنی سخت و ز من آهی خوش

Abulfazl Rashiduddin Maybadi
(12th century C.E.)

1

Draw an arrow from your quiver in my name
And pull it hard with the bow of love.
If you want any target, here is my heart and soul.
A powerful strike from you and a happy sigh from me.

۲

گلها که من از باغ وصالت چیدم
درها که من از نوش لبت دزدیدم
آن گل همه خار گشت در دیده من
وان در همه از دیده فرو باریدم

2

The roses I picked from your garden of union,
All turned into thorns in my eyes.
The pearls I stole from the nectar of your lips,
All poured down from my eyes.

۳

ای ماه بر آمدی و تابان گشتی
گرد فلک خویش خرامان گشتی
چون دانستی برابر جان گشتی
ناگاه فرو شدی و پنهان گشتی

3

O moon, you came out shining brightly,
And moved about in your sky elegantly.
When you found you had become equal to my soul,
You went down and hid yourself suddenly.

۴

بخت از در خان ما در آید روزی
خورشید نشاط ما بر آید روزی
وز تو بسوی ما نظر آید روزی
وین انده ما هم بسر آید روزی

4

Fortune will come from the door of my house one day.
The sun of my happiness will come out one day.
A glance from you will come to me one day.
This sorrow of mine will also come to an end one day.

۵

ز اول که مرا عشق نگارم نو بود

همسایه بشب ز ناله من نغنود

کم گشت کنون ناله که عشقم بفزود

آتش چو همه گرفت کم گردد دود

5

In the beginning, when my love for my sweetheart was new,
My neighbors could not sleep from my laments at night.
Now that my love has increased, my laments are few.
For the smoke goes down when the fire has caught.

۶

بر شاخ طرب هزار دستان توایم

دل بسته بدان نغمه و دستان توایم

از دست مده که زیر دستان توایم

بگذار گناه ما که مستان توایم

6

On the branch of joy, we are your nightingales.
Our hearts are attached to your song and tale.
Do not lose us, for we are your subjects.
Forgive our sins, for we are drunk by you.

خاقانی شروانی
(۵۹۵ هجری قمری)

۱

بختی دارم چو چشم خسرو همه خواب
چشمی دارم چو لعل شیرین همه آب
جسمی دارم چو جان مجنون همه درد
جانی دارم چو زلف لیلی همه تاب

Khâqâni Shervâni
(d. 1199 C.E.)

1

Like the eyes of Khosrow, my luck is full of sleep.
Like the lips of Shirin, my eyes are full of water.
Like the soul of Majnun, my body is full of pain.
Like the tress of Layli, my soul is full of curls.

۲

عشقی که ز من دود بر آورد این است
خون میخورم و بعشق در خورد این است
اندیشه آن نیست که دردی دارم
اندیشه بتو نمیرسد درد این است

2

The love that brought my sighs out is this.
I am drinking blood, and what suits love is this.
I do not mind that I have pain.
The mind can not attain to you, the pain is this.

۳

مرغی که نوای درد راند عشق است
پیکی که زبان غیب داند عشق است
هستی که به نیستیت خواند عشق است
وآنچ از تو ترا باز رهاند عشق است

3

The bird that sings the song of pain is love.
The courier who knows the tongue of the Unseen is love.
The existence that calls you to nonexistence is love.
And that which redeems you from you is love.

۴

بپذیر دلی را که پراکنده تست
بر گیر شکاری که هم افکنده تست
با صد گنه نکرده خاقانی را
گر زنده گذاری ار کشی بنده تست

4

Receive this heart which is distraught for you.
Pick up the prey which is shot down by you.
Whether you leave alive or kill Khâqâni,
Who has a hundred uncommitted sins, he is bonded to you.

۵

دانی ز جهان چه طرف بربستم هیچ
وز حاصل ایام چه در دستم هیچ
شمع خردم ولی چو بنشستم هیچ
آن جام جمم ولی چو بشکستم هیچ

5

Do you know what I benefitted of this world? Nothing.
And what I gained from the days of life? Nothing.
I am a candle of wisdom; but when extinguished, nothing.
I am the cup of Jamshid; but when broken, nothing.

۶

هیچ است وجود و زندگانی هم هیچ
وین خانه و فرش باستانی هم هیچ
از نسیه و نقد زندگانی همه را
سرمایه جوانیست جوانی هم هیچ

6

Being is nothing, and living is also nothing.
This house with this ancient carpet is also nothing.
The cash and credit of each person is youth.
None the less, the youth itself is nothing.

۷

هر روز فلک کین من از سر گیرد
بر دست خسان مرا زبون تر گیرد
با او همه کار سفلگان در گیرد
من سفله شوم بو که مرا برگیرد

7

Everyday heaven resumes its rancor against me,
And makes me more helpless in the hands of the lowly.
It favors the lowly people in everything.
I should become lowly, too, hoping that it favor me.

۸

خاقانی را جور فلک داد آید
گر مرغ دلش زین قفس آزاد آید
در رقص آید چو دل بفریاد آید
در فریادش عهد ازل یاد آید

8

Heaven's cruelty to Khâqâni will be justified
If the bird of his heart is released from this cage.
The heart begins to dance as it cries out,
Recalling the Primordial Pact in his outcry.

٩

هر یک چند از خسان جهان سیر آید

روشن جانی از آسمان زیر آید

خاقانی ازین جنس درین دور مجوی

بر ره منشین که کاروان دیر آید

9

Once in a while, the world becomes fed up with the lowly,
And an enlightened spirit descends from the heaven.
Khâqâni, search not such a spirit in this period.
And do not wait on the road, for the caravan comes late.

١٠

گر بد دارد و گر نکو او داند

گر جرم کند وگر عفو او داند

تا زنده ام از وفا نگردانم سر

من بر سر اینم آن او او داند

10

Whether he treats me well or badly, it is up to him.
Whether he forgives or punishes me, it is up to him.
I will not waver in my fidelity as long as I live.
This is my intention. Whatever his be, it is up to him.

١١

صد بار وجود را فرو بیخته اند

تا همچو تو صورتی برانگیخته اند

سبحان الله ز فرق سر تا قدمت

در قالب آرزوی من ریخته اند

11

A hundred times, existence was sifted
Before a form like you was created.
Praised be God! From head to toe,
You were cast in the mold of my desire.

۱۲

ای بت علم سیه ز شب صبح ربود

بر خیز و می صبوحی اندر ده زود

بر دار ز خواب نرگس خون آلود

بر خیز که خفتنت بسی خواهد بود

12

The morning stole the black banner of the night, my darling.
Get up and bring the morning wine soon.
Remove the sleep from your reddened eyes.
Get up, for you have a long sleep ahead.

۱۳

این بند که بر دلم کنون افکندند

نقبی است که بر خانه خون افکندند

دل کیست کزو صبر برون افکندند

خیمه چه بود چونش ستون افکندند

13

This chain they fastened to my heart now
Is a tunnel they dug into a house of blood.
What is a heart robbed of patience?
What is a tent robbed of its poles?

۱۴

ای ماه شب است پرده وصل بساز

وی چرخ مدر پرده خاقانی باز

ای شب در صبحدم همی دار فراز

وی صبح کلید روز در چاه انداز

14

O moon, it is night, compose the tune of union.
And you, heavens, do not tear Khâqâni's veil open.
O night, keep the door of the morning closed.
And you, morning, throw the day's key in the well.

۱۵

سوزی که در آسمان نگنجد دارم
وان ناله که در دهان نگنجد دارم
گفتی ز جهان چه غصه داری آخر
آن غصه که در جهان نگنجد دارم

15

The fire which cannot be contained in the sky, I have.
The lament which cannot be contained in the mouth, I have.
You asked me, "What in the world is your grief anyway?"
The grief which cannot be contained in the world, I have.

۱۶

در خواب شوم روی تو تصویر کنم
بیدار شوم وصل تو تعبیر کنم
گر هر دو جهان خواهی و جان و دل و تن
بر هر دو و هر سه چار تکبیر کنم

16

I see the image of your face in my dream.
I wake up and interpret that I will be with you.
If you want both worlds, my heart, my soul and body;
I will give up forever the two and the three for you.

۱۷

ای گشته دلم در غم تو صد پاره
عیش و طرب از نزد رهی آواره
من خود که بوم که گشته اند از غم تو
شیران جهان چو روبهان بیچاره

17

O you, whose sorrow has broken my heart to pieces,
And has made delight and pleasure strangers to my heart,
Who am I to complain of your sorrow? For your sorrow
Has rendered the lions of the world, like foxes, helpless.

روزبهان بقلی شیرازی
(۶۰۶ هجری قمری)

۱

کی بو که سر زلف تو در چنگ زنم
صد بوسه بر آن رخان گلرنگ زنم
در شیشه کنم مهر و هوای دگران
در پیش تو ای نگار بر سنگ زنم

Ruzbehân Baqli Shirâzi
(d. 1210 C.E.)

1

When shall I be able to take hold of your tress-tip,
And give a hundred kisses to those rosy cheeks,
And put all the love and desire of the others in a bottle
And knock it on the rock before you, my beloved?

۲

در جستن جام جم جهان پیمودم
روزی ننشستم و شبی نغنودم
ز استاد چو وصف جام جم بشنودم
خود جام جهان نمای جم من بودم

2

I travelled the world in search of the cup of Jamshid.
I did not rest any day nor slept any night.
When I heard my master describe the cup of Jamshid,
I realized I was myself that world-viewing cup of Jamshid.

۳

دی آینه خویش به صیقل دادم
روشن کردم به پیش خود بنهادم
در آینه عیب خویش چندان دیدم
کز عیب کسان هیچ نیامد یادم

3

Yesterday I polished my mirror,
Made it bright and placed it before myself.
I saw so many faults of my own in the mirror
That I forgot other people's faults completely.

۴

تا دولت وصل بر نظام است مرا
کار همه آفاق بکام است مرا
تا می ز لب یار بجام است مرا
راه ازل و ابد دو گام است مرا

4

As long as I possess the wealth of union,
The world is all according to my wish.
As long as my cup is full of wine from my beloved's lips,
The road of eternity is only two steps long for me.

۵

گر تاب در آن زلف نگون اندازی
زهاد ز صومعه برون اندازی
ور عکس جمال خود بروم اندازی
بتها به سجود سرنگون اندازی

5

If you put a twist in that inverted tress,
You will throw ascetics out of monasteries.
And if you cast the reflection of your face in Rome,
You will throw the idols down in prostration.

۶

چشم از رخ خوبت آفتابی دارد
حسن از قبل روی تو تابی دارد
مسکین دل شوریده سرگشته من
از تاب سر زلف تو تابی دارد

6

The eye has its sun from your beautiful face.
Beauty has its radiance by the power of your face.
My poor, frenzied, and wandering heart
Has its support from the curls of your tress.

٧

تا سایه مشک بر گل انداخته ای
بس دل که ز درد عشق بگداخته ای
تا غالیه بر گل و سمن ساخته ای
از جان و دلم صبر بپرداخته ای

7

As long as you are casting the shade of musk on the rose,
Many hearts are being consumed with the pain of love.
As long as you are the *ghâlia* of the jasmine and the rose,
My heart and soul are being deprived of patience.

٨

با لشکر عشاق سواری چه خوش است
با معشوقان سست مهاری چه خوش است
در وقت معاشرت شراب و گل سرخ
با نرگس مست جویباری چه خوش است

8

Riding with the host of lovers, O what a pleasure!
Riding slowly along the beloveds, O what a pleasure!
And when together with the beloved, wine and roses
And the drunk narcissus by the stream, O what a pleasure!

۹

گر با خود بیخود نفسی بنشینی
وز هر چه جز اوست دامن اندر چینی
در هر چه کنی تعقل او را یابی
در هر چه کنی تفکر او را بینی

9

If you sit by yourself without yourself for a moment,
You will abstain from anything that is not Him.
In anything you exercise your reason, you will find Him.
And in anything you meditate about, you will see Him.

۱۰

گل گشت خجل ز روی تو در بستان
وز نرگس خونخوار تو مسکین مستان
زلفین تو در دست رهی افتاده ست
زنهار سر زلف ز مستان مستان

10

The rose in the orchard was humbled before your face
And drunkards felt helpless before your bloodthirsty eyes.
Your twin tresses have fallen in the hands of this your slave.
Beware! Take not your hair out of the hands of the drunk.

شهاب الدین سهروردی

(۵۸۵ هجری قمری)

١

هان تا سر رشته خرد گم نکنی

خود را ز برای نیک و بد گم نکنی

رهرو تویی و راه تویی منزل تو

هشدار که راه خود به خود گم نکنی

Shahâbuddin Sohrvardi
(d. 1189 C.E.)

1

Beware, lest you should lose the thread of your intellect!
Lest you should lose yourself for the sake of good and bad.
You are the traveler, the road, and the destination.
Beware, lest you should lose your way to yourself!

٢

امروز منم در قفس تنگ وجود

محتاج ببوی عدم از ننگ وجود

کو صیقل لطف تا دمی بزداید

از آینه حقیقتم زنگ وجود

2

Today in this tight cage of being, ashamed of existence,
I am in need of the scent of nonexistence.
Where is the varnish of grace to clear for a moment
From the mirror of my reality the rust of existence?

٣

هر گه نظر از سر سودات افتد

لاشک حرکتهای نه بر جات افتد

گر بر سر نفس خویشتن پای نهی

هر جا که شاهدی است در پات افتد

3

Whenever you look at someone sensuously,
You are bound to make improper motions.
If you step on the head of your sensuality,
Everywhere every beauty will fall at your feet.

۴

اصل گهر عشق ز کانی دگر است

منزلگه عاشقان جهانی دگر است

وان مرغ که دانه غم عشق خورد

بیرون ز دو کونش آشیانی دگر است

4

The origin of the gem of love is a different mine.
The lovers' home is in a different world.
The bird that feeds on the seed of longing for love,
Outside this world and the next, has a different nest.

۵

جانا همه وعده های باطل دهی‌ام

وز جام شکر شربت قاتل دهی‌ام

تا چند جگر خورم ز دست ستمت

نامد گه آنکه اندکی دل دهی‌ام

5

My darling, you always give me false promises.
You give me a fatal drink from the cup of sugar.
How long shall I suffer from your cruelty?
Is it not time you gave me a little encouragement?

۶

در کوی خرابات بسی مردانند
کز لوح وجود درسها می خوانند
بیرون ز شتر گربه اسرار فلک
دانند شگفتها و خر می رانند

6

In the street of the tavern, there are many men
Who learn lessons from the tablet of existence.
Beyond the odds and ends of the secrets of heaven,
They know many marvels but do not show them.

ظهیر فاریابی
(۵۹۸ هجری قمری)

۱

گر یک نفست ز زندگانی گذرد
مگذار که جز بشادمانی گذرد
زنهار که سرمایه ملکت بجهان
عمر است چنان کش گذرانی گذرد

Zahir Fâryâbi
(d. 1202 C.E.)

1

Let *not a single* moment of your life
In any way but joyfully pass!
The substance of your reign in this world is your life,
Which will pass as you make it pass.

۲

با گل گفتم ابر چرا می‌گرید
ماتم زده نیست بر کجا می‌گرید
گل گفت اگر راست همی باید گفت
بر عمر من و عهد شما می‌گرید

2

I asked the rose, "Why does the cloud weep?"
"It is not in mourning, why does it weep?"
"To tell the truth," replied the rose,
"It weeps for my [short] life and your era."

۳

ای شب نه ز زلف اوست در پای تو بند
بس دیر و دراز در کشیدی تا چند
ای صبح تو هستی چو من عاشق زار
من میگریم بس است باری تو بخند

3

O night, your feet are not chained by her tress,
Why are you then dallying so long?
O morning, you are a desperate lover like me.
It is enough that I cry. At least, *you* do smile!

۴

اسباب طرب از همه بابی دارم
از دیده و دل می و کبابی دارم
هر گوشه که می نشینم از دولت اشک
در مد نظر جدول آبی دارم

4

All the means of enjoyment have I.
Wine from the eyes and kebab from the heart have I.
Any corner I sit, from the plenitude of tears,
A stream of water in my sight have I.

۵

ای شمع تو صوفی صفتی پنداری
کین شش صفت از اهل صفا میداری
شب خیزی و نور چهره و زردی روی
سوز دل و اشک دیده و بیداری

5

O candle, you are like a Sufi, as it were.
For you have the six qualities of the purified people:
Nocturnal wakefulness, lustrous cheeks, golden face,
Fiery heart, tearful eyes, and vigilance.

۶

ای باد بهار بوی گلزار بیار
وی بلبل مست ناله زار بیار
ای بلبل اگر ملک چمن می طلبی
پروانه مطلق از رخ یار بیار

6

O spring wind, bring the scent of the rose-garden.
And you, drunk nightingale, bring a doleful melody!
O nightingale, if you want to reign in the meadow,
Bring an unconditional permit from the beloved.

۷

جسمی دارم دلی خراب اندر وی
جانی دارم هزار تاب اندر وی
در آرزوی روی تو دارم شب و روز
چشمی و هزار چشمه آب اندر وی

7

I have a body, an intoxicated heart in it.
I have a soul, a thousand flames in it.
Yearning for your face, day and night,
I have an eye, a thousand streams in it.

٨

در ده می لعل لاله گون صافی

بگشای ز حلق شیشه خون صافی

کامروز برون ز جام می نیست مرا

یک دوست که دارد اندرون صافی

8

Give me the pure ruby wine, of the color of the tulip.
Let the pure blood flow from the bottle's throat.
For today, except the bowl of wine,
I have no friend whose inside is pure.

٨

نی برگ شکایت از تو گفتن دارم

نی طاقت درد دل نهفتن دارم

آکنده چو غنچه گشتم از غم در تاب

کز تنگ دلی سر شکفتن دارم

9

Neither the strength to complain of you have I,
Nor the power to hide my heart's pain have I.
My heart is so filled with sorrow that, like a rose-bud,
A desire for blooming have I.

١٠

باد آمد و گل بر سر میخواران ریخت

یار آمد و می در قدح یاران ریخت

آن عنبر تر رونق عطاران برد

وین نرگس مست خوی هشیاران ریخت

10

The wind came and poured flowers on the drinkers' heads.
The beloved came and poured wine in the lovers' cups.
That fresh ambergris stole the perfume-dealers' market.
And this drunk narcissus put the sober ones to shame.

۱۱

دل خیمه غم بر آتش ناب زده است

خونابه دیدگان ره خواب زده است

این تعبیه بین که دل برون آورده است

وین نقش نگر که دیده بر آب زده است

11

My heart has pitched the tent of sorrow in real fire.

My blood-stained tears have cut the road of sleep.

Behold this contrivance which my heart has brought forth!

Behold this design which my eyes have drawn in water!

عین القضاة همدانی

(۵۲۵ هجری قمری)

۱

اندر ره عشق حاصلی باید و نیست

در کوی امید ساحلی باید و نیست

گفتی که به صبر کار تو نیک شود

با صبر تو دانی که دلی باید و نیست

Aynulqozât Hamadâni
(d. 1131 C.E.)

1

In the path of love there must be a gain, but there is not.

In the sea of hope there must be a shore, but there is not.

You told me things would become better with patience.

To have patience there must be a heart, but there is not.

۲

دیشب که بدم با تو نگارا بنهفت
صبح از نفسم نماز خفتن بشکفت
وامشب که شدم با غم هجران تو جفت
گویا که فلک بمرد و خورشید بخفت

2

Last night that I was secretly with you, my sweetheart,
Evening prayers blossomed from my breath in the morning.
And tonight that I am coupled with your separation's grief,
It seems as if the sky is dead and the sun sleeping.

۳

در بتکده گر نشان ز معشوقه ماست
رفتن بطواف کعبه از عقل خطاست
گر کعبه از او بوی ندارد کنش است
با بوی وصال او کنش کعبه ماست

3

If there is a sign of our beloved in the idol-temple,
It is against reason to go to circumambulate Ka'ba.
If Ka'ba lacks his scent, it is an idol-temple.
If the idol-temple possesses his scent, it is our Ka'ba.

۴

ناگه ز درم در آمد آن دلبر مست
جام می لعل نوش کرد و بنشست
از دیدن و از گرفتن زلف چو شست
رویم همه چشم گشت و چشمم همه دست

4

Suddenly from the door came that drunk heart-ravisher.
She drank a cup of ruby wine and sat.
In order to see and catch her curved tress,
My face became all eyes and my eyes all hands.

۵

دوش آن بت من دست در آغوشم کرد

بگرفت و به قهر حلقه در گوشم کرد

گفتم صنما ز عشق تو بخروشم

لب بر لب من نهاد و خاموشم کرد

5

Last night my sweetheart took me in her arms,
Held me tightly and forced a ring on my ear.
I said, "I am boisterous with your love, my darling."
She put her lips upon my lips and made me silent.

۶

تا قبله عشاق جهان روی تو شد

روی بت و بتگران همه سوی تو شد

چوگان سر زلف تو رهبان چو بدید

انگشت بر آورد و یکی گوی تو شد

6

When your face became the lovers' kebla in the world,
All idols and idol-makers turned their faces toward you.
When the monk saw the polo-stick of your tress-tip,
He repented and became a polo-ball before you.

۷

ای برده دلم به غمزه جان نیز ببر

بردی دل و جان نام و نشان نیز ببر

گر هیچ اثر نماند از ما بجهان

تاخیر روا مدار آن نیز ببر

7

You took my heart with one glance, take my soul, too.
You took my heart and soul, take my name and fame, too.
If any trace from me has remained in the world,
Make no delay, take that one, too.

٨

خود را ز برای خویش غمناک مدار

بردار نظر ز خاک و بر خاک مدار

چون قبله تو جمال معشوقه تست

رو سجده کن و ز هیچ کس باک مدار

8

Do not worry about yourself very much.
Take your eyes off the dust and look away from it!
Since your kebla is your beloved's face,
Go prostrate [before him] and fear no one.

٩

آتش بزنم بسوزم این مذهب و کیش

عشقت بنهم بجای مذهب در پیش

تا کی دارم عشق نهان در دل خویش

مقصود رهم تویی نه دین است و نه کیش

9

I will set fire to this creed and religion,
And put your love in place of the religion.
How long should I hide your love in my heart?
My goal is you, not a creed or religion.

١٠

اندر تن من جای نماند ای بت بیش

الا همه عشق تو گرفت از پس و پیش

گر عزم کنم که برگشایم رگ خویش

ترسم که به عشقت اندر آید سر نیش

10

O my idol, no more space remained in my body,
Which was not filled with your love from fore and aft.
If I intend to cut my vein open,
I fear the lancet will run into your love.

۱۱

آن ره که من آمدم کدام است ای دل
تا باز روم که کار خام است ای دل
در هر گامی هزار دام است ای دل
نامردان را عشق حرام است ای دل

11

What road did I take to come here, O heart,
That I may trace it back? For it was all mistake, O heart.
There are a thousand traps in every step, O heart.
Love is forbidden to the unmanly ones, O heart.

۱۲

بستردنی است آنچه بنگاشته‌ایم
افکندنی است آنچه بفراشته‌ایم
سودا بوده است آنچه پنداشته‌ایم
دردا که به هرزه عمر بگذاشته‌ایم

12

What we have written must be erased.
What we have hoisted must be lowered.
What we have thought is an illusion.
Alas, the life we have lived is wasted.

۱۳

چندان غم عشق ماهرویی خوردیم
کاو را بمیان اندهش گم کردیم
اکنون ز وصال وز فراقش فردیم
کو عشق و چه معشوق کرا پروردیم

13

So much suffered I from the love of a moon-faced one
That I lost her in the middle of my suffering.
Now I am free from her union and disunion.
Where is love and where the beloved? Whom did I nurture?

۱۴

یک روز گذر کردم بر کوی تو من

ناگاه شدم شیفته روی تو من

بنواز مرا که از پی بوی تو من

ماندم شب و روز در تکاپوی تو من

14

One day I walked into your street
And was suddenly charmed by your beauty.
Be kind to me. For following your scent,
I have been searching for you day and night.

۱۵

ای آنکه همیشه در جهان می پویی

این سعی ترا چه سود دارد گویی

چیزی که تو جویای نشان اویی

با تست همی تو جای دیگر جویی

15

O you who explore the world all the time,
What good is this struggle for you, tell me?
What you are seeking a sign of is already with you.
Yet, you are searching for it somewhere else.

۱۶

پیری دیدم ز عشق در غرقابی

وز گریه خود به گرد او گردابی

گفتم که ز بهر چیست این گریه تو

گفتا که ز بهر دلبر نایابی

16

I saw an old man drowing in love,
Whose tears had made a whirlpool for him.
I asked him, "What is this weeping for?"
He said, "For a beloved who is hard to find."

١٧

در عشق اگر نیست شوی هست شوی
در عقل اگر هست شوی پست شوی
وین بلعجبی ببین که از باده عشق
هشیار گهی شوی که سر مست شوی

17

In love, if you are annihilated, you will exist.
In reason, if you exist, you will go down.
Behold this wonder how the wine of love
Makes you sober when you are drunk!

اوحدالدین انوری
(۵۸۳ هجری قمری)

١

ای هجر مگر نهایتی نیست ترا
وی وعده وصل غایتی نیست ترا
ای عشق مرا بصد هزاران زاری
کشتی و جز این کفایتی نیست ترا

Ohaduddin Anvari
(d. 1187 C.E.)

1

O separation, is there no end for you?
O promise of union, is there no end for you?
O love, you killed me with many laments,
Is there no other talent for you?

۲

نه صبر بگوشه‌ای نشاند ما را

نه عقل بکام دل رساند ما را

چون یار ز پیش می براند ما را

کو مرگ که زین باز رهاند ما را

2

Neither patience seats me in a corner,
Nor reason gives me my heart's desire.
Since my beloved drives me away from himself,
Where is death that could free me from this [pain]?

۳

هم طبع ملول گشت از آن شعر چو آب

هم رغبت از آن شراب چون آتش ناب

ای دل تو عنان ز شاهدان نیز بتاب

کاریست ورای شاهد و شعر و شراب

3

I am tired of that poetry which was fluent like water.
I have no more relish for that wine which was pure like fire.
O heart, turn away from the beautiful youths, too.
There is a work beyond poetry, wine, and the youth.

۴

آن شد که بنزدیک من ای در خوشاب

دشنام ترا طال بقا بود جواب

جانا پس از این نبینی این نیز بخواب

بر آتش من زد سخن سرد تو آب

4

The time passed, O lustrous pearl,
When my response to your swearing was, "Go on!"
From now on, you will not even dream of it, my dear.
Your cold words poured water on my fire.

۵

بس شب که بروز بردم اندر طلبت
بس روز طرب که دیدم از وصل لبت
رفتی و کنون روز و شب این میگویم
کای روز وصال یار خوش باد شبت

5

Many nights spent I desiring for you till morning.
Many happy days spent I in union with your lips.
You went away, and now day and night I say this:
"O day of the beloved's union, may your night be good."

۶

در کوی تو هیچ کار من ناشده راست
ایام به کین خواستن من بر خاست
واخر بدلت گذر کند چون بروم
کان دلشده کی رفت و چگونه ست و کجاست

6

In your street, nothing has worked out for me.
Time is intent upon taking revenge of me.
When I am gone, will it ever occur to your heart:
When did that lover go? How is he? And where is he?

۷

در وصل تو عزم دل من روز نخست
آن بود که عمر با تو بگذارم چست
کی دانستم که بعد از آن عزم درست
آن روز بخواب شب همی باید جست

7

On the first day of our union, my heart's resolution was:
I am going to spend the rest of my life with you.
How could I know after that right resolution
I would be seeking that day in my dreams at night?

٨

دل در خم آن زلف معنبر بنشست
جان گفت که دل رفت وزین غمکده رست
من هم پی دل روم بهر حال که هست
مسکین چو بلب رسید پایش بشکست

8

When my heart nestled in the curve of that fragrant tress,
My soul said, "The heart is freed from this house of woes.
"I will also go after the heart, whatever might happen."
Poor soul broke its leg as it reached the lip.

٩

چون حسن تو رنج من بعالم سمر ست
کارم چو سر زلف تو زیر و زبرست
دیدم ز غمت بسی جفاها لیکن
نادیدن تو ز هر چه دیدم بترست

9

Like your beauty, my suffering is known to the world.
Like your tress-tip, my affairs are upside down.
While longing for you, I have seen many cruelties.
Not seeing you is worse than anything I have seen.

١٠

دل بر سر عهد استوار خویش است
جان در غم تو بر سر کار خویش است
از دل هوس هر دو جهانم بر خاست
الا غم تو که برقرار خویش است

10

My heart is steadfast in her promise.
My soul is occupied with longing for you.
The desire for both worlds left my heart.
But the desire for you is firm as ever.

۱۱

با آنکه دلم در غم هجرت خونست
شادی بغم توام ز غم افزونست
اندیشه کنم هر شب و گویم یا رب
هجرانش چنین است وصالش چونست

11

Although my heart bleeds from the pain of separation,
My joy exceeds my suffering in longing for you.
I think about it every night and ask myself, *O Lord,*
If her separation is like this, how will her union be?

۱۲

گر شرح نمی دهم که حالم چونست
یا از تو مرا چه درد روزافزونست
پیداست چو روز نزد هر کس که مرا
با این لب خندان چه دل پر خونست

12

If I do not explain how I am,
Or how my suffering increases daily because of you,
It is as clear to everyone as the daylight
How my heart bleeds in spite of these smiling lips!

۱۳

عشقی که همه عمر بماند این است
دردی که ز من جان بستاند این است
کاری که کسش چاره نداند این است
وان شب که بروزم نرساند این است

13

The love that lasts a lifetime is this.
The pain that is going to kill me is this.
The problem whose solution no one knows is this.
And the night that will not take me to the day is this.

۱۴

معشوق مرا عهد من از یاد برفت
وان عهد و وفا بباد بر داد و برفت
پایم بحیل ببست و آزاد برفت
آتش بمن اندر زد و چون باد برفت

14

My love forgot her promise to me and went away.
She threw her loyalty to the wind and went away.
She tied my feet cunningly, and herself freely went away.
She set fire on me, and herself like the wind went away.

۱۵

آن بت که بانصاف نکو بود برفت
حورا صفت و فرشته خو بود برفت
آسایش عمرم همه او داشت ببرد
آرایش جانم همه او بود برفت

15

That idol who was, in all fairness, beautiful is now gone.
She who was houri-like and angel-natured is now gone.
She had all the comfort of my life which she took away.
She who was the adornment of my soul is now gone.

۱۶

دلبر چو دلم بعشوه بربود برفت
غمهای مرا بغمزه بفزود برفت
بس دیر بدست آمد و زود برفت
آتش بمن اندر زد و چون دود برفت

16

My beloved stole my heart coyly and went away.
She added to my sorrows with her glance and went away.
She came too late, and too soon she went away.
She set fire on me, and like smoke she went away.

۱۷

من با تو که عشق جاودانی دارم

یک مهر و هزار مهربانی دارم

با من صنما چو زندگانی نکنی

من بی تو بگو چه زندگانی دارم

17

I, who have an eternal love with you,

Have one love but a thousand favors from you.

If you do not live with me, my darling,

Tell me what kind of life I have without you!

۱۸

روزی که بحیلت بشب تیره برم

میگویم شکر و باز پس می‌نگرم

بنگر که ز عمر در چه خون جگرم

تا روز گذشته را غنیمت شمرم

18

After I lead my day cunningly to the dark night,

I look back and I am thankful.

Behold, how life makes my heart bleed

I am grateful for the day that has passed!

۱۹

چون روی ندارم که برویت نگرم

باری بسر کوی تو بر می‌گذرم

در دیده کشم ز آرزوی رخ تو

گردی که ز کوی تو بدامن سپرم

19

Since I do not have the face to look at your face,

I walk through your street anyway.

Longing for your face, I rub on my eyes the dust

Which has sat on my skirt from your street.

۲۰

در کار تو هر روز گرفتارترم
غمهای ترا بجان خریدارترم
هر روز بچشم من نکوروی تری
هر چند که بیش بینمت زارترم

20

Everyday I am more involved with your affair
And more prepared to bear your sorrows.
Everyday you are more beautiful in my eyes.
The more I see you, the more desperate I am.

۲۱

بازیچه دور آسمانم چه کنم
سرگشته گردش جهانم چه کنم
از هر چه همی کنم پشیمان گردم
آیا چه کنم تا که بدانم چه کنم

21

I am the plaything of the sky's rotation, what shall I do?
I am bewildered by the world's revolution, what shall I do?
Whatever I do, I regret it later.
In order to know what I should do, what shall I do?

۲۲

بر آتش هجر عمری ار بنشینم
بر خاک در تو هم بدل نگزینم
از باد همه نسیم زلفت بویم
در آب همه خیال رویت بینم

22

Even if I sit in the fire of your separation all my life,
I will not trade your door's dust for anything.
I smell only the scent of your tress in the breeze,
And see only the image of your face in the water.

۲۳

من دل بکسی جز از تو آسان ندهم

چیزی که گران خریدم ارزان ندهم

صد جان بدهم در آرزوی دل خویش

وان دل که ترا خواست بصد جان ندهم

23

I will not give my heart easily to anyone but you.
I will not sell cheap what I have bought expensive.
I will give a hundred lives for the desire of my heart.
I won't trade the heart that desires you for a hundred souls.

۲۴

ای دل مگذار عمر چون بی خبران

ایمن منشین ز روزگار گذران

تو طاق نه ای با تو همان خواهد کرد

ایام که کرد و می کند با دگران

24

O heart, spend not your life like the ignorant people.
Do not sit secure from the fleeting time.
You are not an exception. Time will do with you
What it has done and is doing with the others.

فخر رازی
(۶۰۶ هجری قمری)

۱

ای دل ز غبار جهل اگر پاک شوی
تو روح مجردی بر افلاک شوی
عرش است نشیمن تو شرمت ناید
کایی و مقیم عرصه خاک شوی

Fakhr Râzi
(d. 1210 C.E.)

1

O heart, if you clean yourself of the dust of ignorance,
You are a free spirit. You will rise to the heavens.
The empyrean is your seat. Are you not ashamed
You have come and sat in the field of dust?

۲

ترسم بروم عالم جان نادیده
بیرون شوم از جهان جهان نادیده
در عالم جان چون روم از عالم تن
در عالم تن عالم جان نادیده

2

I fear dying before seeing the world of spirit.
I fear going out of the world before seeing the world.
How can I go from the physical world to the spiritual world
Without seeing the world of spirit in the world of the body?

٣

در رهگذرم هزار جا دام نهی

گویی کشمت اگر در او گام نهی

یک ذره زمین ز دام تو خالی نیست

گیری و کشی و عاصی‌ام نام نهی

3

You lay a thousand traps in my way and say:
"I will kill you if you step in any of them!"
Not a bit of land is empty of your traps.
You capture me, kill me, and call me a sinner!

۴

سیر آمدم از ساز کژ آهنگ وجود

زین پرده بی نوای ده رنگ وجود

صد سجده شکر در عدم بیش برم

گر باز رهد نام من از ننگ وجود

4

I am tired of the uncouth music of being,
Of this loud and untuned scale of being.
I will prostrate before nonbeing a hundred times
If my name is redeemed from the infamy of being.

۵

نه از سر و کار باخلل می ترسم

نه نیز ز نقصان عمل می ترسم

ترسم ز گنه نیست که می آمرزند

از سابقه حکم ازل می ترسم

5

I do not fear the shortcomings of my deeds,
Nor do I fear the deficiencies of my acts.
I do not fear my sins, for they can be forgiven.
I fear the precedence of the Primordial Command.

۶

هر جا که ز مهرت اثری افتاده است
سودازده‌ای بر گذری افتاده است
در وصل تو کی توان رسیدن کانجا
هر جا که نهی پای سری افتاده است

6

Wherever a trace of your love has fallen,
There a lover in a passage has fallen.
When can one attain to your union in a place
Where at every step someone's head has fallen?

۷

آن مرد نیم کز عدمم بیم آید
آن نیمه مرا خوشتر ازین نیم آید
جانیست به عاریت مرا داده خدای
تسلیم کنم چو وقت تسلیم آید

7

I am not the one who is afraid of nonbeing.
That half is more pleasant to me than this one.
I have a soul lent to me by God.
I will yield it when the time for surrender comes.

۸

درویشی جوی و روی در شاه مکن
وز دامن فقر دست کوتاه مکن
اندر دهن مار شو و مال مجوی
در چاه بزی و طلب جاه مکن

8

Try to be a dervish and do not turn your face to the king.
Do not deprive yourself of the garment of poverty.
It is better to go into a snake's mouth than seek possessions!
It is better to live in a well than seek luxury!

۹

کنه خردم در خور اثبات تو نیست

آسایش جان بجز مناجات تو نیست

من ذات ترا به واجبی کی دانم

داننده ذات تو بجز ذات تو نیست

9

The essence of my reason is not fit to prove your existence.

My soul's comfort is only in communion with you.

How can I realize your essence by being objective?

Your essence is known to your essence only.

ابوالحسن طلحه

(قرن ششم هجری قمری)

۱

آن دل که کلید گنج هر شادی داشت

در هر کاری هزار استادی داشت

شد بنده تو بدان نمانست که او

هرگز روزی نشان آزادی داشت

Abulhasan Talhe
(12th century C.E.)

1

My heart, which had the key to every joy's treasury

And was mighty masterly in every skill,

Became your slave and did not seem

It had ever had any sign of freedom.

۲

چون صبر رمیده شد پیام تو چه سود
جان رفت ز پرسش و سلام تو چه سود
در آتش هجران تو ای جان جهان
دل سوخته شد وعده خام تو چه سود

2

When patience ran out, what good is your message?
When life finished, what good is your greeting and inquiry?
Now that in the fire of your separation, O soul of the world,
My heart is consumed, what good is your vain promise?

۳

در عشق تو دل نکرد یاد از دگری
دیده ز وفا نشان نداد از دگری
گرچه ستم از تو دید و داد از دگری
غمناک هم از تو به که شاد از دگری

3

In your love, never did my heart recall another,
Nor did my eyes see a sign of fidelity from another.
Although it saw cruelty from you and good from another,
It preferred to be saddened by you than rejoiced by another.

۴

هر چند همی بیش دوی بر در عشق
آزرده شوی تو زود از خنجر عشق
این حرف نوشته‌اند بر دفتر عشق
سر دوست ندارد آنکه دارد سر عشق

4

The faster you run toward the door of love,
The sooner you are struck by the sword of love.
These words are written in the book of love:
He who heads toward love does not love his head.

۵

در کوی تو گم گشت دلم روز نخست

امروز یقینم شد کان در کف تست

زین پس به دل شکسته و عزم درست

دل را و تو را بجان همی خواهم جست

5

My heart was lost in your street the first day.
Today I am sure it is in your hands.
From now on, with a broken spirit but sound determination,
I shall be looking for you and my heart as long as I live.

۶

شادی چو غم توام در این عالم نیست

وان دم که نه در غمت بر آرم دم نیست

آنکس که غم تو خورد او را غم نیست

زیرا که غمت ز هیچ شادی کم نیست

6

There is no joy for me like your sorrow in this world.
The air I do not breathe in your sorrow is not a breath.
He who sorrowed for you has no sorrow.
For your sorrow is not less good than any happiness.

۷

دلدار مرا گفت شنیدم به درست

کز من دل خویشتن همی خواهی جست

گیرم که دل تو در سر زلف من است

آخر نه سر زلف من اندر کف توست

7

"Did I hear it right," asked my beloved,
"That you wanted your heart back from me?
"Supposing your heart is in my tress,
"Is it not true that my tress is in your hand?"

نظامی گنجوی
(۶۰۴ هجری قمری)

۱

گفتم سخنم با تو عیاری بدهاد
در عشق تو ایزدم قراری بدهاد
گفتا که ازین دعا غرض چیست ترا
گفتم وصلت گفت خدایت بدهاد

Nezâmi Ganjavi
(d. 1208 C.E.)

1

"May that my words have some value with you," said I,
"And may that God give me some patience in love."
"What is this prayer for?" asked he. "Your union," said I.
"May that God give it to you," said he.

۲

گر آه کشم کجاست فریادرسی
ور صبر کنم عمر نماندست بسی
بر یاد تو میزنم به هر دم نفسی
کس را اندهد خدای سودای کسی

2

If I sigh, who is going to help me?
If I be patient, not much life is left for me.
Every moment I breathe in your memory.
May God make no one so eager for another.

۳

چون نیست امید عمرم از شام به چاشت

باری همه تخم نیکویی باید کاشت

چون عالمِ را بکس نخواهند گذاشت

باری دل دوستان نگه باید داشت

3

Since there is no hope for life from dusk to dawn,
One must sow only the seed of goodness.
Since this world will not remain for anyone,
One must, at least, be kind to his friends.

۴

بیچاره دلی که او ندارد یاری

بی یاری و بیکسی است مشکل کاری

این یک دو سه دم را که بجان نتوان یافت

گر دل داری مدار بی دلداری

4

Miserable is a heart that has no beloved.
It is difficult to be without a friend or a beloved.
These few moments which you can never find again,
If you have a heart, do not be without a beloved.

۵

از هر چه خورد مرد شراب اولیتر

در بتکده ها باده ناب اولیتر

عالم چو خرابست و در او جایی نیست

در جای خراب هم خراب اولیتر

5

Of all things that man consumes, wine is the best.
In idol-temples, pure wine is the best.
Since this world is in ruins with no sound place therein,
To be ruined (drunk) in the ruins is the best.

۶

تا شربت عاشقی چشیدم ز غمت
هر بد که گمان بری کشیدم ز غمت
قصه چه کنم بجان رسیدم ز غمت
آن به که نگویم که چه دیدم ز غمت

6
Since I tasted the wine of love in your sorrow,
Any pain you may think of I have suffered in your sorrow.
To make a long story short, I died in your sorrow.
It is better I say nothing of what I have seen in your sorrow.

رشید وطواط
(۵۷۳ هجری قمری)

۱

چون ابر ز عشق یار میگریم زار
وز گریه من چو برق میخندد یار
او هست بهار حسن و خالی نبود
از گریه ابر و خنده برق بهار

Rashid Vatvât
(d. 1178 C.E.)

1
In the love of my beloved, like a cloud I am crying.
And my beloved, like a lightning, is laughing at my crying.
She is the spring of beauty, and a spring is not devoid
Of the laughter of the lightning and the crying of the cloud.

٢

بویت شنوم ز باد بیهوش شوم

نامت شنوم ز خلق مدهوش شوم

اول سخنم تویی چو در حرف آیم

واندیشه من تویی چو خاموش شوم

2

I smell your scent from the wind and become unconscious.
I hear your name from the people and become intoxicated.
You are my first word when I begin to speak,
And my only thought when I am silent.

٣

بس شب بدعا دو دست بر داشته‌ام

بس روز براه تو نظر داشته‌ام

از خویشتنم خبر مبادا همه عمر

گر بی تو ز خویشتن خبر داشته‌ام

3

Many a night I have raised both my hands in prayer.
Many a day I have kept my eyes on your road.
If I ever was conscious of myself without you,
Let me have no consciousness of the self the rest of my life.

مجدالدین بغدادی
(۶۰۷ هجری قمری)

۱

ای نسخه نامه الهی که تویی
وی آینه جمال شاهی که تویی
بیرون ز تو نیست هر چه در عالم هست
در خود بطلب هر آنچه خواهی که تویی

Majduddin Baghdâdi
(d. 1211 C.E.)

1

O you who are the transcription of God's scripture
And the mirror of his majestic beauty,
Whatever exists in the world is not outside you.
Seek in yourself anything you want, for you are that.

۲

هر موی تو را هزار صاحب هوس است
تا خود بتو از جمله کرا دسترس است
آنکس که بیافت دولتی یافت عظیم
وانرا که نیافت درد نایافت بس است

2

For every strand of your hair, there are a thousand aspirers.
It remains to be seen who will have access to you.
He who found you, found a great fortune.
And to him who didn't, the pain of not finding is enough.

٣

عشق تو ز من دل و جهان نیز ببرد

عقلی که نبود ناله آن نیز ببرد

گفتم دین هست اگر دل و دنیا نیست

سیلاب قضا در آمد آن نیز ببرد

3

Your love took the heart from me, and the world, too.
And the reason, which did not really exist, my laments took.
I said, "Faith exists if the heart and world do not."
The flood of destiny came and took away that one, too.

۴

آنها که مقیم آستان تو زیند

کی کشته شوند چون بجان تو زیند

از آب حیات خود چنان نتوان زیست

کز آتش عشق دوستان تو زیند

4

Those who live at your presence do not die.
How can they, since they live by your spirit?
One cannot live by the water of life
The way your lovers do by the fire of love.

۵

آن را که بود ز بندگی آزادی

غمگین نبود از غم و شاد از شادی

از حضرت عزت که نظرگاه دل است

باز افتادی بهر چه باز افتادی

5

He who is free from bondage and devotion [to God]
Is not saddened by grief nor rejoiced by joy.
Out of the Divine Presence, which is the heart's viewpoint,
Into anything one fell, one is fallen.

۶

کو دل که بر آرد نفسی اسرارش

کو گوش که بشنود دمی گفتارش

معشوقه جمال می نماید شب و روز

کو دیده که تا بر خورد از دیدارش

6

Where is the heart that can reveal His secrets for a moment?
Where is the ear that can hear His words for moment?
The Beloved reveals His Face day and night.
Where is the eye that can benefit from this sight?

۷

دیوانه نباشد آنکه از زر ترسد

عاشق نبود هر که ز خنجر ترسد

تا چند ز سر بریدنم بیم کنی

آنکس که سر تو دارد از سر ترسد؟

7

He is not mad who is afraid of gold.
He is not a lover who is afraid of the sword.
How long should you frighten me of beheading me?
Is the one who loves you afraid of losing his head?

۸

در بحر محیط غوطه خواهم خوردن

یا غرقه شدن یا گهری آوردن

کار تو مخاطره است خواهم کردن

یا سرخ کنم روی بدان یا گردن

8

I shall be diving in the ocean [of love].
Either I will drown or bring up a pearl.
Your affair is a risk. I shall take it.
I will redden either my cheek or my neck.

٩

از لطف تو هیچ بنده نومید نشد
مقبول تو جز مقبل جاوید نشد
لطفت بکدام ذره پیوست دمی
کان ذره به از هزار خورشید نشد

9

No one who belonged to you lost hope of your favor.
He whom you favored became the eternal favorite.
What particle did your favor join for a moment,
Which did not become better than a thousand suns?

١٠

چرخ و مه و مهر در تمنای تواند
سرو و گل و لاله در تماشای تواند
ارواح مقدسان قدسی شب و روز
ابجد خوانان لوح سودای تواند

10

The moon, the sun, and the sky are aspiring for you.
The cypress, the rose, and the jasmine are looking on you.
Day and night, the holy spirits of the heaven
Are the abecedarians of the board of your love.

١١

تا مرد ز عشق خاک بر سر نکند
از جمله عشاق تو سر بر نکند
روشن نشود با تو سر و کار کسی
کو سر بسر کار تو اندر نکند

11

Unless man soil his head in your love,
He cannot lift his head among your lovers.
Unless man put his head over your affair,
He cannot clear his affair with you.

۱۲

شمع است رخ خوب تو پروانه منم
دل خویش غم تو است و بیگانه منم
زنجیر سر زلف که بر گردن تست
در گردن من فکن که دیوانه منم

12

Your beautiful face is the candle, I am the moth.
The heart is related to your love's pain, I am the stranger.
The chain of your tress, which is on your neck,
Throw on my neck, for I am the insane.

۱۳

من عشق تو در میان جان بنهادم
با مهر غمت بر سر آن بنهادم
تا دل ز همه جهان کناره نگرفت
با او سخن تو در میان ننهادم

13

I placed your love inside my soul,
And sealed it with your love's pain.
As long as my heart had not withdrawn from all the world,
I did not speak with it about you.

۱۴

یک تیر جفا نماند کان زیبا یار
آنرا نزدست بر دل من صد بار
این طرفه که هر لحظه کنم توبه ز عشق
بازم به کرشمه‌ای برد بر سر کار

14

Not a single arrow of cruelty that beautiful friend
Missed to shoot at my heart for a hundred times!
How amazing that any moment I repent of love,
He puts me back to work with another loving look!

رضی الدین نیشابوری
(۵۹۸ هجری قمری)

۱

ای شمع بهرزه چند بر خود خندی
تو سوز دل مرا کجا مانندی
فرق است میان سوز کز جان خیزد
با آنکه به ریسمانش بر خود بندی

Raziuddin Nishâburi
(d. 1202 C.E.)

1

O candle, how long will you laugh by yourself in vain?
How can you be like the fire in my heart?
The fire that rises from the spirit is different from
The one that you fasten to yourself with a string.

۲

یا رب اگرم عشق تو افزون گردد
تا عاقبت کار دلم چون گردد
عشق تو چو کوهیست که از وی یک جو
بر دل نه که بر کوه نهی خون گردد

2

O Lord, if your love increased in me,
How would my heart be by the end of this affair?
Your love is like a mountain, one grain of which if placed,
Not on a heart, but on a mountain, would turn it into blood.

۳

جوری که مرا از آن جفا کیش آید
بر هر چه بر اندازم از آن بیش آید
از کس گله ای نیست مرا هم ز خود است
چون من پی دل روم چنین پیش آید

3

The cruelty which comes to me from that unkind friend
Exceeds anything I use to measure it.
I have no complaint of anyone except myself.
Because I follow my heart, this is what happens.

۴

تا ظن نبری که کم کمت می بینم
بی زحمت دیده هر دمت می بینم
در وصف نگنجد و صفت نتوان داد
آن شادیها که در غمت می بینم

4

In order for you not to suspect that I see you rarely,
I see you every moment without the trouble of looking.
The pleasures, which I experience in longing for you,
Cannot be explained or be contained in any description.

۵

در راه غم تو چند پویم آخر
رخساره به اشک چند شویم آخر
ور پرسندم کز پی چندین تک و تاز
از یار چه یافتی چه گویم آخر

5

How long shall I walk on the road of your love's pain?
How long shall I wash my face with tears?
And if they ask me, What I gained from the beloved,
After all this struggle, what shall I say?

۶

چون صبح مرا ز روی تو یاد دهد
در خونباری دیده من داد دهد:
ای بی معنی کسی چنان دوستیی
بی هیچ سبب به خیره بر باد دهد؟

6
When the morning reminds me of your face,
While shedding blood, my eyes cry out:
O you fool, does anyone throw to the wind
Such a friendship without any cause?

۷

هر نیم شبم درد تو بیدار کند
و اندیشه تو در دل من کار کند
زان می ترسم بتا که درد دل من
روزی به چنین شبت گرفتار کند

7
Every midnight the pain of your love wakes me up,
And your thought does its work in my heart.
What I am afraid of, my darling, is that one day
The pain of my heart might engulf you, too, in such a night.

Chapter Four
13th Century C.E.
7th Century Hejri

جلال الدین مولوی رومی
(۶۰۴-۶۷۲ هجری قمری)

۱

آن دل که شد او قابل انوار خدا

پر باشد جان او ز اسرار خدا

زنهار تن مرا چو تنها مشمر

کو جمله نمک شد به نمکزار خدا

Jalâluddin Molavi Rumi
(1208-1274 C.E.)

1
The heart that became worthy of the light of God
Has its life replete with the secrets of God.
Beware that you do not count my body like other bodies!
For it has entirely turned to salt in the salt-marsh of God.

۲

آنکس که ببسته است ره خواب مرا
تر میخواهد ز اشک مجراب مرا
خاموش مرا گرفت و در آب افکند
آبی که حلاوتی دهد آب مرا

2

He who has closed the road of my sleep
Wants my eyes to be wet with tears.
He picked me up and threw me in the water,
The water that sweetened my life.

۳

ای آنکه چو آفتاب فرد است بیا
بیروی تو برگ و باغ زرد است بیا
عالم بیتو غبار و گرد است بیا
این مجلس عیش بیتو سرد است بیا

3

O you who are like the singular sun, come!
The garden plants are pale without your face, come!
The world without you is ashes and dust, come!
This assembly of joy is cold without you, come!

۴

ایدوست بدوستی قرینیم ترا
هر جا که قدم نهی زمینیم ترا
در مذهب عاشقی روا کی باشد
عالم بتو بینیم و نبینیم ترا

4

O friend, I am close to you in friendship.
I am the ground wherever you step on.
How could it be right in the creed of love
That I see the world through you, but not see you?

۵

ای سبزی هر درخت و هر باغ و گیا
ای دولت و اقبال من و کار و کیا
ای خلوت و ای سماع و اخلاص و ریا
بی حضرت تو اینهمه سوداست بیا

5

O greenness of every tree, plant, and garden,
O my wealth, fortune, pomp, and glory,
O my solitude and music, my sincerity and pretence —
All these are illusions without your presence, come!

۶

با عشق روان شد از عدم مرکب ما
روشن ز شراب وصل دائم شب ما
زان می که حرام نیست در مذهب ما
تا صبح عدم خشک بیابی لب ما

6

In love, my horse walked out of nonbeing.
My night is always bright with the wine of union.
Of the wine, which is not forbidden in our religion,
You will never see my lips dry.

۷

بر رهگذر بلا نهادم دل را
خاص از پی تو پای گشادم دل را
از باد مرا بوی تو آمد امروز
شکرانه آن بباد دادم دل را

7

I laid my heart on the passage of calamity.
Especially for you I let loose of my heart.
The wind brought me your scent today.
In gratitude, I gave my heart to the wind.

٨

تا از تو جدا شده است آغوش مرا

از گریه کسی ندیده خاموش مرا

در جان و دل و دیده فراموش نه ای

از بهر خدا مکن فراموش مرا

8

Since you separated from my arms,

No one has seen me silent from crying.

You are not forgotten from my heart, soul, and sight.

For Heaven's sake, forget me not!

٩

تا با تو بوم نخسبم از یاریها

تا بیتو بوم نخسبم از زاریها

سبحان الله که هر دو شب بیدارم

تو فرق نگر میان بیداریها

9

When I am with you, I cannot sleep because of loving.

When I am not with you, I cannot sleep because of crying.

Glory be to God, I am awake both nights.

Behold the difference between the two awakenments!

١٠

تا نقش خیال دوست با ما است دلا

ما را همه عمر خود تماشا است دلا

ای مکر در آمیخته هر جائی را

یک مکر برای من در انگیز و بیا

10

As long as the image of the Friend is with me, O heart,

I am a sightseer all my life, O heart.

O you who have plotted a design everywhere,

Plot a design for me and come!

۱۱

جز عشق نبود هیچ دمساز مرا
نی اول و نی آخر و آغاز مرا
جان میدهد از درونه آواز مرا
کی کاهل راه عشق در باز مرا

11

Except love there was no other companion for me.
Neither the beginning, nor the first and last for me.
The soul is calling on me from within me:
O indolent of the road of love, lose me!

۱۲

خود را بحیل در افکنم مست آنجا
تا بنگرم آن جان جهان هست آنجا
یا پای رساندم به مقصود و مرام
یا سر بدهم همچو دل از دست آنجا

12

I should throw myself there cunningly,
So that I see if that soul of the world is there.
I will either lead my steps to my desired goal,
Or lose my head, like my heart, there.

۱۳

در سر دارم ز می پریشانیها
با قند لب تو شکر افشانیها
ایساقی پنهان چو پیاپی کردی
رسوا شود ایندم همه پنهانیها

13

I have many agitations in my head because of wine,
And many sweetnesses because of your lips' sugar.
O Sâqi, since you secretly gave wine one cup after another,
Now all the secrets will come to the open.

۱۴

دستان کسی دست زنان کرد مرا

بی حشمت و بیعقل و روان کرد مرا

حاصل دل او دل مرا گردانید

هر شکل که خواست آنچنان کرد مرا

14

Someone's hands made me clap my hands.
They made me without prudence, intellect, and soul.
In short, his heart revolutionized my heart,
And shaped me in any form he wanted.

۱۵

عاشق همه سال مست و رسوا بادا

دیوانه و شوریده و شیدا بادا

با هشیاری غصه هر چیز خوریم

چون مست شویم هر چه بادا بادا

15

May the lover be drunk and infamous all the year.
May he be charmed, frenzied, and mad.
While sober, we suffer for everything.
When we get drunk, we let go of everything.

۱۶

عشق است طریق و راه پیغمبر ما

ما زاده عشق و عشق شد مادر ما

ای مادر ما نهفته در چادر ما

پنهان شده از طبیعت کافر ما

16

Love is the road and the way of our prophet.
We are born from love. Love is our mother.
O mother, you are concealed in our tent.
You are hiding from our denying nature.

۱۷

عمریست ندیده ایم گلزار ترا

وان نرگس پر خمار خمار ترا

پنهان شده ای ز خلق مانند وفا

دیریست ندیده ایم رخسار ترا

17
I have not seen your rose-garden for a long time,
Nor those languishing, drunken eyes of yours.
You are absent from among the people, like fidelity.
I have not seen your face for a long, long time.

۱۸

گر در طلب خودی ز خود بیرون آ

جو را بگزار و جانب جیحون آ

چون گاو چه میکشی تو بار گردون

چرخی بزن و بر سر این گردون آ

18
If you are seeking the Self, come out of your *self.*
Leave the gutter and come toward the Oxus.
Why do you carry the burden of the world, like a cow?
Make a turnaround and rise above the world.

۱۹

نور فلکست این تن خاکی ما

رشک ملک آمده است چالاکی ما

گه رشک برد فرشته از پاکی ما

گه بگریزد دیو ز بیباکی ما

19
This earthly body of ours is the light of heaven.
Our nimbleness is the envy of the angels.
Sometimes, angels envies our piety.
Other times the devil escapes from our intrepidity.

۲۰

آن لقمه که در دهان نگنجد بطلب
وان علم که در نشان نگنجد بطلب
سریست میان دل مردان خدای
جبریل در آن میان نگنجد بطلب

20

Desire the loaf which cannot be contained in the mouth.
Seek the knowledge which cannot be contained in symbols.
Seek the secret which is in the hearts of men of God,
Wherein Gabriel cannot be admitted.

۲۱

آنی که ملک با تو در آید بطرب
گر آدمئی شیفته گردد چه عجب
تا جان دارم بندگیت خواهم کرد
خواهی بطلب مرا و خواهی مطلب

21

You are the one who excites the angels.
If man becomes enamoured of you, what wonder?
I will be bound to you as long as I live,
Whether you want me or not.

۲۲

امروز چو هر روز خرابیم خراب
مگشا در اندیشه و بر گیر رباب
صد گونه نماز است رکوعست و سجود
آنرا که جمال دوست باشد محراب

22

Today, like everyday, I am drunk, so drunk.
Do not open the door of thinking. Pick up the rebeck.
He whose *mehrâb* is the Friend's Face,
Stands, bends, and prostrates in many prayers.

۲۳

ای ماه جبین شبی تو مهوار مخسب

در دور در آ چو چرخ دوار مخسب

بیداری ما چراغ عالم باشد

یکشب تو چراغ را نگهدار مخسب

23

One night, O moon-browed, like the moon, sleep not.
Start whirling, and like the turning sky, sleep not.
Our awakenment is the light of the world.
One night, you keep on the light, sleep not.

۲۴

این باد سحر محرم راز است مخسب

هنگام تضرع و نیاز است مخسب

بر خلق دو کون از ازل تا بابد

اندر که نبسته است باز است مخسب

24

This morning wind is the confidante of secrets, sleep not.
It is time for entreaty and supplication, sleep not.
This door, which never closes, is open, for all eternity,
To the people of both worlds, sleep not.

۲۵

حاجت نبود مستی ما را بشراب

یا مجلس ما را طرب از چنگ و رباب

بی ساقی و بی شاهد و بی مطرب و نی

شوریده و مستیم چو مستان خراب

25

Our intoxication does not need any wine,
Nor does our assembly's joy depend on a harp and a rebec.
Without a Sâqi, a *shâhed*, a minstrel, or a reed,
We are exultant and ecstatic like drunkards.

۲۶

سبحان الله من و تو ای در خوشاب

پیوسته مخالفیم اندر همه باب

من بخت توام که هیچ خوابم نبرد

تو بخت منی که بر نیایی از خواب

26

Glory be to God, O brilliant pearl!
We are always contraries in everything.
I am your luck that never falls asleep.
You are my luck that never wakes from sleep.

۲۷

شب گشت در این سینه چه سوز است عجب

می‌پندارم کاول روز است عجب

در دیده عشق می نگنجد شب و روز

این دیده عشق دیده دوز است عجب

27

It became night. Oh, what a fire is burning in my breast!
It looks like the beginning of the day. How strange!
There is no day and night in the eye of love.
This eye of love is an eye-blinder. How strange!

۲۸

علمی که ترا گره گشاید بطلب

زان پیش که از تو جان بر آید بطلب

آن نیست که هست می‌نماید بگزار

آن هست که نیست می‌نماید بطلب

28

Seek the knowledge that can untie your knot.
Seek it before your soul leaves your body.
Give up the nonbeing that looks like being.
Seek the being that looks like nonbeing.

۲۹

مستند مجردان اسرار امشب

در پرده نشسته اند با یار امشب

ای هستی بیگانه از این ره بر خیز

زحمت باشد بودن اغیار امشب

29

The confidants of secrets are drunk tonight.
They have privacy with the beloved tonight.
O stranger existence, get out of the way!
Having strangers around is a trouble tonight.

۳۰

آسوده کسی که در کم و بیشی نیست

در بند توانگری و درویشی نیست

فارغ ز غم جهان و از خلق جهان

با خویشتنش بذره ای خویشی نیست

30

He has peace who cares not for more or less,
Who is not concerned about poverty or wealth.
Free from the world's sorrow and the world's people,
He has no relationship to himself at all.

۳۱

آن تلخ سخنها که چنان دل شکن است

انصاف بده چه لایق آن دهن است

شیرین لب از تلخ نگفتی هرگز

این بی نمکی ز شوربختی من است

31

Those bitter words which are so heart-breaking,
Be fair, are they proper from that mouth?
Those sweet lips had never uttered a bitter word.
This misfortune is due to my bad luck.

۳۲

آن عشق مجرد سوی صحرا می تاخت
دیدش دل من ز کر و فرش بشناخت
با خود میگفت چون ز صورت برهم
با صورت عشق عشقها خواهم باخت

32

That libral love was dashing toward the desert.
My heart saw it and recognized it by its glory.
My heart said, "If I am released from appearances,
"I will fall in love with the face of love."

۳۳

اندر سر ما همت کاری دیگر است
معشوقه خوب ما نگاری دیگر است
والله که بعشق نیز قانع نشویم
ما را پس از این خزان بهاری دیگر است

33

In my head, there is the determination for another work.
My beautiful sweetheat is another beloved.
By God, I am not content with love either.
For me, after this autumn, there is another spring.

۳۴

انصاف بده که عشق نیکوکار است
زانست خلل که طبع بدکردار است
تو شهوت خویش را لقب عشق نهی
از شهوت تا بعشق ره بسیار است

34

In all fairness, love is benevolent.
The problem is that nature is malevolent.
You call your lust love.
There is a long way from lust to love.

٣۵

ای جان خبرت هست که جانان تو کیست

وی دل خبرت هست که مهمان تو کیست

ای تن که بهر حیله رهی میجوئی

او میکشدت ببین که جویان تو کیست

35

O soul, do you know who your beloved is?

And you, O heart, do you know who your guest is?

O body, who are looking for a way desperately,

He is pulling you toward himself. See, who your seeker is!

٣۶

ای حسرت خوبان جهان روی خوشت

وی قبله زاهدان دو ابروی خوشت

از جمله صفات خویش عریان گشتم

تا غوطه خورم برهنه در جوی خوشت

36

O you, whose lovely face is the envy of the world's beauties,

And whose eyebrows are the kebla of the world's ascetics,

I denuded myself of all my attributes,

So that I can plunge naked in your pleasant stream.

٣٧

ای خواجه ترا غم جمال و جاهست

واندیشه باغ و راغ و خرمنگاهست

ما سوختگان عالم توحیدیم

ما را سر لا اله الا الله است

37

O *khâja*, you are concerned about beauty and glory,

And you think of gardens, meadows, and harvest-times.

We are consumed in the world of unity,

Our only thought is: *There is no god but Allah.*

٣٨

ای طالب اگر ترا سر اینراهست

واندر سر تو هوای اندرگاهست

مفتاح فتوح اهل حق دانی چیست

خوش گفتن لا اله الا الله است

38

O seeker of the Truth, if you are determined on this road,
And have the desire to reach the destination in your head,
Do you know what the key of success of men of Truth is?
It is the cheerful reciting of *There is no god but Allah*.

٣٩

ای عقل برو که عاقلی اینجا نیست

گر موی شوی موی ترا گنجا نیست

روز آمد و روز هر چراغی که فروخت

در شعله آفتاب جز رسوا نیست

39

O reason, go away! There is no wise person here.
Even if you turn into a hair, there is no room for you here.
It is daytime now, and any lamp lit at daytime
Is but defamed before the flame of the sun.

۴۰

ای کز تو دلم پر سمن و یاسمن است

وز دولت تو کیست که او همچو من است

بر خاستن از جان و جهان مشکل نیست

مشکل ز سر کوی تو برخاستن است

40

O you, who have filled my heart with lilies and jasmines,
Who has availed of your fortune as much as I have?
To leave life and the universe is not hard.
To leave your street is hard.

۴۱

اینجمله شرابهای بیجام کراست
ما مرغ گرفته ایم این دام کراست
از بهر نثار عاشقان هر نفسی
چندین شکر و پسته و بادام کراست

41

All these wines without goblets, for whom are they?
We have caught the bird, these snares for whom are they?
Offered to lovers every moment,
So much sugar, pistachios and almonds, for whom are they?

۴۲

این سینه پر مشعله از مکتب اوست
و امروز که بیمار شدم از تب اوست
پرهیز کنم ز هر چه فرمود طبیب
جز از می و شکری که آن از لب اوست

42

This breast, full of flames, is the nurtured of his school.
This illness of mine today is because of his fever.
I shall abstain from all that the physician forbade,
Except from the wine and sugar that come from his lips.

۴۳

این فصل بهار نیست فصلی دیگر است
مخموری هر چشم ز وصلی دیگر است
هر چند که جمله شاخها رقصانند
جنبیدن هر شاخ ز اصلی دیگر است

43

This season is not spring. It is another season.
The lovesickness of each eye is from a different union.
Although all branches are dancing,
The motion of each branch is from a different cause.

۴۴

این مستی من ز باده حمرا نیست
وین باده بجز در قدح سودا نیست
تو آمده ای که باده من ریزی
من آن باشم که باده ام پیدا نیست

44

This intoxication of mine is not from the red wine.
This wine is found only in the goblet of love.
You have come here to pour me wine.
I am the one whose wine is not visible.

۴۵

بر ما رقم خطا پرستی همه هست
بدنامی و عشق و شور و مستی همه هست
ایدوست چو از میانه مقصود توئی
جای گله نیست چون تو هستی همه هست

45

All kinds of demerits can be attributed to me:
Infamy, love, passion, and drunkenness.
O Friend, since of all things you are my goal,
Why complain? Because you are, they all are.

۴۶

بر من در وصل بسته میدارد دوست
دل را بعنا شکسته میدارد دوست
زین پس من و دلشکستگی بر در او
چون دوست دل شکسته میدارد دوست

46

The friend keeps the door of union closed to me.
He loves to see my heart in pain broken.
From now on I shall sit at his door heart-broken.
For the friend loves the heart broken.

۴۷

بیچاره تر از عاشق بیصبر کجاست
کاین عشق گرفتاری بی هیچ دواست
درمان غم عشق نه صبر و نه ریاست
در عشق حقیقی نه وفا و نه جفاست

47

Where is a more wretched person than an impatient lover?
This love is a problem without any solution.
The remedy of love's pain is neither patience nor pretension.
In a true love, there is neither fidelity nor cruelty.

۴۸

بی دیده اگر راه روی عین خطا است
بر دیده اگر تکیه زدی تیر بلا است
در صومعه و مدرسه از راه مجاز
آنرا که نه جا است تو چه دانی که کجا است

48

It is a shere mistake to walk with your eyes closed.
But to rely on the eye is to invite disaster.
How can you find the one who occupies no place
In the monastery or the school by unreal means.

۴۹

بی یار نماند هر که با یار بساخت
مفلس نشد آنکه با خریدار بساخت
مه نور از آن گرفت کز شب نرمید
گل بوی از آن یافت که با خار بساخت

49

He who agreed with the beloved was not deprived of love.
He who got along with the buyer did not go bankrupt.
The moon gained light because it did not avoid the night.
The rose got along with the thorn and gained its fragrance.

۵۰

تا حاصل دردم سبب درمان گشت

پستیم بلندی شد و کفر ایمان گشت

جان و دل و تن حجاب ره بود کنون

تن دل شد و دل جان شد و جان جانان گشت

50

When the effect of my pain became the cause of my remedy,
My downs became ups and my disbelief faith.
The body, the soul, and the heart were obstacles in the way.
The body became heart, the heart soul, the soul the beloved.

۵۱

تا در دل من صورت آن رشک پریست

دلشاد چو من در همه عالم کیست

والله که بجز شاد نمیدانم زیست

غم می شنوم ولی نمیدانم چیست

51

As long as the image of that envy of the fairy is in my heart,
Who on earth is as happy as I am?
By God, I do not know how else but happily to live.
I hear about sorrow, but I do not know what it is.

۵۲

جانی که حریف بود بیگانه شده است

عقلی که طبیب بود دیوانه شده است

میران همه گنجها بویرانه نهند

ویرانه ما ز گنج ویرانه شده است

52

The soul that was my companion has become a stranger.
The reason that was my doctor has become insane.
Kings bury their treasures in the ruins.
Our ruins have become ruins because of treasures.

۵۳

جانی و جهانی و جهان با تو خوش است
ور زخم زنی زخم سنان با تو خوش است
خود معدن کیمیا است خاک از کف تو
هر چیز که ناخوش است آن با تو خوش است

53

You are soul and the world. The world with you is good.
If you inflict a wound, the wound of your spear is good.
From your hand, dust is a mine of elixir itself.
Whatever is not good, with you it is good.

۵۴

چشم تو ز روزگار خونریزتر است
تیر مژه تو از سنان تیزتر است
رازیکه بگفته ای بگوشم واگوی
زانروی که گوش من گرانخیزتر است

54

Your eyes are more bloodthirsty than time.
The arrows of your eyelashes are sharper than spears.
The secret you whispered in my ears, say it again.
Because it is now harder for my ears to hear.

۵۵

خورشید رخت ز آسمان بیرونست
چون حسن تو کز شرح و بیان بیرونست
عشق تو درون جان من جا دارد
و اینطرفه که از جان و جهان بیرونست

55

The sun of your face is out of the sky;
Like your beauty which is beyond description.
Your love has its place inside my soul,
Yet, strangely it is beyond the soul and the world!

۵۶

خورشید و ستارگان و بدر ما اوست

بستان و سرای و صحن و صدر ما اوست

هم قبله و هم روزه و هم صبر ما اوست

عید و رمضان و شب قدر ما اوست

56

Our sun, our stars, and our full moon is he.

Our garden, our home, our yard, and our seat is he.

Our kebla, our fasting, and our patience is he.

Our festival, our Ramazan, and our Night of *Qadr* is he.

۵۷

خیزید که آن یار سلامت بر خاست

خیزید که از عشق غرامت بر خاست

خیزید که آن لطیف قامت بر خاست

خیزید که امروز قیامت بر خاست

57

Rise, for the beloved got up in good health.

Rise, for the compensation for love is over.

Rise, for that delicate-figured got up to his feet.

Rise, for the Resurrection began today.

۵۸

در راه طلب عاقل و دیوانه یکیست

در شیوه عشق خویش و بیگانه یکیست

آنرا که شراب وصل جانان دادند

در مذهب او کعبه و بتخانه یکیست

58

On the way of quest, the sane and insane are one.

On the way of love, relatives and strangers are one.

Whom the wine of the beloved's union was given,

In his religion, the Ka'ba and the idol-temple are one.

۵۹

در ظاهر و باطن آنچه خیر است و شر است
از حکم حقست و از قضا و قدر است
من جهد همی کنم قضا میگوید
بیرون ز کفایت تو کاری دیگر است

59

Inside and out, that which is virtue or vice
Exists by God's command and is destined to be there.
I keep striving, but Destiny says:
"Beyond your power, something else is there."

۶۰

در عشق تو هر حیله که کردم هیچست
هر خون جگر که بیتو خوردم هیچست
از درد تو هیچ روی درمانم نیست
درمان که کند مرا که دردم هیچست

60

Any trick I played in your love was in vain.
Any heart-blood I drank without you was in vain.
There is no remedy whatsoever for your pain.
Who can cure me, for my pain is in vain?

۶۱

در عشق که جز می بقا خوردن نیست
جز جان دادن دلیل جان بردن نیست
گفتم که ترا شناسم آنگه میرم
گفتا که شناسای مرا مردن نیست

61

In love, where one drinks only the wine of eternity,
Nothing leads to life but the surrendering of life.
I said, "First I want to know you and then die."
He said, "He who knows me never dies."

۶۲

در مجلس عشاق قراری دیگر است
وین باده عشق را خماری دیگر است
آنعلم که در مدرسه حاصل کردند
کاری دیگر است و عشق کاری دیگر است

62

In the assembly of lovers, there is a special order.
This wine of love gives a special hangover.
The knowledge, which was acquired in schools,
Is something and love something else.

۶۳

درویشی و عاشقی بهم سلطانیست
گنجست غم عشق ولی پنهانیست
ویران کردم بدست خود خانه دل
چون دانستم که گنج در ویرانیست

63

To be a dervish and a lover at the same time is sultanate.
The sorrow of love is a treasure which is hidden.
I ruined the house of my heart with my own hands,
Because I knew that a treasure is found in ruins.

۶۴

دل در بر من زنده برای غم تست
بیگانه خلق و آشنای غم تست
لطفیست که میکند غمت با دل من
ورنه دل تنگ من چه جای غم تست

64

My heart in my chest is alive for the sake of your sorrow.
Stranger to people but acquainted with your sorrow is.
Your sorrow does a favor to my heart. Otherwise,
How could my lonely heart be the place of your sorrow?

۶۵

دل رفت بر کسیکه بیماش خوش است
غم خوش نبود و لیک غمهاش خوش است
جان میطلبد نمیدهم روزی چند
جانرا محلی نیست تقاضاش خوش است

65

My heart went to someone who is happy without me.
Sorrow is not pleasant, but his sorrows are.
He is asking for my life, but I hold it back a few days.
Life is not important, but his request is good.

۶۶

شاهی که شفیع هر گنه بود برفت
وان شب که به از هزار مه بود برفت
گر باز آید مرا نبیند تو بگوی
او نیز چو تو بر سر ره بود برفت

66

The king who was the intercessor for every sin is gone.
The night which was better than a thousand moons is gone.
If he ever returns and finds out I am not here, tell him:
"He, too, like you, was set for the road. So he is gone."

۶۷

شمشیر ازل بدست مردان خداست
گوی ابدی در خم چوگان خداست
آن تن که چو کوه طور روشن آید
نور خود از او طلب که او کان خداست

67

The sword of eternity is in the hands of men of God.
The eternal ball is in the bend of the polo-stick of God.
The body that comes lit like Mount Sinai,
Seek your light from him, for he is the mine of God.

۶۸

عشق آمد و شد چو خونم اندر رگ و پوست
تا کرد مرا تهی و پر کرد از دوست
اجزای وجود من همه دوست گرفت
نامیست ز من بر من و باقی همه اوست

68

Love came and, like blood, entered into my veins and skin.
It made me empty and then filled me with the Friend.
The Friend occupied all the parts of my being.
Now there is only a name from me. The rest is all him.

۶۹

عشق تو چنین حکیم و استاد چراست
مهر تو چنین لطیف بنیاد چراست
بر عشق چرا سوزم اگر او خوش نیست
ور عشق خوش است اینهمه فریاد چراست

69

Why is your love so wise and skillful?
Why is your kindness so delicately-founded?
If love is not good, why do I burn in it?
And if it is good, what is this much ado for?

۷۰

عقل آمد و پند عاشقان پیش گرفت
در ره بنشست و رهزنی کیش گرفت
چون در سرشان جایگه پند ندید
پای همه بوسید و ره خویش گرفت

70

Reason came and began to counsel the lovers.
He sat on the road and tried to cut off their way.
Since he found no room for advice in their heads,
He kissed their feet all and one and went his own way.

۷۱

عمریست که جان بنده بی خویشتن است
و انگشت نمای عالمی مرد و زن است
بر خاستن از جهان و جان مشکل نیست
مشکل ز سر کوی تو بر خاستن است

71

All my life, my soul has been a selfless slave,
Notorious among a world of men and women.
It is not hard to give up life and the universe.
What is hard is to leave your street.

۷۲

گر جمله آفاق همه غم بگرفت
بیغم بود آنکه عشق محکم بگرفت
یک ذره نگر که پای در عشق بکوفت
وان ذره جهان شد که دو عالم بگرفت

72

If the whole world were full of sorrow,
He who held of love tightly would be without sorrow.
See how one atom, which was persistent in love,
Became the universe and contained all there is!

۷۳

گر شرم همی از آن و این باید داشت
پس عیب کسان زیر زمین باید داشت
ور آینه وار نیک و بد بنمایی
چون آینه روی آهنین باید داشت

73

If one is to be ashamed of this person and that,
One must cover up people's faults.
But if one is to show the good and the bad,
One must be iron-faced like a mirror.

۷۴

کس نیست که اندر هوسی شیدا نیست
کس نیست که اندر سرش این سودا نیست
سر رشته آن ذوق کزو خیزد شوق
پیداست که هست آن ولی پیدا نیست

74

None exists who is not mad with a strong desire.
None exists who does not have this thought in his mind.
The source of this zeal, from which the strong desire arises,
Is obviously *That*, but it is not visible.

۷۵

ما را بجز این زبان زبانی دیگر است
جز دوزخ و فردوس مکانی دیگر است
آزاده دلان زنده بجان دیگرند
آن گوهر پاکشان ز کانی دیگر است

75

In addition to this language, I have another language.
In addition to heaven and hell, I have another place.
The free-spirited ones live with a special soul.
Their genuine gems are from a different mine.

۷۶

ماهی که نه زیر و نی بالاست کجاست
جانی که نه بی ما و نه با ماست کجاست
اینجا آنجا مگو بگو راست کجاست
عالم همه اوست آنکه بیناست کجاست

76

Where is the Beauty who is neither above nor below?
Where is the Soul who is neither with us nor without us?
Don't say, *He is here or there*. Tell the truth, where is He?
He is all the world, but the one who sees Him, where is he?

۷۷

مستی ز ره آمد و بما در پیوست

ساغر میگشت در میان دست بدست

از دست افتاد ناگهان و بشکست

جامی چه زید میانه چندین مست

77

A drunkard came in from the door and joined us.
A chalice passed around from hand to hand.
Suddenly it fell down and broke to pieces.
How can a glass last among so many drunkards?

۷۸

هر روز دلم در غم تو زارتر است

وز من دل بیرحم تو بیزارتر است

بگزاشتیم غم تو نگذاشت مرا

حقا که غمت از تو وفادارتر است

78

Everyday my heart is weaker in its suffering for you,
While your pitiless heart is more hateful of me.
You left me alone, your suffering did not.
Indeed your suffering is more faithful than you are.

۷۹

هرگز ز دماغ بنده بوی تو نرفت

وز دیده من خیال روی تو نرفت

در آرزوی تو عمر بردم شب و روز

عمرم همه رفت و آرزوی تو نرفت

79

Never did your scent go out of my nose,
Nor the image of your face out of my eyes.
Life passed for me in longing for you day and night.
My life came to an end but longing for you did not.

٨٠

آن ذره که جز همدم خورشید نشد

بر نقد زد و سخره امید نشد

عشقت بکدام سر در افتاد که زود

از باد تو رقصان چو سر بید نشد

80

That particle which kept company with only the sun
Chose the cash in hand and was not fooled by hope.
What head ever filled with your love
Which did not dance like the top of a willow tree?

٨١

آنسر که بود بیخبر از وی خسبد

آنکس که خبر یافت از او کی خسبد؟

میگوید عشق در دو گوشم همه شب

ای وای بر آنکسی که بی وی خسبد

81

He sleeps who is unaware of Him.
When does the one who is aware of Him sleep?
Every night love whispers in my ears:
"Woe is him who sleeps without Him."

٨٢

آنکس که بر آتش جهانم بنهاد

صد گونه زبانه بر زبانم بنهاد

چون شش جهتم شعله آتش بگرفت

اه کردم و دست بر دهانم بنهاد

82

He who put me in the fire of the world,
Placed a hundred kinds of flames on my tongue.
When the flames surrounded me from six directions,
I sighed and he put his hand on my mouth.

٨٣

آنکس که ترا شناخت جانرا چه کند
فرزند و عیال و خانمان را چه کند
دیوانه کنی هردو جهانش بخشی
دیوانه تو هر دو جهان را چه کند

83

He who came to know you what need has he for life?
What need has he for children, home, and wife?
You make him mad and give him both worlds.
What need has your mad for both worlds?

٨۴

آن یار که از طبیب دل برباید
او را دارو طبیب چون فرماید
یکذره ز حسن خویش اگر بنماید
والله که طبیب را طبیبی باید

84

The friend who steals the doctor's heart,
How can the doctor prescribe medication for him?
If he displays a particle of his beauty,
By God, the doctor himself will need a doctor.

٨۵

از آتش عشق تو جوانی خیزد
در سینه جمالهای جانی خیزد
گر میکشیم بکش حلالست ترا
کز کشته دوست زندگانی خیزد

85

From the fire of your love, youth arises.
Many spiritual beauties in the bosom arises.
If you want to kill me, do so! It is lawful for you to kill me.
Because from the slain of the beloved, life arises.

۸۶

از شبنم عشق خاک آدم گل شد

صد فتنه و شور در جهان حاصل شد

صد نشتر عشق بر رگ روح زدند

یک قطره از آن چکید و نامش دل شد

86

With the dew of love, Adam's dust turned into clay.
Then many a tumult and frenzy in the world came to play.
A hundred lancets at the vein of the soul was struck.
One drop from it dripped and was named *heart*.

۸۷

از عشق تو دریا همه شور انگیزد

در پای تو ابرها درر میریزد

از عشق تو برقی بزمین افتاده است

این دود بآسمان از آن میخیزد

87

In your love, the sea boils with passion,
And clouds strew pearls at your feet.
In your love, a bolt of lighting has struck the earth,
And this smoke that rises to the sky is the result of that.

۸۸

از عشق دلا نه بر زیان خواهی شد

بیجان ز کجا شوی که جان خواهی شد

اول بزمین از آسمان آمده ای

آخر ز زمین بر آسمان خواهی شد

88

You will not be a loser in love, my dear.
How can you be dead while you will be the life itself?
In the beginning you descended from the sky to the earth.
In the end, you will ascend from the earth to the sky.

۸۹

از لشگر صبرم علمی بیش نماند
وز هر چه مرا بود غمی بیش نماند
وین طرفه تر است کز سر عشق هنوز
دم میدمد و مرا دمی بیش نماند

89

Of my patience's army, except a banner nothing remained.
Of all the things I had, except sorrow nothing remained.
And what is more surprizing is that I am still breathing
Because of love, though except a breath nothing remained.

۹۰

اکنون که رخت جان جهانی بربود
در خانه نشستنت کجا دارد سود
آنروز که مه شدی نمیدانستی
کانگشت نمای عالمی خواهی بود

90

Now that your face stole the heart of a world,
What is the use of your staying at home?
When you became a moon, did you not know
That you will be conspicuous throughout the world?

۹۱

امروز ز ما یار جنون میخواهد
ما مجنونیم و او فزون میخواهد
گر نیست چنین پرده چرا میدرد
رسوا شده از پرده برون میخواهد

91

Today the Beloved wants frenzy from us.
We are already frenzied, but he wants more.
If it is not so, why does he tear our veil?
He wants us to come infamous to the open.

۹۲

امشب شب آن نیست که از خانه روند
از یار یگانه سوی بیگانه روند
امشب شب آنست که یاران عزیز
در آتش اشتیاق مستانه روند

92

This is not the night to go out of the house,
To leave the only beloved and go to strangers.
Tonight is the night when dear friends
Must walk drunken into the fire of love.

۹۳

ایدل اثر صبح گه شام که دید
یک عاشق صادق نکو نام که دید
فریاد همی زنی که من سوخته ام
فریاد مکن سوخته خام که دید

93

O heart, who has seen the morning sign in the evening?
Who has seen a true lover that had a good reputation?
You scream that you have burned?
Don't scream! Who has seen a burned one who was raw?

۹۴

ای سرو روان باد خزانت مرساد
ای چشم جهان چشم بدانت مرساد
ای آنکه تو جان آسمانی و زمین
جز رحمت و جز راحت جانت مرساد

94

O gliding cypress, may the autumn wind never touch you!
O sight of the world, may the evil eye never harm you!
O you who are the soul of heaven and earth,
May that nothing but peace and blessing reach you!

۹۵

با هر که دمی عشق تو آمیخته شد
گویی که بلا بر سر او ریخته شد
منصور ز سر عشق میداد نشان
حلقش بطناب غیرت آویخته شد

95

Whoever mixed with your love for a moment,
It was as if disaster poured over his head.
When Mansur revealed a sign of the secret of love,
His throat was hanged with the rope of *ghayrat*.

۹۶

بی عشق نشاط و عشرت افزون نشود
بی عشق وجود خوب و موزون نشود
صد قطره ز ابر اگر بدریا بارد
بی جنبش عشق در مکنون نشود

96

Joy and pleasure do not flourish without love.
Being does not become beautiful and elegant without love.
Many drops may fall into the sea from the cloud,
Yet none shall become a pearl without the motion of love.

۹۷

تا بنده ز خود فانی مطلق نشود
توحید بنزد او محقق نشود
توحید حلول نیست نابودن تست
ورنه بگزاف باطلی حق نشود

97

Unless a man become totally non-existent,
He will not actually realize *towhid*(the unity of God).
Towhid is not transmigration, but your non-existence.
No falsehood can become a truth by boasting.

۹۸

جودت همه آن کند که دریا نکند
ایندم کرمت وعده بفردا نکند
حاجت نبود از تو تقاضا کردن
کز شمس کسی نور تقاضا نکند

98

Your generosity does what the ocean does not.
Your kindness does not put off this moment till tomorrow.
There is no need for asking of you.
No one asks light of the sun.

۹۹

چون دیده برفت توتیای تو چه سود
چون دل همه گشت خون وفای تو چه سود
چون جان و جگر سوخت تمام از غم تو
آنگه سخنان جانفزای تو چه سود

99

When the eye-sight is gone, what good is your vitriol?
When the heart is bled, what good is your fidelity?
When the whole body is consumed in your sorrow,
What good are your reviving words?

۱۰۰

شور عجبی در سر ما میگردد
دل مرغ شده است و در هوا میگردد
هر ذره ما جدا جدا میگردد
دلدار مگر در همه جا میگردد

100

A marvellous fervor has filled my head.
My heart has become a bird and is soaring in the air.
Each particle of mine is moving separately.
Perhaps the beloved is walking everywhere?

۱۰۱

عشاق بیکدم دو جهان در بازند
صد ساله بقا بیکزمان در بازند
بر بوی دمی هزار منزل بروند
وز بهر دلی هزار جان در بازند

101

Lovers may lose both worlds in one instant.
They may lose a hundred-years' life all at once.
They pass a thousand stations for the scent of one breath.
They lose a thousand lives for the sake of one heart.

۱۰۲

کس واقف آن حضرت شاهانه نشد
تا بیدل و بیعقل سوی خانه نشد
دیوانه کسی بود که آنروی تو دید
وانگه ز تو دور ماند و دیوانه نشد

102

No one became aware of your majestic presence
Until he came home a lover and lost his reason.
That person is really mad who saw your face,
Separated from it, and did not go mad.

۱۰۳

کشتی چو بدریای روان میگذرد
می پندارد که نیستان میگذرد
ما میگذریم زین جهان در همه حال
می پنداریم کاین جهان میگذرد

103

When a ship is moving in a calm sea,
It seems as if the bed of reeds is passing by.
We pass through this world anyway,
And think that this world is passing by.

۱۰۴

کی گفت که آن زنده جاوید بمرد
کی گفت که آفتاب امید بمرد
آن دشمن خورشید در آمد بر بام
دو دیده ببست و گفت خورشید بمرد

104

Who said that the eternally alive is dead?
Who said that the sun of hope is dead?
That enemy of the sun came to the roof,
Closed his eyes and said, *The sun is dead.*

۱۰۵

مردان رهت که سر معنی دانند
از دیده کوته نظران پنهانند
این طرفه تر آنکه هر که حق را بشناخت
مومن شد و خلق کافرش میخوانند

105

Men of the Path, who know the secret of meaning,
Are hidden from the eyes of the short-sighted.
Not only that, but anyone who came to know the truth
Became a believer, and people called him a disbeliever.

۱۰۶

معشوق چو آفتاب تابان گردد
عاشق بمثال ذره گردان گردد
چون باد بهار عشق جنبان گردد
هر شاخ که خشک نیست رقصان گردد

106

When the Beloved begins to shine like the sun,
The lover begins to dance like a particle.
When the spring wind of love begins to blow,
Any branch which is not dead begins to dance.

۱۰۷

من بنده آن قوم که خود را دانند
هر دم دل خود را ز غلط برهانند
از ذات و صفات خویش خالی گردند
وز لوح وجود خود اناالحق خوانند

107

I am humbled before those who know themselves
And free their hearts from falsehood every moment.
They empty themselves of all attributes and essence
And read *I am the Truth* on the board of their being.

۱۰۸

من بیخبرم خدای خود میداند
کاندر دل من مرا چه میخنداند
باری دل من شاخ گلی را ماند
کش باد صبا بلطف میافشاند

108

I am unconscious. God himself knows
What makes me laugh in my heart.
My heart is like a blossoming branch,
Which is lovingly shaken by the zephyr.

۱۰۹

میجوشد دل که تا بجوش تو رسد
بیهوش شده است تا بهوش تو رسد
مینوشد زهر تا بنوش تو رسد
چون حلقه شده است تا بگوش تو رسد

109

My heart is boiling in order to reach to your ebulience.
To reach your consciousness, it has lost consciousness.
It is drinking poison in order to reach to your honey.
It has become like a ring so that it can reach to your ear.

۱۱۰

هستی اثری ز نرگس مست تو بود

آب رخ نیستی هم از هست تو بود

گفتم که مگر دست کسی در تو رسد

چون به دیدم که خود همه دست تو بود

110

Existence was an impression of your intoxicating eyes.
Nonexistence was honored by your existence.
I used to wonder if anyone's hand could reach you.
When I looked well, I saw your hand was all there was.

۱۱۱

هشدار که فضل حق بناگاه آید

ناگاه آید بر دل آگاه آید

خرگاه وجود خود ز خود خالی کن

چون خالی شد شاه بخرگاه آید

111

Beware, the grace of God comes suddenly.
It comes suddenly to an alert heart.
Empty the tent of your being of yourself.
When it is empty, the king will enter the tent.

۱۱۲

یک چند میان خلق کردیم درنگ

زایشان بوفا نه بوی دیدیم نه رنگ

آن به که نهان شویم از دیده خلق

چون آب در آهن و چو آتش در سنگ

112

I spent sometime among the people.
I did not see any sign of fidelity from them.
It is better that I hide from the eyes of the people,
Like water in iron and like fire in stone.

۱۱۳

عشقی بکمال و دلربائی بجمال
دل پر سخن و زبان ز گفتن شده لال
زین نادره تر کجا بود هر گز حال
من تشنه و پیش من روان آب زلال

113

A perfect love and a beautiful sweetheart,
The heart full of words, but the tongue mute:
Where can there be a rarer situation than this
That I be thirsty while limpid water flows in front of me?

۱۱۴

از خویش بجستن آرزو میکندم
آزاد نشستن آرزو میکندم
در بند مقامات همی بودم من
وان بند گسستن آرزو میکندم

115

I desire to jump out of myself.
I desire to be liberated.
I have been chained to the stations of the Path.
I desire to be released from the chain.

۱۱۶

بی دف بر ما میا که ما در سوریم
بر خیز و دهل بزن که ما منصوریم
مستیم نه مست باده انگوریم
از هر چه خیال کرده ای مر دوریم

116

Do not come to us without a tabourine, for we have a party.
Rise and beat the drum, for we are Mansur.
We are drunk, but not drunk by grape-juice.
We are far from anything you have imagined.

١١٧

تا خواسته ام از تو ترا خواسته ام
از عشق تو خوان عشق آراسته ام
خوابی دیدم دوش و فراموشم شد
این میدانم که مست بر خاسته ام

117

As long as I have wanted, all I wanted of you was you.
I have decorated the table of love with your love.
I had a dream last night, but I forgot.
All I know is that I have woken up drunk.

١١٨

اندر ره حق چو چست و چالاک شوی
نور فلکی باز بر افلاک شوی
عرش است نشیمن تو شرمت ناید
چون سایه مقیم خطه خاک شوی

118

Should you become agile on the road of Truth,
You are the light of heavens and will return to heavens.
Your seat is the empyrean. Are you not ashamed
You have resided, like shadow, in the realm of dust?

١١٩

تا در طلب گوهر کانی کانی
تا در هوس لقمه نانی نانی
این نکته و رمز اگر بدانی دانی
هر چیز که در جستن آنی آنی

119

If you are in search of a mine of gems, you are a mine.
If you are desiring a loaf of bread, you are bread.
If you knew this subtle point and secret,
You would realize you are that which you are searching.

۱۲۰

رفتم بطبیب گفتم از بینائی

افتاده عشق را چه میفرمائی

ترک صفت و محو وجودم فرمود

یعنی که ز هر چه هست بیرون آئی

120

I went to a doctor and asked him:
"What do you say about the one fallen in love?"
He said, "Give up your identity and erase your existence.
"That is to say, emerge from all that exists!"

سعدی شیرازی

(۶۹۰-۶۰۶ هجری قمری)

۱

هر ساعتم اندرون جوشد خون را

واگاهی نیست مردم بیرون را

الا مگر آنکه روی لیلی دیدست

داند که چه درد میکشد مجنون را

Sa'di Shirâzi
(1210-1291 C.E.)

1

Every hour blood is boiling in my inside.
Unaware of this are the people of outside.
Only the one who has seen the face of Layli
Knows what pain is killing Majnun.

٢

عشاق بدرگهت اسیرند بیا
بدخوئی تو بر تو نگیرند بیا
هر جور و جفا که کرده ای معذوری
زان پیش که عذرت نپذیرند بیا

2

Lovers are captives at your door, come!
They will not hold your temper against you, come!
You are excused of any cruelty you have done.
Before they do not excuse you anymore, come!

٣

ای چشم تو مست خواب و سرمست شراب
صاحبنظران تشنه و وصل تو سراب
مانند تو آدمی در آباد و خراب
باشد که در آئینه توان دید و در آب

3

O you whose eyes are drunk with sleep and wine,
People of perception are thirsty and your union is a mirage.
The like of you, whether in habitation or in ruins,
Can be seen only in the mirror or in the water.

۴

چون دل ز هوای دوست نتوان پرداخت
درمانش تحملست و سر پیش انداخت
یا ترک گل لعل همی باید گفت
یا با الم خار همی باید ساخت

4

Since the heart cannot avoid desiring the beloved,
The remedy is in tolerance and submission.
One must either forget about the rose
Or put up with the pain of thorns.

۵

روزی گفتی شبی کنم دلشادت
وز بند غمان خود کنم آزادت
دیدی که از آنروز چه شبها بگذشت
وز گفته خود هیچ نیامد یادت

5

One day you told me, "I will make you happy one night
"And free you from the chain of my sorrows."
Do you know how many nights passed since that day
While you did not remember anything of what you had said?

۶

صد بار بگفتم بغلامان درت
تا آینه دیگر نگذارند برت
ترسم که ببینی رخ همچون قمرت
کس باز نیاید دگر اندر نظرت

6

A hundred times I told your servants that
They should not put any mirror in front of you.
I fear that you may look at your moon-like face
And let no one else enter your sight anymore.

۷

آن یار که عهد دوستداری بشکست
میرفت و منش گرفته دامان در دست
میگفت دگر باره بخوابم بینی
پنداشت که بعد از آن مرا خوابی هست

7

My friend who broke the promise of friendship,
Was leaving me and, while I held his skirt, was saying:
"From now on you will see me only in your sleep."
He thought I was going to have any sleep after that.

٨

آن کیست که دل نهاد و فارغ بنشست

پنداشت که مهلتی و تاخیری هست

گو میخ مزن که خیمه می باید کند

گو رخت منه که بار می باید بست

8

Who did ever rest his heart, sat comfortably, and
Thought he had time to relax and chance for leisure?
Do not nail down the tent, for soon you must dismantle it.
Do not unpack, for soon you must pack up again.

٩

شبها گذرد که دیده نتوانم بست

مردم همه از خواب و من از فکر تو مست

باشد که بدست خویش خونم ریزی

تا جان بدهم دامن مقصود بدست

9

Many nights pass when I cannot close my eyes,
While people are drunk with sleep and I with your thought.
I wish you shed my blood with your own hand,
So that I would surrender my soul, having attained my goal.

١٠

هشیار سری بود ز سودای تو مست

خوش آنکه ز روی تو دلش رفت ز دست

بیتو همه هیچ نیست در ملک وجود

ور هیچ نباشد چو تو هستی همه هست

10

That head is sober which is drunk with your love.
That man is blessed who has lost his heart for your face.
Without you nothing exists in the realm of being;
And if nothing exists, when you exist everything does.

۱۱

آنکس که خطای خویش بیند که رواست
تقریر مکن صواب نزدش که خطاست
آن روی نمایدش که در طینت اوست
آئینهٔ کج جمال ننماید راست

11

He who sees his wrongs as rights,
It is a mistake to tell him what is right.
He shows that which is in his nature.
A distorted mirror does not show the face right.

۱۲

وه وه که قیامتست این قامت راست
با سرو نباشد این لطافت که تراست
شاید که تو دیگر بزیارت نروی
تا مرده نگوید که قیامت بر خاست

12

My! My! What a marvellous thing your upright stature is!
Not even the cypress has such an elegance as you do!
It is better that you should not visit a tomb,
Lest the dead may think the Resurrection has started!

۱۳

سرو از قدت اندازه بالا برده است
بحر دهنت لؤلؤ لالا برده است
هر جا که بنفشه ای ببینم گویم
موئی ز سرت باد بصحرا برده است

13

The measure of height the cypress from you has taken.
The glittering pearls the sea from your mouth has taken.
Anywhere I see a violet, I say:
"A strand of your hair the wind to the plains has taken."

۱۴

امشب که حضور یار جان افروز است
بختم بخلاف دشمنان پیروز است
گو شمع بمیر و مه فرو شو که مرا
آنشب که تو در کنار باشی روز است

14

Tonight that my soul-brightening beloved is present,
Contrary to my enemies' wish, my fortune is triumphant.
Let the candle die and the moon go down,
For the night is day when you are at my side.

۱۵

آنشب که تو در کنار مائی روز است
وآنروز که با تو میرود نوروز است
دی رفت و بانتظار فردا منشین
در یاب که حاصل حیات امروز است

15

The night is day when you are at my side.
The day that passes with you is *Nowruz*.
Yesterday is gone. Do not wait for tomorrow.
Capture the moment! For the sum of life is today.

۱۶

خیزم بروم چو صبر نامحتملست
جان در قدمش کنم که آرام دلست
واقرار کنم برابر دشمن و دوست
کانکس که مرا بکشت از من بحلست

16

I must rise and go, for patience is no longer possible.
I must lay my life at his feet, for he is the peace of my heart.
And I must confess before my friends and enemies
That the one who killed me is pardoned by me.

١٧

آن سست وفا که یار دل سخت منست

شمع دگران و آتش رخت منست

ای با همه کس بصلح و با ما بخلاف

جرم از تو نباشد گنه از بخت منست

17

That soft-in-loyalty who is my hard-hearted beloved,
Is the candle of others and fire on my clothes.
O you who are at peace with all but at war with me,
You are not guilty, my luck is.

١٨

از بسکه بیازرد دل دشمن و دوست

گوئی بگناه مسخ کردندش پوست

وقتی غم او بر همه دلها بودی

اکنون همه غمهای جهان بر دل اوست

18

So much did he hurt the hearts of friends and foes
His skin looked as if metamorphosed by his sins.
There was a time when his sorrow was in every heart.
Today all the sorrows of the world are in his heart.

١٩

ای در دل من رفته چو خون در رگ و پوست

هر چه آن بسر آیدم ز دست تو نکوست

ای مرغ سحر تو صبح بر خاسته ای

ما خود همه شب نخفته ایم از غم دوست

19

O you who are in my heart like blood in my veins and skin,
Whatever comes to me from your hand is good.
O morning-bird, you have woken only in the morning.
I have not slept all night, longing for my beloved.

۲۰

گر دل بکسی دهند باری بتو دوست

کت خوی خوش و بوی خوش و روی نکوست

از هر که وجود صبر بتوانم کرد

الا ز وجودت که وجودم همه اوست

20

If I am to give my heart to anyone, better to you, my friend,
Who have a pleasant temper and a beautiful face.
I can do without anyone's being in the world,
Except yours, for that is my whole existence.

۲۱

گر زخم خورم ز دست چون مرهم دوست

یا مغز بر آیدم چو بادام از پوست

غیرت نگذاردم که نالم بکسی

تا خلق ندانند که منظور من اوست

21

If the curing hand of my friend wounds me,
Or if my soul comes out like an almond from its shell,
Jealousy will not allow me to complain to anyone,
So that people should not know he is my desired one.

۲۲

گر خود ز عبادت استخوانی در پوست

زشتست گر اعتقاد بندی که نکوست

گر بر سر پیمان برود طالب دوست

حقا که هنوز منت دوست بروست

22

If worshipping has made you bones and skin,
It is wrong for you to believe you have done some good.
If the aspirer of the Friend dies in his quest,
Truly he should still be much obliged to the Friend.

۲۳

گویند رها کنش که یاری بدخوست
خوبیش نیارزد بدرشتی که دروست
بالله بگذارید میان من و دوست
نیک و بد و رنج و راحت از دوست نکوست

23

They tell me, "Let him go! He is a bad-tempered friend.
"His beauty is not worth his harshness."
For God's sake, do not interfere between me and my friend.
Good or bad, trouble or comfort, I accept from my friend.

۲۴

تا یکسر موئی از تو هستی باقیست
اندیشه کار بت پرستی باقیست
گفتی بت پندار شکستم رستم
آن بت که ز پندار پرستی باقیست

24

Even if an iota of your [ego's] existence remains,
The thought of idol-worshipping does still exist.
You said you broke the idol of illusion and became free.
Yet, the idol you worship in your imagination is still there.

۲۵

شب نیست که چشمم آرزومند تو نیست
وین جان بلب رسیده در بند تو نیست
گر تو دگری بجای من بگزینی
من عهد تو نشکنم که مانند تو نیست

25

Not a single night do my eyes rest from looking for you,
Nor does my soul, which has reached to my lips.
If you choose someone else in my place,
I will not break with you, for no one is like you.

۲۶

بالای قضای رفته فرمانی نیست
چون درد اجل گرفت درمانی نیست
امروز که عهد تست نیکوئی کن
کاین ده همه وقت از آن دهقانی نیست

26

There is no command over what is predestined.
There is no remedy for the pain of death.
Today, while you have a chance, be good!
For this village does not always belong to a villager.

۲۷

ماهی امید عمرم از شست برفت
بیفایده عمرم چو شب مست برفت
عمری که از و دمی بجانی ارزد
افسوس که رایگانم از دست برفت

27

The fish of my life's hope slipped out of my hand.
My life passed in vain, like the night of a drunkard.
My life, each moment of which was worth a fortune,
Free of charge, alas, went out of my hand.

۲۸

دادار که بر ما در قسمت بگشاد
بنیاد جهان چنانکه بایست نهاد
آنرا که نداد از سببی خالی نیست
دانست که سر بخر نمیباید داد

28

God who opened the door of *qesmat* for us,
Laid the foundation of the world as it had to be.
Whom he did not give was not without any reason.
He knew that a donkey should not have a mind.

۲۹

نه هر که زمانه کار او در بندد
فریاد و جزع بر آسمان پیوندد
بسیار کسا که اندرونش چون رعد
مینالد و چون برق لبش میخندد

29

Not everyone whose affairs do not go right
Raises his cries and lamentations to the sky.
There are many whose hearts roar like thunder,
Yet their lips smile like lightning.

۳۰

تو هر چه بپوشی بتو زیبا گردد
گر خام بود اطلس و دیبا گردد
مندیش که هر که یکنظر روی تو دید
دیگر همه عمر از تو شکیبا گردد

30

Whatever you wear looks beautiful on you.
Coarse material becomes satin and silk on you.
Think not that anyone who glanced at your face once
Could be patient without you for the rest of his life.

۳۱

ای باد چو عزم آن زمین خواهی کرد
رخ در رخ یار نازنین خواهی کرد
از ماش بسی دعا و خدمت برسان
گو یاد ز دوستان چنین خواهی کرد؟

31

O wind, since you will be visiting that land,
And will come face to face with that elegant love,
Take plenty of prayers and regards from us and say:
Is this how you remember your lovers?

۳۲

در چشم من آمد آن سهی سرو بلند
بربود دلم ز دست و در پای افکند
این دیده شوخ میبرد دل بکمند
خواهی که بکس دل ندهی دیده ببند

32

That tall upright cypress appeared before my eyes,
Stole my heart and threw it at his feet.
These bold eyes take the heart into a loop.
Shut your eyes if you wish not to give your heart to anyone!

۳۳

در خرقهٔ توبه آمدم روزی چند
چشمم بدهان واعظ و گوش به پند
ناگاه بدیدم آن سهی سرو بلند
وز یاد برفتم سخن دانشمند

33

For a while I wore the cloak of repentance,
Watched the preacher's mouth and listened to his advice.
Suddenly I saw that tall upright cypress
And forgot the words of the man of learning.

۳۴

گویند مرو در پی آن سرو بلند
انگشت نمای خلق بودن تا چند
بی فایده پندم مده ای دانشمند
من چون نروم که میبرندم بکمند

34

They tell me, "Do not go after that tall cypress!
"How long should the people point their fingers at you?"
Do not waste your advice on me, O learned ones!
How can I not go while I am being pulled by a lasso?

۳۵

آنانکه پریروی و شکر گفتارند
حیفست که روی خوب پنهان دارند
فی الجمله نقاب نیز بیفایده نیست
تا زشت بپوشند و نکو بگذارند

35

Those who have cheeks like fairies and words like sugar,
It is a pity they should hide their beautiful faces!
Nevertheless, a veil is not without any benefit either.
It is for the ugly to wear and for the beautiful to remove.

۳۶

آن گل که هنوز نو بدست آمده بود
نشکفته تمام باد قهرش بربود
بیچاره بسی امید بر خاطر داشت
امید دراز و عمر کوتاه چه سود

36

The rose that had just started to grow,
The hostile wind snatched before it could fully bloom.
Poor thing had many hopes in the heart.
What good is it to have a long desire and a short life?

۳۷

افسوس بر آن دل که سماعش نربود
سنگست و حدیث عشق با سنگ چه سود
بیگانه عشق را حرام است سماع
زیرا که نیاید بجز از سوخته دود

37

The heart not captured by music is to be regretted.
It is a rock. What good is the story of love to a rock?
Music is forbidden to the strangers of love.
Smoke rises only from that which burns.

۳۸

جائیکه درخت عشق پر بار بود
در در نظر و گهر در انبار بود
آنجا همه کس یار وفادار بود
یار آن یار است که در بلا یار بود

38

Where the tree of love is full of fruit,
And pearls are in sight and jewels in store,
There everyone is a loyal friend.
He is a friend who is friend in calamity.

۳۹

چون صورت خویشتن در آئینه بدید
وان کام و دهان و لب و دندان لبید
میگفت چنانکه می توانست شنید
بس جان بلب آمد که بدین لب نرسید

39

When she looked at her face in the mirror,
And at her lips, mouth, and white teeth,
She spoke in an audible voice:
Many a soul came to lips before reaching to these lips.

۴۰

من چاکر آنم که دلی برباید
یا دل بکسی دهد که جان آساید
آنکس که نه عاشق و نه معشوق کسیست
در ملک خدای اگر نباشد شاید

40

I am humbled before the one who steals someone's heart
Or gives his heart to someone who comforts the soul.
The kingdom of God would be better off without
The one who is neither a lover nor a beloved.

۴۱

امشب نه بیاض روز بر می آید
نه ناله مرغان سحر می آید
بیدار همه شب و نظر بر سر کو
تا صبح کی از سنگ بدر می آید

41

Tonight the light of the day is not coming,
Nor is the cry of the morning-bird.
All night, wakeful and watching the street,
I am wondering when the morning is coming.

۴۲

از هر چه کنی مرحم ریش اولیتر
دلداری خلق هر چه بیش اولیتر
ایدوست بدست دشمنانم مسپار
گر میکشیم بدست خویش , اولیتر

42

Curing someone's wound than anything else is better.
In consoling people, the more is better.
O friend, leave me not in the hands of my enemies.
If you are to kill me, by your own hand it is better.

۴۳

نامردم اگر زنم سر از مهر تو باز
خواهی بکشم بهجر و خواهی بنواز
ور بگریزم ز دستت ای مایهٔ ناز
هر جا که روم پیش تو می آیم باز

43

I am not a man if I turn away from your love,
Whether you be kind to me or kill me by separation.
And if I run away from you, O gracious one,
I will return to you, no matter where I go.

۴۴

ای ماه شب افروز شبستان افروز

خرم تن آنکه با تو باشد شب و روز

تو خود بکمال خلقت آراسته ای

پیرایه مکن عرق مزن عود مسوز

44

O night-illumining and harem-brightening moon,
Happy is the one who is with you day and night.
You are yourself adorned with the perfection of creation.
You need not dress up, use perfume, or burn incense.

۴۵

یا روی بکنج خلوت آور شب و روز

یا آتش عشق بر کن و خانه بسوز

مستوری و عاشقی بهم ناید راست

گر پرده نخواهی که درد دیده بدوز

45

Either stay in seclusion day and night
Or kindle the fire of love and let your house burn.
Being in love and prudence do not go together.
If you do not wish the veil to be torn, close your eyes.

۴۶

روئی که نخواستم به بیند همه کس

الا شب و روز پیش من باشد و بس

پیوست بدیگران و از من ببرید

یا رب تو بفریاد من مسکین رس

46

He whose face I did not want everyone to see,
But be in front of me day and night,
Joined others and cut off from me.
O Lord, come to the aid of this wretched one!

۴۷

گر بیخبران و عیبگویان از پس

منسوب کنندم بهوا و بهوس

آخر نه گناهیست که من کردم و بس

منظور ملیح دوست دارد همه کس

47

If the ignorant and faultfinders behind me
Accuse me of passion and desire,
After all, this is not a sin only I have committed.
Everyone likes a charming beautiful person.

۴۸

منعم که بعیش میرود روز و شبش

نالیدن درویش نداند سببش

بس آب که میرود بجیحون و فرات

در بادیه تشنگان بجان در طلبش

48

The rich whose days and nights pass in pleasure
Do not know the cause of the laments of the poor.
Plenty of water flows in the Oxus and Euphrates,
While the thirsty in the desert search for it desperately.

۴۹

یا همچو همای بر من افکن پر خویش

تا بندگیت کنم بجان و سر خویش

گر لایق خدمتم ندانی بر خویش

تا من سر خویش گیرم و کشور خویش

49

Either cast your shade on me, like a *homa*,
So that I serve you with all my heart and soul;
Or if you do not think I am worthy of service to you,
Let me go my way and return to my country.

۵۰

ای بی تو فراخای جهان ما را تنگ

ما را بتو فخر ست و ترا از ما ننگ

ما با تو بصلحیم و ترا با ما جنگ

آخر تو نگوئی که دلست این یا سنگ

50

Without you the expanse of the world is a prison for me.

I am proud of you, you are ashamed of me.

I am at peace with you, you are at war with me.

Do you never wonder if your heart is a heart or a rock?

۵۱

تا دل ز مراعات جهان برکندم

صد نعمت او بمنتهی بپسندم

هر چند که نو آمده ام بر سر ذوق

بر کهنه جهان چون گل نو میخندم

51

Since I released my heart from the cares of the world,

I began to appreciate His many blessings with all my heart.

Although I am fresh in my enthusiasm,

I am smiling, like a fresh rose, at the old world.

۵۲

هر سرو قدی که بگذرد در نظرم

در هیئت او خیره بماند بصرم

چون چشم ندارم که جوان گردم باز

آخر کم از آنکه در جوانان نگرم

52

Whenever a cypress-statured one passes into my sight,

My eyes remain gazing at his figure.

Since I do not hope to become young again,

Should I not, at least, look at the young?

۵۳

خیزم که نماند بیش از این تدبیرم

خصم ار همه شمشیر زند یا تیرم

گر دست دهد که آستینش گیرم

ورنه بروم بر آستانش میرم

53

I cannot help it any longer. I must rise and go,
Even if my enemy strike me with a sword or an arrow.
I will get hold of my friend's sleeve if possible.
If not, I will go and die at his threshold.

۵۴

آن دوست که دیدنش بیاراید چشم

بیدیدنش از دیده نیاساید چشم

ما را ز برای دیدنش باید چشم

ور دوست نبیند بچه کار آید چشم

54

My eyes, adorned by seeing the friend,
Do not rest from looking when they do not see him.
I need my eyes for the sake of seeing him.
If I am not to see him, what good are my eyes for?

۵۵

هر گه که نظر بر گل رویت فکنم

خواهم که چو نرگس مژه بر هم نزنم

ور بی تو میان ارغوان و سمنم

بنشینم و چون بنفشه سر بر نکنم

55

Whenever I look at the rose of your face;
I want, like the narcissus, not to blink.
And if I am among Judas-trees and jasmines without you,
I want to sit, like the violet, and not raise my head.

۵۶

آرام دل خویش نجویم چه کنم
واندر طلبش بسر نپویم چه کنم
گویند مرو که خون خود میریزی
مادام که در کمند اویم چه کنم

56

If I do not seek the peace of my heart, what shall I do?
If I do not search him anxiously, what shall I do?
They tell me: *Don't go! You are shedding your own blood.*
As long as I am his captive, what shall I do?

۵۷

گفتم که دگر چشم بدلبر نکنم
صوفی شوم و گوش بمنکر نکنم
دیدم که خلاف طبع موزون من است
توبت کردم که توبه دیگر نکنم

57

I told myself, "I shall no longer gaze at any heart-ravisher.
"I shall become a Sufi and avoid the forbidden."
Then I saw it was against my balanced nature.
I repented that I should not repent again.

۵۸

من بی تو سکون نگیرم و خو نکنم
بی عارض گلبوی تو گل بو نکنم
گویند فراموش کنش تا برود
الحمد فراموش کنم و او نکنم

58

Without you I will not settle nor will I calm down.
Without your rose-scented face, I will not smell a rose.
They say, "Forget about him! Let him go!"
I may forget my daily prayers, but not him.

۵۹

خیزم قد و بالای چو حورش بینم
وآن طلعت آفتاب نورش بینم
گر ره ندهندم که بنزدیک شوم
آخر نزنندم که ز دورش بینم

59

I will go and see her houri-like stature,
And see her face, which is brilliant like the sun.
If they do not allow me to go near her,
At least, they will not beat me for looking at her from far.

۶۰

می آئی و لطف و کرمت می بینم
آسایش جان در قدمت می بینم
و آنوقت که غایبی همت می بینم
هر جا که نگه میکنمت می بینم

60

When you are present, I see your kindness and generosity.
I see the comfort of my soul at your feet.
When you are absent, I can still see you.
Wherever I look, I see you.

۶۱

تنها ز همه خلق و نهان می گریم
چشم از غم دل بر آسمان می گریم
طفل از پی مرغ رفته چون گریه کند
بر عمر گذشته همچنان می گریم

61

Alone, away from all the people, I am crying.
Eyes in the sky, with a doleful heart, I am crying.
How does a child cry after his bird has flown away?
In the same manner, for my lost life I am crying.

۶۲

ما حاصل عمری بدمی بفروشیم

صد خرمن شادی بغمی بفروشیم

در یکدم اگر هزار جان دست دهد

در حال بخاک قدمی بفروشیم

62

I could sell the sum of a lifetime for a single moment
And a hundred harvests of joy for a single sorrow of love.
If a thousand lives could be obtained with each breath,
I would sell them all for the dust under a [beloved's] foot.

۶۳

یاران بسماع دف و نی جامه دران

ما دیده بجائی متحیر نگران

عشق آن منست و لهو از آن دگران

من چشم بر این کنم شما گوش بر آن

63

My eyes gaze, amazed and anxious, while my friends
Tear their shirts to the music of the reed and tambourine.
Love belongs to me, and amusement to the others.
I have my eyes on love, and they their ears to music.

۶۳

من خاک درش بدیده خواهم رفتن

ایخصم بگوی هر چه خواهی گفتن

چون پای مگس که در عسل سخت شود

چندانکه برانی نتواند رفتن

64

I would sweep the dust of his door with my eyelashes.
O enemy, say whatever you wish!
When a fly has its legs stuck in honey,
It cannot move, no matter how you chase it away.

۶۵

مه را ز فلک بطرف بام آوردن

وز روم کلیسیا بشام آوردن

در وقت سحر نماز شام آوردن

بتوان نتوان ترا بدام آوردن

65

To pull the moon from the sky down to the roof,
To bring a church from Rome to Damascus,
And to perform the evening prayers in the morning,
Are all possible, but to allure you is not.

۶۶

در دیده بجای سرمه سوزن دیدن

برق آمد و آتش زده خرمن دیدن

در قید فرنگ غل بگردن دیدن

به زانکه بجای دوست دشمن دیدن

66

To see a needle in the eye in place of collyrium,
To see a lightning descend and strike fire to a harvest,
And to see a yoke around one's neck in a foreign country,
Are all better than seeing the enemy in place of the friend.

۶۷

ایدوست گرفته بر سر ما دشمن

یا دوست گزین بدوستی یا دشمن

نا دیدن دوست گرچه مشکل دردیست

آسانتر از آنکه بینمش با دشمن

67

O you who have taken the enemy as your firend,
Choose either the friend or the enemy for your friendship.
Though it is painful not to see the friend,
It is easier than seeing him with the enemy.

۶۸

آن لطف که در شمایل اوست ببین
و آن خنده همچو پسته در پوست ببین
نی نی تو بحسن روی او ره نبری
در چشم من آی صورت دوست ببین

68

Behold the elegance of her features!
Behold her laughter, like a pistachio in its shell.
No, no. You will never realize the beauty of her face.
Come into my eyes and behold the face of my beloved!

۶۹

چون جاه و جلال و حسن و رنگ آمد و بو
آخر دل آدمی نه سنگست و نه رو
آنکس که نه راست طبع باشد نه نکو
نه عاشق کس بود نه کس عاشق او

69

When glory and glamor, beauty, scent and color appear,
The human heart, after all, is not made of stone or tin.
He who has neither good looks nor right nature
Is neither someone's lover nor someone's beloved.

۷۰

یک روز باتفاق صحرا من و تو
از شهر برون شویم تنها من و تو
دانی که من و تو کی بهم خوش باشیم
آنوقت که کس نباشد الا من و تو

70

One day we should go out of town, you and I.
And head toward the plains, you and I.
Do you know when you and I can be happy together?
When there is no one around, except you and I.

۷۱

نه سرو توان گفت و نه خورشید و نه ماه
آه از تو که در وصف نمی آئی آه
هر کس برهی میرود اندر طلبت
گر ره بتو بودی نبدی اینهمه راه

71

You cannot be described as a cypress, the sun, or the moon.
Alas, nothing can describe you, alas!
Each person takes a road in search of you. Had there been
Any way to you, there would not have been so many roads.

۷۲

ای یار کجائی که در آغوش نه ای
و امشب بر ما نشسته چون دوش نه ای
ای سرو روان و راحت نفس روان
هر چند که غایبی فراموش نه ای

72

Where are you, my love, away from my bosom?
You are not sitting by me tonight, like last night.
O gliding cypress and peace of my soul,
Absent though you are, you are never forgotten.

۷۳

گیرم که بفتوای خردمندی و رای
از دائره عقل برون ننهم پای
با میل که طبع میکند چتوان کرد
عیبست که در من آفریدست خدای

73

Suppose, in accordance with wisdom and discretion,
I do not step out of the circle of reason.
What shall I do then with the desire in my nature?
This is a fault that God has created in me.

۷۴

ایکاش که مردم آن صنم دیدندی

یا گفتن دلستانش بشنیدندی

تا بیدل و بیقرار گردیدندی

بر گریهٔ عاشقان نخندیدندی

74

I wish people had seen that darling,
Or had heard her speech so charming,
Then they would have become restless lovers,
And would not have laughed at the tears of the lovers.

۷۵

گر سنگ همه لعل بدخشان بودی

پس قیمت سنگ و لعل یکسان بودی

گر در همه چاهی آب حیوان بودی

در یافتنش بر همه آسان بودی

75

If all stones were brilliant rubies,
The price of a ruby would be equal to a stone.
If the water of life had existed in every well,
Finding it would have been easy for everyone.

۷۶

فردا که بنامهٔ سیه در نگری

بس دست تحسر که بدندان ببری

بفروخته دین بدنیی از بیخبری

یوسف که به ده درم فروشی چه خری؟

76

Tomorrow, when you look at your black record of deeds,
Many times you will bite your hand in regret.
Having sold your religion for the world through ignorance,
What can you buy when you sell Joseph for ten drachmas?

٧٧

گویند که دوش شحنگان تتری
دزدی بگرفتند بصد حیله گری
امروز به آویختنش می بردند
میگفت رها کن که گریبان ندری

77

They say last night the Turkish police
Arrested a thief after many tricks.
Today when they were taking him to hang, he was saying:
"Take your hands off me! You may tear my collar!"

٧٨

گفتم بکنم توبه ز صاحب نظری
باشد که بلای عشق گردد سپری
چندانکه نگه میکنم ای رشک پری
بار دومین از اولین خوبتری

78

I said to myself, "I must repent of looking at the beautiful,
So that the calamity of love may pass away."
The more I look, O Envy of the Fairy,
You are more beautiful the second time than the first.

٧٩

هر روز بشیوه ای و لطفی دگری
چندانکه نگه میکنمت خوبتری
گفتم که بقاضی برمت تا دل خویش
بستانم و ترسم دل قاضی ببری

79

Everyday you have a new charm and elegance.
The more I look, the more beautiful you look.
I thought I should take you to the court to reclaim my heart.
I fear you might steal the judge's heart, too.

٨٠

ای بلبل خوش سخن چه شیرین نفسی

سرمست هوی و پای بند هوسی

ترسم که بیاران عزیزت نرسی

کز دست و زبان خویشتن در قفسی

80

O sweet-singing nightingale, how sweet is your breath!
You are drunk with desire and captured by fancy.
I fear you may never join your dear friends.
For your own hand and tongue have put you in cage.

٨١

کردیم بسی جام لبالب خالی

تا بو که نهیم لب بر آن لب سالی

ترسنده از آن شدم که ناگاه ز جان

بیوصل لبت کنیم قالب خالی

81

Many a brimful cup did I empty,
So that one year I may put my lips on hers.
I am afraid that suddenly, without reaching those lips,
My body may be emptied of my soul.

٨٢

گر کام دل از زمانه تصویر کنی

بیفایده خود را ز غمان پیر کنی

گیرم که ز دشمن گله آری بر دوست

چون دوست جفا کند چه تدبیر کنی

82

If you picture your heart's desire obtained in the world,
You will grow old in suffering uselessly.
Suppose you complained to your friend about your enemy,
What could you do if the friend himself was cruel to you?

٨٣

ای غائب چشم و حاضر دل چونی
وی شاخ گل شکفته در گل چونی
یکبار نگوئی برفیقان وداع
کاخر تو در آن اول منزل چونی

83

O absent from the eye, present in the heart, how fare you?
O blossoming branch of flowers, how fare you?
Not once you ask your friends whom you bade farewell:
In that first station of the road, how fare you?

٨۴

ای مایهٔ درمان نفسی ننشینی
تا صورت حال دردمندان بینی
گر من بتو فرهاد صفت شیفته ام
عیبم مکن ایجان که تو بس شیرینی

84

O Essence of Remedy, will you not sit for a moment
To see how the sufferers in your love are doing?
If I am captivated by you, like Farhâd,
It is not my fault, my dear, so Shirin as you are.

شیخ فخرالدین عراقی
(۶۱۰-۶۸۸ هجری قمری)

۱

عیشی نبود چو عیش لولی و گدا
افکنده کله از سر و نعلین از پا
پا بر سر جان نهاده دل کرده فدا
بگذاشته از بهر یکی هر دو سرا

Shaykh Fakhruddin Arâqi
(1214-1289 C.E.)

1
There is no pleasure like that of a mendicant
Who has cast his hat off his head and shoes off his feet,
Who has stepped on his life and sacrificed his heart, and
Who has given up both worlds for the sake of the One.

۲

حاشا که دل از خاک درت دور شود
یا جان ز سر کوی تو مهجور شود
این دیده تاریک من آخر روزی
از خاک قدمهای تو پر نور شود

2
Far be it that my heart distance itself from your door,
Or my soul be banished from your street.
One day this darkened vision of mine
Will be brightened by the dust under your feet.

۳

ای روی تو آرزوی دیرینهٔ ما

جز مهر تو نیست در دل و سینهٔ ما

از صیقل آدمی زداییم درون

تا عکس رخت فتد در آیینهٔ ما

3

O you whose face is my long-time desire,

There is nothing but your love in my heart and breast.

I should wipe out the gloss of humanity from my inner self,

So that the picture of your face would appear in my mirror.

۴

بی آنکه دو دیده در جمالت نگریست

در آرزوی روی تو خونابه گریست

بیچاره بمانده ام دریغا بی تو

بیچاره کسی که بی تواش باید زیست

4

Though they never looked at your face,

My eyes shed tears with blood, longing for your face.

Alas! I am left helpless without you.

Helpless is the one who must live without you.

۵

پیری ز خرابات برون آمد مست

دل رفته ز دست و جام می بر کف دست

گفتا می نوش کاندرین عالم پست

جز مست کسی ز خویشتن باز نرست

5

A sage drunken came out of a tavern.

His heart lost, he was holding a cup of wine in his hand.

"Drink wine," said he. "For in this lowly world,

None but the drunkard is freed from his ego."

۶

ماییم که بی مایی ما مایهٔ ماست
خود طفل خودیم و عشق ما دایهٔ ماست
فی الجمله عروس غیب همسایهٔ ماست
وین طرفه که همسایهٔ ما سایهٔ ماست

6

I am the one whose selflessness is his essence.
I am the child of myself, and my love is my nurse.
Meanwhile, the bride of the Unseen is my neighbor.
And how strange that my neighbor is my shadow!

۷

آن دوستی قدیم ما چون گشته است؟
مانده است بجای یا دگرگون گشته است؟
از تو خبرم نیست که بی ما چونی
باری دل من ز عشق تو خون گشته است

7

How is that old friendship of ours?
Has it remained in its place or changed?
I do not know how you are doing without me.
All I know is that my heart is bleeding in your love.

۸

هرگز بت من روی بکس ننموده است
این گفت و مگوی مردمان بیهوده است
آن کس که ترا براستی بستوده است
او نیز حکایت از کسی بشنوده است

8

Never has my idol shown his face to anyone.
All these disputations of the people are in vain.
The person who praised you rightly,
He, too, has heard the story from someone else.

۹

اول قدم از عشق سر انداختن است
جان باختن است و با بلا ساختن است
اول اینست و آخرش دانی چیست
خودی را ز خودی خود بپرداختن است

9

The first step in love is casting one's head.
It is risking one's life and putting up with calamity.
This is the first, and do you know what the last is?
To rid oneself from the selfness of the self.

۱۰

عشق تو ز دست ساقیان باده بریخت
و ز دیده بسی خون دل ساده بریخت
بس زاهد خرقه پوش سجاده نشین
کز عشق تو می بر سر سجاده بریخت

10

Your love wine from the hands of Sâqis poured,
And much blood of the heart pure from the eyes poured.
Many ascetics, who wore cloaks and sat on prayer-rugs,
Because of your love, wine on their prayer-rugs poured.

۱۱

شوقی که چو گل دل شکفاند عشق است
ذهنی که رموز عشق داند عشق است
مهری که ترا از تو رهاند عشق است
لطفی که ترا بدو رساند عشق است

11

The longing that makes the heart bloom like a rose is love.
The mind that knows the secrets of affection is love.
The affection that redeems you from yourself is love.
The grace that takes you to Him is love.

۱۲

اندر ره عشق دی و کی پیدا نیست

مستان شده اند و هیچ می پیدا نیست

مردان رهش ز خویش پوشیده روند

زان بر سر کوی عشق پی پیدا نیست

12

On the way of love, no before and after is visible.
The drunken are gone, and no wine is visible.
The men of his way walk hidden from themselves.
Hence, on the road of love, no footprint is visible.

۱۳

غم گرد دل پر هنران میگردد

شادی همه بر بیخبران میگردد

زنهار که قطب فلک دایره وار

در دیده صاحبنظران میگردد

13

Pain circles around the hearts of the meritorious.
Pleasure circles around the unaware.
Beware! For the axis of the spherical heaven
Pivots in the eye of the man of perception.

۱۴

بی روی تو عاشقت رخ گل چه کند

بی بوی خوشت ببوی سنبل چه کند

آنکس که ز جام عشق تو سرمست است

انصاف بده به مستی مل چه کند

14

What shall your lover do with roses without your face?
What shall he do with hyacinths without your fragrance?
He who is drunk from the cup of your love, in all fairness,
What shall he do with the intoxication of wine?

۱۵

این عمر که برده ای تو بی یار بسر
نا کرده دمی بر در دلدار گذر
جانا بنشین و ماتم خود میدار
کان رفت که آید ز تو کاری دیگر

15

The life you have spent without your beloved,
Without passing by his door for a minute,
Sit down and mourn for it , my dear.
For the time when you could do something is gone.

۱۶

دل ز آرزوی تو بیقرار است هنوز
جان در طلبت بر سر کارست هنوز
دیده بجمالت ار چه روشن شد لیک
هم بر سر آن گریهٔ زارست هنوز

16

My heart is still restless in its desire for you.
My soul is still active in its quest for you.
Although my eyes were brightened by your beauty,
They are still busy in their bitter crying for you.

۱۷

بیزار شد از من شکسته همه کس
من مانده ام اکنون و همان لطف تو بس
فریاد رسی ندارم ای جان و جهان
در جمله جهان بجز تو فریادم رس

17

Everyone grew tired of me, the broken-hearted.
Now I am left alone with your kindness only.
In the whole world, I have no help but you.
So help me, O Soul of the world!

۱۸

ای جان و جهان ترا ز جان می طلبم
سرگشته ترا گرد جهان می طلبم
تو در دل من نشسته ای فارغ و من
از تو ز جهانیان نشان می طلبم

18

O Soul of the world, deep in my soul I am searching you.
Bewildered, all around the world I am searching you.
Though you are sitting relaxed in my heart,
I am asking the people of the world for a trace of you.

۱۹

امشب نظری بروی ساقی دارم
ای صبح مدم که عیش باقی دارم
شاید که بر افلاک زنم خیمه از آنک
با همدم روح هم وثاقی دارم

19

I have my eyes on the Sâqi's face tonight.
O dawn, break not! For I have more enjoyment ahead.
Now that I am in the presence of my soul's companion,
I could pitch my tent in the heavens.

۲۰

در سر هوس شراب و ساقی دارم
تا جام جهان نمای باقی دارم
گر بر در میخانه روم شاید از آنک
با دوست امید هم وثاقی دارم

20

Until I possess the eternal world-viewing cup,
The desire for wine and Sâqi exists in my head.
If I go to the door of the tavern, it is worthwhile,
Because I hope to have a tryst with my friend there.

۲۱

پیری بدر آمد ز خرابات فنای

در گوش دلم گفت که ای شیفته رای

گر می طلبی بقای جاوید مباش

بی باده روشن اندرین تیره سرای

21

A spiritual master came out of the tavern of mortality
And whispered in my ear, "O you, troubled in mind,
"If you are seeking immortality,
"Do not be without clear wine in this murky world."

۲۲

آنم که توام ز خاک برداشته ای

نقشم بمراد خویش بنگاشته ای

کارم بمراد خود چو نگذاشته ای

می رویم از آنسان که توام کاشته ای

22

I am the one whom you have picked up from dust
And have drawn my image according to your wish.
Since you have not allowed me to have my wish,
I am growing the way you have planted me.

۲۳

ای لطف تو دستگیر هر رسوایی

وی عفو تو پرده پوش هر خودرایی

بخشای بدان بندَه که اندر همه عمر

جز درگه تو دگر ندارد جایی

23

O you, whose grace takes the hand of every disgraced one
And whose forgiveness veils every self-conceited one,
Be generous to that slave who, in all his life,
Has no other place except your door.

۲۴

نی کرده شبی بر سر کویت گذری
نی بوی خوشت بمن رسیده سحری
نی یافته از تو اثری یا خبری
عمرم بگذشت بی تو آخر خبری

24

I have neither passed through your street any night,
Nor have smelt your pleasant scent any morning.
I have neither found your trace nor heard your news.
My life wasted without you. At least, send me some news.

۲۵

گفتم که اگر چه آفت جان منی
جان پیش کشم ترا که جانان منی
گفتا که اگر بنده فرمان منی
آن دگران مباش چون زان منی

25

"Although you are the plight of my soul," said I.
"I shall give my life for you because you are my beloved."
"If you are obedient to my command," said he,
"Don't belong to others, because you belong to me."

سراج الدین قمری

(۶۵۰-۵۸۰ هجری قمری)

۱

امروز که رونق جوانی من است
می خواهم از آنکه شادمانی من است
عیبش مکنید اگرچه تلخ است خوش است
تلخ است از آنکه زندگانی من است

Serâjuddin Qomri
(1185-1252 C.E.)

1

Today while my youth is flourishing,
I want of that which gives me joy.
Do not criticize it. For though it is bitter, it is good.
It is my life. Therefore, it is bitter.

۲

هر غم که بمن رسد ز عشقت شادیست
داد آیدم از تو هر چه آن بیدادیست
در بندگیت چو سرو ثابت قدمم
کز بندگی توام چو سرو آزادیست

2

Any sorrow that reaches me from your love is joy.
Any injustice from you is justice to me.
In my devotion to you, I am stable like a cypress.
In my bondage to you, I am free like a cypress.

۳

از وصل تو عمر جاودانی دارم

وز عشق تو لذت جوانی دارم

شادی جهان در دل من غم بادا

گر جز بغم تو شادمانی دارم

3

I have eternal life because of your union.
I have the pleasure of youth because of your love.
If I have any joy except in your sorrow,
Let the pleasure of the world be pain to me.

۴

هر می که خورم با تو فتوحم باشد

شادی دل و راحت روحم باشد

تو با منی و چهرهٔ تو صبح منست

هر گه که خورم باده صبوحم باشد

4

Any wine I drink with you is a victory for me.
It is the joy of my heart and comfort of my soul.
When you are with me, your face is my morning.
Any wine I drink with you is a morning-draught.

۵

در خواب مرا با تو وصالی باشد

هر چند وصال تو محالی باشد

خود دولت این زمانهٔ لعبت باز

چون نیک نگه کنی خیالی باشد

5

I have union with you in my dream,
Even though union with you is impossible.
The fortune of this trickster world itself,
If one looks carefully, is a illusion.

۶

صبح است و مرا آرزوی خواب نماند
رغبت بجز از سوی می ناب نماند
باشد که از این آب جگر تازه کنم
چون بر جگر تشنه مرا آب نماند

6

It is morning and no more desire in me for sleep is left.
No desire except for pure wine is left.
Perhaps I could refresh my liver with this water.
For no more water for my thirsty liver is left.

سعدالدین حموی
(۶۵۰ هجری قمری)

۱

اندر دل من درون و بیرون همه اوست
اندر تن من جان و دل و خون همه اوست
آنجای چگونه کفر و ایمان گنجد
بیچون باشد وجود من چون همه اوست

Sa'duddin Hamavi
(d. 1252 C.E.)

1

In my heart, within and without, all is him.
In my body, the soul and heart and blood, all is him.
How can faith and blasphemy be contained in me?
My existence is incomparable because all is him.

٢

این هستی تو هستی هستی دگرست
وین مستی تو مستی مستی دگرست
رو سر بگریبان تفکر در کش
کاین دست تو آستین دستی دگرست

2

This your being is the being of another existent.
This your intoxication is the intoxication of another drunk.
Go thrust your head in your collar and meditate.
For this your hand is the sleeve of another hand.

٣

ای قد تو معتدل نه بالا و نه پست
وی چشم تو مخمور نه هشیار نه مست
با لجمله چنانی که چنان می باید
کس را چو تو محبوب نه بودست و نه هست

3

O you who are moderate in stature, neither tall nor short,
Your languishing eyes are neither drunk nor sober.
After all, you are just as you should have been.
No one has ever had a darling like you.

۴

بی تو نفسی قرار و آرامم نیست
بی نام تو ذات و صفت و نامم نیست
بی چاشنی تو در جهان کامم نیست
بی روی تو صبح و زلف تو شامم نیست

4

Without you, not a moment of rest or calmness have I.
Without your name, no essence, attribute, or name have I.
Without your spice, no taste for the world have I.
Without your face and tress, no morning and night have I.

۵

کس نیست که او شیفته روی تو نیست

سرگشته چو من در شکن موی تو نیست

گویند بهشت جاودان خوش باشد

دانم به یقین که خوشتر از کوی تو نیست

5

Unattracted by your face, there is none.
Bewildered like me in your hair's curls, there is none.
They say the eternal paradise is pleasant.
I know certainly it is not more pleasant than your street.

۶

وقت است که یار ما به بستان آید

سلطان جمال او بمیدان آید

پیدا و نهان در دل و در جان آید

کفر همه کافران به ایمان آید

6

It is time our beloved came to the orchard,
The sultan of his beauty appeared in the field,
And the visible and invisible entered the heart and soul,
When the disbelief of all disbelievers became belief.

۷

دل وقت سماع ره به دلدار برد

جان را به سراپردهٔ اسرار برد

این فتنه چو مرکبی است مر روح ترا

بردارد و خوش به عالم یار برد

7

During the *samá'*, the heart finds its way to the Beloved,
And takes the soul to the harem of secrets.
This charming music is like a horse for your soul.
It picks your soul up and takes it to the Beloved's world.

٨

بر مرکب عشق اگر سوار آید دل
بر جمله مراد کامکار آید دل
گر دل نبود کجا وطن سازد عشق
ور عشق نباشد به چه کار آید دل

8

If the heart rides on the steed of love,
It will attain to all that it desires.
Where could love make its home if the heart did not exist?
And of what use the heart would be if love did not exist?

٩

در دل ز فراق خستگی ها دارم
در کار ز چرخ بستگی ها دارم
با این همه غم تو نیز پیمان وفا
مشکن که جز این شکستگی ها دارم

9

I have many wounds in my heart because of separation.
I have many knots in my affairs because of the world.
With all this suffering, don't break your promise of loyalty!
For I have many other broken things in my life.

١٠

من دوست براستی ترا داشته ام
جز از تو کسی دگر نپنداشته ام
چندان بتو من امید بر داشته ام
کافعال تو فعل خویش انگاشته ام

10

I have always truly loved you.
I have never thought of anyone except you.
I have developed so much hope in you that
I have considered your acts my own.

١١

بی تو نه بهشت بایدم نه رضوان
نی کوثر و سلسبیل و بحر حیوان
با قهر تو دوزخ است دار رضوان
با لطف تو دوزخ همه روح و ریحان

11

Without you, I want neither paradise nor heaven,
Neither *Kosar* nor *Salsabil*, nor the water of life.
When you are not friend with me, heaven is hell.
When you are kind to me, hell is pleasant and exciting.

١٢

در هر چه نظر کنم ترا بینم من
در دیدهٔ من تویی کرا بینم من؟
جز از تو که باشد کرا بینم من؟
کی باشد و گر بود چرا بینم من؟

12

Whatever I look at, it is you whom I see.
It is you in my eyes, who else can I see?
Who is there except you that I might see?
And if there is one, why should I see?

١٣

در من نگرد دلم بجوش آید ازو
صبرم برود بانگ و خروش آید ازو
گر یک سخنی مرا بگوش آید ازو
باشد که دلم باز بهوش آید ازو

13

When he looks at me, my heart becomes excited.
It loses patience and begins to clamor and shout.
If only a word from him reached my ear,
Perhaps my heart would regain its consciousness.

۱۴

ذکریست مرا که بوی جان آید ازو
بوی خوش یار مهربان آید ازو
در وی نفسی گر به بیان آید ازو
کلی رموز در عیان آید ازو

14

The name I repeat the scent of life comes from it.
The pleasant scent of the kind sweetheart comes from it.
If a waft of this fragrance could express itself,
Many secrets would be revealed by that.

۱۵

خورشید حق است و هر دو عالم سایه
آن سایه که نور باشد آن را مایه
افتاده ز پای ما و او بر سر ما
ما غایب ازو او بما همسایه

15

Truth is the sun and both worlds are its shadow,
The shadow whose essence is light.
We have fallen to ground while the sun is above our heads.
We are away from him while he is our neighbor.

۱۶

ای بلبل مست چند آواز کنی
در عالم عشق چند پرواز کنی
دانم که همی نه آگهی از رخ یار
ورنه در صبر همچو من باز کنی

16

O drunk nightingale, how long are you going to sing?
How long are you going to fly in the world of love?
I know that you are not aware of the beloved's face.
If you were, you would run out of patience, like me.

۱۷

با ضعف بساز تا قوی دست شوی

گرد در نیست گرد تا هست شوی

در کاهش جسم کوش تا جان گردی

وز دردی عشق نوش تا مست شوی

17

Put up with weakness until you become strong.
Stay with nonbeing until you become being.
Try to reduce your body until you become spirit.
Drink from the dregs of love until you become drunk.

۱۸

بی تو نظری نیست مرا در کاری

در باغ رضای چون تو زیبا یاری

پیدا و نهان روی تو دیدم باری

بی روی تو خوش نیامدم گلزاری

18

Without you, I have no interest in any work
In the garden of satisfaction of a beautiful friend like you.
I have seen your face both secretly and openly.
Besides your face, no rose-garden pleases me.

۱۹

کافر شوی ار زلف نگارم بینی

مؤمن شوی ار عارض یارم بینی

در کفر میاویز و در ایمان منگر

تا عزت یار و افتقارم بینی

19

If you see my beloved's tress, you will be a disbeliever.
If you see my beloved's face, you will be a believer.
Do not hang on to disbelief, nor look at belief,
So that you may see the beloved's glory and my poverty.

۲۰

گر جمله جهان به خویش مقرون بینی
در کل جهان خدای بیچون بینی
چون کل جهان آیهٔ کل تو بود
پس در دو جهان غیر خدا چون بینی

20
If you see the whole world related to yourself,
You will see the ineffable God in the whole world.
Since the whole world is the sign of your wholeness,
How can you see anyone but God in both worlds?

سیف الدین باخرزی
(۶۲۹ هجری قمری)

۱

من با تو چنانم ای نگار ختنی
کاندر غلطم که من توام یا تو منی
از ما دوری و در یکی پیرهنی
پس من کیم ایجان جهان گر تو منی

Sayfuddin Bâkharzi
(d. 1232 C.E.)

1
I am so with you, O beauty of Khotan,
I am wrong if I say I am you or you are me.
You are far from me, yet in the same garment with me.
If you are me, then who am I, O Soul of the World?

٢

پیریم ولی چو عشق را ساز آید
از ما همه بوی طرب و ناز آید
از زلف دراز تو کمندی فکنیم
در گردن عمر رفته تا باز آید

2

I am old, but if love be kind to me,
I will be all exuberance and pride.
I will make a lasso of your long tress and throw it
On the neck of the expired life and bring it back.

٣

هر چندگهی ز عشق بیگانه شوم
با عافیت آشنا و همخانه شوم
ناگاه پری رخی به من برگذرد
برگردم از آن حدیث و دیوانه شوم

3

Once in a while, I estrange myself from love,
Make acquaintance with prudence, and stay with it.
Suddenly a fairy-faced one passes by me.
I forget all prudence and become mad again.

۴

از دیدهٔ سنگ خون چکاند غم تو
بیگانه و آشنا نداند غم تو
دم در کشم و همه غمت نوش کنم
تا از پس من بکس نماند غم تو

4

Your love's sorrow makes the eye of a rock bleed.
It does not differentiate between friends and strangers.
I would say nothing and joyfully drink all of your sorrow,
So that none of it could be left for anyone after me.

۵

چون صبح ولای حق دمیدن گیرد
جان از همه آفاق رمیدن گیرد
جایی برسد مرد که در هر نفسی
بی زحمت دیده دوست دیدن گیرد

5

When the morning of God's love begins to dawn,
The spirit turns away from the whole world.
Man reaches a point where, at every moment,
He sees the Beloved without bothering to look.

۶

بی خویش و تبار و بی قرینم کردی
با فاقه و فقر همنشینم کردی
این مرتبهٔ مقربان در تست
یا رب به چه خدمت این چنینم کردی

6

You took me from my relatives, parents, and friends,
And put me in the company of poverty and penury.
This is the position of those who are near to you.
O Lord, what good had I done that you made me so?

۷

عشق است که شیر نر زبون آید ازو
بحری است که طرفه ها برون آید ازو
گه دوستیی کند که روح افزاید
گه دشمنیی که بوی خون آید ازو

7

Love is it that can make a lion helpless.
It is an ocean from which many wonders emerge.
Sometimes it is so friendly it elates the spirit.
And sometimes so hostile it smells blood.

٨

با عشق تو من به خرمی می سازم
با غم به امید بی غمی می سازم
در من اثر هلاک پیداست ولی
میدانم و خود را عجمی می سازم

8

I am getting along with your love happily.
I am putting up with sorrow, hoping for the lack of sorrow.
The sign of death is apparent in me.
I know this, but I pretend that I do not.

٩

هر دم که دلم با غمت انباز شود
صد در ز طرب بر دل من باز شود
به زان نبود که جان فدای تو کنم
تیهو که فدای باز شد باز شود

9

A hundred doors of joy open to my heart
Any time it takes part in the sorrow of your love.
Nothing is better for me than being sacrificed for you.
When a partridge falls prey to an eagle, it becomes an eagle.

١٠

دانی چه بود شرط خرابات نخست
اسب و کمر و کلاه در بازی چست
چون مست شوی و پایها گردد سست
گویند نشین هنوز باقی بر تست

10

Do you know what the first requirement of a tavern is?
To lose one's horse, girdle, and helmet all at once.
And when you have become drunk and your legs are weak,
They will tell you, "Sit, the remainder is still for you."

۱۱

زان می خواهم که خرمی را سبب است
نامش می و کیمیای شادی لقب است
سرخ است چو عناب و ز آب عنب است
آبی که به رخ بر آتش آرد عجب است

11

I want that wine which is the cause of happiness,
Whose name is wine and surname the elixir of happiness.
It is red like jujube and made from the juice of the grape.
The water that can bring fire to the face is an amazing thing.

۱۲

ای عادت تو یار موافق بودن
وی پیشهٔ تو بوعده صادق بودن
بر موجب این دو خوی نیکو که تراست
جز بر تو حلال نیست عاشق بودن

12

O you, whose habit is to be an agreeable friend
And whose custom is to keep promises;
Because of these two traits that you have,
It is not good to be in love with any other than you.

۱۳

ما را بتو از بخت نویدست هنوز
نومید شدن از تو که دیدست هنوز
گر روز فراق تو درازست رواست
ما را شب وصل از تو امیدست هنوز

13

I still have hope of my luck that I will be with you.
Who has ever been disappointed with you?
If the day of your separation is long, it is all right.
I still have hope for the night of union with you.

دختر سالار

(قرن هفتم هجری قمری)

۱

بر دیدهٔ من چو اشک گلگون بچکد

هر لحظه هزار قطرهٔ خون بچکد

بر آتش عشق تو کباب است دلم

چون گرم شود کباب از او خون بچکد

Dokhtar Sâlâr
(13th Century C.E.)

1

As the rose-colored tears drip from my eyes,
A thousand drops of blood fall down every moment.
My heart is like kebab in the fire of your love.
When the kebab is heated, it drips blood.

۲

چندانکه بکار خویش وا می بینم

خود را بغم تو مبتلا می بینم

وین طرفه که در آینهٔ دل شب و روز

من می نگرم ولی تو را می بینم

2

The more I look back at my life,
The more I see myself afflicted with your [love's] sorrow.
It is strange that in the mirror of the heart,
It is I who look, but you whom I see day and night!

خواجه نصیرالدین طوسی
(۶۷۲ هجری قمری)

۱

ای بیخبر این شکل مجسم هیچ است
وین دایرهٔ سطح مخیم هیچ است
خوش باش که در نشیمن کون و فساد
وابستهٔ یک دمی و آنهم هیچ است

Khâja Nasiruddin Tusi
(d. 1274 C.E.)

1

O unaware one, this embodied form is nothing.
And this circular campground is nothing.
Be happy! For in this abode of becoming and unbecoming,
Your life depends on one breath, and that, too, is nothing.

۲

چون در سفریم ای پسر هیچ مگوی
احوال حضر در این سفر هیچ مگوی
ما هیچ و جهان هیچ و غم و شادی هیچ
می دان که نئی هیچ و دگر هیچ مگوی

2

My son, now that we are traveling, say nothing.
In this trip, of the condition of life at home, say nothing.
We and the world are nothing, joy and sorrow are nothing.
Know that you are nothing, and then say nothing.

۳

گر زانکه بر استخوان نماند رگ و پی

از خانهٔ تسلیم منه بیرون پی

گردن منه ار خصم بود رستم زال

منت مکش ار دوست شود حاتم طی

3

Even if only veins, vessels, and bones remain from you,
Do not step out of the house of submission.
Do not bow even if Rostam, Son of Zâl, is the enemy.
Do not stoop to favor even if Hatam Tâi is the friend.

۴

موجود بحق واحد اول باشد

باقی همه موهوم و مخیل باشد

هر چیز جز او که آمد اندر نظرت

نقش دومین چشم احول باشد

4

The One truly existent is the first.
The rest are all illusions and imaginings.
Anything except Him that comes to your view
Is the second image of an squint eye.

۵

تا چند سر خود چو سر میم کنی

تسلیم و رضا را سپر بیم کنی

آخر تو کئی که تا رضاییت بود

گو چیست ترا که تا تو تسلیم کنی

5

How long shall you bow and lower your head?
And make surrender and consent a shield for your fear?
Who are you to consent or not?
What do you own that you may surrender?

۶

زین گوشه و ایوان که برافراشته‌ای

وین خواستهٔ خلق که برداشته‌ای

چه فایده بد ترا چو نایافته کام

بگذشتی و اینها همه بگذاشته‌ای

6

Of this lofty palace you have raised
And all these desired things you have collected,
What do you gain if you pass away
And leave all without having enjoyed any?

۷

هر چند همه هستی خود می‌دانیم

چون کار بذات می‌رسد حیرانیم

بالجمله بدوک پیرزن می مانیم

سررشته بدست ما و ما حیرانیم

7

Although we consider everything part of our existence,
When it comes to the essence, we are bewildered.
In short, we are like the spindle of an old woman.
We have the end of the thread in hand, yet wandering.

۸

اندر ره معرفت بسی تاخته‌ام

واندر صف عارفان سر افراخته‌ام

چون پرده ز روی دل برانداخته‌ام

بشناخته‌ام که هیچ نشناخته‌ام

8

I have galloped much on the road of knowledge,
And have stood tall in the line of the mystics.
Yet, when I have removed the veil from my heart,
I have realized that I have not realized anything.

٩

از هر چه که نه از بهر تو کردم توبه
ور بی تو غمی خورم از آن غم توبه
وان نیز که بعد از این برای تو کنم
گر بهتر از آن توان از آنهم توبه

9

Of anything I did which was not for your sake I repent.
And if I suffered for anyone other than you I repent.
Also of what I will do for you from now on,
If I could have done it better, I repent.

کمال الدین اسماعیل
(۶۳۵ هجری قمری)

١

ای شب ره صبحدم بزنجیر ببند
بر چهرهٔ چرخ چادر تیره ببند
امشب که دو دست یار در گردن ماست
تو نیز دو پای خود بزنجیر ببند

Kamâluddin Ismâil
(d. 1238 C.E.)

1

O night, block the road of the dawn with a chain.
And cover the face of the sky with a black veil.
Tonight when my beloved's arms are around my neck,
You should tie your feet with a chain.

٢

در حالت عشق بس نکو رقص کنم
واندر غم تو از هزار تو رقص کنم
دست است و دل است آلت رقاصی
کو دست و دلی که من بدو رقص کنم

2

I can dance very well when I am in the ecstasy of love.
I can dance a thousand-fold in your love's sorrow.
The heart and hands are the tools of dancing.
Where are the hands and heart with which I may dance?

٣

هر شب ز غمت تو ای نگارین یارم
وز مهر رخ چو ماهت ای دلدارم
تا وقت سحر بماه در می نگرم
وز دیده ستارگان فرو می بارم

3

Every night, longing for you, O my beautiful sweetheart,
And from the love of your moon-like face, O my darling,
I look at the moon until morning
And rain stars from my eyes.

۴

اشکم که ز خون چو دردی شیره شدست
وز رفتن او دو چشم من خیره شدست
از دیدهٔ بیچاره نمی باید دید
کاین آب ز سرچشمه دل تیره شدست

4

My poor eyes should not be held responsible for the tears,
Which have become like molasses with blood and
Whose flow has dimmed my vision.
For this water was darkened in my heart's fountainhead.

۵

درد‌ی است اجل که نیست درمان او را
بر شاه و وزیر هست فرمان او را
شاهی که بحکم دوش کرمان می خورد
امروز همی خورند کرمان او را

5

Death is an ailment without remedy.
She rules over kings and viziers.
The king whose order conquered Kermân last night
Is being conquered by *kermân* (worms) tonight.

۶

در باغ شدم سحرگه از درد نهفت
بلبل بزبان حال با گل میگفت
از غنچه برون آی و بخنده خوش باش
ای بس گل رعنا که در این باغ شکفت

6

I went to the garden at dawn because of a hidden pain.
The nightingale, in its own language, was telling the rose:
"Come out of the bud, smile, and have a good time.
"Many beautiful roses have bloomed in this garden."

۷

راز تو به نزد این و آن نتوان گفت
آسان آسان بترک جان نتوان گفت
این با که توان گفت که درد دل من
تو نشنوی و با دگران نتوان گفت

7

I cannot tell your secret to this person or that.
I cannot give up my soul slowly and gradually.
Whom should I tell that the story of my heart
You will not listen to and cannot be told to others?

٨

گل خواست که چون رخش نکو باشد و نیست
چون دلبر من به رنگ و بو باشد و نیست
صد روی فراهم آورد هر سالی
باشد که یکی چو روی او باشد و نیست

8

The rose wanted to be beautiful like her face, but it is not;
To be of the same color and scent as my love, but it is not.
The rose puts up a thousand faces every year,
So that one face, at least, may be like hers, but it is not.

٩

کو دیده که تا بر وطن خود گرید
بر حال دل و واقعهٔ بد گرید
دی بر سر یک مرده دو صد گریان بود
امروز یکی نیست که بر صد گرید

9

Where is the eye that may cry for its homeland?
And cry for the condition of the heart and for this disaster?
Yesterday, two hundred people would cry for one dead.
Today, not one person will cry for a hundred dead.

١٠

گل ساخته بد ز غنچه پیکانی چند
تا با تو کند مصاف حسن ای دلبند
خورشید رخت چو تیغ بنمود ز دور
پیکان سپری کرد سپر هم بفکند

10

The rose had made several arrows in its bud
In order to battle with you for beauty, my love.
When the sun of your face showed the sword from afar,
The rose-bud used up its arrows and dropped its shield, too.

۱۱

هنگام صبوح است حریفان خیزید
وان باقی دوشین بقدح در ریزید
یک لحظه زبند نیک و بد بگریزید
در بی خبری و بی خودی آویزید

11

Rise, O challengers! It is time for the morning drink.
And pour the wine remaining from last night in your cups!
Escape from the fetters of good and bad for a moment,
And hang on to ecstasy and unawareness.

۱۲

یارم ز جفا هیچ رها کرد نکرد
یک وعده که فرمود وفا کرد نکرد
هر تیر که چشم مستش انداخت بمن
گویی به خطا یکی خطا کرد نکرد

12

Did my beloved ever let go of cruelty? Never.
Did she ever make a promise and keep it? Never.
Did any of the arrows she aimed at me
From her languishing eyes ever miss the target? Never.

۱۳

آلوده مشو که پاک می باید شد
ماسای که دردناک می باید شد
از باد چو آتش ار بری سر بفلک
چون آب بزیر خاک می باید شد

13

Do not be contaminated. You must be clean.
Do not indulge in comfort. You must be full of pain.
If you raise your head to the sky like a flame in the wind,
[In the end] like water, you must sink beneath the earth.

۱۴

همچون آواز یک زمانم بر کش
وآنگاه چو چنگ تنگم اندر بر کش
ور در تن من رگی نه بر پردهٔ تست
بیرون کن و دیگری بجایش بر کش

14

Sing me a little while like a song,
And tightly hold me in your arms like a harp;
And if a single vein in my body is out of tune with you,
Pull it out and replace it with another.

۱۵

از گردش چرخ بی خرد می ترسم
در هر حالی ز نیک و بد می ترسم
زان روی که بر کس اعتمادی بنماند
از همرهی سایهٔ خود می ترسم

15

I fear the revolution of this stupid wheel.
I fear the good and bad in every situation.
Since no one can be trusted any longer,
I fear the accompaniment of [even] my own shadow.

۱۶

وقت است که قصد عالم پاک کنیم
وین پشت دوتا گشته بر افلاک کنیم
خرپشته نشین قالبم می گوید
وقت است که روی خیمه در خاک کنیم

16

It is time to head toward the immaculate world,
And lift this folded back to the heavens.
The dweller in the form of my body is telling me:
It is time for the tent to be lowered to the ground.

۱۷

ای یاد غمت مونس تنهایی من
وی خاک درت سرمهٔ بینایی من
مگذار که فاش گردد اندر عالم
چون حسن تو حال دلَ سودایی من

17

O you, whose love's memory is my companion in loneliness,
And whose door's dust is the collyrium of my vision,
Do not let the condition of my melancholic heart
Be divulged, like your beauty, around the world.

۱۸

در بند جهان مباش و آزاد بزی
وز باده خراب گرد و آباد بزی
تا زنده‌ای از مرگ نباشی ایمن
یکبار بمیر و تا ابد شاد بزی

18

Do not be tied to the world. Live freely.
Become broken by wine, and live soundly.
As long as you are alive, you are not secure from death.
Die once, and live happily ever after.

۱۹

گر باز آیی دلم بمن باز آری
هوشم بدل و روان بتن باز آری
جانی که ز تن برفت اگر رای کنی
از نیمه رهش بیک سخن باز آری

19

If you come back, you will bring my heart back to me
And return consciousness to my heart and soul to my body.
The soul which left my body, if you decide, with one word
You will bring it back from the middle of the road.

۲۰

دی بلبلکی لطیفکی خوش گویی

می گفت نشته بر کنار جویی

کز لعل و زمرد و زر خرده توان

بر ساخت گلی ولی ندارد بویی

20

Yesterday, a little nightingale, delicate and sweet-singing,
Was sitting on the bank of a brook and singing:
From the pieces of ruby, emerald, and gold,
One can make a rose, but it will not have any perfume.

نجیب گنجه‌ای

(قرن هفتم هجری قمری)

۱

هر چند که دل را غم عشق آیین است

چشم است که آفت دل مسکین است

من معترفم که شاهد دل معنی است

لیکن چکنم که چشم صورت بین است

Najib Ganjei
(13th Century C.E.)

1

Although the sorrow of love is the creed of the heart,
It is the eye that is the plight of the wretched heart.
I know that it is the essence that the heart loves,
But what should I do if the eye sees only the appearance?

۲

ای دل هوست به گفت و گو ننشیند
وین لابه گری در دل او ننشیند
ای دیده مریز آب کاین آتش عشق
هر گز به چنین آب فرو ننشیند

2

O heart, words will not quell your passion.
And this imploring will not impress his heart.
Shed no tears, O my eyes! For this fire of love
Will not be extinguished by such water as this.

۳

ای عشق تو در هر نفسی مایهٔ من
وی درد و غمت بروز و شب دایهٔ من
در مذهب عاشقی روا کی باشد
کت سایه ببینم و تو همسایهٔ من

3

O love, you are the substance of my every breath.
And your pain is my nurse day and night.
Where is it allowed in the creed of lovers
That you be my neighbor and I see only your shadow?

شمس الدین سجاسی
(قرن هفتم هجری قمری)

۱

گر یک نظر از تویی بمن برفکنی
آثار منی همه بهم برشکنی
چون در نگرم بچشم بی خویشتنی
در خود غلطم که من توام یا تو منی

Shamsuddin Sajâsi
(13th Century C.E.)

1

If you cast a glimpse of "thou-ness" at me,
You will erase all the traces of "I-ness" from me.
When I look at myself with the eye of selflessness,
I cannot tell whether I am you or you are me.

۲

در عشق خود از غایت بی خویشتنی
می نشناسم که من توام یا تو منی
هم با من و هم بی منی آری چه عجب
جانی که نه در تنی نه بیرون تنی

2

In my love, because of extreme selflessness,
I do not know whether I am you or you are me.
How strange that you are both with me and without me!
You are the spirit that is neither inside nor outside the body.

٣

خود دیدهٔ ره بین تو بس تاریک است
ورنه بتو جانان تو بس نزدیک است
یک پرده حجاب است میان تو و او
اندیشه قوی کن که سخن باریک است

3

Your pathfinder vision is very dull,
Or else your beloved is very close to you.
There is only one veil between you and him.
Sharpen your mind, for this is a delicate point!

۴

زآنروی که عشق از دو جهان حاصل ماست
گویی تن ما ز عشق و عشق از گل ماست
از غایت عشق فرق می نتوان کرد
کاندر دل ماست عشق یا خود دل ماست

4

Since my harvest from both worlds is love,
It is as if my body is from love and love from my clay.
So intense is my love that I cannot tell
Whether it is in my heart or it is my heart itself.

۵

ای دل ز وصال او نشان نیست پدید
چیزی مطلب که در جهان نیست پدید
جان و دل و دیده هر سه از دست برفت
وین طرفه که دوست در میان نیست پدید

5

O heart, no sign of his union is visible.
Do not seek what in this world is not visible.
My soul, my heart, and my vision — all three are lost.
How strange that the beloved is not still visible!

۶

آن دوست که هست عشق او دشمن جان
بر باد همی دهد خمش خرمن جان
من میدوم اندر طلبش کوی به کوی
او در دل و دست کرده در گردن جان

6

That friend, whose love is the enemy of my life,
Is silently throwing to the wind the harvest of my life.
I am running after him from street to street,
While he is in my heart, attempting at my life.

۷

مرکب به رهٔ عشق مرانیت شما
کان راه دراز است بمانیت شما
با عشق موافقت ز جان بیزاری است
سریست در این شیوه ندانیت شما

7

Do not ride your horse on the road of love!
This is a long road. You will not make it.
Agreement with love is disagreement with life.
There is a secret in this point you do not know.

۸

بر خیز که عاشقان بشب راز کنند
گرد در و بام دوست پرواز کنند
هر در که بود جمله بشب در بندند
الا در عاشق که بشب باز کنند

8

Rise! For lovers bill and coo at night.
They fly around the beloved's door and roof at night.
Every door is closed at night,
Except the lover's door, which is opened at night.

٩

دل بی غم تو جام طرب نوش نکرد

جز یاد تو با هیچ کسی گوش نکرد

از لذت خوبی تو آگاه نشد

تا مستی خویش را فراموش نکرد

9

My heart drank not from the cup of joy without your love,
And listened not to any person without remembering you.
It became not aware of the pleasure of your beauty
Without forgetting its own drunkenness first.

١٠

دل گر غم تو بر نگزیند چه کند

تنهاست چو با غم ننشیند چه کند

او مرغ غم است درد تو چینهٔ اوست

بیچاره که درد تو نچیند چه کند

10

If my heart does not choose your sorrow, what must it do?
It is lonely. If it be not with your sorrow, what must it do?
It is a bird of sorrow, and the pain of your love is its seed.
If the poor thing does not peck your pain, what must it do?

١١

هر دل که تو را بباخت در تاب بود

هر دیده که بی تو گشت بیتاب بود

در چشم منی دایم و این نیست شگفت

زیرا که پری همیشه در آب بود

11

Any heart that lost you is in trouble.
Any eye that fell far from you is anxious.
You are always in my eye, and this is not unusual.
For the fairy is always in water.

۱۲

دی از برم آن یار پسندیده برفت
آرام و قرار از دل شوریده برفت
نتوانستم ز اشک دیدن رویش
تا چشم زدم چو اشکم از دیده برفت

12

Yesterday when that lovely friend of mine was leaving me,
Peace and comfort deserted my frenzied heart.
I could not see his face because of my tears.
With one blink, like tears from my eyes, he went away.

۱۳

تا کی ز فراق دیده پر خون بینم
وز کاهش جان درد دل افزون بینم
گویند خیال او همی بین در خواب
خوابم ناید خیال او چون بینم

13

How long should I see eyes full of blood in separation?
And see my heartache increase as my life decreases?
They tell me to be happy with his image in my dreams.
I cannot sleep. How can I see his image in my dreams?

۱۴

یاری که به خواب بی طلب شاید یافت
خفتم مگرش بدین سبب شاید یافت
در خواب شدم خیالش آمد که مخسب
معشوقه به بیداری شب شاید یافت

14

The friend who may be found in sleep without searching,
I slept so that perhaps I find him in this way.
He appeared in my dream and said: "Sleep not!
"In the wakefulness of the night one may find the beloved."

۱۵

ای دوست که عاشق کشی و زار کشی
یاران گنه نکرده بسیار کشی
من طاقت زخم پر ندارم زنهار
مزدت باشد گرم به یکبار کشی

15

O Friend who kill lovers and kill painfully,
Who kill innocent lovers and kill plentifully,
Beware, I have no tolerance for many wounds.
May you be rewarded if you kill me at once!

نجم الدین رازی
(۶۵۱ هجری قمری)

۱

عشقت که دوای جان این دلریش است
زاندازه هر هوس پرستی بیش است
چیزی است که از ازل مرا در سر بود
کاری است که تا ابد مرا در پیش است

Najmuddin Râzi
(d. 1253 C.E.)

1

Your love, which is the remedy of the soul of this heartsore,
Measures beyond any kind of sensuality. It is something
Which has been in my head since the Primordial Day.
It is some work I have before me for all eternity.

٢

از ما تو هر آنچه دیده‌ای سایهٔ ماست

بیرون ز دو کون ای پسر پایهٔ ماست

بی مایی ما به کار ما مایهٔ ماست

ما دایهٔ دیگران و او دایهٔ ماست

2

Whatever you have seen of me is my shadow.
My rank is beyond the two worlds, my son.
Selflessness is the substance of my work.
He is my nurse while I am the others'.

٣

مقصود وجود انس و جن آینه است

منظور نظر در دو جهان آینه است

دل آینهٔ جمال شاهنشاهی است

وین هر دو جهان غلاف آن آینه است

3

The purpose of existence of jinn and men is a mirror.
That which is viewd in both worlds is a mirror.
The heart is a mirror for the majestic Face.
And the two worlds are the cover of that mirror.

۴

عشاق تو از الست مست آمده‌اند

سرمست ز بادهٔ الست آمده‌اند

می مینوشند و پند می ننیوشند

کایشان ز الست می پرست آمده‌اند

4

Your lovers have come drunk since the Primordial day.
They have come drunk with the wine of *Alast*.
They drink wine and listen to no admonishing.
For they have come drunk since the Primordial Day.

۵

زان پیش که نور بر ثریا بستند
وین منطقه بر میان جوزا بستند
در عهد ازل بسان آتش بر شمع
عشقت بهزار رشته بر ما بستند

5

Before light was tied to the Pleaides
And this region was put in the middle of the Gemini,
On the Primordial Day, like fire to a candle,
Your love was tied to us with a thousand strings.

۶

گه هشیارم ز باده گاهی مستم
گاهی چو فلک بلند و گاهی پستم
گه مؤمن کعبه‌ام گهی کافر دیر
من ز آن خودم چنانکه هستم هستم

6

Sometimes I am drunk with wine and sometimes sober.
Sometimes I am high as the sky and sometimes low.
Either a believer in Ka'ba or an infidel in a tavern,
I belong to myself. I am as I am.

۷

در عشق تو شادی و غمم هیچ نماند
با وصل تو سور و ماتمم هیچ نماند
یک نور تجلی توام کرد چنان
کز نیک و بد و بیش و کمم هیچ نماند

7

In your love, neither joy nor sorrow remained for me.
In your union, neither feast nor mourning remained for me.
One ray of your epiphany made me so that
Neither good and bad, nor much and little remained for me.

٨

مردان رهش زنده بجانی دگرند

مرغان هواش ز آشیانی دگرند

منگر تو بدین دیده بدیشان کایشان

بیرون ز دو کون در جهانی دگرند

8

The men of his path are alive by a different soul.
The birds in his air are from a different nest.
Do not look at them with these eyes.
For outside both worlds, they are from a different world.

بابا افضل

(قرن هفتم هجری قمری)

١

افضل دیدی که آنچه دیدی هیچ است

هر چیز که گفتی و شنیدی هیچ است

سرتا سر آفاق دویدی هیچ است

وان نیز که در کنج خزیدی هیچ است

Bâbâ Afzal
(13th Century C.E.)

1

Afzal, did you see that what you saw was nothing?
Whatever you said or heard was nothing.
Your running around the whole world was nothing.
And your crawling into a corner also was nothing.

۲

بگذر ز ولایتی که آن آن تو نیست
زان درد نشان مده که در جان تو نیست
از بی خردی بود که با جوهریان
لاف از گهری زنی که در کان تو نیست

2

Stay away from a province that does not belong to you.
Do not display a pain which is not in your soul.
It is a folly to boast to jewelers
Of a gem which is not in your mine.

۳

تا گردش گردون فلک تابان است
بس عاقل و با هنر که سرگردان است
تو غره مشو ز شادئی گر داری
در هر شادی هزار غم پنهان است

3

As long as the wheel of the sky turns,
Many men of intellect and art are bewildered.
If you have any pleasure, do not be proud of it.
In every pleasure, a thousand pains lurk.

۴

حلوای جهان غلام کشکینهٔ ماست
دیبای جهان خرقهٔ پشمینهٔ ماست
از جام جهان نمای تا کی گویی
صد جام جهان نمای در سینهٔ ماست

4

The sweetmeat of the world is the slave of my barley bread.
The silk-robe of the world is my woolen cloak.
How long will you talk about the world-viewing cup?
There are a hundred world-viewing cups in my breast.

۵

چندین غم مال و حسرت دنیا چیست
هرگز دیدی کسی که جاوید بزیست
این یک نفسی که در تنت عاریت است
با عاریتی عاریتی باید زیست

5

What is all this worry about property and worldly desires?
Have you ever seen anyone who lived forever?
Your body has borrowed this one breath [that is your life].
What is borrowed must be dealt with as a borrowed thing.

۶

آنانکه مقیم حضرت جانانند
یادش نکنند و بر زبان کم رانند
و آنانکه مثال نای باد انبانند
دورند از او از آن ببانگش خوانند

6

Those who are in the presence of the Beloved,
Seldom mention it or speak about this matter.
And those who are full of wind, like a reed,
Call him loudly because they are far from him.

۷

دل نعره زنان ملک جهان می طلبد
پیوسته حیات جاودان می طلبد
مسکین خبرش نیست که صیاد اجل
سر در پی او نهاده جان می طلبد

7

The heart demands the kingdom of the world roaringly.
It demands immortal life constantly.
The poor thing does not know that
The hunter of death is after it and demands its life.

٨

ای از همه آزرده بی آزار گذر

و ای مست فریب خورده هشیار گذر

آرامگه نهنگ مرگ است دهنت

بر خوابگه نهنگ بیدار گذر

8

O you who were hurt by all, pass by without hurting.
O you who are deceived drunk, pass by soberly.
Your mouth is the resting place of the whale of death.
Over the sleeping place of the whale, pass by wakefully.

٩

روزی که برند این تن پر آز به خاک

وین قالب پرورده بصد ناز به خاک

روح از پی تن نعره زنان خواهد گفت

خاک کهن است میرود باز به خاک

9

The day when they carry this greedy body to the grave
And lay this cherished and nurtured form under the earth,
My soul will say roaringly to my body:
"It is the old earth returning to the earth."

١٠

در جستن جام جم جهان پیمودیم

روزی ننشستیم و شبی ناسودیم

ز استاد چو وصف جام جم پرسیدیم

خود جام جهان نمای جم ما بودیم

10

We traversed the world in search of the Cup of Jamshid.
We did not rest one day and did not sleep one night.
When we asked our master to describe the Cup of Jamshid,
We realized we ourselves were the Cup of Jamshid.

۱۱

در جستن جام جم ز کوته نظری

هر لحظه گمانی نه به تحقیق بری

رو دیده بدست آر که هر ذره خاک

جامی است جهان نما چو در وی نگری

11

In search of the Cup of Jamshid, in your short-sightedness,
You imagine something uncertain every minute.
Obtain a vision! For every particle of dust is a cup
That shows the world if you look carefully.

۱۲

تا در نزنی به هر چه داری آتش

هر گز نشود حقیقت وقت تو خوش

اندر یک دل دو دوستی ناید خوش

ما را خواهی خطی به عالم در کش

12

Until you set fire to everything you have,
You will never have a true enjoyment.
It is not good to have one heart and two loves.
If you want the beloved, cross a line over the world.

۱۳

آن کس که درون سینه را دل پنداشت

گامی دو نرفته جمله حاصل پنداشت

علم و ورع و زهد و تمنا و طلب

این جمله رهند خواجه منزل پنداشت

13

He who thought that the inside of the breast is heart,
Before walking two steps, he fancied the destination.
Knowledge, piety, ascesis, desire, and search —
These are all the road. He thought it was the destination.

اوحد الدین کرمانی
(۶۳۵ هجری قمری)

١

آتش نزند در دل ما الا او
کوته نکند منزل ما الا او
گر جمله جهانیان طبیبم گردند
حل می نکند مشکل ما الا او

Ohaduddin Kermâni
(d. 1238 C.E.)

1

No one sets fire to my heart except him.
No one shortens the road to my destination except him.
If all the people of the world became my doctors,
No one would solve my problem except him.

٢

مؤمن که بصدق از او نرنجد چیزی
در پیش دلش جز او نسنجد چیزی
حق بر عرش است و عرش دانی چه بود
آن دل که درو جز او نگنجد چیزی

2

He is a believer who truly hurts nothing,
And except God his heart reckons nothing.
God is seated in the empyrean. What is the empyrean?
The heart that contains nothing except Him.

٣

گفتم که ز رخ پردهٔ عزت بردار
بسیار کسند منتظر آن دیدار
نیکو سخنی بگفت آن زیبا یار
دیدار قدیم است برو دیده بیار

3

I said, "Take the veil of glory off your face,
"There are many who are anxious to see it."
That beautiful beloved gave a good response:
"The face is always apparent. Go find a vision!"

۴

در عشق اگرچه شور و شر بسیار است
بودن بی عشق رهروان را عار است
عشق است حیات عالم و عالمیان
و آنرا که نه عشق میکشد مردار است

4

Although there is much frenzy in love,
It is a shame for the wayfarers to be without love.
Love is the life of the world and humans.
He whom love does not kill is a carrion.

۵

مجنون پریشان توام دستم گیر
چون میدانی کان توام دستم گیر
هر بی سر و پای دستگیری دارد
من بی سر و سامان توام دستم گیر

5

I am your distressed Majnun, take my hand.
You know that I am yours, take my hand.
Anyone who is in distress has a helper.
I am in distress for you, take my hand.

۶

یارب ز شراب عشق سرمستم کن

یکباره به بند عشق پابستم کن

در هر چه نه عشق است تهیدستم کن

در عشق خودت نیست کن و هستم کن

6

O Lord, make me drunk with the wine of love.
Fasten my feet at once with the chain of love.
Empty my hands from everything except love.
Give me existence. Annihilate me in your love.

۷

دل پرتو لطف تست رایش بفزای

در مقعد صدق خویش جایش بفزای

شهباز سپید عالم پاک است او

این زنگلهٔ خاک ز پایش بگشای

7

My heart is a ray of your grace, increase its awareness.
Open more room for it in the seat of your truth.
It is the white royal hawk of the immaculate world.
Untie this little bell of the earth from its feet.

۸

از تست فتاده در خلایق شر و شور

در پیش تو درویش و توانگر همه عور

ای با همه در حدیث و گوش همه کر

وی با همه در حضور و چشم همه کور

8

It is from you that frenzy has fallen in the creation.
The rich and the poor are all naked in front of you.
You are conversing with all, and all are deaf.
You are present before all, and all are blind.

٩

جز در غم تو شادی من نفزاید

جز در طلبت جان و دلم ناساید

خاک در تو چو سرمه در چشم کشم

ملک دو جهان به چشمم اندر ناید

9

My joy does not increase except in suffering for you.
My heart and soul do not rest except in searching for you.
I rub your door's dust like collyrium on my eyes,
The kingship of both worlds is nothing in my eyes.

١٠

تا با خودم از هر دو جهان بیرونم

چون بی خودم از هر دو جهان افزونم

این حال که هست شرح نتوانم داد

دانم که خوشم ولی ندانم چونم

10

When I am in my *self*, I am out of both worlds.
When I am out of my *self*, I am beyond both worlds.
I cannot describe this condition of mine.
I know I am happy, but I do not know how I am.

١١

هر مرد که او پای در این راه فشرد

در شیشهٔ جام او چه صافی و چه درد

تا سر ننهی پای در این راه منه

کاین راه به بی سری بسر شاید برد

11

Any man who planted his foot on this road,
Pure wine and dregs made no difference in his cup.
Step not on this road if you are afraid of losing your head.
For this road should be traveled without fear for the head.

۱۲

در عشق هزار جان و دل بس نکند

جان خود چه بود حدیث جان کس نکند

این راه کسی رود که در هر قدمی

صد جان بدهد که روی واپس نکند

12

In love, a thousand hearts and souls are not enough.
What is life? It is not even mentioned there.
He who travels this road sacrifices a hundred lives
At every step and never looks back.

۱۳

در دل همه شرک و روی بر خاک چه سود

با جسم پلید و جامهٔ پاک چه سود

زهر است گناه و توبه تریاک وی است

چون زهر بجان رسید تریاک چه سود

13

What good is the face on the dust and the heart full of gods?
What good is clean clothes on a filthy body?
Sin is like poison, repentance its antidote.
What good is antidote when the poison reaches the soul?

۱۴

در راه خدای دو کعبه آمد حاصل

یک کعبهٔ صورتی و یک کعبهٔ دل

تا بتوانی زیارت دلها کن

کافزون ز هزار کعبه آید یک دل

14

There are two Ka'bas in the path of God:
One the apparant Ka'ba, the other the heart's ka'ba.
Perform pilgrimage of hearts as many times as you can,
Because one heart is greater than a thousand Ka'bas.

۱۵

هستم بوصال دوست دلشاد امشب

وز غصهٔ هجر گشته آزاد امشب

با یار نشسته و به دل میگویم

یا رب که کلید صبح گم باد امشب

15

I am happy I am united with my beloved tonight.

I am free from the grief of separation tonight.

I am sitting with my beloved and saying in my heart:

O Lord, may the key of the dawn be lost tonight.

۱۶

زنهار پی طبع هوس پیمایت

تاریک مکن روان روشن رایت

تو از سر صدق یک نفس با او باش

تا هر که جز اوست سر نهد در پایت

16

Beware of darkening your brilliant spirit

By following your capricious nature!

Be with Him in all truthfulness for a moment,

So that everyone but Him may put his head at your feet.

۱۷

در بادیهٔ عشق دویدن چه خوش است

وز عیب کسان نظر بریدن چه خوش است

زین سان که من احوال جهان می بینم

دامن ز زمانه در کشیدن چه خوش است

17

To dash in the desert of love, how pleasant!

To look away from the people's faults, how pleasant!

The way I see the conditions of this world,

To turn aside from the world, how pleasant!

۱۸

گر دل ز تو بگسلد به غم بشکنمش
یا از بر خویشتن برون افکنمش
گر دیده بغیر تو بکس در نگرد
یا پر کنمش ز خون و یا بر کنمش

18

If my heart cuts off from you, I will break it with sorrow,
Or I will cast it away from myself.
If my eyes behold anyone except you,
I will either fill them with blood or gouge them.

۱۹

تا ظن نبری که خان و مان محتشمی است
یا خواسته و حکم روان محتشمی است
در درویشی اگر تو قانع باشی
حقا و بجان تو که آن محتشمی است

19

Do not suspect that having a house is richness,
Or having whatever you desire is richness.
If you be content with poverty,
Truly, and I swear by your soul, *that* is richness.

۲۰

افکند بتی به بت پرستی ما را
او راست خبر که نیست هستی ما را
زان می که شب وصال با هم خوردیم
تا روز قیامت است مستی ما را

20

The idol who threw me into idol-worshipping
Knows that I have no existence [without him].
From the wine we drank together the night of union,
I will be intoxicated till the day of Resurrection.

٢١

اندر همه عمر من شبی وقت نماز
آمد بر من خیال معشوق فراز
بگشود ز رخ نقاب و میگفت براز
باری بنگر که از که میمانی باز

21

One night in my whole life, during my prayers,
The beloved's image appeared before me.
He removed the veil from his face and said,
Behold from whom you are staying away!

٢٢

گر کافر از آن کسی که او دشمن تست
بنگر تو بکافری که اندر تن تست
با کافر رومی تو خصومت چه کنی
چون کافر تو درون پیراهن تست

22

If you consider your enemy an infidel,
Behold the infidel who is in your own body.
Why are you so hostile to the Roman infidel
While your infidel is under your garment?

٢٣

عمر از پی افزودن زر کاسته گیر
گنجی به هزار حیله آراسته گیر
تو بر سر آن گنج چو در صحرا برف
روزی دو سه بنشسته و برخاسته گیر

23

Suppose you have spent your life accumulating gold
And have built a treasure through a thousand tricks,
And suppose you have sat on that treasure for a few days,
Like snow in a desert, and then have stood up!

۲۴

در عشق سری و سرفرازی نخرند
خود بینی و کبر و بی نیازی نخرند
سرمایهٔ عشق عجز و بیچارگی است
کانجا جلدی و چاره سازی نخرند

24

In love, pride and vanity have no buyers;
Selfishness, arrogance, and needlessness have no buyers.
The capital of love is destitution and helplessness.
There cleverness and stratagem have no buyers.

۲۵

هر دل که درو عشق نگاری نبود
مرده شمرش که زنده باری نبود
هر دل که درو نباشد از عشق اثر
در هیچ حسابی و شماری نبود

25

Any heart wherein no love of a beauty exists,
Count it dead. For it cannot be considered alive.
Any heart wherein no trace of love is found
Should not be included in any counting or sensus.

۲۶

آنها که مدام شاهدی می جویند
تا ظن نبری کز پی صورت پویند
لطفی که دل کسی بیاساید ازو
آن را به زبان حال شاهد گویند

26

Those who always seek a *shâhed*,
You should not suspect that they are after an appearance.
The beauty from whom someone's heart finds peace,
They call *shâhed* in a figurative language.

٢٧

ای دلشدگان رخت به بستان آرید
چون ژاله سرشک خویش بر گل بارید
روزی دو سه گل پیش شما مهمان است
مهمان دو روزه را گرامی دارید

27

O lovers, bring your chattels to the orchard,
And shed your tears like dewdrops on the rose.
The rose is your guest for only a few days.
Hold dear the guest who stays only a few days.

٢٨

آبی که خللهای دماغ انگیزد
او را چه خوری که آبرویت ریزد
مستی خواهی بادهٔ معنی مینوش
کز بادهٔ گندیده چه مستی خیزد

28

Why should you drink something that should disturb
Your mind and make you lose your honor?
If you want intoxication, drink of the wine of the spirit.
What intoxication can you get from some stinking wine?

٢٩

تا از دم خواجگی و میری نرهی
گر میر سپاهی ز اسیری نرهی
چون طوطی آن خواجه که آن رمز شنید
زین بند قفس تا بنمیری نرهی

29

Until you get rid of the pride of mastership or rulership,
You are not free of slavery even if you are a commander.
Like that man's parrot who heard the secret, unless you die,
You will not be free from the confinement of the cage.

۳۰

نه مهر تو در دل حزین می گنجد
نه مهر تو در هیچ نگین می گنجد
جان خوانمت ارچه بیش ازینی لیکن
در کالبد جسد همین می گنجد

30

Neither can your love in a doleful heart be contained,
Nor can your seal in the bezel of a ring be contained.
I call you my soul, though you are more than that.
Yet in the frame of a body, that is what can be contained.

۳۱

جز حق حکمی که حکم ر اشاید نیست
هستی که ز حکم او برون آید نیست
هر چیز که هست آنچنان می باید
و آن چیز که آنچنان نمی باید نیست

31

Except God there is no judge who deserves to rule.
There is no existent that can escape his rule.
Everything that exists must be as it is.
And what must not be as it is does not exist.

۳۲

خوابی که ندیده ای تو تعبیر مکن
حرفی که نخوانده ای تو تفسیر مکن
پیران حقیقت از تو معنی طلبند
از دیده بگو روایت از پیر مکن

32

Do not interpret the dream you have not had.
Do not comment on the words you have not read.
Spiritual masters want the essence of matter from you.
Speak of what you have seen. Do not quote masters.

۳۳

بستردنی است هر چه بنگاشته‌ام
و افکندنی است هر چه برداشته‌ام
سودا بوده است هر چه پنداشته‌ام
دردا که بعشوه عمر بگذاشته‌ام

33

Erasable is whatever I have written.
Discardable is whatever I have picked.
Fanciful is whatever I have imagined.
Alas, I have lived my life in darkness.

۳۴

در میکده جز بمی وضو نتوان کرد
و آن نام که زشت شد نکو نتوان کرد
افسوس که این پردهٔ مستوری ما
از بس که دریده شد رفو نتوان کرد

34

In a tavern, ablutions but with wine cannot be done.
And when a name is defiled, it cannot be cleaned.
Alas, so many times was this veil of chastity torn
That it can not be mended any longer.

۳۵

ما دوش در مغانه بی باک زدیم
عالی علم کفر بر افلاک زدیم
از بهر بت مغانه‌ای کافر کیش
صد پاره کلاه توبه بر خاک زدیم

35

Last night, I knocked at the tavern's door recklessly,
And raised the banner of blasphemy to the heavens.
For the sake of an infidel Magian idol,
I threw to the ground the ragged hat of repentance.

۳۶

اول ره عشق تو مرا سهل نمود

پنداشت رسد به منزل وصل تو زود

گامی دو سه رفت راه را دریا دید

چون پای در او نهاد موجش بربود

36

At first, the road of your love looked easy to me.
I thought I could soon reach to my destination — your union.
After I had taken a few steps, I saw the road led to a sea.
And when I stepped in, I was snatched by the waves.

۳۷

نام تو برم کار مرا ساز آید

یاد تو کنم عمر شده باز آید

هرگه که حدیث عشق گویم با خود

با من در و دیوار به آواز آید

37

When I mention your name, my work delights me.
When I remember you, my past life returns to me.
And when I tell myself the story of love,
Doors and walls begin to sing with me.

۳۸

ای آمده گریان ز تو خندان همه کس

از آمدن تو گشته شادان همه کس

امروز چنان باش که فردا که روی

خندان تو بدر روی و گریان همه کس

38

O you who came crying while everyone was laughing,
And your arrival made all your people happy,
Be so good today that when you are going tomorrow,
You be laughing while everyone else is crying.

۳۹

جهدی بکن ار پند پذیری دو سه روز

تا پیشتر از مرگ بمیری دو سه روز

دنیا زن پیر است چه باشد گر تو

با پیرزنی انس نگیری دو سه روز

39

Accept this good advice if you would:
Try to die a few days before your death.
The world is an old woman. What happens
If you are not intimate with her for a few days?

همام تبریزی

(۷۱۴ هجری قمری)

۱

ای بیخبران شکل مجازی هیچ است

احوال فلک بدین درازی هیچ است

بر گیر بعقل پرده از چشم خیال

تا بشناسی کاین همه بازی هیچ است

Homâm Tabrizi
(d. 1315 C.E.)

1

O unaware ones, the transient form is nothing.
The story of the universe, though long, is nothing.
Remove the veil from the eye of illusion by your reason,
So that you realize this whole game [of being] is nothing.

٢

میلت بمن ای ای یار موافق عجب است

مهرت بمن ای نگار صادق عجب است

عاشق دیدی در انتظار معشوق

معشوق در انتظار عاشق عجب است

2

Your interest in me, O my favorite friend, is unsusal.
Your love to me, O my true beloved, is unusual.
You have seen a lover waiting for his beloved.
The beloved's waiting for the lover is unsusal.

٣

ای دل مطلب دوا ز معلولی چند

مشغول مشو به مهر مشغولی چند

پیرامن آستان درویشان گرد

باشد که شوی قبول مقبولی چند

3

O heart, ask not for medicine from some sick people.
Do not occupy yourself with some occupied people's love.
Stay around the threshold of dervishes,
So that you become accepted by some accepted people.

۴

در بزم تو هر آنکه ترک هستی نکند

از بادهٔ لبهای تو مستی نکند

در مذهب عاشقی مسلمان نشود

با روی تو هر که بت پرستی نکند

4

Whosoever does not abandon his being in your party,
Does not become drunk with the wine of your lips.
Whosoever does not worship your face, like an idol,
Does not become a believer in the religion of love.

۵

باد سحری رقص کنان می آید

با مژدهٔ یار مهربان می آید

برخیز که تا بر سر ره بنشینیم

کاواز درای کاروان می آید

5

The morning wind dancingly is coming.
With tidings from my kind friend is coming.
Let us rise and sit along the road.
For the sound of the caravan's bell is coming.

۶

شد دوش بر یار حکایت آغاز

از هر بن موییم بر آمد آواز

شب رفت و حدیث ما بپایان نرسید

شب را چه گنه قصهٔ ما بود دراز

6

Last night as my story unfolded before my beloved,
Every root of my hair began to sound.
The night passed but my story did not finish.
It was not the night's fault. My story was long.

۷

یک جوهر روشن است جان من و تو

آگه نشود کس از نهان من و تو

ای دوست میان من و تو فرقی نیست

حیفیم من و تو در میان من و تو

7

One brilliant gem is your soul and mine.
No one can know what is hidden in you and me.
O friend, there is no difference between you and me.
It is a pity to let *you* and *me* stand between you and me.

Chapter Five
14th Century C.E.
8th Century Hejri

علاإالدوله سمنانی

(۷۳۶-۶۵۹ هجری قمری)

۱

یا رب چه خوش است این دل روشن ما

گویی همه نور گشت پیراهن ما

مشکات چراغ ایزد است این تن ما

احسنت زهی روشنی گلشن ما

Alâeddoleh Semnâni
(1261-1336 C.E.)

1
O Lord, how joyful this my lustrous heart is!
It is as if my whole garment has turned into light.
This my body is a niche for the lamp of God.
Well done! How glamorous my rose-garden is!

۲

آن دل که نه عاشق است در عین بلاست

بیچاره کسی که وصل دلدار نخواست

در آرزوی وصل تو باشم لیکن

این کار به آرزو نمی آید راست

2

The heart that is not in love is in real trouble.

He who has no desire for the beloved's union is miserable.

I am desiring your union,

But this work will not be done by only desiring.

۳

ای دوست چو یار بر سر عهد و وفاست

از شحنه و قاضیان مرا بیم چراست

ساقی تو بیا ز جام وحدت در ده

مطرب تو بزن نوا که امشب شب ماست

3

O friend, since my love is keeping his promise and fidelity,

Why should I be afraid of the magistrate and judge?

Sâqi, come and serve the wine from the cup of unity.

Minstrel, play a tune because tonight is my night.

۴

نادیدنت از بخت بشولیدهٔ ماست

ورنه همه عمر مسکنت دیدهٔ ماست

نا دیدن ما برای نزدیکی تست

وین عیب هم از چشم ستمدیدهٔ ماست

4

Your not seeing me is because of my confounded fortune.

Otherwise, you always have your place in my sight.

My not seeing you is because of your nearness.

This, too, is the fault of my oppressed eyes.

۵

چون بی تو دمی زدن محال است ای دوست
بیهوده کدام قیل و قال است ای دوست
تو با همه و همه ترا می جویند
لطفی بکن و بگو چه حال است ای دوست

5

Since it is impossible to take a breath without you,
What commotion is in vain, my friend?
You are with all while all are looking for you.
Kindly explain this condition for me, my friend.

۶

آنرا که نظر بر آن جمال است ای دوست
در هر چه نگه کند حلال است ای دوست
جز روی تو روی دیگری کی بیند
در دیدهٔ او جز تو محال است ای دوست

6

He who has his eyes on your face, O friend,
Whatever he looks at is legitimate for him, O friend.
How can he see any face but yours?
Other than you is impossible in his eyes, O friend.

۷

مگذار که عمرت به تمنا برود
وین جان عزیز از پس سودا برود
آنکس که نشست با تو دی دوش برفت
امروز هر آنکه ماند فردا برود

7

Do not allow your life to pass in wanting
And your dear soul to go after a fancy.
He who sat with you yesterday went away last night.
He who has stayed today will go away tomorrow.

٨

این ذوق و سماع ما مجازی نبود
وین رقص که میکنیم بازی نبود
با بی خبران بگو که ای بی خبران
بیهوده سخن بدین درازی نبود

8

This our excitement and *samâ'* is not a pretence.
This our dancing is not a game.
Tell the ignorant ones, "O unaware ones,
"A discourse can not be so long without any reason."

٩

گر عهد تو بشکند دلم بشکنمش
وز دایرهٔ وجود بیرون کنمش
من دیده برای دیدنت دارم دوست
در غیر تو گر نگه کند بر کنمش

9

I will break my heart if it breaks my promise to you,
And expel it from the sphere of existence.
I love my eyes for the purpose of seeing you.
I will gouge them if they look at any other than you.

١٠

وقت سحری در آمد آن مهرویم
در گوش دلم گفت که ای دلجویم
تو هیچ مباش تا همه من باشم
تو هیچ مگوی تا همه من گویم

10

One morning my moon-faced sweetheart came up to me
And whispered in my ear, "O my desired one,
"You be nothing, so that I be everything.
"You say nothing, so that I say everything."

١١

من شاد زیم چو او بود غمخوارم
آسوده شوم چو او بود تیمارم
فارغ گردم من از غم هر دو جهان
گر در دل خویش یاد او بنگارم

11
I will live happily if he sympathizes with me.
I will be comfortable if he cares for me.
I will be saved from the sorrow of both worlds
If I inscribe his memory in my heart.

١٢

بسیار رهی نیست از اینجا تا او
خود دور نبودست دمی از ما او
اسرار مکن فاش که نیکو نبود
دزدیده خوش است عشقبازی با او

12
It is not a long way from here to him.
Not a single instant was he ever far from us.
Do not disclose secrets! It is not good.
What is good is to love him secretly.

١٣

گفتم صنما نشسته اندر جانی
بیچارگی و عجز مرا میدانی
گر از تو جدا شوم کجا خواهم شد
گفتا تو ز من جدا شدن نتوانی

13
I said, "My darling, you are seated in my soul.
"You know how powerless and helpless I am.
"If I separate from you, where can I go?"
He said, "You can never separate from me."

۱۴

گر پند و نصیحت مرا گوش کنی

روزی می وصل یار من نوش کنی

بر قحبهٔ دنیا تو اگر دل ننهی

با دلبر من دست در آغوش کنی

14

If you listen to my advice and guidance, one day
You will joyfully drink the wine of my beloved's union.
If you do not attach your heart to this world's prostitute,
You will take my beloved in your arms.

۱۵

صد خانه اگر به طاعت آباد کنی

به زان نبود که خاطری شاد کنی

گر بنده کنی ز لطف آزادی را

بهتر که هزار بنده آزاد کنی

15

To build a hundred houses of worship
Is not any better than making one heart happy.
To enslave a free man with kindness,
Is better than to free a thousand slaves.

۱۶

گر بادهٔ وصل یار ما نوش کنی

ذوق می انگور فراموش کنی

کوته گردد زبان جانت به یقین

گر از بدی خلق تو خاموش کنی

16

If you drink the wine of my beloved's union,
You will forget your desire for the grape wine.
And if you stop speaking ill of people,
Your spirit will certainly be at peace.

۱۷

آنرا که ز جام عشق مدهوش کنی
بر وی همه لذتی فراموش کنی
گویاش کنی به ذکر در عالم سر
وز گفت و مگو زبانش خاموش کنی

17

Whom you intoxicate with the wine of love,
You make him forget all other pleasures.
You make him eloquent with *zekr* in the unseen world,
And make his tongue silent from speech.

۱۸

مقصود منم ز کعبه و بتخانه
محروم بود از این سخن بیگانه
در نه قدمی در این میان مردانه
تا کشف شود حقیقت افسانه

18

Of the Ka'ba and the idol-temple, I am the goal.
These words are not for strangers.
Step in this field like a man,
So that the truth of the myth can be revealed to you.

خواجوی کرمانی
(۷۵۰-۶۸۹ هجری قمری)

۱

گر زانکه ترا بکام دل دسترس است
خوش باش که از جهان همین باب بس است
فرصت شمر این نفس که چون در نگری
عالم نفسی و این نفس آن نفس است

Khâjuye Kermâni
(1290-1349 C.E.)

1

If you have obtained your heart's desire, be happy.
For this much is enough from the world.
Know the value of this breath. For if you look carefully,
Existence is but a breath, and this is that breath.

۲

دل در طلبِ محرم و محرم همه اوست
جان بیخبر از همدم و همدم همه اوست
هر چند که او نیست ز عالم خالی
عالم همه ز و پر است و عالم همه اوست

2

The heart is after a confidant while the sole confidant is He.
The soul is unaware of it while the only companion is He.
Although He is not empty of the world,
The world is full of Him and all the world is He.

۳

تا کی دل شوریده مشوش داریم
رخساره بخون دل منقش داریم
چون نیست یقین که حال فردا چه شود
امروز به نقد عیش خود خوش داریم

3

How long should I keep my frenzied heart in anguish,
And keep my face painted with my heart's blood?
Since it is not certain how tomorrow will be,
I shall enjoy my life right today.

۴

آن لعل که گنج شایگان است کجاست
وان آب که آتش روان است کجاست
تا چهرهٔ جان در آن ببینم روشن
آن جام که آیینهٔ جان است کجاست

4

That ruby which is the royal treasure, where is it?
That water which is the liquid fire, where is it?
In order for me to see the face of my soul clearly,
That cup which is the mirror of the soul, where is it?

۵

روزی که من از جهان روم با دل تنگ
گردون زندم شیشهٔ هستی بر سنگ
بر تربت من کسی نگرید جز جام
در ماتم من کسی ننالد جز چنگ

5

The day I leave this world with a doleful heart,
When the heaven knocks the glass of my being on the rock,
Let no one weep over my grave except the cup of wine.
Let no one lament for me except the harp.

سلمان ساوجی
(۷۰۹-۷۷۸ هجری قمری)

۱

از بسکه شکسته باز بستم توبه
فریاد همی کند ز دستم توبه
دیروز به توبه ای شکستم ساغر
و امروز به ساغری شکستم توبه

Salmân Sâvaji
(1310-1377 C.E.)

1

So many times I broke my repentance and remade it
That repentance now cries out against me.
Yesterday I broke a goblet over a repentance.
Today I broke that repentance over a goblet.

۲

ای آنکه تو طالب خدایی بخود آ
از خود بطلب کز تو جدا نیست خدا
اول بخود آ چون بخود آیی بخدا
کاقرار نمایی به خدایی خدا

2

O you, who are seeking God, come to yourself.
Search him in yourself, for God is not separate from you.
First come to yourself. For if you do so,
By God, you will confess to the godhead of God.

۳

درویش برو جامهٔ صورت بر کن

تا در ندهی بجامهٔ صورت تن

رو کهنه گلیم فقر بر دوش افکن

در زیر گلیم کوس سلطانی زن

3

Dervish, go take off the garb of appearance,
So that you do not surrender to the outward form.
Throw the old mat of poverty on your shoulder,
And beat the drum of kingship under the mat.

۴

از جام توام بهره خمار آمد و بس

وز باغ توام بهرهٔ خار آمد و بس

از هر چه در آید بنظر مردم را

در دیدهٔ من خیال یار آمد و بس

4

My share from your cup of wine was headache only.
My share from your garden was a thorn only.
Of all the things that appear in the human vision,
My share was the image of the Beloved only.

عبید زاکانی
(۷۷۱ هجری قمری)

۱

قومی ز پی مذهب و دین میسوزند
قومی ز برای حور عین میسوزند
من شاهد و می دارم و باغی چو بهشت
ویشان همه در حسرت این میسوزند

Obayd Zâkâni
(d. 1370 C.E.)

1

Some people pine for a faith or a doctrine.
And some people pine for the houris of the heaven.
I have wine, a lovely companion, and a garden like paradise.
And all those people jealously pine for these.

۲

در کوچه فقر گوشه‌ای حاصل کن
وز کشت حیات خوشه‌ای حاصل کن
در کهنه رباط دهر غافل منشین
راهی پیش است توشه‌ای حاصل کن

2

Obtain a corner in the street of poverty.
Pick a bunch of crop from the field of life.
Do not stay negligent in the old guest-house of the world.
There is a road ahead of you, obtain some provisions.

۳

از کار جهان کناره خواهم کردن

رو در می و و در مغانه خواهم کردن

تا خلق جهان دست بدارند ز من

دیوانگیی بهانه خواهم کردن

3

I will withdraw from the affairs of the world
And head to the Magians' tavern and wine.
So that the people of the world take their hands off me,
I will make an excuse of insanity.

۴

از دل نرود شوق جمالت بیرون

وز سینه هوای زلف و خالت بیرون

این طرفه که با اینهمه سیلاب سرشک

از دیده نمیرود خیالت بیرون

4

From my heart, yearning for your beauty will not go.
From my breast, desire for your tress and mole will not go.
It is amazing that in spite of all this flood of tears,
From my eyes your image will not go.

شمس مغربی
(۷۴۹-۸۰۹ هجری قمری)

۱

نابرده به صبح در طلب شامی چند
ننهاده برون ز خویشتن گامی چند
در کسوت خاص آمده‌ای عامی چند
بد نام کنندهٔ نکو نامی چند

Shams Maghrebi
(1349-1407 C.E.)

1

Without staying up till dawn a few nights in quest of Him,
And without taking a few steps outside their lower selves,
Some common people, clothed like the special ones,
Have soiled the names of some well-reputed persons.

۲

مردان همه در سماع و نی پیدا نیست
مستان همه ظاهرند و می پیدا نیست
صد قافله بیشتر در این ره رفتند
وین طرفه که هیچ گونه پی پیدا نیست

2

Men are all in *samâ'*, but the reed is not visible.
The drunks can be seen, but the wine is not visible.
A hundred caravans or more have traveled on this road.
It is strange that no traces are visible.

٣

در خانقه از بهر جهت می پویی

در وی همه ذکر از این جهت می‌گویی

تا در جهتی ز بی جهت بی خبری

بگذر ز جهت چو بی جهت می جویی

3

In the monastery, you look for the direction of kebla.
There you do all your prayers facing that direction.
Seeking directions, you are unaware of the Directionless.
Relinquish directions if you are seeking the Directionless.

۴

ای آنکه طریق عشق ما می سپری

باید که بکل ز خویشتن درگذری

تا با خبری ز خویشتن بی خبری

تا بی خبری ز خویشتن با خبری

4

O you, who are traveling in our path of love,
You must let go of your [lower] self completely.
As long as you are aware of yourself, you are unaware.
You are aware when you are unaware of yourself.

۵

بر چهرهٔ یار ما نقاب است جهان

بر بحر وجود او حباب است جهان

در دیدهٔ تشنگان آب هستی

در بادیهٔ طلب سراب است جهان

5

The world is a veil over the face of our Beloved.
It is a bubble in the ocean of his existence.
In the eyes of the thirsty for the water of existence,
The world is a mirage in the desert of quest.

۶

خیزم طرب و نشاط و عیش آغازم
خود را به خرابات مغان اندازم
ز آنجا بقمار خانه راهی سازم
تا هر چه مرا هست بکل در بازم

6

I am going to get up and have some fun and excitement.
I am going to throw myself in the Magains' tavern.
And from there find my way to a gambling house,
And lose completely whatever I possess.

٧

ای حسن تو در کل مظاهر ظاهر
وی چشم تو در کل مناظر ناظر
از نور رخ و ظلمت زلفت دایم
قومی همه مؤمند و قومی کافر

7

O you whose beauty is apparent in all appearances
And whose eye is the seer of all views,
From the light of your face and the darkness of your hair,
Some people are all believers, others disbelievers.

٨

هر چند که در ملک فنا آمدهای
در ملک فنای بی بقا آمدهای
اندر پی تحصیل بقا باید بود
چون از پی تحصیل لقا آمدهای

8

Although you have come to the land of mortality,
The land of transience and no permanence,
You must endeavor to acquire immortality.
For you have come here to obtain a visit .

٩

كس نيست كزو بسوى تو راهى نيست
بى هستى تو سنگ و گل و كاهى نيست
يك ذره ز ذرات جهان نتوان يافت
كاندر دل او ز مهر تو ماهى نيست

9

There is no one from whom there is no path toward you.
There is no stone, no clay, no straw devoid of your being.
It is impossible to find a particle in this world
In whose heart a moon is not shining by your light.

١٠

تو مست خودى و ما همه مست بتو
تو هست خودى و ما همه هست بتو
تا نسبت ما بتو بود از همه روى
داديم از اين سبب همه دست بتو

10

You are drunk by your own self and we by you.
You are existent by your own self and we by you.
In order for our connection with you to be total,
We have all allowed our hands to be held by you.

١١

با آنكه دو كون سر بسر هستى اوست
انسان ز چه مغز گشت عالم ز چه پوست
زين است كه او مردمك چشم وى است
يا ز آنكه بود آينهٔ چهرهٔ دوست

11

If it is only He who exists throughout both worlds,
Why did man become the kernel and the world the shell?
The reason is that man is the pupil of the eye of God,
Or that man is the mirror for the face of the Friend.

۱۲

در روی پری رخان چو در مینگرم
جز روی تو می نیاید اندر نظرم
هر لحظه ز هر پریرخی حسن رخت
بر دیده کند جلوه بوجهی دگرم

12
When I look at the faces of the fairy-faced ones,
Except your face nothing appears in my sight.
The beauty of your face, from every fairy-faced one,
Appears in my eyes in a different way every moment.

خواجه شمس الدین حافظ
(۷۲۷-۷۹۲ هجری قمری)

۱

جز نقش تو در نظر نیامد ما را
جز کوی تو رهگذر نیامد ما را
خواب ارچه خوش آمد همه را در عهدت
حقا که به چشم در نیامد ما را

Khâja Shamsuddin Hâfez
(1327-1390 C.E.)

1
Except your image nothing appeared in my view.
Except your street no passage opened in front of me.
Although everyone slept happily in your time,
To tell the truth, my eyes did not sleep at all.

۲

بر گیر شراب طرب انگیز و بیا
پنهان ز رقیب سفله بستیز و بیا
مشنو سخن خصم که بنشین و مرو
بشنو ز من این نکته که بر خیز و بیا

2

Pick up the pleasure-evoking wine and come.
Secretly from the mean rival, strive and come.
Do not listen to the enemy who says: "Sit down, don't go!"
Listen to these subtle words: "Get up and come!"

۳

گفتم که لبت گفت لبم آب حیات
گفتم دهنت گفت زهی حب نبات
گفتم سخن تو گفت حافظ گفتا
شادی همه لطیفه گویان صلوات

3

I said, "Your lip." She said, "My lip is the water of life."
I said, "Your mouth." She said, "Oh, a lump of candy!"
I said, "Hafez's words were uttered for you
She said, "Joy to all the speakers of subtlties."

۴

ماهی که قدش به سرو می ماند راست
آیینه بدست و روی خود می آراست
دستارچه ای پیشکشش کردم گفت
وصلم طلبی زهی خیالی که تراست

4

That beauty, whose stature truly resembles a cypress,
Was making her face up with a mirror in her hand.
I gave her a towel as a present. She said:
"Are you seeking union with me? You must be dreaming."

۵

تو بدری و خورشید ترا بنده شدست

تا بندهٔ تو شدست تابنده شدست

زانروی که از شعاع نور رخ تو

خورشید منیر و ماه تابنده شدست

5

You are the full moon for whom the sun is a slave.
The sun grew radiant since it became your slave.
It is from the rays of the light of your face
That the sun has become radiant and the moon shining.

۶

هر روز دلم بزیر باری دگرست

در دیدهٔ من ز هجر خاری دگرست

من جهد همی کنم قضا می گوید

بیرون ز کفایت تو کاری دگرست

6

Everyday another burden falls upon my heart,
And another thorn of separation penetrates my eye.
I keep struggling while the destiny tells me:
There is another work beyond your ability.

۷

ماهم که رخش روشنی خور بگرفت

گرد خط او چشمهٔ کوثر بگرفت

دلها همه در چاهٔ زنخدان انداخت

وانگه سر چاه را به عنبر بگرفت

7

My moon, whose face became radiant like the sun,
And whose *Khatt* the stream of *Kosar* surrounded,
Threw every heart in the pit of his chin,
And then sealed the top of the pit with ambergris.

۸

امشب ز غمت میان خون خواهم خفت

وز بستر عافیت برون خواهم خفت

باور نکنی خیال خود را بفرست

تا در نگرد که بی تو چون خواهم خفت

8

Tonight, I will sleep in the middle of blood
And out of the bed of safety while longing for you.
If you do not believe me, send your vision over,
So that it can see how I sleep without you!

۹

نی قصهٔ آن شمع چگل بتوان گفت

نی حال دل سوخته دل بتوان گفت

غم در دل تنگ من از آنست که نیست

یک دوست که با او غم دل بتوان گفت

9

Neither the story of that elegant candle can be told,
Nor the state of the consumed heart can be told.
The sorrow in my heart is there because I have no friend
With whom I can tell the sorrow of my heart.

۱۰

اول به وفا می وصالم در داد

چون مست شدم جام جفا را سر داد

پر آب دو دیده و پر از آتش دل

خاک ره او شدم به بادم در داد

10

First he kindly gave me the wine of union.
When I became drunk, he gave me the wine of cruelty.
With my eyes full of water and my heart of fire,
I became the dust of his road, he cast me to the wind.

١١

نی دولت دنیا به ستم می ارزد
نی لذت مستیش الم می ارزد
نه هفت هزار ساله شادی جهان
این محنت هفت روزه غم می ارزد

11

Neither the wealth of the world is worth its cruelty,
Nor the pleasure of its intoxication worth its pain.
Nor the seven thousand years of joy in the world
Is worth the trouble of seven days of suffering.

١٢

هر دوست که دم زد ز وفا دشمن شد
هر پاک روی که بود تر دامن شد
گویند شب آبستن و اینست عجب
کو مرد ندید از چه آبستن شد

12

Any friend who boasted of loyalty became an enemy.
Any pious one there was became impious.
They say the night is pregnant. How strange!
She did not see a man. How did she become pregnant?

١٣

چون غنچهٔ گل قرابه پرداز شود
نرگس به هوای می قدح ساز شود
فارغ دل آنکسی که مانند حباب
هم در سر میخانه سر انداز شود

13

When the rosebud turns into a flask of wine,
The narcissus makes a goblet in her desire for the wine.
Free is that person's heart who, like a bottle,
Throws his head at the entrance of the tavern.

۱۴

با می بکنار جوی می باید بود

وز غصه کناره جوی می باید بود

این مدت عمر ما چو گل ده روزست

خندان لب و تازه روی می باید بود

14

Beside a stream with wine one must be,
And aside from sorrow one must be.
This our lifetime is ten days long, like that of the rose.
Lips smiling and face refreshing one must be.

۱۵

این گل ز بر همنفسی می آید

شادی به دلم ازو بسی می آید

پیوسته از آن روی کنم همدمیش

کز رنگ ویم بوی کسی می آید

15

This rose from beside a kindred spirit is coming.
Much happiness from it to my heart is coming.
The reason I always keep this rose with me is that
From its color someone's scent is coming.

۱۶

از چرخ بهر گونه همی دار امید

وز گردش روزگار می لرز چو بید

گفتی که پس از سیاه رنگی نبود

پس موی سیاه من چرا گشت سپید

16

Expect anything from the wheel of time.
Tremble like a willow at the revolution of time.
You said there was no color beyond black.
If so, why did then my black hair turn white?

۱۷

ایام شبابست شراب اولیتر
با سبز خطان بادهٔ ناب اولیتر
عالم همه سر بسر رباطیست خراب
در جای خراب هم خراب اولیتر

17

On these days of youth wine is preferable.
With young adults pure wine is preferable.
The world from end to end is a ruined inn.
In a ruined place being ruined is preferable.

۱۸

خوبان جهان صید توان کرد به زر
خوش خوش بر از ایشان بتوان خورد به زر
نرگس که کله دار جهانست ببین
کو نیز چگونه سر در آورد به زر

18

The comely ones of the world can be hunted with gold.
Happily and joyously their fruit can be eaten with gold.
The narcissus, which is the crowned one of the world,
Behold how she, too, lowered her head with gold.

۱۹

سیلاب گرفت گرد ویرانهٔ عمر
و اغاز پری نهاد پیمانهٔ عمر
بیدار شو ای خواجه که خوش خوش بکشد
حمال زمانه رخت از خانهٔ عمر

19

Flood surrounded the ruins of life.
The cup of life began to fill.
Wake up, O *Khâja*! For the porter of time is pulling
Your chattles gradually out of the house of life.

۲۰

عشق رخ یار بر من زار مگیر

بر خسته دلان رند خمار مگیر

صوفی چو تو رسم رهروان می دانی

بر مردم رند تکیه بسیار مگیر

20

Do not blame poor me for the love of the beloved's face.
Nor blame the drunken heart-wounded *rends*.
Sufi, since you know the custom of the wayfarers,
Do not place much reliance on the *rends*.

۲۱

در سنبلش آویختم از روی نیاز

گفتم من سودا زده را کار بساز

گفتا که لبم بگیر و زلفم بگذار

در عیش خوش آویز نه در عمر دراز

21

I hung on her tress supplicantly and said:
"Solve the problem of this lovelorn me!"
She said, "Take my lip and let go of my tress.
"Hang on to pleasant living, not on to a long life."

۲۲

چشم تو که سحر بابلست استادش

یا رب که فسونها برواد از یادش

آن گوش که حلقه کرد در گوش جمال

آویزهٔ در ز نظم حافظ بادش

22

Your eyes, whose master is the Sorcerer of Babylon,
Would that they forgot their sorcery!
Your ears, whose rings are made of beauty,
Would that they made pearl-rings from Hafez's verse!

٢٣

ای دوست دل از جفای دشمن در کش

با روی نکو شراب روشن در کش

با اهل هنر گوی گریبان بگشای

وز نا اهلان تمام دامن در کش

23

O friend, do not support the cruelty of the enemy.
Drink pure wine in front of a beautiful face.
Bare your breast before the people of merit.
And stay away from the unworthy people completely.

٢۴

ماهی که نظیر ندارد به جمال

چون جامه ز تن بر کشد آن مشکین خال

در سینه دلش ز نازکی بتوان دید

ماننده سنگ خاره در آب زلال

24

When that moon, who is peerless in beauty
And has a musky mole, takes off his clothes,
One can see his heart in his transparent chest,
Like a granite stone in limpid water.

٢۵

در باغ چو شد باد صبا دایهٔ گل

بر بست مشاطه وار پیرایهٔ گل

از سایه بخورشید اگرت هست امان

خورشید رخی طلب کن و سایهٔ گل

25

When the zephyr became the rose's nurse in the garden,
It adorned the rose like a beautician.
If you could choose to move between the sun and the shade,
Look for a sun-faced one and the shade of the rose.

۲۶

لب باز مگیر یک زمان از لب جام
تا بستانی کام جهان از لب جام
در جام جهان چو تلخ و شیرین بهم است
این از لب یار خواه و آن از لب جام

26

Do not withdraw your lips from the bowl's lip
Until it grants your desire from the world.
Since bitter and sweet are mixed in the world's bowl,
Take the sweet from love's lip and bitter from the bowl's.

۲۷

در آرزوی بوس و کنارت مردم
وز حسرت لعل آبدارت مردم
قصه نکنم دراز کوتاه کنم
باز آ باز آ کز انتظارت مردم

27

In desire for your kiss and embrace I died.
Pining for your juicy ruby I died.
To make a long story short,
Come back, come back, while waiting for you I died.

۲۸

عمری ز پی مراد ضایع دارم
وز دور فلک چیست که نافع دارم
با هر که بگفتم که ترا دوست دارم
شد دشمن من وه که چه طالع دارم

28

I wasted my whole life in pursuit of my goal.
What benefit have I got from the revolution of the sky?
Whoever I called my friend became my enemy.
Oh, what a luck, what a luck I have!

٢٩

من حاصل عمر خود ندارم جز غم

در عشق ز نیک و بد ندارم جز غم

یک همدم با وفا ندیدم جز درد

یک مونس نامزد ندارم جز غم

29

Of the product of life, I have nothing but suffering.
Of the good and bad of love, I have nothing but suffering.
I saw no faithful companion except pain,
No intimate spouse I have but suffering.

٣٠

ای شرم زده غنچهٔ مستور از تو

حیران و خجل نرگس مخمور از تو

گل با تو برابری کجا یارد کرد

کو نور ز مه دارد و مه نور از تو

30

The veiled rosebud is ashamed of you.
The languishing narcissus is amazed at you.
How can the rose dare to claim equality with you?
For it has its light from the moon, and the moon from you.

٣١

چشمت که فسون و رنگ می بارد ازو

افسوس که تیر جنگ می بارد ازو

بس زود ملول گشتی از همنفسان

آه از دل تو که سنگ می بارد ازو

31

Your eyes, from which enchantment and wizardry rain,
Alas, the arrows of war from them rain.
You took offence from your companions too quickly.
Oh, what a heart you have, from which stones rain!

۳۲

ای باد حدیث من نهانش می گو

سر دل من به صد زبانش می گو

می گو نه بدانسان که ملالش گیرد

می گو سخنی و در میانش می گو

32

O wind, tell her my story secretly.
Tell her my heart's secret in a hundred tongues.
Tell her, but not in a way that may offend her.
Speak to her and between the words tell her my story.

۳۳

ای سایهٔ سنبلت سمن پرورده

یاقوت لبت در عدن پرورده

همچون لب خود مدام جان می پرور

زان راح که روحیست به تن پرورده

33

O you, in whose tress's shade the jasmine is nurtured,
And in whose lips' rubies the pearl of Eden is cultured,
Like your lips, nourish my soul constantly
With the wine which is a soul nurtured in the body.

۳۴

گفتی که ترا شوم مدار اندیشه

دل خوش کن و بر صبر گمار اندیشه

کو صبر و چه دل کانچه دلش می خوانند

یک قطرهٔ خونست و هزار اندیشه

34

You said, "I will be yours, have no anxiety.
"Let your heart rejoice and focus your mind on patience."
Where is patience and what heart? What they call a heart
Is a drop of blood with a thousand anxieties.

۳۵

آن جام طرب شکار بر دستم نه
وان ساغر چون نگار بر دستم نه
آن می که چو زنجیر بپیچد بر خود
دیوانه شدم بیار بر دستم نه

35

Put that pleasure-capturing cup in my hand.
Put that sweetheart-like goblet in my hand.
That wine, which twists around itself like a chain,
Bring forth and put in my hand, for I am mad.

۳۶

با شاهد شوخ شنگ و با بربط و نی
کنجی و فراغتی و یک شیشهٔ می
چون گرم شود ز باده ما را رگ و پی
منت نبریم یک جو از حاتم طی

36

A jolly sweetheart and a harp and a reed,
A cozy corner, some leisure time, and a glass of wine.
When my veins and vessels become warm with wine,
I will not care a barley-corn for Hâtam Tâi.

۳۷

ای کاش که بخت سازگاری کردی
با جور زمانه یار یاری کردی
از دست جوانیم چو بربود عنان
پیری چو رکاب پایداری کردی

37

I wish my luck cooperated with me,
And the friend helped me against the cruelty of time.
When youth stole the bridle out of my hand,
I wish the old age could stand fast like a stirrup.

۳۸

گر همچو من افتادهٔ این دام شوی
ای بس که خراب باده و جام شوی
ما عاشق و رند و مست و عالم سوزیم
با ما منشین اگر نه بدنام شوی

38

If you fall into this net like me,
Many a time shall you be ruined by the cup of wine.
I am a lover, a *rend*, a drunkard, and a world-renouncer.
Do not sit beside me, or else you will lose your good name.

Chapter Six
15th Century C.E.
9th Century Hejri

شاه نعمت الله ولی
(۷۳۰-۸۳۴ هجری قمری)

١

از آتش عشق صنم دلکش ما
افتاده مدام آتشی در کش ما
پروانهٔ سوختهٔ ما را داند
تو پخته نه ای چه دانی این آتش ما

Shâh Ne'matullâh Vali
(1330-1431 C.E.)

1
From the fire of my charming idol's love,
A constant flame has fallen in my breast.
The wing-scorched moth knows my condition.
You are not cooked, what do you know about my fire?

۲

مطلوب خود از خود طلب ای طالب ما
خود را بشناس یکزمانی به خود آ
گر عاشق صادقی یکی را دو مگو
کافر باشی اگر بگوئی دو خدا

2

O you who seek me, search in yourself your desired one.
Know yourself and come to yourself for a while.
If you are an honest lover, do not call the One two.
You will be a blasphemer if you say there are two gods.

۳

در جام جهان نما نظر کن همه را
آنگه ز وجود خود خبر کن همه را
گفتی که خیال غیر باشد در دل
لطفی کن و از خانه بدر کن همه را

3

In the world-viewing cup behold all.
Then of your existence inform all.
You said the thought of the other is in your heart.
Do yourself a favor. Expel from your house all.

۴

علمی که ترا پاک کند از من و ما
ما القدسش نام کند مرد خدا
خواهی که حدث پاک شود از تو تمام
بر خیز و بشو جامهٔ هستی و بیا

4

The knowledge that cleans you of *I* and *we*,
The man of God calls it *divine knowledge*.
If you want all the filth to be cleaned from you,
Get up, wash the garment of existence, and come.

۵

در دیدۀ ما نور خدا را بطلب

در بحر در آ و عین ما را بطلب

سلطان سراپردۀ توحید بجو

ور درد دلت هست دوا را بطلب

5

Discover the light of God in my eyes.
Come to the ocean and look for my real being.
Search for the sultan of the palace of unity.
And if there is any pain in your heart, ask for remedy.

۶

عالم چو سراب است و نماید سر آب

نقشی و خیالیست که بینند بخواب

در بحر محیط چشم ما ر ابنگر

کان آب حیات را نموده به حباب

6

The world is like a mirage that looks like water.
It is a phantom or an apparition seen in a dream.
In the ocean of existence, look at my eyes
That make the water of life look like a bubble.

۷

عشقست که جان عاشقان زنده از اوست

نوریست که آفتاب تابنده از اوست

هر چیز که در غیب و شهادت یابی

موجود بود ز عشق و پاینده از اوست

7

Love is what makes lovers live.
It is the light that makes the sun shine.
Anything that you find in the open or in the secret
Exists and is sustained by love.

٨

در دیدهٔ ما نقش خیالش پیداست

نوریست که روشنائی دیدهٔ ماست

در هر چه نظر کند خدا را بیند

روشنتر از این دیده دگر دیده کراست

8

The impression of his image is apparent in my eyes.
Its radiance is the light of my sight.
My eye sees God at anything it looks.
Who else has a sharper eye than this?

٩

صبح و سحر و بلبل و گلزار یکیست

معشوقه و عشق و عاشق و یار یکیست

هر چند درون خانه را می نگرم

خود دایره و نقطه و پرگار یکیست

9

The dawn, morning, nightingale, and rose-garden are one.
The beloved, love, lover, and sweetheart are one.
However I look inside the house,
The circle, the center, and the compasses are one.

١٠

در مذهب ما محب و محبوب یکیست

رغبت چه بود راغب و مرغوب یکیست

گویند مرا که عین او را بطلب

چه جای طلب طالب و مطلوب یکیست

10

In my faith, the lover and the beloved are one.
The aspiration, the aspirer, and the aspired are one.
They tell me: "Seek His Essence!" What room is there
For seeking? For the seeker and the sought are one.

۱۱

گر کشته شوم بتیغ عشقش غم نیست
ور در هوسش مرده شوم ماتم نیست
گر جامهٔ خلق بر کشند از سر من
تشریف خدائی خدایم کم نیست

11

If I am killed by his love's sword, there is no need to grieve.
If I die in his desire, there is no need to lament.
If they pull out these ragged clothes off my head,
I will still have God's gift of the divine garment.

۱۲

طاعت ز سر جهل بجز وسوسه نیست
احکام وصول ذوق در مدرسه نیست
عارف نشوی بمنطق و هندسه تو
برهان و دلیل عشق در هندسه نیست

12

Worshiping from ignorance is nothing but temptation.
The rules of acquiring yearning are not found in school.
You will not become a gnostic through logic and geometry.
The logic and reason of love are not found in geometry.

۱۳

این عین که عین جملهٔ اعیانست
عینی است که آن حقیقت انسانست
در آینهٔ دیدهٔ ما بتوان دید
اما چکنم ز دیده ها پنهانست

13

This essence, which is the essence of all appearances,
Is that essence which is the reality of man.
It can be seen in the mirror of my eyes.
But what shall I do? It is hidden from the eyes.

۱۴

دل همچو کبوتر است و شاهد باز است

تا ظن نبری که شیخ شاهد باز است

بر شاهد اگر ز روی معنی نگری

بر تو در حق ز روی شاهد باز است

14

The heart is like a pigeon and the *shâhed* like an eagle.
Do not suspect that the Shaykh is a *shâhed*-lover.
If you behold the *shâhed* with your inner eye,
The door of God opens to you from the *shâhed*'s face.

۱۵

او بر دل تو همه دری بگشاده است

در گوشهٔ دل گنج خوشی بنهاده است

در بندگیش ز عالم آزاد شدیم

مقبول غلامی که چنین آزاد است

15

He has opened every door before your heart,
And has laid a pleasant treasure inside your heart.
In slavery to him, I became free from the world.
Blessed is the slave who is so free as this.

۱۶

یاری که دلش ز حال ما با خبر است

او را با ما همیشه حالی دگر است

ما تشنه لبیم بر لب بحر محیط

وین طرفه لب بحر ز ما تشنه تر است

16

The friend who is aware of our hearts
Each time has a different attitude toward us.
We are standing with thirsty lips at the lip of the ocean.
How strange that the ocean's lip is thirstier than ours!

۱۷

آئینهٔ حضرت الهی دل تو است
گنجینه و گنج پادشاهی دل تو است
دل بحر محیط است و در او در یتیم
در صدفی چنین که خواهم دل تو است

17

The mirror of the Divine Presence is your heart.
The royal treasury with its treasures is your heart.
The heart is an ocean containing an *orphan pearl*.
The pearl of such an oyster as I want is your heart.

۱۸

گنجینه و گنج پادشاهی دل تو است
وان مظهر الطاف الهی دل تو است
مجموعهٔ مجموع کمالات وجود
از دل بطلب که هر چه خواهی دل تو است

18

The royal treasury with its treasures is your heart.
The manifestation of God's grace is your heart.
Ask of your heart for all the perfections of being.
For whatever you desire is in your heart.

۱۹

نقشی بخیال بسته کاین علم من است
وان لذت او در این زبان و دهن است
عقل ار چه بسی رفت در این راه ولی
یوسف نشناخت عارف پیرهن است

19

You have called a picture of your mind your knowledge.
This is for the enjoyment of the mouth and the tongue.
Although the intellect traveled far on this road,
It did not see Joseph but only his shirt.

۲۰

در گلشن ما نالهٔ بلبل چه خوشست

نوشیدن مل بموسم گل چه خوشست

گوئی چه خوشست طاعت از بهر خدا

می نوش ببین که خوردن مل چه خوشست

20

How pleasant the nightingale's lament in our rose-garden is!
How pleasant drinking wine in the season of roses is!
You say how pleasant the worshipping of God is.
Drink wine and see how pleasant the drinking of wine is!

۲۱

ذات و صفت و فعل همه آن ویست

بود همه خلق بفرمان ویست

جمعیت عالم و پریشانی او

در مرتبهٔ جمع و پریشان ویست

21

Essence, attribute, and action all belong to him.
The existence of the whole creation is by his command.
The order and the chaos of the world are due to
His states of unity and diversity.

۲۲

عالم بر رندان بمثل جام می است

ساقی و حریف و جام می جمله ویست

دریا و حباب و موج آبست بما

خود جام حباب خالی از آب کی است

22

In the eyes of *rends*, the world is like a wine-cup.
The Sâqi, the drinker, and the wine-cup are all Him.
Bubbles, waves, and the sea are all water for us.
When is the bowl of a bubble empty of water?

۲۳

گم کردن و یافتن همه گردن تست
گر باطل و گر حق همه پروردن تست
گوئی صنم گم شده را یافته‌ام
این یافتن تو عیش گم کردن تست

23

Losing and finding are both up to you.
Either truth or falsehood is of your own doing.
You say that you have found your lost idol.
The joy of your finding is the result of your losing.

۲۴

عشق آمد و عقل رخت بر بست و برفت
آن عهد که بسته بود بشکست و برفت
چون دید که پادشه در آمد سرمست
بیچاره غلام زود برجست و برفت

24

When love came, reason packed up and left.
Reason broke the promise it had made and left.
When the poor slave saw the king walk in drunk,
He jumped to his feet and left.

۲۵

خوش آینه ایست مظهر ذات و صفات
در وی غیری کجا نماید هیهات
هر ساغر می که ساقیم می بخشد
جامیست جهان نما پر از آب حیات

25

The reflector of the essence and attributes is a fine mirror.
How can any image except His appear in it?
Any cup of wine my Sâqi gives is
A world-viewing cup, filled with the water of life.

۲۶

رندان ز وجود و عدم دم نزنند

از ملک حدوث وز قدم دم نزنند

باشند مدام همدم جام شراب

می مینوشند و دمبدم دم نزنند

26

Rends do not speak of being and non-being.

Nor do they speak of the transient and the permanent.

They are always companions of the cup of wine.

They drink wine but do not brag about it every moment.

۲۷

هر باده که از حضرت الله دهند

بی منت ساقی به سحرگاه دهند

خواهی که کمال معرفت دریابی

از خود بگذر تا بخودت راه دهند

27

Any wine which is from Allah the Exalted,

Is given at dawn without being obliged to Sâqi.

If you wish to obtain the perfection of mystical knowledge,

Cross over your ego so that you can enter your real self.

۲۸

رند آن باشد که میل هستی نکند

وز خویش گذشته خودپرستی نکند

در کوی خرابات مغان رندانه

می نوش کند مدام و مستی نکند

28

He is a *rend* who is not desirous of existence.

Having gone beyond his ego, he is not an egotist.

In the street of the Magians' tavern,

He constantly drinks wine but does not act drunkenly.

۲۹

در عشق تو شادی و غمم هیچ نماند
با وصل تو سود و ماتمم هیچ نماند
یک نور تجلی توام کرد چنان
کز نیک و بد و بیش و کمم هیچ نماند

29

In your love, no joy and no sorrow remained for me.
In your union, no gain and no loss remained for me.
One ray of your manifestation made me so that
Neither good nor bad, nor much nor little remained for me.

۳۰

دل میل به صحبت نگاری دارد
با ساقی و مستی سر و کاری دارد
چون بلبل مست در چمن میگردد
گویا که هوای گلعذاری دارد

30

My heart has a desire for the company of a lovely one.
She wants to be involved with the Sâqi and drunkenness.
She wanders like a drunk nightingale in the meadow.
She is after a rosy-cheeked one, as it were.

۳۱

بودش بکمال خویش بودم بخشید
لطفش بکرم شهد و شهودم بخشید
او طالب من که ظاهرش گردانم
من طالب او که تا وجودم بخشید

31

His being in its perfection granted me my being.
His grace in its generosity sweetened me with his presence.
He wanted me so that I would make him manifest.
I wanted him so that he would give me my being.

۳۲

در مجلس ما که ترک می نتوان کرد
با عقل بیان عشق وی نتوان کرد
چون اوست حقیقت وجود همه چیز
ادراك وجود هیچ شیئ نتوان کرد

32

In our assembly, where wine cannot be avoided,
It is impossible to explain His love to reason.
Since He is the reality of the being of all things,
It is impossible to understand the being of anything.

۳۳

عمری بخیال تو گذاریم دگر
جانرا بهوای تو سپاریم دگر
باز آ که بجان دل همه مشتاقیم
بی تو نفسی صبر نداریم دگر

33

We would spend another lifetime thinking of you,
And end another life aspiring for you.
With all our souls, we are longning for you.
Come back, for we cannot wait another moment for you.

۳۴

کو دل که بداند نفسی اسرارش
کو گوش که بشنود ز من گفتارش
معشوق جمال می نماید شب و روز
کو دیده که تا بر خورد از دیدارش

34

Where is the heart that would understand his secrets?
Where is the ear that would hear his words from me?
The Beloved is showing His face day and night.
Where is the eye that would delight in seeing his face?

ابوالوفا خوارزمی
(۸۳۵ هجری قمری)

۱

ای آنکه تو عقل و جان جانی
چه جای چنین سخن که صد چندانی
چون روی تراست نور روی تو حجاب
زان روی ز پیدایی خود پنهانی

Abulvafâ Khârazmi
(d. 1432 C.E.)

1

You are the reason of reason and the soul of soul.
But why say such words? You are much more than these.
Because the light of your face veils your face,
You are hidden from the eyes, being so glaringly apparent.

۲

در چشم تو گرچه شکل بسیار آمد
چون در نگری یکی به تکرار آمد
گر قدرت و فعل هست ما را نه ز ماست
زان است که حق بما پدیدار آمد

2

Although many forms appear to your eyes,
If you look carefully, it is One which is repeated.
If we have any power or action, it is not from us.
It is because God has manifested himself through us.

۳

من از تو جدا نبوده‌ام تا بودم

وین هست دلیل طالع مسعودم

در ذات تو ناپدیدم ار معدومم

در نور تو ظاهرم اگر موجودم

3

As long as I have been, never was I separate from you.
And this is the proof of my happy fortune.
When I am nonexistent, I am invisible in your essence.
When I am existent, I am visible in your light.

۴

او هست نهان و آشکارست جهان

بل عکس بود شهود اهل عرفان

بل اوست همه چه آشکار و چه نهان

گر اهل حقی غیر یکی هیچ مدان

4

He is hidden and the world is apparent.
Yet the mystics' testimonies are different.
He is all, whether hidden or apparent.
If you are a man of Truth, know none but the One.

۵

جز عشق ز عشق هیچ مقصود مجوی

از جان و جهان بگذر و بهبود مجوی

آن کس که زیان نکرد سودی نکند

چون هیچ زیان نکرده ای سود مجوی

5

In love seek no purpose except love!
Let life and the universe go, and seek no recovery!
He who had no loss will have no profit.
If you have not had any loss, seek no gain!

۶

در جان منی و از تو هستم دور
چشمم بتو روشن وز دیدار تو کور
مشکلتر از این کرا فتد واقعه‌ای
تو با من و من از تو جدا و مهجور

6

You are in my soul, yet I am far from you.
My eyes are illumined by you, yet I am blind before you.
To whom could occur a more difficult event than this
That you be with me and I be separate and distant from you?

۷

در سینه کسی که درد پنهانش نیست
چون زنده نماید او ولی جانش نیست
رو درد طلب که علت بیدردی
دردیست که هیچگونه درمانش نیست

7

He who has no hidden pain in his breast,
Looks alive but has no soul.
Go seek the pain! For the disease of painlessness
Is an illness with no cure whatsoever.

۸

در مذهب آنکه عقل او هست تمام
هستی‌ها را جز به عدم نیست قیام
تا نیست نگردی نشوی هست از آنک
هستی است که نیستی نهادندش نام

8

In the creed of the one whose wisdom is complete,
Existents are erected upon but nonexistence.
Unless you become nonexistent, you will not exist.
Because what is called nonexistence is existence.

٩

بنگر که چه گفت عشق با عقل سلیم
من خضر زمان و تو موسی کلیم
خواهی که شوی ز صحبتم برخوردار
یکسوی نه اعتراض و بنما تسلیم

9

See what love said to reason:
I am Elias, the Immortal; and you Moses, the Interlocutor.
If you want to benefit from my company,
Put aside all objections and surrender.

١٠

از تست هم انتظار و هم بذل مراد
از تست غم غمزده و شادی شاد
هر جا که دریست بسته یا بگشاده
جز قدرت کاملت نبست و نگشاد

10

Desiring and granting of the desire are both from you.
So are the woe of the woeful and the joy of the joyful.
Any door which is opened or closed,
But your absolute power opened not and closed not.

١١

بر عقل چو کشف پرده ها بود محال
عقل از پس پرده کرد از عشق سؤال
تا هست رونده هستی اوست حجاب
ور نیست شود که بهره یابد ز وصال

11

Because it could not possibly see behind the veils,
Reason asked love from behind the curtain:
"As long as a wayfarer exists, his existence is an obstacle;
"And if he becomes nonexistent who benefits of the union?"

۱۲

آنکس که اسیر ننگ و نام است هنوز
اندر ره عشق ناتمام است هنوز
دردا که مرا دلیست کز آتش عشق
عمریست که میسوزد و خام است هنوز

12

He who is concerned about fame or infamy
Is still incomplete in the path of love.
My heart has been burning in the fire of love all my life,
But, alas, it is still uncooked.

۱۳

تا نگذری ای دل ز سر جان و جهان
ننمایدت آن جان جهان روی عیان
تا با خبری ز هستیت بی خبری
زان هستیها که هست بیرون ز گمان

13

O heart, unless you give up life and the universe,
That Soul of the World will not reveal his face to you.
As long as you are aware of your own existence,
You are unaware of the existences beyond imagination.

۱۴

خاموش نشین و گفت و گو را بگذار
کز راه سخن به دل در آیند اغیار
دل خانهٔ حق است نگاهش میدار
تا غیر خدا در او نباشد دیار

14

Stop talking and be silent!
For strangers enter your heart by way of words.
Your heart is the house of Truth.
Take care no one be there but God.

۱۵

ای سر تو در سینهٔ هر محرم راز

پیوسته در رحمت تو بر همه باز

هر کس که به درگاه تو آید به نیاز

محروم ز درگاه تو کی گردد باز

15

O you, whose secret is in every confidant's heart,
And whose door of blessing is open all the time,
When does anyone who comes in need to your door
Ever return disappointed from it?

۱۶

جهدی بنمای تا دلت دل گردد

استاد فنون مشکلت دل گردد

گر حامل دفتر نشوی در رهٔ عشق

محمول شوی و حاملت دل گردد

16

Make an effort to make a true heart of your heart.
Let your master of difficult skills be your heart.
If you do not carry a book in the path of love,
You will be the carried and your heart the carrier.

۱۷

آزاد شو ای دل این و آن را بگذار

پابستهٔ تن مباش جان را بگذار

کم باش و بشوی دفتر فضل و هنر

گم باش و علامت و نشان را بگذار

17

O heart, become free and let everything go.
Be not chained to the body, let life go.
Be little, wash the book of knowledge and art.
Lose yourself, let the marks and signs go.

۱۸

چون کار تو نیست صبر بر محنت و درد
رو نامهٔ فقر و نیستی را بنورد
بگذار حدیث ترک و تجرید و سلوک
زنهار بگرد این عبارات مگرد

18

If you have no patience for pain and tribulation,
Go close the book of poverty and inexistence.
Forget the story of renunciation, devotion, and liberation.
Beware of carelessly using such terms of expression!

۱۹

آمد بر من خیال او نیم شبان
گفتم که نثار پای تست این دل و جان
گفتا چه دل و چه جان ترا ملک کجاست
آسان باشد سخاوت از مال کسان

19

His vision came to me in the middle of the night.
"I shall offer my heart and soul at your feet," said I.
"What heart? What soul? What do you own?" said he.
"It is easy to be generous with other people's possessions."

۲۰

بیرون ز جهان تو جهانی است عجب
کو را نتوان شرح و بیان کرد به لب
اسباب مسببات از آنجاست و لیک
آنجا نه مسببی ببینی نه سبب

20

An amazing world outside your world exists,
To describe which no word or phrase exists.
The cause of all causes is from there.
Yet there neither cause nor effect exists.

۲۱

از حضرت بیکران رسد حد و کران

از عالم بی نشان رسد نام و نشان

آنجا که از او زمان رسیدست و مکان

آنجا نه مکان است پدید و نه زمان

21

All borders and boundaries are from the boundless.
All names and signs are from the signless.
The place from where space and time have originated,
There neither space nor time is visible.

۲۲

از شادی بی قیاس بر رغم حسود

گر چرخ زنم رواست چون چرخ کبود

زانروی که ذاتی و صفاتی که مراست

از ذات و صفات پاک او شد موجود

22

In this incomparable joy of mine, it is all right if I whirl,
Like the blue sky, and against the jealous one's wish.
For the reason that my essence and attributes
Came into existence from His pure essence and attributes.

۲۳

بی حکم و ارادت خداوند جواد

چیزی ز عدم به هستی ما ننهاد

چون اوست مرید و غیر او جمله مراد

پیوسته ز بود خویش خوشوقتم و شاد

23

Without the will and command of the generous God,
Nothing came into being from nonbeing.
Since He is the willer and all else the willed,
I am always happy and pleased with my own being.

۲۴

از سلسله های قیدها آزادم

زیرا که من از وجود مطلق زادم

چون هستی من از اثر هستی اوست

از هستی خویشتن همیشه شادم

24

I am free from the chains of bondages.
Because I was born from the Absolute Being.
Since my being is effected by his Being,
I am ever pleased with my being.

۲۵

تا از ره و رسم خلق گشتم آزاد

عیشی است مرا همیشه بر وفق مراد

در ظاهر اگر غمین نمایم خود را

بهر غرض است ورنه من هستم شاد

25

Since I freed myself from the people's habits and customs,
My life has always been according to my wish.
If I show myself sad in appearance,
It is intentional. Otherwise I am happy indeed.

۲۶

خوشوقتم و شادم که از آن شاه شهان

هر لحظه رسد رسولم از راه نهان

گوید دو سه روز باش بر حبس هنوز

تا باز رهانمت ازین جان و جهان

26

I am cheerful and joyful that from the King of kings
A messenger comes to me secretly every moment and says:
"Stay in this prison a few more days yet
"Before I deliver you from this life and world."

۲۷

ای آنکه تویی مقصد مجموع امم
بر تر ز وجودی و منزه ز عدم
در راه تو هست عقل بینا اکمه
در وصف تو هست نفس ناطق ابکم

27

O you who are the goal of all nations,
You are higher than being and free from nonbeing.
The seeing reason is blind in your way.
The eloquent self is mute in your description.

۲۸

در وادی حیرت هر که افتاد چو من
عقل و دل و دین ببا د بر داد چو من
دینش همه کفر گشت و کفرش همه دین
تا لاجرم از هر دو شد آزاد چو من

28

Whoever fell in the valley of amazement like me,
Cast his reason, faith, and heart to the wind like me.
His faith became blasphemy, and his blasphemy faith,
Until he inevitably became free from both like me.

۲۹

ای روی تو در هر آینه بنموده
وی آینهٔ جمال خود خود بوده
خود دیده بهر دیده جمال خود را
خود گفته بهر زبان و خود بشنوده

29

O you whose face is visible in every mirror,
You who are your own face's mirror,
You yourself see your own face in every mirror.
You yourself speak and hear in every language.

۳۰

ای آنکه به جز تو نیست در هر دو جهان

برتر ز خیالی و منزه ز گمان

هرچند که عین هر نشانی لیکن

اینست نشانت که ترا نیست نشان

30

O you who alone exist in both worlds,
You are higher than imagination and beyond doubt.
Although you are the reality behind every sign,
Your only sign is that you have no sign.

عبدالرحمن جامی

(۸۱۷-۸۹۸ هجری قمری)

۱

در صورت آب و گل عیان غیر تو کیست

در خلوت جان و دل نهان غیر تو کیست

گفتی که ز غیر من بپرداز دلت

ای جان و جهان در دو جهان غیر تو کیست

Abdurrahmân Jâmi
(1414-1493 C.E.)

1

Who is visible in the forms of water and earth except you?
Who is hidden inside the heart and soul except you?
You said, "Polish your heart from everything except me."
O Soul of the world, who exists in both worlds except you?

۲

روزم به غم جهان فرسوده گذشت

شب در هوس بوده و نابوده گذشت

عمری که ازو دمی جهانی ارزد

القصه به فکرهای بیهوده گذشت

2

My days in suffering for this decrepit world passed.

My nights in desiring for what is and what isn't passed.

A lifetime, each moment of which was worth a world,

To put it in a nutshell, in having futile thoughts passed.

۳

خوش آنکه ز قید خودپرستی برهیم

وز تنگدلی و تنگدستی برهیم

بینیم فضای راحت آباد عدم

وز محنت تنگنای هستی برهیم

3

How pleasant it would be if we were free from

The fetters of egotism and from misery and poverty!

How pleasant if free from the sorrow of the prison of being,

We could see the peaceful and open space of nonbeing!

۴

دیدار تو ای یار پسندیدهٔ من

حیف است بدین دیدهٔ غمدیدهٔ من

در دیدهٔ من نشین و بگشای نقاب

خود بین رخ خویش لیکن از دیدهٔ من

4

It is a pity, O my beloved friend,

To see you with these sorrowful eyes of mine.

Enter my eyes and take off your veil.

See your face yourself but through my eyes.

۵

چون دیده ببندم بخیال تو خوشم
ور بگشایم به خط و خال تو خوشم
القصه چه در خواب و چه در بیداری
دایم به تماشای جمال تو خوشم

5

If I close my eyes, I am happy with your thought.
If I open my eyes, I relish your beautiful features.
In short, whether I am awake or asleep,
I am always happy watching your beauty.

۶

در دیده ز تو ابر بهاری دارم
بر چهره شکفته لاله‌زاری دارم
لطفی بنما و برقع از طلعت خویش
بگشا که عظیم انتظاری دارم

6

Because of you I have a spring cloud in the eye,
And a blooming tulip-field in the face.
Do me a favor, take off the veil from your face,
For I have a great expectation from you.

۷

یا رب ز دو کون بی نیازم گردان
وز افسر فقر سرفرازم گردان
در راه طلب محرم رازم گردان
زان ره که نه سوی تست بازم گردان

7

O Lord, make me needless of both worlds,
And honor me with the crown of poverty.
In the path of the quest, make me confidant to your secrets.
And turn me back from the way which does not lead to you.

٨

ای خواجه بسوی اهل دل منزل کن

در پهلوی اهل دل دلی حاصل کن

خواهی که ببینی جمال معشوق ازل

آیینهٔ تو دل است رو در دل کن

8

O *khája*, settle down in the street of the men of heart.

Acquire a heart beside the men of heart.

If you want to see the face of the Eternal Beloved,

Your mirror is your heart, turn your face toward your heart.

٩

ای حسن بتان ماه سیما از تو

وی جانبشان میل دل ما از تو

خون شد دل ما ز دست ایشان یا رب

ز یشان نالیم یا ز خود یا از تو؟

9

O Lord, the beauty of the moon-faced idols is from you.

And our hearts' tendency toward them is from you.

O Lord, our hearts bled because of them.

Should we complain of them, of ourselves, or of you?

١٠

ای از تو مرا گوش پر و دیده تهی

خوش آنکه ز گوش پای در دیده نهی

تو مردم دیده‌ای نه آویزهٔ گوش

از گوش به دیده آ که در دیده بهی

10

O you, from whom my ears are full but my eyes empty,

It would be nice if you stepped into the eye from the ear.

You are the pupil of the eye, not the ring of the ear.

Come from the ear to the eye, for you are better in the eye.

۱۱

خون میگریم و ز تو چه پنهان دارم
وز بهر چه این دو چشم گریان دارم
هر چند دلی به وصل شادان دارم
صد چاک در او ز بیم هجران دارم

11

I am weeping blood. How can I hide it from you?
Why do I have these two tearful eyes for?
Although my heart is rejoicing at your union,
It has a hundred misgivings from the fear of disunion.

۱۲

گر در دل تو گل گذرد گل باشی
ور بلبل بیقرار بلبل باشی
تو جزوی و او کل است اگر روزی چند
اندیشهٔ کل پیشه کنی کل باشی

12

If a rose occurs to your heart, you will become a rose;
And if a restless nightingale, you will become a nightingale.
You are a part, He is the whole. If you make a habit to think
Of the whole for a while, you will become the whole.

۱۳

ای آنکه به قبلهٔ بتان روست ترا
بر مغز چرا حجاب شد پوست ترا
دل در پی این و آن نه نیکوست ترا
یک دل داری بس است یک دوست ترا

13

O you whose face is toward the *qebla* of idols,
Why has a shell become the veil over the kernel for you?
It is not good for you to let your heart go after this and that.
You have one heart. One beloved is enough for you.

۱۴

همسایه و همنشین و همره همه اوست
در دلق گدا و اطلس شه همه اوست
در انجمن فقر و نهانخانهٔ جمع
بالله همه اوست ثم بالله همه اوست

14
The neighbor, the companion, and co-traveler are all him.
Under the beggar's rags and the king's silk-robe is all him.
In the assembly of *faqr* and the seclusion of meditation,
It is all him. By God, it is all him.

Chapter Seven
16th Century C.E.
10th Century Hejri

بابا فغانی شیرازی

(۹۲۵ هجری قمری)

۱

ساقی قدحی که از میان خواهم رفت

آشفته و مست از میان خواهم رفت

در آمدنم نبود از هیچ خبر

آندم که روم نیز چنان خواهم رفت

Bâbâ Faghâni Shirâzi
(d. 1519 C.E.)

1

A cup of wine, Sâqi! For I will be gone.
Amazed and drunk, I will be gone.
When I arrived, I was not aware of anything.
When I depart, the same way I will be gone.

۲

می نوش که شد چمن زرافشان ز خزان

رخ چون گل آتشین کن از آب رزان

کز خاک بسی سرو قد لاله عذار

آیند روان روند چون باد وزان

2

The autumn scattered gold in the meadow, drink wine!
Make your face like the red rose with grape wine.
For many with statures like cypress and cheeks like tulip
Come out of the dust and go with the wind.

۳

آن قوم که اسرار ازل بنهفتند

در پردهٔ دل گوهر وحدت سفتند

گر غیرت آن نبودی و ترک ادب

آن نکته که بود گفتنی می گفتند

3

Those who kept the eternal secrets hidden
Pierced the pearl of unity in the seclusion of their hearts.
If it had not been against their guardianship and politeness,
They would have told the subtlety which was worth telling.

میر نصرت کرمانی
(۹۲۰ هجری قمری)

۱

افسوس که آنچه برده‌ام باختنی است
بشناخته ها تمام نشناختنی است
انداخته‌ام هر آنچه باید بر داشت
برداشته‌ام هر آنچه انداختنی است

Mir Nosrat Kermâni
(d. 1514 C.E.)

1

Alas, what I have won must be lost.
All that is learned must be unlearned.
I have discarded everything which had to be taken.
I have taken everything which must be discarded.

اهلی شیرازی
(۸۵۸-۹۴۲ هجری قمری)

١

ساقی دل ما که شادی از غم نشناخت
جز جام می از نعیم عالم نشناخت
می ده که دم صبوح جانبخش دمی است
کس غیر مسیح قدر این دم نشناخت

Ahli Shirâzi
(1454-1536 C.E.)

1

O Sâqi, my heart, which could not tell joy from sorrow,
Of the pleasures of the world, has known nothing but wine.
Give wine, for the breath of the morning wine is life-giving.
None but the Messiah knew the value of this breath.

٢

ساقی می لعل قوت روح است مرا
دیدار تو خورشید صبوح است مرا
برخیز که در پای تو مردن نفسی
بهتر ز هزار عمر نوح است مرا

2

Sâqi, ruby wine is the food for spirit for me.
Your face is the sun of the morning for me.
Rise! For one moment of dying at your feet is
Better than a thousand lifetimes of Noah for me.

۳

ساقی قدحی که کار دنیا همه هیچ

این گفت و شنید و جنگ و غوغا همه هیچ

طوفان فنا چو بشکند کشتی عمر

عالم همه هیچ و حاصل ما همه هیچ

3

A cup of wine, Sâqi! For the world's affairs are nothing.
These arguments, conflicts, and tumults are nothing.
When the storm of annihilation breaks the ship of life,
This whole world and all our gains from it are nothing.

۴

ساقی قدحی که من به بستان نروم

بی روی تو در روضهٔ رضوان نروم

تا سر بودم قدم در این راه نهم

تا جان بودم ز کوی جانان نروم

4

A cup of wine, Sâqi! To the orchard I will not go.
Without you, to the paradise I will not go.
As long as I have my head, my feet will walk on this way.
As long as I live, out of the beloved's lane I will not go.

۵

ساقی قدحی که هست عالم نفسی

وین یک نفس آن به که شود صرف کسی

نیکان گل عالمند و باقی خس و خار

با شاخ گلی نشین نه با خار و خسی

5

A cup of wine, Sâqi! For the world is but one breath.
And this one breath better be spent beside someone.
Good people are the flowers of the world, the rest weeds.
Sit beside a branch of flowers, not throns and weeds.

۶

عمر تو اگر به خواب غفلت گذرد

آن عمر کسی بزندگی کی شمرد

گر فهم کنی که ذوق بیداری چیست

شاید که دگر ز ذوق خوابت نبرد

6

The life spent in the sleep of negligence,
How can one count it as living?
If you ever realize the thrill of wakefulness,
You may not fall asleep again from enthusiasm.

فکری خراسانی

(۹۷۳ هجری قمری)

۱

فانی شو و اقلیم بقا آر بدست

در دوست کسی رسید کز خویش برست

از هستی خویش بود سرگشته حباب

آن لحظه که نیست شد بدریا پیوست

Fekri Khorâsâni

(d. 1566 C.E.)

1

Become annihilated and acquire the realm of eternity.
He reached to the friend who became free from himself.
A bubble is bewildered because of its being.
The moment its being is gone, it merges with the ocean.

٢

بر صفحهٔ هستی چو قلم می گذریم
حرف غم خود کرده رقم می گذریم
زین بحر پرآشوب که بی پایان است
پیوسته چو موج از پی هم می گذریم

2

Like a pen on the page of existence, we are passing.
Having written about our sorrows, we are passing.
In this tumultuous ocean, which has no boundaries,
Constantly, like waves, one after another, we are passing.

٣

سرمایهٔ دولت گرامی عشق است
طغرای نشان نیکنامی عشق است
بی عشق تمام ناتمام آمده‌ای
در مذهب عشاق تمامی عشق است

3

The wealth which is to be cherished is love.
The fame which is the sign of respectability is love.
You are imperfect without perfect love.
In the creed of lovers, perfection is love.

۴

از مملکت وجود می باید رفت
دیر آمده‌ایم و زود می باید رفت
زین بحر هر آنکه سر برون زد چو حباب
تا چشم ز هم گشود می باید رفت

4

From the country of being, we needs must go.
We have come late, and soon we needs must go.
Whoever stuck his head out of this ocean like a bubble,
As soon as he opened his eye, he needs must go.

۵

زهر است شراب ارغوانی بی تو
مرگ است حیات جاودانی بی تو
چون می که جدا ز بزم احباب خورند
تلخ است و حرام زندگانی بی تو

5

Without you the purple wine is poison.
Without you the immortal life is death.
Like the wine drunk outside the friends' party,
Life is bitter and forbidden without you.

۶

ای آنکه ترا بطرف بستان گذریست
بگشای نظر اگر ز خویشت خبریست
هر غنچه حنا بسته سرانگشت بتی است
هر شاخ شکوفه ساعد سیمبریست

6

O you, who are passing through the orchard,
Open your eyes if you have any awareness of yourself!
Every bud is the fingertip of a beloved, dyed with henna.
Every blossoming branch is the forearm of an elegant youth.

۷

یا رب مددی کن که ز هستی برهم
وز نخوت نفس و ننگ مستی برهم
یعنی ز می شوق خودم بیخود ساز
شاید که ز قید خودپرستی برهم

7

O Lord, help me become free from existence,
From the vanity of the self and the shame of unawareness.
I mean, make me selfless by the wine of yearning,
So that I become free from the chain of selfishness.

٨

پیوسته عروس دهر را آرایند

هر لحظه بصورتی دلی بربایند

ما غافل و باهم شده میزان مه و مهر

بر ما شب و روز عمر می پیمایند

8

The bride of the world is adorned continuously.

Every moment someone's heart is somehow stolen.

We are unaware that the sun and the moon have agreed

To carry our lives to their ends through days and nights.

٩

آن قوم که از قید من و ما گذرند

ز اندیشهٔ سود و فکر سودا گذرند

گردند چو خورشید سرآمد که نهند

پا بر سر دنیا و ز دنیا گذرند

9

Those who transcend the bondage of *I* and *we*,

And leave the thoughts of trade and profit behind,

Become prominent like the sun,

For they step on the head of the world and rise above it.

١٠

ای گوشه نشین نرگس جادویی بین

در حلقهٔ ذکر حلقهٔ مویی بین

تا چند بمحراب نماز آری روی

بگذار نماز و طاق ابرویی بین

10

O secluded one, look at the magical eyes.

And see a ringlet of hair in the ring of incantation.

How long shall you face the *mehrâb* of prayers?

Quit the prayers and look at the arch of an eyebrow.

۱۱

ای راحت جان بی تو ز جان دلگیریم

در سلسلهٔ تو بستهٔ زنجیریم

دیدیم ترا یک نظر و جان دادیم

بنگر که برای یک نظر می میریم

11

O comfort of the soul, I am tired of life without you.
I am chained by your chains [of hair].
I looked at you only once and gave my soul.
Look! For I am dying for one look.

۱۲

در خانهٔ خمار صلای عشق است

در پردهٔ عشاق نوای عشق است

بی عشق دلا زندگیت باد حرام

زآنروی که زندگی برای عشق است

12

In the tavern, they are calling for love.
Lovers in their privacy are singing of love.
O heart, may life be forbidden to you without love.
For the reason that life is for the sake of love.

۱۳

آنرا که قضا ز خیل عشاق سرشت

آزاد ز مسجد است و فارغ ز کنشت

دیوانهٔ عشق را چه هجر و چه وصال

از خویش گذشته را چه دوزخ چه بهشت

13

Whom the destiny put in the crowd of lovers,
Is free from mosques and synagogues.
For the frenzied of love, there is no union or disunion.
For the one without self, there is no heaven or hell.

۱۴

سروی که ز خوبی علم افراخته است
رخساره چو شمع لاله گون ساخته است
از باده بیاض دیده گلگون کرده
در خانهٔ مردم آتش انداخته است

14

That cypress who has hoisted the flag of beauty,
Who has made her face, like a candle, the color of the tulip,
Who has made the white of her eyes rosy with wine,
Has set fire to the houses of the people.

۱۵

زاهد می صاف ارغوانی بکف آر
سرمایهٔ عمر جاودانی بکف آر
دایم به کفت رشتهٔ تسبیح چه سود
سر رشتهٔ عمر جاودانی به کف آر

15

O Ascetic, obtain some pure, purple wine.
Obtain the substance of the immortal life.
What good is it to ever hold a rosary in your hand?
Hold in your hand the string of the immortal love.

۱۶

ایام دمی می وصالت ندهد
کز رنج خمار گوشمالت ندهد
این دم که مجالست دمی شاد نشین
شاید نفس دگر مجالت ندهد

16

The world never gives you the wine of union
Without punishing you with the pain of a hangover.
If you have a chance to rejoice this moment, do!
For you may not have another chance the next moment.

١٧

مجنون تو کوه را ز صحرا نشناخت
سودا زده عشق سر از پا نشناخت
هر کس بتو ره یافت ز خود گم گردید
و آنکس که ترا شناخت خود را نشناخت

17
Your Majnun could not tell a mountain from a desert.
The frenzied of love could not tell head from foot.
Whoever found his way to you became lost to himself.
Whoever came to know you became unknown to himself.

سحابی استرآبادی
(۱۰۱۰ هجری قمری)

١

بشتاب پی دیده گشودن خود را
زنگار ز آیینه زدودن خود را
هر چند تو او را نتوانی دیدن
او بتواند بتو نمودن خود را

Sahâbi Astarâbâdi
(d. 1602 C.E.)

1
Hasten to open your eyes up to yourself,
And to wipe out the rust from your mirror!
Even though you are not able to see him,
He is able to show himself to you.

٢

صاحب نظران که زندۀ جاویدند
وارسته ز بیم و فارغ از امیدند
در هر چه نظر کنند او را بینند
ذرات جهان آینۀ خورشیدند

2

The people of perception, who are alive eternally,
Are released from fear and free from hope.
At whatever they look, they see him.
The particles of the world are mirrors of the sun.

٣

وصل تو بهر صفت که گویند خوش است
راه تو بهر قدم که پویند خوش است
روی تو بهر چشم که بینند نکوست
نام تو بهر زبان که گویند خوش است

3

Your union, in any manner they describe it, is good.
Your road, in any way they walk it, is good.
Your face, in any eye they see it, is pleasant.
Your name, in any language they say it, is good.

۴

غم نیست نکو ولی اثرهاش نکوست
تاریکی شب بد و سحرهاش نکوست
عالم پی آن خوش است کاثار وی است
دلاله نکو نیست خبرهاش نکوست

4

Suffering is bad, but its results are good.
The nights' darkness is bad, but their dawns are good.
The world is good because it is His work.
The matchmaker is not good, her news is.

۵

عالم بخروش لا اله الا هوست
غافل به گمان که دشمن است این یا دوست
دریا به وجود خویش موجی دارد
خس پندارد که این کشاکش با اوست

5

The universe is roaring with *There is no God but He*
The unaware suspects one person enemy another friend.
The sea has waves in itself.
The twig [riding the waves] imagines this struggle is hers.

۶

آنها که شراب عاشقی نوش کنند
از هر چه بجز دوست فراموش کنند
آنرا که زبان دهند دیدی ندهند
وآنرا که دهند دید خاموش کنند

6

Those who drink the wine of love
Forget everything but the one they love.
He who is given a tongue is denied vision.
He who is given vision is denied speech.

۷

توحید چو آفتاب تابان شدن است
زین شب پره طبعان چه هراسان شدن است
گر خلق اینند عزلتی حاجت نیست
از کور چه احتیاج پنهان شدن است

7

To believe in Unity is to shine like the sun.
Why fear these people who have the nature of bats?
If these are the people, there is no need for seclusion.
What need is there to hide from the blind?

۸

هان تا که درین آینه آن رو بینی
این هستی این سوی از آن سو بینی
این پردهٔ پندار ز پیشت چو رود
هر چند بخلق بنگری او بینی

8

Behold, see *that* face in *this* mirror,
See the existence of this side from that side.
If this veil of illusion is removed from before you,
However you look at the creation, you see Him.

فیض فیاضی
(۹۵۴-۱۰۰۴ هجری قمری)

۱

باید به ره عشق تکاپو کردن
پیوسته به خورشید ازل رو کردن
زین سان که بود ظهور حق از همه سو
باید ز چه روی روی یکسو کردن

Fayz Fayyâzi
(1547-1596 C.E.)

1

One must strive in the path of love,
And always turn his face toward the primordial sun.
Since the Truth makes its appearance in all directions,
From what direction should one turn his face away?

۲

یا رب قدمی براه توحیدم ده
شوقی به نهانخانهٔ تجریدم ده
دلبستگیی به سر تحقیقم بخش
آزادگیی ز قید تقلیدم ده

2

O Lord, give me strength to walk on the road of Unity.
Give me a yearning for the secret place of freedom.
Grant me an affection for the mystery of Truth.
Grant me a freedom from the bondage of imitation.

۳

آن نیست که ما ارض و سما نشناسیم
تیر قدر و راز قضا نشناسیم
این هژده هزار عالم و هر چه در اوست
نشناخته به اگر ترا نشناسیم

3

It is not that I do not know the earth and the sky,
Or the arrow of fate and the secret of destiny.
These eighteen thousand worlds and all that exists in them,
It is better not to know if I do not know you.

۴

آن ذات که عقل از آن نشان دید نهای
وان نور که دیدهٔ گمان دید نهای
جز نور نهای ولی چو نیکو نگرم
نوری که به این دیده توان دید نهای

4

That essence of which reason saw a sign, you are not.
The light the eye of imagination saw, you are not.
Except light you are not, but when I look carefully,
The light which can be seen by these eyes, you are not.

وحشی بافقی
(۹۹۱ هجری قمری)

۱

وحشی که همیشه میل ساغر دارد
جز باده کشی چکار دیگر دارد
پیوسته کدویش ز می ناب پر است
یعنی که مدام باده در سر دارد

Vahshi Bâfaqi
(d. 1583 C.E.)

1

Vahshi who always tends toward the cup of wine,
What work does he have except drinking wine?
His gourd is always full of pure wine.
That is to say, he always has wine in his head.

۲

میخواست فلک که تلخ کامم بکشد
ناکرده می طرب به جامم بکشد
بسپرد به شحنهٔ فراق تو مرا
تا او به عقوبت تمامم بکشد

2

Heaven wanted to kill me bitterly
Without putting the wine of pleasure in my cup.
He put me in the hands of your separation's ececutor,
So that he kill me with utmost torment.

۳

شد یار و به غم ساخت گرفتار مرا

بگذاشت بدرد دل افگار مرا

چون سوی چمن روم که از باد بهار

دل می ترکد چو غنچه بی یار مرا

3

My beloved went away and made me a captive of sorrow.
He left me with the pain of a wounded heart.
How can I go to the meadow where, without my love,
The wind of the spring bursts my heart open like a rosebud?

۴

فریاد که سوز دل عیان نتوان کرد

با کس سخن از داغ نهان نتوان کرد

اینها که من از جفای هجران دیدم

یک شمه بصد سال بیان نتوان کرد

4

Alas! One cannot make the fire of the heart visible.
One cannot speak of the hidden fire to anyone.
What I saw from the cruelty of separation,
Even one episode of it cannot be told in one hundred years.

۵

تا کی ز مصیبت غمت یاد کنم

آهسته ز فرقت تو فریاد کنم

وقت است که دست از دهن بردارم

از دست غمت هزار بیداد کنم

5

How long should I recall the hardship of your sorrow?
And lament quietly in your separation?
It is time I took my hand off my mouth
And shouted a thousand cries in your sorrow.

Chapter Eight
17th Century C.E.
11th Century Hejri

شیخ بهائی

(۱۰۳۰-۹۵۳ هجری قمری)

۱

از دست غم تو ای بت حور لقا

نه پای ز سر دانم و نه سر از پا

گفتم دل و دین ببازم از غم برهم

این هر دو بباختیم و غم ماند بجا

Shaykh Bahâ'i
(1546-1621 C.E.)

1

Because of your love, O my houri-faced idol,
I am so lost I cannot tell my feet from my head.
I said if I lose my heart and faith, I'll be free from sorrow.
I lost both, but the sorrow is still there.

۲

ای عقل خجل ز جهل و نادانی ما
درهم شده خلقی ز پریشانی ما
بت در بغل و بسجده پیشانی ما
کافر زده خنده بر مسلمانی ما

2

O reason who are ashamed of my ignorance,
Many people are confused about my distracted mind.
With my arms holding an idol and forehead in prostration,
The disbeliever laughs at my being a Moslem.

۳

دنیا که ازو دل اسیران ریش است
پامال غمش توانگر و درویش است
نیشش همه جانگزاتر از شربت مرگ
نوشش چو نکو نگه کنی همه نیش است

3

Both rich and poor are trampled by the agony of the world
Which makes the hearts of its captives sore.
Its sting is more injurious than the potion of death.
Its honey, if you look carefully, is all sting.

۴

شیرین سخنی که از لبش جان میریخت
کفرش ز سر زلف پریشان میریخت
گر شیخ به کفر زلف او پی بردی
خاک سیهی بر سر ایمان میریخت

4

The sweet-spoken one, from whose lips life
And from her dishevelled hair blasphemy was pouring,
If the Shaykh could understand the irreligion of her hair,
He would pour black dirt over the head of his religion.

۵

دی پیر مغان آتش صحبت افروخت
ایمان مرا دید و دلش بر من سوخت
از خرقهٔ کفر رقعه واری بگرفت
آورد و بر آستین ایمانم دوخت

5

Yesterday the Magians' master lit the fire of conversation,
Found about my faith, and felt pity for me.
He cut a piece from the cloak of unbelief,
Brought it over, and patched it on the sleeve of my belief.

۶

حاجی بطواف کعبه اندر تک و پوست
وز سعی و طواف هر چه کردست نکوست
تقصیر وی آن است که آرد دگری
قربان سازد بجای خود در ره دوست

6

Hâji runs around, circumambulating the Ka'ba.
He has done well in his ceremonies of Hajj,
Except that he has failed in his pilgrimage.
For he has sacrificed other than himself in the Friend's way.

۷

در میکده دوش زاهدی دیدم مست
تسبیح بگردن و صراحی در دست
گفتم ز چه در میکده ها جا کردی گفت
از میکده هم بسوی حق راهی هست

7

Last night I saw an ascetic drunk in a tavern,
A rosary around the neck and a cup of wine in hand.
I asked the reason for his being in a tavern. He replied:
"From the tavern, too, there is a path toward God."

٨

در مزرع طاعتم گیاهی بنماند
در دست بجز ناله و آهی بنماند
تا خرمن عمر بود در خواب بدم
بیدار کنون شدم که کاهی بنماند

8

In my devotion's farm, not a single plant has remained.
Nothing but a lament and sigh has remained.
I was asleep when my life was in crop.
Now that I have woken up not a single straw has remained.

٩

آن حرف که از دلت غمی بگشاید
در صحبت دل شکستگان می باید
هر شیشه که بشکند ندارد قیمت
جز شیشهٔ دل که قیمتش افزاید

9

Words that remove sorrow from your heart
Must be used in speaking to the broken-hearted.
Any glass that breaks loses its value,
Except the glass of the heart that gains in value.

١٠

عشاق بغیر دوست عاری دارند
از حسرت آرزوی او می زارند
و آنانکه کنند طاعت از بهر بهشت
عشاق نیند بهر خود در کارند

10

Lovers disdain to be with anyone but the Friend.
They cry and wail in their desperate desire for the friend.
Those who worship for the sake of paradise are not lovers.
They are after their own interests.

۱۱

او را که دل از عشق مشوش باشد

هر قصه که گوید همه دلکش باشد

تو قصهٔ عاشقان همی کم شنوی

بشنو بشنو که قصه شان خوش باشد

11

He whose heart is in turmoil with love,
Any story he says is wholly fascinating.
You seldom listen to the lovers' story.
Listen! Listen! Their story is interesting.

۱۲

تا نیست نگردی ره هستت ندهند

این مرتبه با همت پستت ندهند

چون شمع قرار سوختن گر ندهی

سررشتهٔ روشنی به دستت ندهند

12

Unless you become naught, you're not admitted into being.
You will not be given this high rank with your low effort.
Like a candle, if you do not resolve to burn,
You are not given the radiance of light.

۱۳

بر درگه دوست هر که عاشق برود

تا حشر ز خاطرش علایق برود

صد ساله نماز عابد صومعه دار

قربان سر نیاز عاشق برود

13

Whoever goes to the Friend's door in love,
All attachments leave his heart forever.
A hundred years of prayers by the monastery's ascetic
Is sacrificed for a lover's supplication.

۱۴

گفتم که کنم تحفه‌ات ای لاله عذار
جان را چو شوم ز وصل تو برخوردار
گفتا که بهایی این فضولی بگذار
جان خود ز من است غیر جان تحفه بیار

14

I said, "O rosy-cheeked one, if I be united with you,
"I will offer my life as a present."
He said, "Stop this meddling, Baha'i.
"Your life itself is from me. Bring another present."

۱۵

از نالۀ عشاق نوایی بردار
وز درد و غم دوست دوایی بردار
از منزل یار تا تو ای سست قدم
یک گام زیاده نیست پایی بردار

15

Take some profit from the lovers' lamentation.
Let the pain and grief for the Friend be your medication.
From the Beloved's home to you, O feeble-footed one,
The distance is but one step. Take that step!

۱۶

یک چند میان خلق کردیم درنگ
زایشان به وفا نه بوی دیدیم نه رنگ
آن به که ز چشم خلق پنهان گردیم
چون آب در آبگینه آتش در سنگ

16

For sometime, I dallied among the people, and neither
Smelt the scent nor saw the color of fidelity from them.
It is better that I hide from the eyes of the people,
Like water in glass and fire in stone.

۱۷

یک چند در این مدرسه ها گردیدم

از اهل کمال نکته ها پرسیدم

یک مسئله که بوی عشق آید از آن

در عمر خود از مدرسی نشنیدم

17

For some time, I went around in these schools
And asked of the wise many subtle questions.
Not one subtlety that had a sign of love
Did I ever hear from a theologian.

۱۸

هر چند که رند کوچه و بازاریم

ای خواجه مپندار که بی مقداریم

سری که به آصف سلیمان دادند

داریم ولی به هر کسی نسپاریم

18

Although I am the *rend* of the street and bazaar,
O *Khâja*, do not think that I am worthless.
The secret which was given to Solomon's Asaf,
I possess, but I will not give it to just anyone.

۱۹

ای دل که ز مدرسه به دیر افتادی

واندر صف اهل زهد غیر افتادی

الحمد که کار را رساندی تو بجای

صد شکر که عاقبت به خیر افتادی

19

O heart, who fell from the school to the tavern
And became a stranger among the ascetics,
Thank God you reached somewhere in your career.
A hundred thanks that you fell to the good in the end.

۲۰

ای چرخ که با مردم نادان یاری

هر لحظه بر اهل فضل غم میباری

پیوسته ز تو بر دل من بار غمی است

گویا که ز اهل دانشم پنداری

20

O Wheel of the sky, friend of the ignorant,
Every moment you rain grief upon the learned.
A burden of grief from you always weighs upon my heart.
Apparently you consider me one of the learned.

۲۱

از فتنهٔ این زمانهٔ شورانگیز

برخیز و بهر جا که توانی بگریز

ور پای گریختن نداری باری

دستی زن و در دامن خلوت آویز

21

From the disaster of these tumultuous times,
Rise and escape wherever you can.
And if your feet are not able to escape,
At least, hang on to the skirt of seclusion with your hands.

۲۲

خوش آنکه صلای جام وحدت در داد

خاطر ز ریاضی و طبیعی آزاد

بر منطقهٔ فلک نزد دست خیال

در پای عناصر سر فکرت ننهاد

22

Happy is the one who called for the grail of unity
And freed his mind from mathematics and biology.
Happy is the one whose mind was not lost in the sky,
Nor his thought troubled over the nature of elements.

۲۳

کاری ز وجود ناقصم نگشاید
گویی که ثبوتم انتفا می زاید
شاید ز عدم من بوجودی برسم
زآنروی که ز نفی نفی اثبات آید

23

I can achieve nothing of this imperfect being of mine.
It is as if my proving adds to my negation.
Perhaps I can attain to some being through non-being.
Because the negation of the negative results in positive.

۲۴

فرخنده شبی بود که آن دلبر مست
آمد ز پی غارت دل تیغ بدست
غارت زده‌ام دید و خجل گشت دمی
با من ز پی رفع خجالت بنشست

24

Blessed was the night when that intoxicated beloved
Came to plunder my heart with a sword in hand!
He found me already plundered and was ashamed,
So he sat beside me in order to get over his shame.

محمد داراشکوه

(۱۰۶۹–۱۰۲۴ هجری قمری)

۱

یک ذره ندیدیم ز خورشید جدا

هر قطرهٔ آب هست عین دریا

حق را به چه نام کس تواند خواندن

هر اسم که هست هست ز اسماءِ خدا

Mohammad Dârâshkuh
(1615-1659 C.E.)

1

I have not seen a particle separate from the sun.
Every drop of water is identical with the sea.
By what name should one call God?
Any name that exists is one of the names of God.

۲

ای آنکه خدای را بجویی همه جا

تو عین خدایی نه جدایی بخدا

این جستن تو به آن همی می ماند

قطره بمیان آب جوید دریا

2

O you, who search for God everywhere,
By God, you are one with God, not separate from him.
This quest of yours is like that of a drop of water,
Which searches for the sea in the middle of water.

٣

ای بی تو مرا قرار و آرام کجاست

اندر تو گمم از آن مرا نام کجاست

بی خواهش تو مرا چه خواهش باشد

کامم چو تو گشته‌ای مرا کام کجاست

3

Without you, what peace and calm do I have?

Since I am lost in you, what name do I have?

Besides desiring you, what desire do I have?

Since you have become my goal, what other goal do I have?

۴

چیزی که فلک برای آن گردان است

چیزی که ملک ز وصف آن حیران است

چیزی که زمین چو فرش گشته بهرش

آن چیز به پیش حضرت انسان است

4

That for whose sake the wheel of the sky is revolving,

That in whose description angels are bewildered,

That for which the Earth has become like a carpet,

That thing is in front of the honorable Man.

۵

کی زهد تو در شمار حق می آید

کی قلب تو در عیار حق می آید

باید که تو عین خویش دانی حق را

فانی شدنت چه کار حق می آید

5

What does your piety matter to God?

What value does your fake coin have for God?

You must know God as identical with your own self.

What good is your annihilation for God?

۶

اندر دو جهان بغیر یارم نبود

شاهنشهی چو شهریارم نبود

گر پرده ز روی کار افتد ای دوست

معلوم شود که جز نگارم نبود

6

In both worlds, I have nothing but my Beloved.
There is no king-of-kings like my King.
If the veil drops off the reality, my friend,
It will be known that nothing exists but my Beloved.

۷

هر دم برسد به عاشقان ذوق جدید

خود مجتهدند نی ز اهل تقلید

شیران نخورند جز شکار خود را

روباه خورد فتاده و لحم قدید

7

Every moment a new ecstasy comes to lovers.
They are themselves leaders, not followers.
Lions do not eat anything but their own hunt.
Foxes eat the crumbs and the remnant meat.

۸

عارف دل و جان تو مزین سازد

خاری که کند بجاش گلشن سازد

کامل همه را ز نقص بیرون آرد

یک شمع هزار شمع روشن سازد

8

An âref will adorn your heart and soul.
The thorn which he plucks replaces with a flower garden.
A perfect man will bring everyone out of imperfection.
A thousand candles can be lit from one candle.

٩

دردیست مرا که هیچ درمان نبود
کفری دارم که ذکر ایمان نبود
بیزار شدم برای او از همه چیز
یک روی شدن به یار آسان نبود

9

I have a pain that has no remedy at all.
I have a blasphemy that has no sign of faith.
For his sake, I became estranged from everything.
To be true to the bleoved is not easy.

١٠

او در نظر است رو به هر چیز کنی
کوری تو چرا به خویش تجویز کنی
حق گفت چو «اینما تولوا» با تو
باید که نظر بسوی خود نیز کنی

10

Whatever you turn your face to, he is in your sight.
Why do you prescribe blindness to yourself?
Since God told you, *Any direction you face* [you see him]
You must turn your face toward yourself, too.

١١

خواهی که شوی داخل ارباب نظر
از قال به حال بایدت کرد گذر
از گفتن توحید موحد نشوی
شیرین نشود دهانت از نام شکر

11

If you want to join the people of perception,
You must move from speech to state.
You will not be a Unitarian by repeating the word *unity*.
The word *sugar* will not make your mouth sweet.

سرمد کاشانی
(۱۰۷۰ هجری قمری)

۱

سرمد که ز جام عشق مستش کردند
بالا بردند و باز پستش کردند
می خواست خداپرستی و هشیاری
مستش کردند و بت پرستش کردند

Sarmad Kâshâni
(d. 1660 C.E.)

1

Sarmad, who was made drunk with the wine of love,
Was carried up high, then brought down low.
He wanted soberiety and God-worshipping.
They made him drunk and turned him to an idol-worshipper.

۲

راضی دل دیوانه به تقدیر نشد
فارغ ز خیال فکر و تدبیر نشد
ایام شباب رفت و باقی است هوس
ما پیر شدیم و آرزو پیر نشد

2

My crazy heart was not content with its fate.
It did not rest from devising and planning.
The days of youth went, yet the passion stayed.
I grew old, but my desire did not.

٣

آن شوخ بمن نظر ندارد چکنم
آه دل من اثر ندارد چکنم
با آنکه همیشه در دلم می باشد
از حال دلم خبر ندارد چکنم

3

That charming one does not look at me, what shall I do?
My heart-felt sighs have no effect on him, what shall I do?
Although he is always in my heart,
He is not aware of the state of my heart, what shall I do?

۴

سرمد تو حدیث کعبه و دیر مکن
در کوچهٔ شک چو گمرهان سیر مکن
رو شیوهٔ بندگی ز شیطان آموز
یک قبله گزین و سجدهٔ غیر مکن

4

Sarmad, speak not of the Ka'ba and idol-temple.
Wander not in the street of doubt, like lost people.
Go learn the way of devotion from Satan.
Choose one kebla and prostrate before no other.

۵

تنها نه همین دیر و حرم خانهٔ اوست
این ارض و سما تمام کاشانهٔ اوست
عالم همه دیوانهٔ افسانهٔ اوست
عاقل بود آن کسی که دیوانهٔ اوست

5

His home is not only this church and sanctuary.
His residence is the whole earth and heaven.
The whole world is crazy for his fable.
He is wise who is mad for him.

۶

یاری بگزین که بی وفایی نکند
دلخسته ترا در آشنایی نکند
پیوسته در آغوش و کنارت گردد
هرگز ز تو یک گام جدایی نکند

6

Choose a companion who will not be unfaithful to you,
And who will not wound your heart with his acqaintance —
A companion who is always beside you and in your bosom,
One who never takes even one step away from you.

٧

سرمد اگرش وفاست خود می‌آید
ور آمدنش رواست خود می‌آید
بیهوده چرا در پی او می‌گردی
بنشین اگر او خداست خود می‌آید

7

Sarmad, if he has loyalty, he himself will come.
If his coming is for the best, he himself will come.
Why do you in vain wander around after him?
Sit down. If he is God, he himself will come.

محقق اردبیلی بیدگلی
(قرن یازدهم هجری قمری)

١

عالم همه عشق است و ازو هیچ نشان نیست
این نکته بجز در دل عشاق عیان نیست
سرمایهٔ سودای غمش سوز نهان است
پیداست که سودی بجز این در دو جهان نیست

Mohaqqeq Ardabili Bidgoli
(17th Century C.E.)

1

The world is all love, yet there is no trace of him.
This subtlety is not clear to anyone but lovers.
To be his lover, one needs to have a hidden fire within.
Obviously there is no other gain than this in both worlds.

٢

جان بادهٔ حیرت است و تن ساغر اوست
کی رست ز حیرت آنکه شد تا بر دوست
شوریدهٔ عشق پا ز حیرت نکشد
گردد چو محقق ار بگردد بر دوست

2

The soul is the wine of amazement and the body its goblet.
When was he who went to the friend free of amazement?
The frenzied of love never withdraws from amazement.
He becomes like Mohaqqeq if he wanders around the friend.

٣

مهر رخ او گرفت پهنای وجود
ببرید ز خود سایه تمنای وجود
امکان و حدوث را ز هستی چه خبر
چون شخص وجوب است سراپای وجود

3

The light of His face spread over the expanse of existence.
And the shade cut off from itself the desire to exist.
What do forms and phenomena have to do with existence?
The essence is the whole reality of existence.

۴

ما دیده بجز جلوه‌گه یار نداریم
بر کار کس از نیک و بد انکار نداریم
کار دو جهان بار دل ار نیست عجب نیست
با هر چه جز آن یار چو ما کار نداریم

4

We see nothing but the manifestation of the Friend.
We do not defy anyone's work whether it is good or bad.
If the labor of both worlds is not a burden on our hearts,
It is no wonder, for our work is with none but the friend.

۵

ای دل نه فساد جسم فانی مرگ است
نادانیت ار نیک بدانی مرگ است
با علم ز مرگ هر دمت جان نویست
با جهل حیات جاودانی مرگ است

5

O heart, the deterioration of the transient body is not death.
Your ignorance, if you know well, is death.
With knowledge, each breath gains a new life from death.
With ignorance, the eternal life is death.

۶

معشوق به رخ پردهٔ اعیان چو کشید
جز خویش به زیر پرده موجود ندید
می خواست که شور عشق گیرد بجهان
با خود سخنی گفت و ز خود باز شنید

6

When the beloved drew the veil of manifestation on his face,
He saw no existent under the veil but himself.
He wanted the frenzy of love to fill the world,
He spoke a word to himself and heard it back from himself.

ملا شاه بدخشانی
(۱۰۷۲ هجری قمری)

۱

دامان بقا فتاده در قبضهٔ ما
از دامن ما خلاص شد دست فنا
با بیرنگی جوان جاوید شدیم
پیری نرسد بگرد ما مرگ کجا

Mullâ Shâh Badakhshâni
(d. 1662 C.E.)

1

The skirt of immortality has fallen in our hands.
The hand of mortality has fallen short of our skirts.
We became eternally young through sincerity.
Old age can not catch us, let alone death.

۲

تا نگذری از شریعت عام ای دوست
بر شرع خواص کی نهی گام ای دوست
آنجا که شریعت اخص الخاص است
از هر دو گذر در اوست آرام ای دوست

2

Unless you leave the religion of the pupulace, my friend,
How can you enter into the religion of the special people?
Wherein the religion of the most special of specials is,
Let both religions go, my friend, for therein is your peace.

۳

ای بند بپای قفل بر دل هشدار
وی دوخته چشم پای در گل هشدار
عزم سفر مشرق و رو با مغرب
ای راهرو پشت بمنزل هشدار

3

O you who have chain on feet and lock on heart, beware!
O you who have eyes closed and feet in mud, beware!
Intent upon traveling East, you are facing West?
O traveler who have your destination behind you, beware!

۴

زنهار به هرزه تخم اسرار مپاش
ترسم که شود مزرع اسرار تو فاش
خواهی ز شریعت به حقیقت افتی
بی شرع مباش و بستهٔ شرع مباش

4

Beware of scattering the seed of secrets in vain!
I fear your field of secrets will be known to all.
If you want to proceed from religion to Truth,
Be neither without religion nor tied to religion.

۵

آنرا که به ماست بر سر ایمان جنگ
او مؤمن و ز ایمان من او را صد ننگ
مؤمن نشود تا که برابر نشود
با بانگ نماز بانگ ناقوس فرنگ

5

He who is at war with me over my faith,
Calls himself a believer and is ashamed of my faith.
One does not become a believer until he equals
The call to prayers with the toll of bell.

۶

از دوری او همیشه در آزاری
آزار ز جهل تست اگر هشیاری
میخانه که هست کعبهٔ تست یقین
وصل است هر آنچه هجر می پنداری

6

You are always in pain because of his distance.
Your pain is caused by your ignorance if you only knew.
The tavern is certainly your Ka'ba.
Whatever you think is separation is union.

۷

ای طالب ذات از چه رو دربدری
جویای خدا چرا ز خود بی خبری
عین همه‌ای و جملگی عین توان
این است حقیقت ار بخود در نگری

7

O seeker of the essence, why are you wandering?
O seeker of God, why are you unaware of yourself?
You are the essence of all and all is your essence.
This is the truth if you look at yourself carefully.

٨

دریا چو رود خس نرود پس چه کند
پس با دریای بیکران خس چه کند
عرفان سریست بایدش پوشیدن
می پوشم لیک مشک را کس چه کند

8

If the ocean moves, what can a twig do but move, too?
What should a twig do with the boundless ocean?
Mystic knowledge is a secret which must be covered.
I am covering it, but what can one do with musk?

٩

از بستگی خویش اگر واگردی
بر وارسی خویش مهیا گردی
واگرد به گرد خویش مانند حباب
تا واگردی ز خویش و دریا گردی

9

If you open up of your closedness,
You will be prepared to examine yourself.
Turn around yourself like a bubble,
So that you open up and become the ocean.

١٠

تا می نکنی ز معرفت شیرین کام
حاصل نشود کام تو از نقل کلام
حلوا حلوا اگر بگویی صد سال
از گفتن حلوا نشود شیرین کام

10

Unless you sweeten your mouth with self-realization,
You will not achieve this goal with the comfit of the word.
If you repeat *sweetmeat, sweetmeat* for a hundred years,
You will not sweeten your mouth with the word *sweetmeat*.

واعظ قزوینی
(۱۰۸۹ هجری قمری)

۱

هر ذره ز مهر تست جانی بی تاب
هر شبنمی از یاد تو چشمی پر آب
هر برگ گلی است یک کتاب از سخنت
هر غنچه کتابخانه‌ای پر ز کتاب

Vâez Qazvini
(d. 1678 C.E.)

1

Every particle is a restless spirit with your love.
Every dewdrop is a tearful eye with your remembrance.
Every rose-petal is a book [written] with your words.
Every rose-bud is a library filled with books.

۲

ای دل رخ از این سرای فانی برتاب
جز در طلب جهان باقی مشتاب
دنیا لفظ است و آخرت معنی آن
در لفظ مپیچ اینهمه معنی دریاب

2

O heart, turn your face away from this transient world.
Do not go after anything but the permanent world.
This world is a word and the hereafter its meaning.
Do not be entangled with the word. Find the meaning.

٣

خوش آنکه به غم شکفته باشی همه شب

در خون جگر نهفته باشی همه شب

شرمت باد از خروس ای طایر جان

کو بیدار و تو خفته باشی همه شب

3

You are blessed if you bloom with sorrow all night,
If you are drowned in the heart-blood all night.
O bird of the soul, have shame of the rooster,
Who is awake while you are asleep all night.

۴

آیینهٔ روی دلبران مظهر اوست

چشم سیهٔ خوش نگهان منظر اوست

منظور حقیقت است از حسن مجاز

ابروی بتان طاقنمای در اوست

4

His image is in the mirrors of the faces of the lovely ones.
His vision is in the dark eyes of the good-looking ones.
The beauty of appearance is intended to show the Truth.
The eyebrows of the idols are the decorations atop his door.

۵

امید ز هر چه هست باید برداشت

دل ز آنچه بجز حق است باید برداشت

در وقت دعاست دست برداشتنت

رمزی که ز جمله دست باید برداشت

5

One must cut off hope from whatever there is.
One must take away one's heart from everything but God.
Raising your hands at the time of praying is a sign that
You must take your hands off from everything there is.

۶

تا کی ز شراب خواب مستی برخیز

از بستر نرم تن پرستی برخیز

با بانگ بلند شب خروسان گویند

ننشسته ز پا شعلهٔ هستی برخیز

6

How long should you be drunk with the wine of sleep?
Rise! Rise from the soft bed of body-loving.
Cocks crow loudly at night and say:
Rise before the flame of your existence sinks down.

٧

ای از مرض حرص ترا دل مرده

اندیشهٔ زر ز دیده خوابت برده

نفس تو ز خار خار دنیا شب و روز

هر سوی رود چون سگ سوزن خورده

7

O you whose heart has died from the disease of greed,
And whose sleep is robbed from the eye by desire for gold,
Your passion, anxious for the world day and night,
Dashes about in every direction, like a prickled dog.

٨

شاهی خواهی گدایی از دست مده

آیین برهنه پایی از دست مده

خواهی که به جذبه‌ای کشد یار ترا

سررشتهٔ آشنایی از دست مده

8

If you want kingship, do not give up mendacity.
Do not give up the way of barefootedness.
If you want the beloved to pull you with one attraction,
Do not lose track of your acquaintance with him.

۹

نبود چو حضور قلب و مژگان تری
فیضی ز نماز خویش چندان نبری
خاکت بر سر این حضور است که تو
در پیش حق استاده و جای دگری

9

Without moist eyelashes and the presence of heart,
You will not take much profit of your prayers.
Shame on you! Is this called presence:
While you stand before God your heart is somewhere else?

۱۰

دنیاست سرای غم تو یکسر شعفی
این خانهٔ ماتم است و تو همچو دفی
چون شاد توان نشست جایی که در او
خیزد هر لحظه شیونی از طرفی؟

10

The world is a house of sorrows, but you are full of mirth.
This is a house of mourning, but you are like a tambourine.
How can one rejoice in a place where
A lament rises every moment from some direction?

Chapter Nine
18th Century C.E.
12th Century Hejri

عبدالقادر بیدل

(۱۰۵۴-۱۱۳۳ هجری قمری)

۱

بر وضع گهر ز موج خندد دریا

جز آزادی نمی پسندد دریا

عارف نشود شیفتهٔ عالم رنگ

بر طرهٔ موج دل نبندد دریا

Abdulqâder Bidel
(1644-1721 C.E.)

1

The sea laughs through waves at the plight of the pearl.
The sea cares for nothing but freedom.
The enlightened one is not fascinated by the world of colors.
The sea does not attach its heart to the tress of the wave.

۲

تا کی بهوای خلد خوانی ما را

یا در غم دوزخ بنشانی ما را

عمریست ز بیدلی بخود ساخته‌ایم

یا رب ز در خویش نرانی ما را

2

How long would you lure us with the desire for paradise?
Or put us in the grief of hell?
Being a lover, we have put up with ourselves for a lifetime.
O Lord, do not expel us from your door.

۳

حرف اینجا بود می شنودم آنجا

آیینه به پیش و می نمودم آنجا

چون گردون سیر من برون از من نیست

جایی نرسیدم که نبودم آنجا

3

The word was here. I was hearing it there.
The mirror was before me. I was reflected over there.
Like the wheel of the sky, my motion is not outside me.
I never arrived at any place I was not already there.

۴

بیدل اسرار کبریائی دریاب

رمز به حقیقت آشنائی دریاب

غافل ز حقی بعلت صحبت خلق

یکدم تنها شو و خدائی دریاب

4

Bidel, the divine mysteries discover!
The secret of acquaintance with Truth discover!
Association with people has made you negligent of God.
Become alone for a moment and godhead discover!

۵

آن حسن که آیینهٔ امکان پرداخت
هر ذره به صد هزار خورشید نواخت
با اینهمه جلوه بود در پردهٔ غیب
تا انسان گل نکرد خود را نشناخت

5

That beauty which adorned the mirror of creation
And caressed every particle with a hundred thousand suns,
In spite of all its glory, was behind the veil of the unseen
And did not know itself until man blossomed.

۶

ای جوش بهار قدس رنگ و بویت
بالیدن حسن مطلق از هر مویت
هر چند جهات دهر وجه الله است
آن به که بسوی خویش باشد رویت

6

O you whose charm is the thrill of the spring of paradise
And whose hair is the pride of the absolute beauty,
Although the Face of God is in all directions of the world,
It is better that your face be toward your own self.

۷

ای سرخوش بادهٔ تردد جامت
مشکل که توان رفع نمود ابرامت
آخر تو همانی که دم طفلی هم
بی جنبش گهواره نبود آرامت

7

O you who are drunk with the wine of hesitation,
It is hard to get rid of your insistence.
Anyway, you are that same person who, even in infancy,
Had no rest without the swing of the cradle.

٨

بی اسم و صفت دلت بخود محرم نیست

بی رنگ و بو بهار جز مبهم نیست

عالم بوجود من و تو موجود است

گر موج و حباب نیست دریا هم نیست

8

Without nouns and adjectives, your heart is alien to you.
Without colors and scents, spring is only an abstract.
The world exists because of your existence and mine.
With no waves or bubbles, there would be no sea either.

٩

بیدل نه‌ای آگاه دلت خانهٔ کیست

وین صوت و صدا چراغ کاشانهٔ کیست

تا صبح قیامت مژه بر هم نزنی

گر دریابی که هستی افسانهٔ کیست

9

Bidel, you are not aware whose home your heart is,
And whose cottage's lamp this voice and sound is.
You would not blink till the morning of Resurrection,
If you knew whose story existence is.

١٠

تا کی پرسی مقام دلدار کجاست

وان شاهد نانموده رخسار کجاست

مژگان تو گر حجاب بینش نشود

در خانهٔ آفتاب دیوار کجاست

10

How long should you ask, "Where is the Beloved's place?
"And where is that Beauty who has not shown His Face?"
If your eyelashes do not veil your vision,
Where is a wall in the house of the sun?

۱۱

در پردهٔ هر ریشه چمن سازی هست
در هر بالی کمین پروازی هست
چون ماهٔ نو از وهم نگردی باریک
در جیب کلید تو در بازی هست

11

Beneath the skin of every root there is a gardener.
In every wing there is a potential of flight.
Do not let illusion narrow you like the new moon.
In the loop of your key there is an open door.

۱۲

در پردهٔ ساز ما نوا بسیار است
عیب و هنر و زنگ و صفا بسیار است
خواهی کف گیر و خواه گوهر بردار
ما دریائیم و موج ما بسیار است

12

In the scale of our instrument, there are many tunes.
There are many virtues and vices, purities and impurities.
Whether you obtain foam or find pearls,
We are a sea and we have many waves.

۱۳

زین بحر که طوفانکدهٔ ما و من است
خلقی گرم تلاش بر در زدن است
کس نیست که دوش غیر گیرد بارش
هر موج پل گذشتن از خویشتن است

13

From this sea where the storms of *I* and *we* arise,
Some people struggle hard to get out.
There is none whose burden another's shoulders may carry.
Every wave is a bridge for crossing over oneself.

۱۴

زین بحر جهانی خطر اندیش گذشت
آسوده همین کشتی درویش گذشت
محو است کنار عافیت با تسلیم
باید نفسی پل شد و از خویش گذشت

14

Through this sea, a world apprehensively passed.
It was only the dervish's boat that peacefully passed.
The shore of safety is destroyed by submission.
One must become a bridge to cross over oneself.

۱۵

زاهد میگفت کسب تقوی دین است
شیخ آینه بر کف که سلوک آیین است
دیوانهٔ ما برغم این بی‌خبران
عریان گردید و گفت مردی این است

15

The ascetic said religion is in obtaining virtue.
The shaykh held a mirror in his hand that this is the creed.
Our mad one, contrary to these unaware ones,
Became naked and said, "This is manliness."

۱۶

عالم غرض آلود جنون من و ماست
اینجا عشق هوس نیالوده کجاست
فرهادی و مجنونی اگر می شنوی
خود اینهمه نیست حرف و صوت شعراست

16

The world is spiteful with the craze of *I* and *we*.
Here, where is a love uncontaminated by lust?
All these tales you hear about Farhâd and Majnun
Are little more than the words and sounds of poets.

۱۷

گر ریشه کنی خیال تخمش وطن است
ور تخم همان به ریشه‌اش انجمن است
ای تجدید آشنای آثار قدیم
هر طرز نوی که می تراشی کهن است

17

If you think of the root, its origin is the seed.
If you think of the seed, its origin is the root.
O new acquaintance of the ancient works,
Any new design you carve is old.

۱۸

اعیان که بهار عز و شان می بینند
در پردهٔ رنگ امتحان می بینند
چون آینه قطره های از بحر جدا
خود را دریای بیکران می بینند

18

The lords, in their spring of pomp and glory,
Are being tested with the canvas of color.
Like a mirror, the drops separated from the sea,
See themselves as a boundless ocean.

۱۹

امروز نسیم یار من می‌آید
بوی گل انتظار من می‌آید
وقت است از آن جلوه برنگی برسم
آیینه ام و بهار من می‌آید

19

Today the scent of my beloved is coming to me.
The fragrance of my expectations' rose is coming to me.
It is time I profitted by that display of glory.
I am a mirror and my spring is coming.

۲۰

از ساغر هستی هوسی آب نخورد

زین گلشن نیرنگ خسی آب نخورد

چشم طمع از سراب امکان بردار

کز چشمهٔ آیینه کسی آب نخورد

20

No desire ever drank water from the goblet of existence.
No plant ever drank water from this rose-garden of deceit.
Take your eye of greed off the mirage of the contingent.
No one ever drank water from the fountain of a mirror.

۲۱

این بزم جنون که نازنینی دارد

غوغای قیامت آفرینی دارد

پر در فکر نوای منصور مرو

هر پشه برای خود طنینی دارد

21

This feast of madness, which is so tender and lovely,
Has a Resurrection-creating tumult.
Do not go deep into the thought of Mansur's voice.
Every mosquito has an echo of its own.

۲۲

تا در کف نیستی عنانم دادند

از کشمکش جهان امانم دادند

چون شمع سراغ عافیت می‌جستم

زیر قدم خویش نشانم دادند

22

When my rein was placed in the palm of nonbeing,
I was granted quarter from the struggle of the world.
Like a candle, I was searching for my well-being.
It was pointed out to me under my feet.

۲۳

تا پای طلب بدامن دل نرسید

هر چند ز خود رفت بمنزل نرسید

هشدار کزین محیط گم گشته کنار

جز موج گهر کسی به ساحل نرسید

23

Until the quest's foot reached the skirts of the heart,
It had not arrived at its destination far as it walked.
Beware! From this ocean whose boundaries are lost,
No one reached the shore except the wave of the essence.

۲۴

حرصت اگر آرزوی شانی دارد

روشنگری دل امتحانی دارد

رو آینه پرداز که در بحر صفا

هر قطره بدامن آسمانی دارد

24

If you have a passion for dignity,
You must pass the test of purifying the heart.
Go polish your mirror! For in the ocean of purity,
Every drop has a sky on its lap.

۲۵

در وادی عشق اگر دویدن باشد

بر جادهٔ غیر خط کشیدن باشد

ما و سفری که همچو خط پرگار

هر جا برسی بخود رسیدن باشد

25

If we are to run in the valley of love,
We must cross out the road of the other.
We are traveling like the compasses which draw a line.
Anywhere we arrive, we arrive at ourselves.

۲۶

زین پیش که دل قابل فرهنگ نبود
از پیچ و خم تعلقم ننگ نبود
آگاهیم از هر دو جهان وحشت داد
تا بال نداشتم قفس تنگ نبود

26

Before now when my heart was not capable of knowledge,
I felt no shame for the meanders of my attachments.
My awareness terrified me of both worlds.
The cage was not tight as long as I had no wings.

۲۷

صد بست و گشاد با هم آمیخته‌اند
تا رنگ بنای این جهان ریخته‌اند
دلتنگ مباشید که مانند هلال
پیش هر در کلیدی آویخته‌اند

27

A hundred knots and loops have joined
To paint the color of the foundation of this world.
Do not worry! For like a crescent moon,
There is a key hanging in front of every door.

۲۸

هوشی که سفیدی و سیاهی فهمید
مپسند که سر حق کماهی فهمید
گفتم سخنی لیک پس از کسب کمال
خواهی فهمید چون نخواهی فهمید

28

If an intelligence understood black and white,
Do not presume it likewise understood the secret of God.
I say this, but after the acquisition of perfection,
You will understand how you would not understand.

۲۹

آنرا که کند حکم ازل محرم کار
بر دل ز تمنا نپسندد آزار
کاری گر می گشود از دست دعا
بار از هر نخل بیش میداشت چنار

29

Whom the Primordial Command made a confidant
Would not bother his heart with praying.
If raising hands for praying solved any problem,
The elm tree would have had more fruit than any date tree.

۳۰

زان پیش که گردم آشنای زنجیر
آزادگیم داشت هوای زنجیر
گفتند حدیثی از خم گیسویی
کردند اسیرم به صدای زنجیر

30

Before I became acquainted with chains,
My freedom had had a fancy for a chain.
They told me a story about the curl of a tress
And captured me with the sound of a chain.

۳۱

یکسان بود امداد حقیقت به ظهور
افهام به صد فهم کند کسب شعور
یاقوت و بلور رنگ استعداد است
از چشمهٔ آفتاب جوشد همه نور

31

The contribution of the Truth to all manifestation is equal.
Minds acquire intelligence by many ways of understanding.
The ruby and the crystal display the color of their nature.
From the fountain of the sun, only light boils out.

۳۲

کلک هوس تو هر چه زاید بنویس
از نقطه و خط آنچه نماید بنویس
دارد این دشت و در سیاهی بسیار
هر چیز که در خیالت آید بنویس

32

Whatever is born from the pen of your fancy, write!
Whatever it shows of dots and lines, write!
This dale and vale has a lot of blackness.
Whatever comes to your imagination, write!

۳۳

کیفیت روز و شب ز افلاک بپرس
گر می در خم نیابی از تاک بپرس
تا چند سراغ رفتگان خواهی کرد
یاران همه حاضرند از خاک بپرس

33

The quality of days and nights, of the skies, ask!
If you do not find wine in the vat, of the vine, ask!
How long are you going to inquire about the dead?
The friends are all present, of the dust, ask!

۳۴

اسرار قدم به فهم یکتائی خویش
کرد انسان را دلیل دانائی خویش
خود را تا قطره بر نیاورد محیط
آگه نشد از شکوه دریائی خویش

34

The mysteries of eternity, by their unified intelligence,
Made man the witness of their wisdom.
The ocean, until it brought forth the drop,
Did not become aware of its oceanic splendor.

۳۵

بیدل سخنی چند که داری یادش

از خلق گذشته است استعدادش

امروز تو نیز حرفی از فطرت خویش

بنویس بخاک تا بخواند بادش

35

Bidel, the few words which you remember,
You owe their meaning to the people of the past.
Today you, too, about your nature
Write a word in the dust for the wind to read.

۳۶

زان نسخه که وارسند سر تا پایش

هر سطر به نقطه میکشد ایمایش

از کثرت خلق وحدتی جلوه گر است

دریا همه قطره قطره است اجزایش

36

If a script is thoroughly studied,
It will be seen that every line of it is composed of dots.
The multiplicity of creation displays a unity.
The sea has the drops of water as its parts.

۳۷

عارف به تماشای چمنزار کمال

جز در قفس دل نگشاید پر و بال

هر چند ز امواج قدم بردارد

از خویش برون رفتن دریاست محال

37

To view the meadow of perfection, an âref,
Except in the cage of the heart, spreads not his wings.
No matter how many steps the sea takes with its waves,
It is impossible for the sea to go out of itself.

۳۸

هر سانحه‌ای که شد به افسانه دلیل
بیکاری خلق شهرتش راست کفیل
موسی تا حال می شکافد دریا
فرعون هنوز میخورد غوطه به نیل

38

Any accident which gives birth to fable,
People's idleness secures its popularity.
Even now Moses is splitting the sea,
And the Pharaoh is plunging in the Nile.

۳۹

از نفی خود اثبات تو خرمن کردیم
در رنگ شکسته سیر گلشن کردیم
خاکستر ما چو صبح گر رفت بباد
آیینهٔ آفتاب روشن کردیم

39

By negating ourselves, we harvested your confirmation.
We traversed a rose-garden in a broken color.
As the wind took our ashes in the morning,
We lighted the mirror of the sun.

۴۰

بیدل سحری بجهد دامن چیدیم
با مهر سپهر هم عنان گردیدیم
دیدیم تلاش خلق عجز است آخر
او سر به غروب برد و ما خوابیدیم

40

Bidel, one dawn I made an effort and gathered my skirt
And rode alongside the sun of the sky.
I realized people's struggle was helplessness in the end.
The sun proceeded to set and I went to sleep.

۴۱

بیدل نه غرور عز و شانی دارم
نی دعوی تابی و توانی دارم
در گوشهٔ تسلیم جهانی دارم
از خاک فروتر آسمانی دارم

41

Bidel, I neither pride at a high rank,
Nor claim power and ability.
I have a world in the corner of submission.
I have a sky which is lower than the earth.

۴۲

دی سیر خیال این گلستان کردیم
محو تو شدیم و گل بدامان کردیم
واشد مژه‌ای که همچو بال طاووس
ایجاد هزار چشم حیران کردیم

42

Yesterday my mind made an excursion to this rose-garden.
I became lost in you and filled my lap with roses.
An eyelash opened, which like the wing of a peacock,
Created a thousand astonished eyes.

۴۳

یا رب ز کجا محرم آداب شدم
آفتکش این برق جگرتاب شدم
یعنی چو عرق به کارگاه انصاف
آگه ز تب هر که شدم آب شدم

43

O Lord, how did I become the confidant of mysteries?
And the endurer of this liver-burning lightning?
Like the sweat in the workshop of justice,
When I became aware of someone's fever, I turned to water.

۴۴

از موج سراب آب خوردن نتوان
می در قدح حباب خوردن نتوان
از خوان فلک به وهم قانع می باش
قرص مه و آفتاب خوردن نتوان

44

From the wave of a mirage, drinking water is impossible.
From the goblet of a bubble, drinking wine is impossible.
From the table of the sky, be content with an illusion.
Eating the globes of the moon and the sun is impossible.

۴۵

ای مردهٔ انتظار محشر بردن
حیفست بهر فسانه‌ات خون خوردن
در صورت آفاق نظر کن کاینجا
هر روز قیامت است و هر شب مردن

45

O you, who are dying in anticipation of the Resurrection,
It is a pity that you should suffer because of every myth.
Look at the face of the universe. For here,
Every day is a resurrection and every night a dying.

۴۶

ای هوش تو آوارهٔ نافهمیدن
از علم علی چه بایدت پرسیدن
آنکس که رموز لوکشف کرد بیان
او بود که دیده بود قبل از دیدن

46

O you whose consciousness is wandering in ignorance,
How can you question about Ali's knowledge?
The man who explained the secrets of lo kushef
Was the one who had seen before looking.

۴۷

با ما ستم است آشنایی کردن
آنگاه ارادهٔ جدایی کردن
هر چند که زندگی بود زندانت
مرگ است ازو فکر رهایی کردن

47

It is cruel to become acquainted with us
And then to want to separate from us.
Even if life were your prison,
To contemplate escape from it is death.

۴۸

تا کی به غبار وهم پنهان گشتن
زین بیش نقاب جلوه نتوان گشتن
ای سایه ز خویش چشم پوشیدن تست
در کسوت آفتاب عریان گشتن

48

How long should we hide beneath the dust of illusion?
One cannot cover the display of the glory anymore.
O shade, your self-renunciation is:
To become naked under the attire of the sun.

۴۹

آنرا که برون ز خویش می جویی کو
یا آن سوی خود رهی که می‌پویی کو
خود را پر دور دیده‌ای چشم بمال
ای بیخبر اویی که تو می‌گویی کو

49

Where is the one whom you seek outside yourself?
Where is the road you search beyond yourself?
You have seen yourself very far away. Rub your eyes!
O unaware one, you are he and ask, where is he?

۵۰

راحت خواهی به خار و خس یکسان شو

با دیده نگاه با بدنها جان شو

مضمون عبارت دو عالم می باش

بر هر چه رسی به رنگ او عریان شو

50

If you want comfort, be equal to the thorn and straw.
Be vision to the eye and soul to the body.
Be the meaning of the phrase of *both worlds*.
Anything you meet, bare yourself to its color.

۵۱

آیینهٔ عالم بقاییم همه

نیرنگ جهان کبریاییم همه

کو موج و چه گرداب و چه دریا چه حباب

هر جا نم جلوه‌ای است ماییم همه

51

The mirror of the eternal world are we all.
The magic of the divine world are we all.
What is a wave, a vortex, a sea, or a bubble?
Wherever there is a trace of manifestation, that are we all.

۵۲

امروز رسیده فکر فردا کرده

فردا شده لب به حیف دی واکرده

ای بیخبران چه برگ و ساز است اینجا

جز خجلت کرده و غم ناکرده

52

Today, having arrived, you worry about tomorrow.
Tomorrow, having arrived, you regret losing yesterday.
O unaware ones, what accoutrements are here except
The shame of what is done and the worry of what is not?

۵۳

تا چند به این هستی غارت برده
می باید زیست بی حس و افسرده
خجلت کش تهمت ظهوریم عبس
چون ناخن و مو نه زنده و نه مرده

53

How long should one live in this looted existence,
Unfeeling and depressed?
In vain we are ashamed of being accused of manifestation.
Like nails and hair, we are neither alive nor dead.

۵۴

ای رهرو اگر ز خویش غافل باشی
سرگشته تر از راه به منزل باشی
چون گوهر اگر به ضبط خود پردازی
در دریا هم مقیم ساحل باشی

54

O wayfarer, if you be negligent of your own self,
You will be more lost at home than on the road.
If you attend to your self, like a pearl,
Even in the sea you will be on the shore.

۵۵

تا همسبق مزاج طفلان نشوی
آزاد ز قید این دبستان نشوی
دانائی و آسوده دلی خصم همند
ای محو خرد مباد نادان نشوی

55

Unless you become of the same nature as children,
You will not be free from the bondage of this school.
Learnedness and calmness are enemies one to the other.
O lost-in-wisdom, beware lest you avoid becoming unlearned.

۵۶

دریایی صید هر تلاطم نشوی
خورشیدی پایمال انجم نشوی
یعنی در عالم فریب کر و فر
مردی به هجوم خلق اگر گم نشوی

56

You are a sea if you do not fall prey to every turbulence.
You are a sun if you are not trampled by the stars.
That is to say, in the deceiving world of power and glory,
You are a man if you are not lost in the rush of the crowd.

۵۷

ما را نه زری است نی نثار سیمی
جز تحفهٔ عجز بندگی تقدیمی
چون شاخ گلی که خم شود پیش نسیم
از دوست سلامی و ز ما تسلیمی

57

I have neither gold nor silver to present.
I have no offering but the gift of humble devotion.
Like a branch of flowers, which bends before the breeze,
A greeting from the friend and a surrender from me.

عاشق اصفهانی

(۱۱۸۱ هجری قمری)

۱

امشب که به ساغرت شراب ناب است

زان ماه دو هفته خانه پر مهتاب است

عاشق بطرب کوش نه جای خواب است

در یاب که وقت خرمی نایاب است

Âsheq Isfahâni
(d. 1768 C.E.)

1

Tonight when your cup is full of pure wine
And the house full of the light of that fortnight's moon,
It is no time to sleep, Âsheq. Enjoy yourself.
Beware that the time for enjoyment is rare.

۲

سروی و رخ تو ماه آراسته است

ماهی و قد تو سرو نوخاسته است

چندانکه ز پای تا سرت می بینم

آنی که دل من از خدا خواسته است

2

You are a cypress and your face is a moon bedecked.
You are beautiful and your stature is a newly-risen cypress.
However I look at you, from head to toes,
You are exactly what my heart had asked of God.

۳

هر جا باشم گریه رخم می شوید
هر جا که روی طرب ز پی می پوید
کانجا که منم غم از هوا می بارد
و آنجا که تویی دل از زمین می روید

3

Wherever I am, tears wash my face.
Wherever you go, delight follows you.
Wherever I am, grief rains from the sky.
Wherever you are, excitement grows from the earth.

۴

ای زاهد پاکدامن ای یار عزیز
از پیش نمی رود صلاح و پرهیز
جایی که دهد ساقی گلچهره قدح
وقتی که بود باد صبا مشک آمیز

4

My dear friend, O pious ascetic,
Where the rose-cheeked Sâqi offers wine,
And when the zephyr carries the scent of the musk,
Piety and abstinence will not work.

مشتاق اصفهانی
(۱۱۷۱ هجری قمری)

۱

پیدا چو گهر ز قطرهٔ آب شدیم
پنهان به صدف چو در نایاب شدیم
بودیم خراب در شبستان عدم
بیدار شدیم باز در خواب شدیم

Moshtâq Isfahâni
(d. 1758 C.E.)

1

As I appeared, like a pearl, from a drop of water,
I hid myself, like a rare pearl, inside an oyster.
I was unconscious in the harem of nonexistence.
I woke up and went to sleep again.

۲

مرغان چو دل از سیر چمن شاد کنید
آنگاه نوای عیش بنیاد کنید
پرواز به گرد سرو شمشاد کنید
از حال اسیران قفس یاد کنید

2

O birds, when you are joyfully flying in the meadow;
And in all excitement, singing your songs of joy,
Fly around that box-tree cypress
And have a sympathy for the captives of the cage.

۳

ای ساده دلی که گفتن حق فن تست
منصور صفت هر که بود دشمن تست
حق گنج بود چو یابی‌اش پنهان دار
ور فاش کنی خون تو در گردن تست

3

O simple-hearted one, whose skill is in speaking the Truth,
You are like Mansur and everyone else is your enemy.
Truth is a treasure. Hide it when you find it.
If you display it, you are responsible for your own blood.

۴

عالم همه هیچ و کار عالم همه هیچ
نفع و نقصان و شادی و غم همه هیچ
با مهروشی دمی زنی گر چون صبح
باشد همه آن دم و جز آن دم همه هیچ

4

The world is nothing, and its affairs are all nothing.
Profit and loss, joy and suffering are all nothing.
If you spend a moment with an elegant one,
Life is that very moment, and the rest is all nothing.

۵

نه تاج و نه تخت و نه نگین خواهد ماند
نه سلطنت روی زمین خواهد ماند
ساقی تو ز لطف شیشه و ساغر را
خالی کن و پر کن که همین خواهد ماند

5

Neither crowns, nor thrones, nor signets will remain.
Not even the kingship of the Earth will remain.
Sâqi, kindly empty and fill the decanter and the goblet,
Because, of all things, only this will remain.

۶

آنانکه نه از خیل خردمندانند
نیک و بد خویش را ز گردون دانند
از چرخ مکن شکوه که هر گردنده
گردد بهمان روش که می گردانند

6

Those who are not of the group of the wise think that
The wheel of the sky is responsible for their good and bad.
Do not complain of the wheel of the sky,
For anything that turns turns the way it is turned.

٧

در عشق به لب خموش می باید بود
در عالم دل بجوش می باید بود
چشمی نه هزار چشم می باید بود
گوشی نه هزار گوش می باید بود

7

In love, lips silent must be.
In the world of the heart one boisterous must be.
With two eyes, nay with a thousand eyes,
With two ears, nay with a thousand ears one must be.

٨

ای دلبر بی نظیر من دستم گیر
در کشور جان امیر من دستم گیر
افتاده ام از پا و نباشد دستی
جز دست تو دستگیر من دستم گیر

8

O my peerless beloved, hold my hand.
In the world of the spirit, you are my emir, hold my hand.
I have fallen down, and except your hand,
There is no other help for me. Hold my hand.

٩

هرگز غم یار را به اغیار مگو
ور میگویی بغیر دلدار مگو
اسرار به نامحرم اسرار مگو
زنهار مگو هزار زنهار مگو

9

Never speak to strangers about the sorrow of love.
And if you do, never speak to anyone but the beloved.
Never tell the secrets to the non-confidante of the secrets.
Beware! A thousand times beware! Never tell!

١٠

غم بیحد و درد بیشمار و من فرد
یا رب چکنم که صبر نتوانم کرد
یا درد به اندازهٔ طاقت بفرست
یا حوصله ای بده به اندازهٔ درد

10

Suffering limitless, pains countless, and I all alone!
O Lord, I cannot tolerate, what should I do?
Give either pain in proportion to tolerance,
Or tolerance in proportion to pain.

هاتف اصفهانی

(۱۱۹۸ هجری قمری)

۱

گر فاش شود عیوب پنهانی ما

ای وای به خجلت و پریشانی ما

ما غره به دینداری و شاد از اسلام

گبران متنفر از مسلمانی ما

Hâtef Isfahâni

(d. 1784 C.E.)

1

If our hidden faults came to the open,
What a shame and embarrassment!
We are proud of our faith and happy with Islam,
While the Zoroastrians are disgusted with our Islam.

۲

ای غیر برغم تو در این دیر خراب

با یار شب و روز کشم جام شراب

از ساغر هجر و جام وصلش شب و روز

تو خون جگر خوری و من بادهٔ ناب

2

O stranger, contrary to your wish, in this ruined house,
I drink wine with my beloved day and night.
From the cup of his separation, you drink the heart's blood.
From the cup of his union, I drink pure wine day and night.

٣

از عشق کزوست بر لبم مهر سکوت
هر دم رسدم بر دل و جان قوت و قوت
من بندهٔ عشق و مذهب و ملت من
عشق است و علی ذلک احیی و اموت

3

From love, which has sealed my lips, every moment come
Strength and nourishment to my heart and soul.
I am love's slave, and love is my religion and nationality.
This is how I have lived, and this is how I will die.

۴

روی تو که رشک ماه ناکاسته است
باغیست که از هر گلی آراسته است
گر زانکه خدا نیز وفائی بدهد
آنی که دل من از خدا خواسته است

4

Your face, which is the envy of the unwaned moon,
Is a garden adorned with all kinds of flowers.
If God also gave you fidelity,
You would be the one my heart has asked of God.

۵

ساقی فلک ارچه در شکست من و تست
خصم تن و جان می پرست من و تست
تا جام شراب و شیشهٔ می باشد
در دست من و تو دست من و تست

5

Sâqi, although the heaven is after my defeat and yours,
And is the enemy of our wine-loving bodies and souls,
As long as there is the decanter and the cup of wine,
In your hand and mine is my hand and yours.

۶

یک لحظه کسیکه با تو دمساز آید

یا با تو دمی همدم و همراز آید

از کوی تو گر سوی بهشتش خوانند

هر گز نرود و گر رود باز آید

6

He who became your intimate for a moment,
Or your companion and confidant for an instant,
If called from your lane to paradise, he would never go.
And if he did, he would come back.

۷

هر شب بتو با عشق و طرب میگذرد

بر من ز غمت به تاب و تب میگذرد

تو خفته به استراحت و بی تو مرا

تا صبح ندانی که چه شب میگذرد

7

For you every night passes with love and pleasure,
For me with tossing and glowing in your sorrow.
While you are comfortably asleep, you do not know
What a night passes for me without you.

۸

یا رب رود از تنم اگر جان چه شود

وز رفتن جان رهم ز هجران چه شود

مشکل شده زیستن مرا بی یاران

از مرگ شود مشکلم آسان چه شود

8

O Lord, if the soul goes out of my body, what happens?
And if I am thus relieved from separation, what happens?
Life has become difficult for me without the loved ones.
If my difficulty is solved by death, what happens?

۹

ای مستمعان را ز حدیث تو سرور

وی دیدهٔ صاحب‌نظران را ز تو نور

جز حرف و رخت گر شنوم ور بینم

گوشم کر باد الهی و چشمم کور

9

O you, whose story captivates the audience,
You, who give light to the eyes of men of perception,
If I ever hear anything but your word and see but your face,
May God make my ears deaf and my eyes blind!

۱۰

باز آی و بکوی فرقتم فرد نگر

وز درد فراق چهره ام زرد نگر

از مرگ دوای درد خود میطلبم

بیمار نگر دوا نگر درد نگر

10

Come back and see my loneliness in the lane of separation.
See my face sallow with the pain of separation.
I am asking of death the remedy of my pain.
See the patient, the remedy, and the pain!

۱۱

باز آی و دلم ز هجر پردرد نگر

در سینهٔ گرمم نفس سرد نگر

در گوشهٔ بی مونسیم تنها بین

در زاویهٔ بیکسیم فرد نگر

11

Come back and see my heart full of the pain of separation.
See the cold breath in my warm breast.
See my loneliness in the corner of friendlessness.
See how I am alone in the corner of loneliness.

۱۲

ای در حرم و دیر ز تو صد آهنگ
بیرنگی و جلوه میکنی رنگ برنگ
خواننده ترا مؤمن و ترسا شب و روز
در مسجد اسلام و کلیسای فرنگ

12

O you, who play many tunes in the sanctuaries and taverns,
Though colorless, you appear in different colors.
Moslems and Christians call you day and night
In the mosques of Islam and the churches of the West.

۱۳

از عشق تو جان بیقراری دارم
در دل ز غم تو خار خاری دارم
هر دم کشدم سوی تو بیتابی دل
میپنداری که با تو کاری دارم

13

I have a restless soul because of your love.
I have discomfort in my heart because of your sorrow.
My heart's impatience pulls me towards you every moment,
And you think that I have something to do with you.

۱۴

اول بودت برم گذر مسکن هم
دست از دستم کشی کنون دامن هم
من نیز بر آن سرم که گیرم سر خویش
با من تو چنان نه ای که بودی منهم

14

Previously you used to visit me and also stay with me.
Now you pull your hand and also your skirt out of my hand.
I have in my mind to go my own way.
You are not with me as you used to be, nor should I.

۱۵

هر گل که شمیم مشکبار آید ازو

بی روی تو خاصیت خار آید ازو

جانیکه گرامیتر از آن چیزی نیست

ای جان جهان بی تو چکار آید ازو

15

Any flower that exudes musky fragrance,
Without your face, has the quality of a thorn.
The soul, than which nothing is dearer,
Without you, O soul of the world, what good is it?

۱۶

هر چند که گلچهره و سیمین بدنی

حیف از تو ولی که شمع هر انجمنی

ای یار وفا دار اگر یار منی

با غیر مگو حرفی و مشنو سخنی

16

Although you have a rosy face and a silvery body,
It is a pity that you are the candle of every assembly.
O my loyal beloved, if you are my love,
Speak not to any stranger, nor listen to any.

Chapter Ten
19th Century C.E.
13th Century Hejri

نشاط اصفهانی
(۱۲۴۴ هجری قمری)

۱

آنانکه ز جام عشق مدهوش شدند

از خاطر خویشتن فراموش شدند

از بهر شنیدن همه تن گوش شدند

بستند لب از حدیث و خاموش شدند

Neshât Isfahâni
(d. 1829 C.E.)

1

Those who became drunk with the wine of love,
Became forgotten from their own minds.
Their whole bodies turned to ears in order to hear.
They closed their lips to speech and became silent.

٢

در هجر تو گر دمی به کامم باشد
در وصل تو زندگی حرامم باشد
بی لعل لبت گر هوس باده کنم
خون دل خویشتن بجامم باشد

2

If one moment way from you passes according to my wish,
Let life be denied to me in your union.
If I desire wine without the ruby of your lip,
Let the blood of my heart fill my cup.

٣

گر ره بخدا جویی در گام نخست
نقش خودی از صفحهٔ جان باید شست
گم گشته ز تو گوهر مقصود و تو خود
تا گم نشوی گم شده نتوانی جست

3

If you are looking for a path to God; in the first step,
You must wash your ego's imprint from your soul's page.
The gem of your goal is lost from you.
Unless you are lost, you cannot seek what is lost.

۴

پیوند غمت تا به دل و جان بستم
از دل ببریدم و ز جان بگستم
اندوه ترا چه شکر گویم کز وی
از شادی و اندوه دو عالم رستم

4

When I attached your love to my heart and soul,
I detached myself from my heart and soul.
How can I be thankful for your love's grief,
Which freed me from both worlds' joy and grief?

۵

فارغ ز غم سود و زیانم کردی
آسوده ز محنت جهانم کردی
ای عشق ترا چه شکر گویم که چنانک
میخواستم آخر آنچنانم کردی

5

From the care of profit and loss, you redeemed me.
From the troubles of the world, you released me.
O love, how can I show you my gratitude?
For what I really wanted to be, *that* you made me.

۶

گر با تو بود کس همه عالم راه است
ور بی تو رود جهان سراسر چاه است
با خاک سر و گریبان پیوست
آن دست که از دامن تو کوتاه است

6

If one is with you, every road is the right road.
And if he walks without you, the whole world is a well.
He whose hand failed to reach you,
Poured dust over his head and tore his collar.

مدرس رفسنجانی
(۱۳۱۴ هجری شمسی)

۱

مستان جهان از می دنیا مستند
مستان بهشت از می عقبا مستند
چون نیک نظر بهر دو ما اندازیم
بینیم همه از می خرما مستند

Modarres Rafsanjâni
(d. 1936 C.E.)

1

The world's drunkards are drunk with the world's wine.
The heaven's drunkards are drunk with the heaven's wine.
If we look at both groups carefully,
We will see that they are all drunk with the date wine.

۲

مستان تو از بند دو دنیا رستند
بر محض لقای حضرتت دل بستند
در امر جهان اگر چه آنها پستند
لیکن ز می وصال تو سرمستند

2

Your drunkards broke the fetters of both worlds
And attached their hearts to your pure presence only.
Although they are low in the affairs of this world,
They are high with the wine of your union.

٣

یک جذبهٔ تو ز صد عبادت خوشتر

یک نفخهٔ تو ز صد ریاضت خوشتر

یک ذره عنایتت اگر رو آرد

از سیر و سلوک و جمله طاعت خوشتر

3

A single attraction by you is better than a hundred prayers.
A single breath of you is better than â hundred austerities.
One bit of attention that you pay to someone
Is better than any devotion and worship.

۴

گر یار طلب کنی ز اغیار گریز

گر خیر طلب کنی ز اشرار گریز

اغیار که است آنچه در وهم تو است

گر نور طلب کنی تو از نار گریز

4

If you want the beloved, escape from the others.
If you want the good, escape from the evil.
The others are those who exist in your imagination.
If you want to see the light, escape from the fire.

۵

معشوق مگو آنکه یکی عاشق اوست

آنرا تو بگو که عالم عاشق اوست

مطلوب اگر طلب نمایی تو ز شوق

آنرا بطلب که عالم شائق اوست

5

Whom someone loves do not call him the beloved.
Whom the whole world loves call him the beloved.
If you are avidly looking for your desired one,
Look for the one whom the whole world calls the Beloved.

۶

کوته نکنم سخن ز وصف دلدار
کاندر دل من نشسته باشد دلدار
گر رفت ز دل دگر سخن نسرایم
تا باز بدیدنم بیاید دلدار

6

I can not stop praising my beloved,
For he is seated in my heart.
If he left my heart, I would say no more,
Unless he comes back to see me again.

۷

نارش همه نور است ز نورش تو مپرس
زهرش همه شهد است ز شهدش تو مپرس
زین نکته بکن رقص که محبوب جهان
قهرش همه لطف است ز لطفش تو مپرس

7

His fire is all light, ask not about his light.
His poison is all honey, ask not about his honey.
Dance, for the wrath of the world's beloved is all grace.
Do not ask about his grace!

۸

یوسف وارم ز چه به زندان افکند
زاهد بودم به چنگ رندان افکند
معشوق بود چه باکش از سختیهاست
او عاشق خود بما کجا او در بند

8

Like Joseph, he threw me in a well.
I was an ascetic, he put me in the hands of *rends*.
He is the beloved, what cares he for my hardships?
He is in love with himself, what cares he for me?

٩

راحت بود آن کسی که از صورت رست
در رنج فتد هر آنکه دل بر وی بست
صورت چه بود هر چه به دل غیر خداست
کز وی دل تو بود چو ماهی در شست

9

Comfortable is the one who freed himself from appearances.
Troubled is the one who attached his heart to appearances.
What is an appearance? Anything but God in your heart
Shall make your heart like a fish on a hook.

١٠

شرب می من از لب نوشین تو بود
ماه نو من ابروی مشکین تو بود
امروز دلم اگر قراری دارد
ز آنروست که در فتنهٔ دوشین تو بود

10

My wine was from your delectable lips.
My new moon was your musky eyebrow.
If my heart has any rest today,
It is because it was under your charm last night.

Chapter Eleven
20th Century C.E.
14th Century Hejri

ملک الشعراٳ بهار

(۱۳۳۰ هجری قمری)

۱

پرهیز از خود که جای پرهیز اینجاست

وز کس مطلب چیز که هر چیز اینجاست

تا چند پی راز خدا می گردی

راز دل خود جو که خدا نیز اینجاست

Malekushshoarâ Bahâr
(d. 1912 C.E.)

1

Abstain from your ego, for the place of abstinence is here.
Ask not anything of anyone, for everything is here.
How long will you be searching for the mystery of God?
Search for the mystery of your heart, for God is also here.

۲

زاغی می‌گفت اگر بمیرد شهباز

من جای کنم بدست شاهان از ناز

بلبل بشنید و گفت کای بندهٔ آز

رو لاف مزن با وزغ و موش بساز

2

"If the royal falcon dies," said a crow,
"I will proudly perch on the king's hand."
A nightingale heard this and said, "Stop bragging,
"You, slave of greed! Go put up with frogs and mice."

۳

ما بادهٔ عزت و جلالت نوشیم

در راه شرف از دل و از جان کوشیم

گر در صف رزم جامه از خون پوشیم

آزادی را به بندگی نفروشیم

3

We drink the wine of honor and glory,
And strive to save our dignity with all our hearts.
Even if blood may cover us in the line of battle,
We will not trade our freedom for slavery.

۴

برخیز که خود را ز غم آزاده کنیم

تا کی طلب روزی ننهاده کنیم

آخر که گل ما به سبو خواهد رفت

کن فکر سبویی که پر از باده کنیم

4

Rise and let us free ourselves from suffering.
How long shall we seek the undestined sustenance?
In the end, our dust will be made into a jug.
Now let us find a jug and fill it with wine.

۵

آزادی ماست اصل آبادی ما
اینست نتیجهٔ خدا دادی ما
آزاد بزی ولی نگر تا نشود
آزادی تو رهزن آزادی ما

5

Our freedom is the principle of our development,
Which is the purpose intended by God.
Live freely, but be careful not to allow
Your freedom to be the brigand of the others' freedom.

۶

ما درس صداقت و صفا می خوانیم
آیین محبت و وفا می دانیم
زین بی هنران سفله ای دل مخروش
کانها همه می روند و ما می مانیم

6

We have taken the lessons of honesty and sincerity
And have learned the ways of love and fidelity.
O heart, complain not of these artless and mean people.
For they will all go, but we will remain.

ابوالقاسم حالت

۱

گر زانکه بیاد حق زدی پیمانه
باید که ز غیر حق شوی بیگانه
یا دل به جهاندار بده یا به جهان
یا خانه بخواه یا که صاحب خانه

Abulqâsem Hâlat

1

If you drank wine to the remembrance of God,
You must estrange yourself from anything other than God.
Love either the world or the possessor of the world.
Choose either the house or the owner of the house.

۲

مؤمن ز خدا جدا شدن نتواند
هم زو بهراسد و هم او را خواند
هر ذکر که می کنی خدا میشنود
هر فکر که می کنی خدا میداند

2

A believer cannot separate himself from God.
He both fears him and calls him.
Any word you say God hears it.
Any thought you think God is aware of it.

۳

حیوان درنده ای که خونخوار بود
بهتر ز امیری که ستمکار بود
کز آن گاهی به جسم آسیب رسد
وز این همه گاه جان در آزار بود

3

A rapacious and bloodthirsty beast
Is better than a cruel ruler.
The beast may hurt the body sometime.
The cruel ruler hurts the soul all the time.

۴

یک چند اگر کنی به خوش بینی زیست
دانی که خوشی بغیر خوش بینی نیست
گر صحبت جسم است و اگر راحت دل
هر دو بر و برگ شاخهٔ خوش بینی ست

4

If you live optimistically for a while,
You will realize that happiness is nothing but optimism.
Both the enjoyment of the body and the peace of the mind
Are the leaves and fruit of the branch of optimism.

۵

اندر پی هر خوشی ملالی و غمی ست
در صورت هر نشاط چین المی ست
در گردن هر زنده طناب اجل است
بر دامن هر وجود گرد عدمی ست

5

In the wake of every joy, there is a sorrow and a grief.
In the face of every pleasure, there is a wrinkle of pain.
On the neck of every living being, there is a noose of death.
On the skirt of every existent, there is the dust of nonbeing.

۶

در حق رفیق هر که وجدان دارد

تن در ندهد به خدعه تا جان دارد

کفر است اگر خیانت و خدعه کنی

در کار کسی که بر تو ایمان دارد

6
He who has conscience
Will never in his life deceive his friend.
It is a blasphemy to deceive and cheat
Someone who believes in you.

٧

بگزین ره مردم حقیقت جو را

بر بند لب مردم باطل گو را

هر جا که ستم رسیده‌ای را دیدی

بر رغم ستمکار مدد کن او را

7
Choose the way of the people who seek the Truth.
Close the lips of the people who speak falsehood.
Wherever you see an oppressed person,
Help him against the oppressor.

٨

هرگز به سه کس نیفکند چشم خدا

آن مرد که کار اوست بیداد و جفا

آن کس که به بیدادگران کرد مدد

وان کس که به بیدادگری داد رضا

8
Upon three persons, God never casts a look:
The person who is cruel and unjust,
The person who helps the unjust, and
The person who consents to injustice.

۹

آن از همه خلق گرانمایه تر است
کازاد ز اندیشهٔ نفع و ضرر است
دنیای دنی بدست هر کس که در است
او را نه بدان میل و نه بر آن نظر است

9

He is the most respectable of all humans
Who is free from the thought of profit and loss.
He has no interest in and no expectation of the world,
No matter in whose hand this lowly world may be.

۱۰

ز آنجا که ثبات نیست آیین جهان
نه مهر جهان ماند و نه کین جهان
ای شیفتگان خوان رنگین جهان
خواب است و خیال تلخ و شیرین جهان

10

Since there is no stability in the affairs of the world,
Neither the love nor the hatred of the world will remain.
O you, who are fascinated by the world's colorful table,
The bitter and sweet of the world are illusions and dreams.

۱۱

آتش مفکن ز غم به کاشانهٔ دل
پر کن ز می نشاط پیمانهٔ دل
شادی است چو گنجینه بویرانهٔ دل
خنده است چو آفتاب در خانهٔ دل

11

Cast not fire in your heart with sorrow.
Fill the bowl of your heart with the wine of joy.
Joy is like a treasure in the ruins of the heart.
Laughter is like sunlight in the house of the heart.

۱۲

دانا همه پی بر هنر خلق برد

نادان همه سوی عیب مردم نگرد

افسوس که عیب جوئی بیخردان

بیش است ز عیب پوشی اهل خرد

12

The wise seek out the people's merits.
The unwise seek out the people's demerits.
Alas, the fault-finding of the unwise
Exceeds the fault-covering of the wise.

۱۳

تا سر تهی از فهم و ذکا می باشد

در لب همه لاف و ادعا می باشد

پر معرفت از لاف زدن مستغنی است

ظرفی که پر است کم صدا می باشد

13

When the head is devoid of intelligence and understanding,
The lips are busy boasting and bragging.
The one who is full of knowledge is needless of boasting.
The vessel which is full makes less sound.

۱۴

زین شوق که پر کنی ز گل دامن خود

بس خار در افکنی به پیراهن خود

تا خلق گرفتار هوا و هوسند

هر کس خود اوست بدترین دشمن خود

14

In the excitement of filling your lap with roses,
You will let many thorns pierce your garment.
When people are caught in their passions and desires,
Each person is his own worst enemy.

صغیر اصفهانی
(۱۳۴۹هجری شمسی)

۱

شد دور چو از نظر غبار من و ما
آن یکه سوار ناگهان شد پیدا
یعنی که شدیم نیست و اندر همه جا
دیدیم خدا هست خدا هست خدا

Saghir Isfahâni
(d. 1971 C.E.)

1

When the dust of *I* and *we* went out of sight,
That Sole-rider appeared all at once.
That is, we became nonexistent and saw everywhere
It is God that exists, God that exists, God.

۲

خرم دل آن کس که ز خود آگاه است
نفی‌اش سوی اثبات دلیل راه است
بر هر چه نظر کند خدا بیند و بس
این معنی لا اله الا الله است

2

Blissful is the heart of the one who is aware of himself.
His negation [of himself] leads him toward his affirmation.
Whatever he looks at, he sees only God.
This is the meaning of *Lâ ilâha illAllâh*.

٣

افلاک نه مست ماست مست دگری است

وین خاک نه پست ماست پست دگری است

زان کار گره خورد بدست من و تو

تا کشف شود که کار دست دگری است

3

Heavens are not made drunk by us, but by another.
This Earth is not lowered by us, but by another.
Things do not go right in your hand and mine,
So that it be known they are in the hand of another.

۴

ای سجده‌گه اهل وفا ابرویت

وی قبلهٔ جان حق پرستان کویت

هر سو که کنم روی و بهر جا که روم

باشد بخدا روی دل من سویت

4

O you, whose eyebrow is the altar of the faithful,
And whose lane is the qebla of Truth-worshippers,
Any direction I turn and any place I go,
By God, my heart faces toward you.

۵

این مرده دلان مردهٔ مرده پرست

وقعی ننهند بر بزرگی تا هست

از گرسنگی چو او در افتاد ز پای

آنگاه به گور میبرندش سر دست

5

These worshippers of the dead, whose hearts are dead,
Pay no attention to a great person while he is alive.
When he succumbs to starvation and dies,
They carry him to his grave upon their hands.

۶

بی اهل دلی مرا سر بستان نیست
میلم به کنار لاله و ریحان نیست
با بودن اهل حال اندر نظرم
فرقی بمیان گلشن و زندان نیست

6

Without an enlightened person, I desire not an orchard,
Nor the fields of tulips and fragrant flowers.
When I am with an enlightened person, in my view,
There is no difference between a rose-garden and a prison.

۷

می آمد و شهد از لب خندان میریخت
میرفت و به دل تیر ز مژگان میریخت
از حسرت موی و روی خود خون جگر
از دیدهٔ کافر و مسلمان میریخت

7

As she came, honey from her lips poured.
As she went, arrows from her lashes to the heart poured.
Sadly longing for her hair and face, from the eyes of
Moslems and non-Moslems, blood of the heart poured.

۸

هر دل که اسیر عشق دلبر گردد
هر دم گذرد غمش فزونتر گردد
هر غم به زمانه کاهد اما غم عشق
هر روز فزون ز روز دیگر گردد

8

Any heart captured by the love of a lovely one
Experiences more pain with the passing of every moment.
Every sorrow decreases in time, except the sorrow of love,
Which grows everyday more than the day before.

٩

رو سوی حقیقت کن و بگذر ز مجاز

یعنی که مبر بسوی کس دست نیاز

با غیر خدا مگوی راز دل خویش

چون نیست بغیر او کسی محرم راز

9

Turn your face toward the Truth and ignore the untruth.
In other words, do not extend a needy hand toward anyone.
Do not tell your heart's secret to anyone but God.
For there is no confidant of secrets except God.

١٠

پرسید کسی ز من بگو عرش کجاست

گفتم که فراز این سپهر میناست

گفتا که ز عرش اعظمت هست خبر

گفتم دل با صفای مردان خداست

10

Someone asked me, "Where is the empyrean?"
"Above this blue sky," said I. He asked again,
"Do you know where the highest empyrean is?"
"It is in the sincere heart of a man of God," I replied.

١١

خفت به کسان مده کسان محترمند

از خرد و کلان پیر و جوان محترمند

گر راه به توحید بیابی دانی

کافراد بشر یکان یکان محترمند

11

Do not humiliate people. They are respectable.
Children and adults, the young and the old are respectable.
If you find your way to unity, you will know that
Human beings, each and all, are respectable.

۱۲

آن استر بارکش که خود باری برد
وان اشتر بیزبان که خود خاری خورد
صد ره به از آدمی که از مادر خویش
زاد آدم و ظالم شد و چون ماری مرد

12

That draught mule that carries loads
And that mute camel that eats thorns
Are a hundred times better than the one who was born
As a human, lived as an oppressor, and died as a snake.

۱۳

جان عشق و محبت است جان را بشناس
حق بیخودی است این بیان را بشناس
هر جا من و ما ز در در آید نفس است
با این دو نشان خاص آنرا بشناس

13

The soul is love and affection. Know your soul.
Truth is selflessness. Know this expression.
Wherever *I* and *we* enter, there is the ego.
With these two special signs, know the ego.

۱۴

چون گنج نهان کن غم پنهانی خویش
منما بکسی بی سر و سامانی خویش
جمعیت خاطر خود ار می طلبی
با غیر خدا مگو پریشانی خویش

14

Hide your secret like a treasure.
Reveal to no one your destitution.
If you want a peace of mind,
Tell your affliction to no one but God.

۱۵

ای ساقی ماه وش در این ماه صیام

ده باده که روزه بهر من گشت حرام

افطار کنم که دیده ز ابرو و رخت

هم شکل هلال دید و هم ماه تمام

15

O moon-like Sâqi, give me wine in this month of fasting.
For fasting became forbidden to me now.
Let me break my fast. For my eyes saw the crescent moon
Of your eyebrow and the full moon of your face.

۱۶

تا کی به زمانه نیک و بد می بینی

از چشم قبول و چشم رد می بینی

اینها همه پرتو جمال ازلی است

کز صبح ازل تا به ابد می بینی

16

How long will you see good and bad in the world?
Or see with approving and disapproving eyes?
These are all the rays of the face of the Primordial One,
Which are seen from the dawn of time till eternity.

۱۷

جز صلح و صفا نباشدم کرداری

با رد و قبول کس ندارم کاری

آزار جهانی ار کشم آن خواهم

کز من نرسد بهیچ کس آزاری

17

I do not do anything except with a pure and sincere heart.
I do not care for anyone's approval or disapproval.
Even if I am hurt by the whole world,
I want no one to be hurt by me.

شیخ الرئیس افسر
(۱۳۱۹ هجری شمسی)

۱

زاهد گوید کسی که نوشید شراب
در عالم دیگر ببرد رنج و عذاب
گر باده یدالله دهد هست ثواب
از دست خدا چرا ننوشیم شراب

Shaykhorrais Afsar
(d. 1941 C.E.)

1
The ascetic says, "Whoever drinks wine
"Will have pain and torment hereafter."
Wine is permissible if given by the hand of God.
Why shall we not drink wine from the hand of God?

۲

تا پیرهن ستم کشی در تن ماست
آزادی ما دستخوش دشمن ماست
ما را کشتند و دست و پا هم نزدیم
خون شهدا تمام در گردن ماست

2
As long as the garment of tolerance of injustice is on us,
Our freedom is a victim in the hand of the enemy.
They killed us and we did not even twitch.
The blood of martyrs is on our neck.

٣

از خرمن علم و معرفت خوشه بگیر

از همت خویش بهر ره خوشه بگیر

تا چند اسیر وهم و نخجیر خیال

پرواز کن از دو عالم و گوشه بگیر

3

Take your share from the harvest of knowledge and gnosis.
Make a provision for the road with your effort.
How long will you be the captive of illusion and fancy?
Fly out of the two worlds and stay away.

رعدی آذرخشی

١

فرزانه کسی که تخم نیکویی کاشت

وز خلق جهان بجز بدی چشم نداشت

بد دید و نرنجید که خود خواست چنان

ور زانکه بدی ندید نیکی انگاشت

Ra'di Âzarakhshi

1

He is wise who sowed the seed of good
And expected nothing but evil from the people.
If they were bad to him, he was not hurt. He expected it.
And if they were not bad to him, he considered it good.

۲

هر دستگهی گریز پایی دارد
هر خواسته مایهٔ از گدایی دارد
از دستگه و خواسته در عشق گریز
کاین خانه دری به روشنایی دارد

2

Every organization has a runaway.
Every desire has its substance in begging.
Escape from every organization and desire into love.
For this house has a door that opens to light.

۳

دانی چه بود مایهٔ گمراهی ما
دزد خرد و رهزن آگاهی ما
در جامهٔ رنگ رنگ مردم خواهی
این دیو دو روی خویشتن خواهی ما

3

Do you know what the cause of our bewilderment is?
Do you know what robs us of our reason and intelligence?
It is this double-faced demon of selfishness
That comes in the colorful garment of philanthropism.

۴

کودک که بود اسیر زهدان چندی
باشد ز اسارتش دل خرسندی
ای در رحم عادت و اوهام اسیر
کی در رخ عشق عالم آرا خندی

4

A child, imprisoned in the womb for a while,
Is content with its imprisonment. And you,
Who are imprisoned in the womb of habits and illusions,
When will you smile at the face of the world-adorning love?

۵

از عادت و اوهام قدم بالا نه

جهدی کن و پا به عالم والا نه

دیروز گذشت و نیست فردا پیدا

گر دل تو به عشق مینهی حالا نه

5

Step out of your habits and illusions!
Make an effort and step up to a higher world!
Yesterday passed and tomorrow is not in sight.
If you want to give your heart to love, do it now!

حمید سبزواری

۱

یا رب که براه رهروان دام مباد

ور دام سزد جز که بهر گام مباد

آنرا که تویی طبیب درد افزون باد

آنرا که تویی قرار آرام مباد

Hamid Sabzvâri

1

O Lord, let there be no trap on the path of wayfarers.
But if they deserve, let there be a trap at every step.
Let the one whose physician is you have more pain.
Let the one whose peace is you have no rest.

۲

تن چیست حجاب جان گرش چاک کنی
زر بینی اگر نگاه بر خاک کنی
در هر چه نظر کنی خدا را بینی
وز عالم خاک سیر افلاک کنی

2

What is a body? The veil of the spirit.
If you tear it, you will see gold when you look at dust.
Anything you look at, you will see God therein,
And you will rise to heavens from the world of earth.

۳

عاشق شو اگر صبر و شکیب است ترا
وز توشهٔ رهروی نصیب است ترا
درد ار رسد از سوی طبیب است ترا
آنکس که طبیب است حبیب است ترا

3

Fall in love if you have patience and tolerance,
And if you have provisions for the trip.
If you find pain, it is from the doctor.
He who is your doctor is your friend.

۴

خواهی که قدم نهی به سر منزل عشق
اول سر عشق باید آنگه دل عشق
اندیشه مکن ز سهل و از مشکل عشق
بر دریا زن مپرس از ساحل عشق

4

If you wish to step on the road of love,
You must first have the mind for love, then the heart for it.
Think not of the comforts and difficulties of love.
Take to the sea and ask not where the shore is.

۵

آن کس که بچشم دل جهان را نگرد

هر سو به نشانه بی نشان را نگرد

زین بادیه گردی به دلش ننشیند

الا که گذار کاروان را نگرد

5

He who looks at the world with the eye of the heart
Sees the sign of the Signless in every direction.
No dust from this desert settles in his heart,
Except when he watches the caravans pass.

۶

سنگ است دلی که نیست در سنگر عشق

خاک است بسر آنکه ندارد سر عشق

بدنام کسی که منشیان خط دوست

نامش ننوشته اند در دفتر عشق

6

The heart which is not in the trench of love is a rock.
The head which is empty of love is buried with dust.
Defamed is the one whose name is not registered
In the book of love by the scribes of the Friend.

۷

بگشای قفس فضای خود را بنگر

در عرصهٔ عمر جای خود را بنگر

ای گوهر جان بهای خود را بنگر

در خود بنگر خدای خود را بنگر

7

Open the cage and behold your space.
Behold your position in the field of life.
O essence of the spirit, behold your value.
Look at yourself and behold God.

طوطی همدانی

۱

ای شاه یگانه مهر هرجایی من
وی خاک رهت سرمهٔ بینایی من
دانا چو شدم بتو بحق تو شده است
حیرانی من حاصل دانایی من

Tuti Hamadâni

1

O my universal sun and the one and only king,
Whose road's dust is the collyrium of my eyes,
Since I came to know you, I swear by your truth,
My knowledge has become the cause of my amazement.

۲

جز مهر تو نیست در جهانم هنری
جز تو نبود روی دلم با دگری
تا با خبرم از تو ز خود بی خبرم
وز بی خبری بیافتم هر خبری

2

Except loving you, I have no other art.
Except you, I have no other desire in my heart.
As long as I am aware of you, I am unaware of myself.
Any awareness I found was from this unawareness.

۳

ای ذات تو ماورای ادراک عقول

در وصف تو محو و مات انسان جهول

توصیف ترا هر که نمود از ره عجز

بر عجز وی از لطف زدی مهر قبول

3

O you, whose essence is beyond the intellect's ken,

The ignorant man is confused and lost in describing you.

Whoever described you in his helplessness,

You accepted his helplessness kindly.

۴

مالی که نه بهر دین بود باشد مار

کاری که نه بهر حق بود باشد زار

نامی که نه از کمال شد آمد ننگ

فخری که نه از خدا بود باشد عار

4

The property which is not for the sake of faith is a snake.

The work which is not for the benefit of Truth is a failure.

The fame which is not from excellence is an infamy.

The honor which is not from God is a shame.

۵

مردان خدا خدای را مرآتند

شاهند ولی ز عشق جانان ماتند

چون نور خدا گرفته جان و دلشان

ز آنروی برای نور حق مشکوتند

5

Men of God are the mirrors of God.

They are kings, but checkmated by the love of God.

Since God's light has pervaded their hearts and souls,

They are the lamps of the light of God.

۶

روی تو مرا قبله و عشقت دین است
دیدار تو خواهم و مرادم این است
طوطی صفتم ثنای تو قند من است
مهر تو مرا چو شمع بر بالین است

6

Your face is my kebla and your love my creed.
I want to see you. This is my goal.
I am like a parrot, and your praise is my sugar.
Your love is like a candle to me at my bedside.

۷

من مهر ترا چراغ جان می بینم
پیوند تو عیش جاودان می بینم
گر پرتوی از نور تو تابد به دلم
دل را چو یکی باغ جنان می بینم

7

I see your love as the lamp of my spirit,
And your union as the eternal life.
If a ray of your light shines upon my heart,
I will see my heart as the garden of heaven.

۸

از بادهٔ عشق خود مرا مجنون کن
وین کاسهٔ هستی مرا وارون کن
بر چشم دلم سرمهٔ بینایی بخش
دل خانهٔ تست غیر را بیرون کن

8

Make me frenzied with the wine of love.
Turn this bowl of my existence upside down.
Bestow to my heart's eye the collyrium of vision.
My heart is your home. Put the strangers out.

٩

شاهم اگر از صدق گدای تو شوم
باقی شده ام اگر فنای تو شوم
منحوس زمانی که بغفلت بگذشت
مسعود دمی که من برای تو شوم

9

I will be a king if I sincerely become your beggar.
I will be eternal if I become annihilated by you.
Dismal was the time that passed in negligence.
Blessed will be the moment I become yours.

١٠

چون جلوه نمود عشقت اندر دل ما
از هجر تو شد غم جهان حاصل ما
ای دوست بود شبی که در خلوت دل
روشن کنی از جمال خود محفل ما

10

When your love displayed its glory in my heart,
My gain was a world of suffering in your separation.
O friend, will it ever happen that one night with your beauty
You illuminate my dwelling in the *khalvat* of the heart?

١١

بیگانه شدم ز خلق تا یار توام
آزاد شدم تا که گرفتار توام
معروف شدم تا شده ام عارف تو
رستم ز هوس تا که هوادار توام

11

I became estranged from the people as I befriended you.
I became free when I was captured by you.
I have become well-known since I came to know you.
I was freed from desire when I became desirous for you.

۱۲

تو با همه و خلق ز تو بی خبرند
تو در دل و خلق سوی تو رهسپرند
گر پرده برافتد ز میان گردد فاش
بی پرده تویی و خلق در پرده درند

12

You are with all, but people are unaware of you.
You are in the heart, yet people are traveling toward you.
If the curtain between you and people falls down,
It will be known that people were veiled, not you.

۱۳

ای دوست مرا بجز تو دلداری نیست
جز فکر تو و ذکر توام کاری نیست
گفتی که بکن نفی و به اثبات برس
نفی که کنم که جز تو دیاری نیست

13

O my love, I have no sweetheart except you.
I do nothing but think of you and remember you.
You told me, "Negate so that you can affirm."
Whom should I negate? For you are the only one there is.

۱۴

تو شاهی و خوبان همگی مات تواند
تو شمسی و ماسوی چو ذرات تواند
تو نوری و اعیان همه مشکوة تواند
تو ذاتی و عالم همه آیات تواند

14

You are the king and all the lovely ones are amazed at you.
You are the sun and all the rest are your particles.
You are the light and all manifestations are your lamps.
You are the essence and all things are your appearances.

عبدالحسین نصرت

١

دنیا چو حباب است و لیکن چه حباب

نه بر سر آب بلکه بر روی سراب

وان نیز سرابی که ببینند به خواب

وان خواب چه خواب خواب بد مست خراب

Abdulhosayn Nosrat

1

The world is like a bubble. What kind of a bubble?

A bubble, not on water, but on the surface of a mirage.

A mirage which is seen in a dream.

A dream which is seen by someone who is dead drunk.

٢

جز در ره خود قدم نمی باید زد

هیچ از بد و نیک دم نمی باید زد

چون نیک نظر کنی جهان مزبله‌ایست

این مزبله را بهم نمی باید زد

2

One should not walk except in one's own road.

One should not talk of good and bad at all.

If one looks carefully, the world is a pile of rubbish.

One should not stir this pile of rubbish at all.

٣

هر روز به محنتی و رنجی بودیم
هر شب به مشقت و شکنجی بودیم
خوش خوش چو بویرانهٔ فقر آسودیم
دیدیم که ما شگفت گنجی بودیم

3
Everyday I had some kind of pain and grief.
Every night I had some kind of torment and hardship.
But when I slowly began to rest in the ruins of *faqr*,
I realized I was a wonderful treasure.

محمد مهدی فولادوند

١

ما در بن غاریم و ز حق بی خبریم
عاجز که قفای خویشتن را نگریم
هر سایهٔ باطل که بدیوار افتد
از کثرت جهل خود حقیقت شمریم

Mohammad Mehdi Fulâdvand

1
We are at the end of a cave, unaware of truth,
And unable to look behind our heads.
We are so ignorant that any false shade
That falls on the wall, we take it for truth.

۲

خوشبخت کسی که جاودان جوید عشق

فارغ ز جفای این و آن جوید عشق

این گوهر نایاب برو در خود جوی

بیچاره کسی که در مکان جوید عشق

2

Happy is the one who always seeks love.

Heedless to the people's unkindness, he seeks love.

Search for this rare gem in your own self.

For you will be disappointed if you search for love in space.

۳

خوشتر که جهان برای ما راز بود

در مجلس زیرکان صد آواز بود

گر پرده برافتد از رخ شاهد راز

دیگر چه نیاز و جلوه و ناز بود

3

It is better that the world be a mystery for us,

Better that a hundred voices be in the assembly of the wise.

If the veil drops from the face of the mysterious Beloved,

What more need is for supplication, glorification, and pride?

جلال بهی زاد

۱

بر خیز و نظاره کن چهرهٔ دوست
هر جا نگری نشانی از جلوهٔ اوست
خیر است هر آنچه در وجود است نه شر
مغز است هر آنچه در حیات است نه پوست

Jalâl Behizâd

1

Rise and behold the face of the Friend.
Wherever you look, there is a sign of his glory.
Whatever is in existence is good, not bad.
Whatever is in life is a kernel, not a shell.

۲

گل آمده تا نشانی از یار دهد
هجران زده را مژده بدیدار دهد
بلبل همه جا ترانهٔ عشق زند
تا که خبر از جلوهٔ دلدار دهد

2

The rose has come to bring a token from the beloved,
And to give the news of union to the one who is separated.
Everywhere the nightingale is singing the song of love
In order to announce the beloved's display of glory.

٣

از دیدن روی یار جان مست شود
هر نیستی از هستی او هست شود
صد حیف که این بادهٔ پر نشئهٔ وصل
در بزم حیات دست بر دست شود

3

The spirit is intoxicated when it sees the beloved's face.
Any nonbeing becomes being by his existence.
Alas, alas, this exhilarating wine of union
Goes from one hand to another in the feast of life.

۴

شوریده سری که دل نهاده ره دوست
آن زنده دلی که عاشق روی نکوست
هر سو نگرد جمال او بیند و بس
هر جا که رود همیشه دیوانهٔ اوست

4

The frenzied who has laid his heart in the beloved's way,
That young in heart who is in love with beautiful faces,
At any direction he looks, sees only His face,
And anywhere he goes, he is always mad after Him.

۵

دریای کمال ما بجز قطره نبود
جز حیرت ما ز معرفت بهره نبود
دنیای تصور من و تو به وجود
چون نیک نظر کنی بجز ذره نبود

5

The sea of our perfection was no more than a drop.
Our share of knowledge was no more than amazement.
The world as it was conceived by you and me,
When examined carefully, was no more than a particle.

۶

این مدعیان از همه خودخواه ترند
مغرور به علم گشته گمراه ترند
وین ساده دلان عاری از فضل و کمال
چون پاک دلانند پس آگاه ترند

6

These claimants to knowledge are the most arrogant.
Proud of their knowledge, they are the most astray.
And these simple-hearted ones who lack learning and talent,
Because of their sincere hearts, are the most conscious.

۷

زین بند قفس اگرچه پرواز کنم
عشق ابدیت خود آغاز کنم
اینجا چو مرا نبوده آزادی عشق
آنجا روم و تجلی راز کنم

7

If I ever fly out of the confinement of this cage,
I will commence my love of eternity.
Since I have had no freedom of love here,
I will go there and manifest the mystery.

آذر اصفهانى

۱

دل زنده و هر دو دیده بیدار خوش است

در پای خم شراب با یار خوش است

یک دست پیاله دیگری گردن یار

اینجاست که هر چه عمر بسیار خوش است

Âzar Isfahâni

1

It is good to have a lively heart and both eyes fully awake.
It is good to be with one's beloved beside a wine vat.
One hand holding a cup, another around the beloved's neck,
It is this kind of life that the longer the better is.

۲

رندی بدر میکده دیدم سرمست

یک کوزه می به پیش و تسبیح به دست

گفتم رندا شراب و سجاده چرا

گفتا که بدین طریق هم راهی است

2

I saw a *rend*, drunk at the door of a tavern,
A jug of wine in front of him and a rosary in his hand.
"Wine and prayer-mat? Why?" asked I.
"This, too, is a road toward Him," said he.

۳

هر کس به دیار خویش یاری دارد
هر شاخهٔ گل به پای خاری دارد
ما هم ز بهار خویش گل می چینیم
گویند که هر گلی بهاری دارد

3

Every person has a friend in his homeland.
Every rosebush has a thorn at its foot.
I, too, am picking roses in my spring.
Every flower has a spring, as they say.

۴

آذر همه اجرام سماوی مستند
مستند که این چنین بهم پیوستند
گردون و سپهر و چرخ و چنبر همگی
در آمدن و رفتن ما همدستند

4

Azar, all the celestial bodies are drunk.
Being drunk, they have thus joined to each other.
The wheel, the sky, the sphere, and the circle
Have all joined hands to make us come and go.

۵

میخانهٔ عشق زیر و رو باید کرد
در جستن یار جستجو باید کرد
هر مطلب خویش مختصر باید گفت
می خوردن خود سبو سبو باید کرد

5

One must turn the tavern of love upside down.
One must search in order to find one's beloved.
One must say briefly what one wants to say:
One must drink wine one jug after another.

۶

تا یار نبینم انبساطم نبود
تا می نخورم روی نشاطم نبود
جز جام و پیاله ای و معشوقه ناز
ای بی خبر آه در بساطم نبود

6

Until I see my beloved, I am not cheerful.
Until I drink wine, I am not joyful.
Except a decanter, a bowl, and a coy sweetheart,
I have nothing else, O unaware ones.

۷

وقت خوش من شب است در خلوت یار
ای ساقی شب زنده دلان باده بیار
ما بر کرم پیر مغان تکیه زنیم
دنیای پر از حادثه انگار انگار

7

My happy time is at night when I am alone with my beloved.
Bring wine, O Sâqi of the live-at-night!
I rely on the generosity of the Magians' master.
I do not care if this eventful world exist or not.

۸

بر خیز و غم جهان فرسوده مخور
غم بهر زمان بود و نابوده مخور
می خور که ز بند هر دو عالم برهی
خوش باش و غمی که هست بیهوده مخور

8

Rise to your feet and for this wearied world grieve not.
Over the time which was or was not, grieve not.
Drink wine to be free from the bondage of both worlds.
Be happy and in vain grieve not.

٩

ما دلبر خود به هر دو عالم ندهیم
سری که ز باده دیده در پرده نهیم
بر فرض که ما ز اهل دوزخ باشیم
از عابد خودنمای بیداد بهیم

9

I will not trade my sweetheart for both worlds.
I will keep hidden the secret I know about wine.
Even if I may be of the people of hell,
I am better than the pretentious and cruel ascetic.

فؤاد کرمانی
(۱۳۴۰ هجری قمری)

١

هر چند که در هزار و یک پرده در است
نور رخش از هزار و یک پرده در است
از پرده برون شدیم و در پرده درون
بیرون و درون پرده آن پرده در است

Fuâd Kermâni
(d. 1922 C.E.)

1

Though covered by a thousand and one veils,
The light of his face shines out of a thousand and one veils.
I came out from behind the veil and went in behind it.
I saw the veil-tearer behind and in front of the veil.

۲

پرسید جوانی شبی از حضرت پیر

خواهم که نمیرم و ندانم تدبیر

فرمود که مرگ خلق در زندگی است

خواهی که چو من زنده شوی زنده بمیر

2

One night a young man asked a spiritual master:
"I want to be immortal, but I do not know how."
"People's death is in life," said the master,
"If you want to become alive like me, die alive."

۳

این نقطهٔ دل را که تو گویی خون است

صد عالم حس درون او مکنون است

از چون بدر آی و چشم بی چون بگشای

وین عالم چون نگر که در بی چون است

3

This little thing called heart, which you say is blood,
Has a hundred worlds of sense hidden within it.
Come out of the causality and open the causeless eye,
And see this caused world inside the causeless one.

۴

ما در رخ جان جمال جانان دیدیم

آنرا که ندیده این و آن آن دیدیم

طومار سموات ظنون پیچیدیم

تا عرش خدا را دل انسان دیدیم

4

We saw the beloved's beauty in the face of the spirit.
We saw what this person and that have not seen.
We rolled up the scroll of many suspicions
When we saw the heart of man was the empyrean of God

۵

یک عمر به جستجوی دلبر گشتیم
سرگشته به هر بحر و به هر بر گشتیم
دلبر دل ما بود و دل اندر بر ما
با دلبر دل بسوی دل برگشتیم

5

A lifetime I searched for the beloved.
Bewildered, I roved over the sea and land.
The beloved was my heart, and my heart was in my breast.
I returned to my heart with the beloved of my heart.

۶

دیدار تو هر مرتبه دیدی دارد
در هر نظری حسن جدیدی دارد
رخسار تو جز به چشم دل نتوان دید
پیداست که هر دری کلیدی دارد

6

Seeing you, each time presents a different view.
With each view, it reveals a different beauty.
Your face cannot be seen except with the eye of the heart.
Obviously, each door has its own key.

۷

اوضاع جهان نقش بر آب است حکیم
بیداری دنیا همه خواب است حکیم
این باده که ما ز جام کثرت نوشیم
گوییم شراب است و سراب است حکیم

7

The world's phenomena are like sketches in water, O sage.
The world's wakefulness is only sleep, O sage.
The wine we drink from the cup of multiplicity,
We call it wine, but, in fact, it is a mirage, O sage.

٨

جان کندنت ای خواجه ز دلبستگی است
دل بر کن و جان مکن که این رستگی است
گر طالب معرفت نئی زود بمیر
حمال مشو که زندگی خستگی است

8

Your struggling is because of your attachment, O khâja.
Detach your heart and struggle not. Freedom is this.
If you are not after enlightenment, die soon.
Do not be a porter, for life is exhausting.

٩

وارسته دلی که بسته بر یزدان است
عرشی است که مستوی بر او رحمن است
در او بنگر خدا و جز او منگر
کآیینهٔ حق نما همین انسان است

9

That heart is free which is tied to God.
Such a heart is the abode of the All-merciful.
Behold God there and nowhere else!
For this same man is the mirror that shows God.

١٠

می میری و در دم دم عیسی با تست
در بندگیت کوری و مولا با تست
عاشق نشود ز عشق معشوق جدا
مجنون که شدی همیشه لیلی با تست

10

At the moment of death the breath of Jesus is with you.
You are blind in your slavery while the master is with you.
The lover is never separate from the beloved's love.
When you are Majnun, the love of Layli is always with you.

۱۱

گفتم ز لبت بوسهٔ دیگر خواهم
من طوطی ام و مدام شکر خواهم
گفتا که ز قند لعل من هر که خورد
گوید که از این قند مکرر خواهم

11

I said, "I want another kiss from your lips.
"I am a parrot. I want sugar constantly."
She said, "Whoever tastes the sugar of my lips says,
"'I want more of this sugar and more.'"

۱۲

دریاست وجود و ما در او غوطه‌وریم
در بحر وجود خود ز خود بی خبریم
هر لحظه بچشم سر و بینایی سر
در بحر دریم و گویی از بحر دریم

12

Existence is an ocean and we are floating in it.
We are unaware of ourselves in the ocean of existence.
With the eyes of the head and the sight of the head,
While in the ocean, we think we are out of the ocean.

۱۳

معنی به سخن در است چون باده به جام
عارف نشوی کلیم را جز به کلام
اعجاز رسل نمانده باقی به جهان
وین معجزه باقی است تا صبح قیام

13

The meaning is inside the word, like the wine inside the cup.
A speaker is not known except by his words.
No more miracles of the prophets remain in the world,
Except this miracle of words, which will last till doomsday.

۱۴

هر کشته شدن نه شرط مردانگی است

در مهلکه تاختن ز دیوانگی است

تا زنده نگردی بخدا کشته مشو

گر کشته شوی خلاف فرزانگی است

14

Not every kind of being killed is the sign of courage.
To rush into a death-trap is madness.
Until you have become alive in God, do not get killed.
If you do so, it is contrary to wisdom.

۱۵

عاشق که سرشته از حقیقت گل اوست

از دوست نخواهد بحقیقت جز دوست

حق از همه رو گرچه هویداست ولی

پنهان بود از کسی که در عشق دو روست

15

The lover, whose clay was kneaded from truth,
Wants nothing of the friend except the friend himself.
Although Truth is visible in everything,
It is hidden from the one who is double-faced in love.

۱۶

دانای زمانه بر جهان غم نخورد

لقمان حکیم لقمهٔ سم نخورد

دنیا همه هیچ و جاهل اندر غم اوست

عالم غم هیچ را به عالم نخورد

16

He who knows the world suffers not for the world.
The Sage Loqmân eats not a poisonous morsel.
The whole world is nothing, yet the ignorant suffers for it.
The learned in the world suffers not for the *nothing*.

۱۷

وارسته ز قید شو عبادت این است
دلبسته بدوست شو سعادت این است
از دعوت اهل حق بجز رویت حق
مطلب مطلب که خرق عادت این است

17

Be free from attachments! This is worship.
Be attached to the Friend! This is happiness.
Of the invitation of the men of God,
Seek no goal but the seeing of God! This is paranormal.

احمد سروش

۱

این وحشتت از فرشتهٔ مرگ چراست
آنکس که نمرده و نمیرد بکجاست
مرگ است چو خواب خستگان در شب درد
هر چیزی بجای خویش خوب و زیباست

Ahmad Srush

1

What is your terror of the angel of death for?
Where is the man who has not died and will not die?
Death is like the sleep of the wounded in the night of pain.
Everything is good and beautiful in its own place.

۲

مرگ از تو جدا نیست فراموش مکن
باور سخن مردم کم هوش مکن
مرگ است ز روز ازل همزاد حیات
این است و جز این قصه دگر گوش مکن

2

Death is not separate from you. Don't forget it.
Don't believe the words of the less intelligent people.
Death is the twin of life from the first day of creation.
This is the story. Listen to no other story anymore.

۳

یا رب دردم به عجز و زاری نکشد
زنهار به صبر و بردباری نکشد
خواهم که به اوج همچو شاهین میرم
کارم به جهان به لاشخواری نکشد

3

O Lord, allow not my pain to end in disability and misery.
Allow not that I be forced into endurance and patience.
I want to die like an eagle in the climax.
Allow not my life to end in scavenging.

۴

گر نام خدا بریم نز بهر خداست
محتاج کجا خدا به دینداری ماست
بی نور یقین چسان سپارم راهی
کانرا نه نهایت نه بدایت پیداست

4

If I mention the name of God, it is not for the sake of God.
God is not in need of our religiousness.
Without the light of Truth, how can I travel the road,
Whose beginning and end is out of sight?

محمد باقر طاهری
(۱۳۳۱ هجری شمسی)

١

تا چند دل به هیچ در پیچ و خمی

از بهر دو روزه وهم در بیش و کمی

چون ابر بهار عمر تو در گذر است

بگذار تو هم در چمن دهر نمی

Mohammad Bâqer Tâheri
(d. 1953 C.E.)

1

O heart, how long will you meander for nothing
And wax and wane for the sake of a transient illusion?
Your life is passing like a spring cloud.
You, too, leave some moisture in the meadow of the world.

٢

وحدت طلبی در عشقها کم باشد

از بحر حقیقت این جهان نم باشد

از جزء به کل تا نگیری پیوند

هر جا که نظر کنی همه غم باشد

2

Quest for unity is rare in loves.
This world is a drop from the sea of the Truth.
Until you are grafted from the part to the whole,
There is only suffering wherever you look.

۳

دلدار گر از دیده نهانی باشد

ز آلودگی چشم جهانی باشد

در دایرهٔ وجود عشق و مستی

در ظل نشان بی نشانی باشد

3

If the beloved is hidden from the eye,
It is because of the infection of this worldly eye.
In the circle of existence, love and ecstasy
Are under the sign of the Signless.

۴

عالم به خیال یا که در خواب گذشت

روز و شب عاقلان در این باب گذشت

تا فلسفی از آب کشد دستارش

دیوانه هم از آتش و هم آب گذشت

4

Time passed either in a dream or imagination.
This is how the days and nights of the wise passed.
Before the philosopher could salvage his hat from the water,
The mad one passed through both fire and water.

مهدیهٔ الهی قمشه ای

۱

در دولت گل توبه ز می گشت حرام
ساقی ز شراب لاله گون ریز به جام
زان می که بیک جرعه فراموش کنیم
یک عمر خیال ننگ و اندیشهٔ نام

Mahdiyya Elâhi Qamshei

1

In the season of the rose, repentance of wine is forbidden.
Sâqi, pour the red wine in the glass.
Pour the wine, a gulp of which should make me forget
A lifetime of fear of shame and hope for name.

۲

تا عاشق و رند و لابالی شده ایم
از هر چه بغیر دوست خالی شده ایم
مستیم چنان که تا رسد هشیاری
بر کوزه گر دهر سفالی شده ایم

2

Since I became a lover, a *rend*, and a vagrant,
I have been empty of everything except the beloved.
I am so drunk that by the time I sober up
I will be the clay of the jug-maker of the world.

۳

هنگام سحر چو یاد روی تو کنم

با هر سر مویم آرزوی تو کنم

هر صبح که سر ز خواب خوش بردارم

با دل همه لحظه گفتگوی تو کنم

3

In the morning when I recall your face,
I desire you with every strand of my hair.
Every morning when I lift my head from the sweet dream,
I constantly speak to my heart about you.

۴

ای عشق تو مایهٔ نشاط دل من

یادت همه نقد عمر بیحاصل من

تنها نه ز جان و دل حدیث تو کنم

کاین زمزمه بشنوی ز آب و گل من

4

O you, whose love is the cause of my happiness
And whose remembrance the only product of my futile life,
I am not only speaking about you from my heart and soul,
You will hear this song from my earth and water, too.

۵

ساقی می صاف ارغوانیم بیار

زان آب حیات جاودانیم بیار

از بهر رضای دوست تاخیر مکن

زان پیش که بگذرد جوانیم بیار

5

Sâqi, bring me the clear purple wine.
Bring me of that eternal water of life.
Dally not, for the friend's sake.
Bring it before my youth passes away.

۶

در دولت گل بیار ساقی جامی
زان پیش که چرخ گستراند دامی
مطرب بنواز چنگ تا باده خوریم
تا دور دگر ز ما نماند نامی

6

In the bounty of roses, O Sâqi, bring a cup
Before the heaven spread a net.
O minstrel, play the harp so that we drink.
Our names may be forgotten by the next round.

۷

هر جا که توان نشست خوش خانهٔ ماست
هر جا که گل است و سبزه میخانهٔ ماست
شادیم و خوش امروز که فردای زمان
حرفی که بیاد نیست افسانهٔ ماست

7

Wherever I can be happy is my home.
Wherever there are flowers and grass is my tavern.
I am joyful and happy today, because tomorrow
That which will not be remembered is my story.

محمدرضا مرتضوی

١

جز ذکر تو هیچ کار نتوانم کرد
درمان دل بیقرار نتوانم کرد
گر هر نفسی هزار شکرت گویم
شکر تو یک از هزار نتوانم کرد

Mohammad Rezâ Mortazavi

1

Except praising you, I cannot do any other work,
Nor can I relieve this restless heart.
If I thank you a thousand times in every breath,
I can not thank you one thousandth of what I should.

٢

ای درگه تو پناهگاه همه کس
مهر و کرم تو عذرخواه همه کس
لطف تو بیک نظر دو صد چاره کند
درد دل و سوز اشک و آه همه کس

2

O you, whose gate is everyone's refuge,
And whose kindness and generosity everyone's excuse,
Your grace, with one glance, can totally redress
Everyone's heartache, burning tears, and sighs.

۳

از غیر خدا جمله فراموشی به

از بادهٔ وحدت همه بیهوشی به

در محفل فقر و حلقهٔ اهل ولا

دم نازدن و حیرت و خاموشی به

3

All except God is best to be forgotten.
It is better to be totally unconscious with the wine of unity.
In the assembly of *faqr* and the ring of lovers,
It is better to be speechless, silent, and amazed.

۴

هرگز نزنم دری بغیر از در دوست

در دیده و دل نیست بجز منظر دوست

در محفل او پای ز سر نشناسم

سر دوست ندارد آنکه دارد سر دوست

4

I never knock any door except that of the Friend.
In my eyes and heart, there is only the image of the Friend.
I cannot tell head from foot in his presence.
He whose goal is the Friend loves not his head.

۵

آن کس که ترا شناختِ کس را نشناخت

مشتاق گل روی تو خس را نشناخت

آن کس به یقین بهشت عشق تو گزید

واصل شد و دوزخ هوس را نشناخت

5

He who knew you, none other he knew.
Eager for the rose of your face, no thorn he knew.
That person chose your love's paradise with certainty,
Attained it, and no inferno of passion he knew.

۶

یا رب تو به خلق مهربان دار مرا
از آتش خشم در امان دار مرا
ای مظهر نور آسمانها و زمین
آیینهٔ نور جاودان دار مرا

6

O Lord, keep me kind to people.
Save me from the fire of anger.
O source of the light of the Earth and heavens,
Keep me as the mirror of eternal light.

۷

دل کعبهٔ عشق لایزال تو بود
جان شیفتهٔ ذات و جمال تو بود
ای وصل توام غایت آمال وجود
بپذیر مرا وقت وصال تو بود

7

My heart is the Ka'ba of your imperishable love.
My soul is fascinated by your essence and beauty.
O you, whose union is the end of my desires of existence,
Receive me, it is time for union.

۸

تا جرعه ای از جام الستت ندهند
آگاهی از این بلند و پستت ندهند
تا کشتهٔ وادی محبت نشوی
سررشتهٔ عاشقی بدستت ندهند

8

Until you are served a cup of the *Alast* wine,
You are not made aware of this high and low.
Unless you are killed in the valley of love,
You are not given the expertness of a lover.

۹

میمیرم اگر که جستجویت نکنم
تا با همه خلق گفتگویت نکنم
چندان بتو عاشقم که نبود نفسی
کز غایت عشق آرزویت نکنم

9

I will die if I do not search for you
Or if I do not speak about you with the people.
So much in love am I with you and so intense is my love
That not a single moment passes without longing for you.

۱۰

یا رب بتو آنچنان منم پیوسته
کز خویش بریده ام ز خود بگسسته
چندان بتماشای رخت مشتاقم
کز دیدن غیر تست چشمم بسته

10

O Lord, I am so attached to you
That I have cut off and separated from myself.
I am so eager to watch your face
That my eyes are closed to any other than you.

۱۱

ما را بجمال خویش بینایی ده
ما را بکمال خویش دانایی ده
ما بندهٔ ناتوان و مشتاق توایم
ما را ز وصال خویش برنایی ده

11

Give us vision to see your beauty.
Give us knowledge to know your perfection.
We are your desirous and powerless bondsmen.
Give us youth with your union.

هوشنگ حکمتی (سروی)

۱

مستی من از بادهٔ انگوری نیست

یک ذره در آن صحبت مخموری نیست

این بادهٔ جان ز جام جانان من است

فاش این سخن است و جای مستوری نیست

Hushang Hekmati (Sarvi)

1

My drunkenness is not from the grape wine.
There is no talk of languishing in this wine at all.
This wine of the soul is from my beloved's goblet.
I say this openly with no covering at all.

۲

تا چند بوی ز دور گردون دلخون

بستان به بهای عقل یک جام جنون

درکش همه یکباره و آنگاه به وجد

صد قهقهه زن بر فلک آبله گون

2

How long shall you be distraught by the heaven's rotation?
Obtain a cup of wine at the expense of your reason.
Drink it up all at once, and then in your rapture,
Laugh roaringly at the pock-marked firmament.

۳

از باغ جهان سرو روان ما را بس
هم صحبتی پیر مغان ما را بس
گر کام کسان پر نکند دریایی
یک جام ز میخانهٔ جان ما را بس

3

One cypress from the world's garden is enough for me.
The companionship of the Magians' *Pir* is enough for me.
If a sea of water cannot fill the mouths of people,
One cup of wine from the soul's tavern is enough for me.

۴

با پختگی از دختر رز کام بگیر
با شرط ادب می از لب جام بگیر
با سرو قد لاله رخ غنچه لبی
بر سبزه نشین و می گلفام بگیر

4

Fulfill your desire from the daughter of the vine expertly.
Sip the wine from the lip of the bowl politely.
With a cypress-statured, tulip-cheeked, rosebud-lipped
Sweetheart, sit on the grass and drink rosy wine.

۵

تا خرقهٔ خود پرستیت می ندری
بر کار خرابات مغان ره نبری
یک جرعه بکش ز جام ما چرخ زنان
تا چرخ فلک را به پشیزی نخری

5

Until you tear your cloak of selfishness,
You will not understand the work of the Magians' tavern.
Drink one gulp from our goblet so that, whirling,
You do not give a penny for the wheel of the sky.

۶

چون خندهٔ عمر ماست مانند حباب
شرط است همه سبک برقصیم بر آب
یعنی که به بانگ رود و آوای رباب
لب را بنهیم بر لب رود شراب

6

Since the laughter of our life is like a bubble,
We must all dance lightly on the water.
That is, to the sound of music and strain of the rebec,
We must all put our lips on the lip of the river of wine.

۷

گهگاه بتایید کسان شاد شویم
گهگاه به خرده ای غم آباد شویم
این رسم عجب ز اصل خودبینی ماست
آن لحظه خوش است کز خود آزاد شویم

7

Sometimes we are happy because of the others' approval.
Other times we are unhappy because of their disapproval.
This strange habit is due to our selfishness.
That moment is happy when we are free from our egos.

۸

برخیز بتا می دل افروز بیار
آن گوهر شبچراغ چون روز بیار
تا عمر چو گل نگشته بازیچهٔ باد
زان بادهٔ آتشین غم سوز بیار

8

Rise, my sweetheart! Bring that gleeful wine.
Bring that gem which shines at night, like day.
Before my life, like a rose, turn to a plaything of the wind,
Bring of that grief-burning, fire-like wine.

۹

من یاوهٔ هر بیهده گو نتوانم
من جز بمی ناب وضو نتوانم
ساقی بده ساغری که برپاست نماز
من مهلت از خم به سبو نتوانم

9

I cannot tolerate the nonsense of every idle-talker.
I cannot make my ablutions except with pure wine.
Sâqi, give me a goblet. For the prayers are in progress.
I can't wait for wine to pour from the vat to the decanter.

۱۰

من بادهٔ ناب ارغوان خواهم و بس
نوش از لب آن غنچه دهان خواهم و بس
هو هو کنم و هی هی و می می، می می
می می چه میی می مغان خواهم و بس

10

I want pure purple wine, that's all.
I want honey from the lips of that bud-like mouth, that's all.
I will shout: Ho, ho! Wine, wine! Hey, hey! Wine, wine!
What kind of wine? I want the Magians' wine, that's all.

۱۱

تا عقل بکار بیش و کم خواهد بود
جان من و تو عرصهٔ غم خواهد بود
می نوش و به عشق کوش کاین جوهر ناب
جان داروی دلهای دژم خواهد بود

11

As long as reason is concerned with *more or less,*
Life is a field of suffering.
Drink wine and try to love, for this rare substance is
The life-giving medicine of the sorrowful hearts.

۱۲

یک جرعهٔ می مملکت جم ارزد
یک خندهٔ وی به نقد حاتم ارزد
گنج دو جهان به آب انگور دهید
کاین آب بخاک همه عالم ارزد

12

One gulp of wine is worth the kingdom of Jamshid.
One laughter of wine is worth the wealth of Hatam.
Trade the treasures of both worlds for grape-juice.
This water is worth all the land in the world.

۱۳

ما آب حیات از لب جانان زده ایم
از ساغر وحدتش می جان زده ایم
نه کفر شناسیم و نه ایمان هی هی
با عشق گره بکفر و ایمان زده ایم

13

I have drunk the water of life from my beloved's lip.
I have drunk the wine of spirit from the cup of unity.
I know neither disbelief nor belief.
I have tied belief and disbelief with the knot of love.

۱۴

تا سخت نکوشی به نوائی نرسی
تا درد ننوشی به صفائی نرسی
تا خویش بنشکنی و خود گم نکنی
منزل بنیابی و بجائی نرسی

14

Unless you work hard, you will not accomplish anything.
Unless you drink the dregs you will not have the pure.
Unless you break your ego and lose yourself,
You will not find your destination or reach anywhere.

۱۵

دیگر نبود مرا ز هجرش المی
دیگر نبود مرا به دل هیچ غمی
من غیبت دوست را ندانم ز حضور
چون دم نزنم بدون او هیچ دمی

15

I do not suffer any pain of separation any longer.
Nor do I have any sorrow in my heart any longer.
I cannot tell the friend's absence from his presence.
For I do not breathe without him any longer.

۱۶

تا کی به غمان آب و نان باید بود
تا کی نگران جسم و جان باید بود
چند از پی کار و بار غم باید شد
تا چند اسیر این جهان باید شد

16

How long shall we suffer for bread and water?
And worry about the body and life?
How long shall we concern ourselves with sorrow?
How long shall we be the captives of this world?

ادیب الممالک فراهانی
(۱۳۳۶ هجری قمری)

۱

خویشش مشمر چو پیش بیگانه نشست
کز دوست برید چون به دشمن پیوست
پرهیز ز پارسای میخانه نشین
بگریز ز آشنای بیگانه پرست

Adibulmamâlek Farâhâni
(d. 1918 C.E.)

1

Do not count him a relative who sat before a stranger,
For he cut off from the friend and joined the enemy.
Avoid that pious man who sat in a tavern.
Run away from the acquaintance who loves strangers.

۲

دل را به حضورت خبر از خویش نبود
جز عشق توام عقیده و کیش نبود
من سجده کنم بخاک کویت کادم
از خاک درت مشت گلی بیش نبود

2

At your presence, my heart was not conscious of itself.
There I had no faith or creed except your love.
I prostrate on the dust of your lane. For Adam was
No more than a handful of clay from the dust of your door.

۳

حق گوی و بدار از درون حق را پاس

حق گو نکند ز هیچ کس وهم و هراس

گر مرد حقی ز حیله حق را بشناس

حق عریان است و حیله پنهان بلباس

3

Speak the truth and guard it from within.
The speaker of truth is not afraid of anyone.
If you are a man of truth, distinguish truth from untruth.
Truth is naked and untruth is hidden by a garment.

۴

ما مست و خراب بر درت تاخته ایم

نقد دل و جان به درگهت باخته ایم

غیر از تو ندیده ایم و نشناخته ایم

با خاک درت از دو جهان ساخته ایم

4

Drunk and ruined, we have rushed to your door.
We have lost our hearts and souls at your door.
We have neither seen nor known anyone except you.
Of the two worlds, we have put up with your door's dust.

۵

اول که مرا بدام خویش آوردی

صد گونه وفا و مهر پیش آوردی

چون دانستی که من گرفتار توام

بیگانه شدی و ناز پیش آوردی

5

In the beginning when you caught me in your snare,
You brought forth a hundred kinds of love and kindness.
When you realized that I was your captive,
You became a stranger and brought forth your pride.

۶

ایام جوانی شد و آن ناز شکست
وز شهپر مرغ عمر پرواز شکست
بنشین بنشین کدام رقص و چه سماع
آن جلوه فرو نشست و آن ناز شکست

6

The days of youth expired and their pride broke.
And flight from the wings of the bird of life broke.
Sit down, sit down! What is this dancing and music?
That display of glory settled down and that pride broke.

۷

ما دستخوش ستمگرانیم هنوز
وز بادهٔ عجب سرگرانیم هنوز
کی دست توان بکار خود زد کز جهل
بازیچه دست دیگرانیم هنوز

7

We are still the victims of the oppressors.
We are still drunk with the wine of arrogance.
How can we attend to our own business
If we are still playthings in the others' hands?

نظمی تبریزی

۱

شیدای رخت به جست و جوی دگر است

وز هر دو جهانش آرزویی دگر است

از خوردن صد پیاله مستی نکند

سرمستی عاشق از سبویی دگر است

Nazmi Tabrizi

1

The crazed for your face is in search of something special.
His desire from the two worlds is something special.
A hundred cups of wine will not make him drunk.
The lover's drunkenness is from a different jug.

۲

خرم دل آنکه چون تو یاری دارد

با همچو تویی بوس و کناری دارد

هر کس که غم ترا خریدست بجان

با شادی دیگران چه کاری دارد

2

Happy is the one who has a sweetheart like you.
Happy is the one who kisses and hugs someone like you.
What cares he for the others' pleasures who has accepted
With all his heart the pain of the love of someone like you?

۳

ای شیخ به گفت و گو نمی گنجد عشق

در معنی تو به تو نمی گنجد عشق

ظرفیت عشق را ندارد دل تو

دریاست بیک سبو نمی گنجد عشق

3

O Shaykh, love can not be contained in an argument,
Nor can it be enclosed in a complex definition.
Your heart does not have the capacity of love.
Love is an ocean. It cannot be contained in a jug.

۴

جز وصف تو نیست هر چه من میگویم

جز راه تو نیست هر کجا می پویم

هر سنبل و گل که در چمن می بویم

مقصود دلم تویی ترا می جویم

4

Whatever I say is nothing but your praise.
Wherever I walk is only your road.
Any rose and hyacinth I smell in the meadow,
You are the goal of my heart. I am looking for you.

۵

در پنجهٔ نفس خستگانیم همه

مرغ پر و پا شکستگانیم همه

از خواهش نفس اگر اطاعت نکنیم

با خیل ملک نشستگانیم همه

5

Wounded by the claws of desire we all are.
Like the birds with broken wings and legs we all are.
If we do not obey the demand of our desires,
Seated in the company of angels we all are.

۶

ما تشنه لبانیم بیا ای ساقی

در ساغر ما ریز شراب باقی

صد حیف که از عمر نشد حاصل ما

جز حسرت و نامرادی و مشتاقی

6
Our lips are thirsty, Sâqi, come!
Pour in our cups the wine remaining.
Alas! A hundred times alas! Our gain from life was
Nothing but yearning, disappointment, and longing.

۷

ما عاشق و دل شکسته ایم ای ساقی

وز هر دو جهان گسسته ایم ای ساقی

ما را ز کمند غم کسی نرهاند

دل بر کرم تو بسته ایم ای ساقی

7
We are in love and broken-hearted, O Sâqi.
We have cut off from both worlds, O Sâqi.
No one will free us from the noose of suffering.
We have our hope for your kindness, O Sâqi.

سید محمد بهشتی

١

خیره است دو چشمم که مگر باز آیی
خندید خیالم که تو با ناز آیی
گفتم تو هزار ناز بر من بنواز
من می کشم این ناز اگر باز آیی

Sayyed Mohammad Beheshti

1

I am gazing at the door, hoping that you will come back.
My fancy is laughing that coyly you will come back.
I said, "Sell me a thousand coquetries, if you wish.
"I will buy them all if you ever come back."

٢

دیریست کنار چشمه چشمم نگران
ناگاه مگر ببینمت چون دگران
پوشی رخ و گویی که گنهکاری تو
بخشنده تویی گناه خونین جگران

2

My eyes have long been anxious for you beside a spring,
So that perhaps I see you suddenly, like other people.
You cover your face and tell me that I am a sinner.
You are the forgiver of the sins of the bleeding hearts.

۳

خورشید به عزم سجده بر خاک افتاد
گل ریخت به سبزه رعشه بر تاک افتاد
روز ازل از پرتو حسنت پیدا
شد عشق و چنین شعله در افلاک افتاد

3

The sun fell to the ground in order to prostrate.
The rose petals scattered on the grass and the vine trembled.
On the Primordial Day, from the radiance of your beauty,
Love appeared and such a flame fell in the skies.

۴

در خلوت خانه بوی یار آمده است
در ظلمت جان نور نگار آمده است
آتش بقلم زد و سخن سوخت مرا
خاموش ز قیل و قال یار آمده است

4

The beloved's scent has reached the privacy of the house.
The light of love has pierced the darkness of the soul.
He set fire to my pen and the words burned me.
The beloved has come silently without discussions.

۵

در خلوت شب آینهٔ آب شکست
در چشمهٔ چشم عاشقان خواب شکست
بر خواست چو عزم رقص را شاخهٔ نور
آیینه غزلخوان شد و مهتاب شکست

5

In the solitude of the night, the mirror of the water broke.
In the fountain of the lovers' eyes, the dream broke.
When a beam of light moved to dance,
The mirror began to sing and the moonlight broke.

۶

گفتم ز چه دیر آمدی و زود روی
گفتا شاید ز خواب بیدار شوی
گفتم نظری بمن بینداز و برو
گفتا نظرم بتوست هر جا که روی

6

I asked, "Why did you come late and are going soon?"
He replied, "So that you may wake up from your sleep."
I said, "Cast a look on me first, and then go!"
"My look is always on you wherever you go," said he.

٧

گفتم به خیال دیدنت مستم من
گفتا که به هر چه بنگری هستم من
گفتم که به هر چه رو نمودی جز من
گفتا کوری تو، نورم و هستم من

7

I said, " I am ecstatic with the thought of seeing you."
He said, "Whatever you look at, I am in existence."
"You look at everything except me," said I.
"You are blind. I am the light. I am the existence," said he.

عشرت قهرمان

١

ای زندهٔ ظاهر و به باطن مرده
وی آنکه شدی همچو خزان افسرده
بر گیر مدد ز اشک تا تازه شوی
با آب گیاه کی شود پژمرده

Ishrat Qahramân

1

O you who are alive outwardly and dead inwardly,
And you who have become wearied like autumn,
Get help from your tears so that you freshen.
When does a plant wither in water?

٢

جان تو ز عاشقی فروزان گردد
پا تا به سرت ز عاشقی جان گردد
چون باد بهار عشق جنبان گردد
هر شاخ که خشک نیست رقصان گردد

2

Your life will become radiant through love.
You will become spirit from head to foot through love.
When the spring wind of love comes into motion,
Any branch which is not dry starts dancing.

۳

شبها که ز اشک من چراغان گردد
یاد تو ز راه آید و مهمان گردد
دانی به چه ماند هوس تو در دل
چون عطر که در باغ پریشان گردد

3

During the nights which are lit with my tears,
Your memory arrives from the road and becomes my guest.
Do you know what your desire in the heart is like?
It is like the perfume that scatters in the garden.

۴

پیوسته به جوشم و خموشم چو حباب
با رخت فنا جلوه فروشم چو حباب
تا بحر وجود این چنین طوفانیست
جز خویش بگو با که بجوشم چو حباب

4

I am always excited and silent like a bubble.
I display my glory in the garb of nonbeing.
As long as the ocean of being is so stormy,
Tell me with whom except myself shall I conjoin?

۵

پروانه صفت سینه برافروزم من
در آتش شوق دوست می سوزم من
گویید به معنی نگر ای بی خبران
معنی ز جمال دوست آموزم من

5

Like a moth, I glow my breast and burn
In the fire of my yearning for the friend.
You tell me to see the reality. O unaware ones,
I see the reality in the face of the friend.

۶

کو یاد تو تا چارهٔ این هوش کنم
رخ را ز سرشک باغ گل پوش کنم
کو یاد تو تا به صد هزاران جلوه
آید ز ره و خویش فراموش کنم

6

Where is your remembrance so that I cure my memory
And turn my face to a rose-garden with my tears?
Where is your memory so that it may come in from the road
With a hundred thousand glories to make me forget myself?

ادیب کرمانی
(۱۳۰۸ هجری شمسی)

۱

دریاست ظهور و ما در آن چون ماهی
هر سو نگریم نیست جز گمراهی
چون جز تو نبینیم تو را نشناسیم
ماهی از آب کی دهد آگاهی

Adib Kermâni
(d. 1930 C.E.)

1

Manifestation is a sea wherein we are like fish.
At any direction we look we see nothing but bewilderment.
Since we do not see anything except you,
We do not know you. How can the fish know the water?

۲

دیدار خدا بچشم دل سهل بود
خود بینی و خود نمایی از جهل بود
گر اهل دلی خدات پیداست ولی
پنهانی او همی ز نااهل بود

2

Seeing God with the eye of the heart is easy.
Self-conceit and flaunting are due to ignorance.
If you are enlightened, your God is visible.
He is invisible to the unenlightened ones.

سید حسن میرخانی
(۱۳۶۹ هجری شمسی)

۱

بس گوهر قیمتی ز اسرار نخست
اندر صدف دل گرانمایهٔ تست
تا نشکند این صدف بسنگ همت
هرگز نشود مراد و کار تو درست

Sayyed Hasan Mirkhâni
(d. 1991 C.E.)

1

Many priceless pearls of primordial secrets are
In the shell of your precious heart.
Until this shell is broken with the stone of endeavor,
Never will your goal and affair be right.

۲

درویش کسی بود که بی کینه بود

پاک از همه آلودگیش سینه بود

اخلاق خوشش عادت دیرینه بود

وز صدق و صفا دلش چو آیینه بود

2

A dervish is a person without rancor.
His breast is clean from all kinds of defilements.
Good nature is his old habit and his heart is like a mirror
Because of his sincerity and purity.

۳

هر کس که دلی سوختهٔ هو دارد

خوشبوی دلی چو ناف آهو دارد

بی بو نبود سوخته ای در عالم

دل سوخته و سوخته دل بو دارد

3

Anyone whose heart is consumed by God
Has a pleasant-smelling heart, like the navel of a musk-deer.
Nothing that burns is without a smell.
The burned heart of the lover has a smell.

۴

تا شمع محبت به دل افروخته ایم

پروانه صفت به شعله اش سوخته ایم

جان و دل ذره ذره اندوخته را

یکباره به بازار تو بفروخته ایم

4

Since the day I lit the candle of affection in my heart,
I have been ablaze in its flame, like a moth.
The soul and heart, which I had accumulated little by little,
I have sold in your market all at once. ·

۵

اسرار خدا ز تیز هوشان بشنو

از دیده وران عیب پوشان بشنو

مشنو ز خمش دلان پر جوش لبان

از جوش دلان لب خموشان بشنو

5

Hear the secrets of God from the sharp-witted.
Hear them from the fault-covering seers.
Hear not from the silent-hearted and boisterous-lipped.
Hear from the boisterous-hearted and silent-lipped.

۶

آن به که بنزد عام بدنام شوی

حق گویی و مستحق دشنام شوی

آیین کژ زهد ریا بگذاری

رندانه مرید مطرب و جام شوی

6

It is better to be infamous before the common people,
To say the truth and deserve bad names.
It is better to drop the false creed of pretentious piety
And be, like a *rend*, a devotee of the minstrel and wine.

منصور اوجی

۱

عشق آمد و در سینهٔ ما خانه گرفت
وز مردم هر دو چشم ما دانه گرفت
خون شد دل ما و عشق ازین بادهٔ سرخ
بر نطع سپید صبح پیمانه گرفت

Mansur Oji

1

Love came and took residence in my breast
And took seed from the pupils of my eyes.
My heart bled, and love took a cup of this red wine
At the white table of the dawn.

۲

خورشیدی از آسمان مشرق گم شد
انگور شرابخانه شد در خم شد
چون آب درون چشم مردم بنشست
چون نان بمیان سفرهٔ مردم شد

2

A sun disappeared from the sky of the East,
Turned to a tavern's grapes and entered a vat.
It settled in the people's eyes as water,
And sat on the people's bread-cloth as bread.

۳

در دکهٔ عاشقان شرابی زد و رفت

بر چهره ز خون خود گلابی زد و رفت

در ظلمت شب چو گل برآمد از خود

بر فرق سپیده آفتابی زد و رفت

3

He took a drink at the lovers' bar and went.
He splashed the rose-water of blood to his face and went.
In the dark of the night, like a rose, he came out of himself,
And over the head of the dawn, like a sun, shone and went.

۴

برخیز شبانه ترک ما و من کن

از اطلس سرخ پیرهن بر تن کن

هنگام رسیده است هنگام صبوح

آفاق سپیده را به خون روشن کن

4

Get up at night and leave the *I* and *we*.
Put on a shirt made of red silk.
The time for the morning wine has arrived.
Brighten the horizons of dawn with blood.

۵

برخیز شبانه پرده دیگرگون کن

از عقل درآی و کار صد مجنون کن

خواهی که نماز عاشقان بر تو برند

هنگام سپیده دم وضو در خون کن

5

At night, rise and change the drape.
Emerge from reason and do a hundred Majnuns' work.
If you want people to perform the lovers' prayers for you,
Make ablutions with blood at dawn.

۶

در خلوت عاشقان شرابی خوردیم
بر بال سماع پیچ و تابی خوردیم
خورشید به نعره ای بر آمد از ما
گویی که شبانه آفتابی خوردیم

6

I took some wine in the lovers' seclusion,
And turned and twisted on the wings of music.
With one roar, the sun came out of me,
As if I had swallowed it in the evening.

۷

ناگاه شبی ز خواب بیدار شدیم
آیینهٔ راز و رمز اسرار شدیم
با بانگ اناالحقی که بر خاک زدیم
منصور شدیم و باز بر دار شدیم

7

Suddenly one night I woke from my sleep
And became the mirror of mystery and the code of secrets.
As I shouted *I am the Truth* to the Earth,
I became Mansur and went back to the gallows.

۸

حالیست مرا که عشق نامش کردند
آنکس که خرید خون بجامش کردند
بر منظر خلق روزگارش بردند
انگشت نمای خاص و عامش کردند

8

The state I am in is called love.
Whoever fell in this state his cup filled with blood.
He was paraded before the eyes of people,
So that he be known to all — common and special people.

٩

حالیست مرا که شور می بارد از او
خورشید خوشم که نور می بارد از او
این چیست بجز عشق که بر جانم زد
بنگر به رخم سرور می بارد از او

9

I am in a state from which frenzy is pouring.
I am a pleasant sun from which light is pouring.
Is this anything other than love that struck at my soul?
Behold my face from which happiness is pouring.

١٠

حالیست مرا که شرح حالش همه خوش
راهش همه خوش رسم و روالش همه خوش
عشق است چنین حال و هر آنکس که وراست
هجرش همه خوش صبح وصالش همه خوش

10

I am in a state whose description is pleasant.
Its path is pleasant and its rites are pleasant.
Such a state is love, and whoever has it,
His separation is all pleasant, so is the morning of his union.

١١

حالیست مرا که سر بسر جان شده ام
نشناخته پا ز سر بمیدان شده ام
ای خلق جهان به شکر و شورم نگرید
من لایق خاکبوس جانان شده ام

11

Mine is a state in which I am wholly become spirit.
Bewildered from head to foot, I have entered the arena.
O people of the world, look at my enthusiasm and gratitude!
I have become worthy of kissing the ground of the beloved.

۱۲

حالیست مرا که باده نوشم شب و روز
با یاد خوشت جمله خموشم شب و روز
عشق است چنین حال و در این حال طرب
با هیچ کسی جز تو نجوشم شب و روز

12

Mine is a state in which I drink wine day and night.
I am silent with your happy memory day and night.
Such a state is love, and in this state of pleasure,
I cannot conjoin with anyone except you.

۱۳

حالیست مرا که آتش و نور بود
از سینهٔ غیر اهل مستور بود
زیبندهٔ کیست این شور عظیم
آن خسرو عاشقان که منصور بود

13

Mine is a state which is fire and light,
Which is hidden from the strangers.
Who deserves this grand ecstasy?
That king of lovers, Mansur.

۱۴

حالیست مرا که سینه بی کینه شده ست
آن ماه کجاست دل چو آیینه شده ست
وین دیده چرا بهانه جویی کندم
او طالب آن نگار دیرینه شده ست

14

Mine is a state in which my breast is devoid of rancor.
Where is that moon? My heart has become like a mirror.
Why should I complain of this vision?
For it has become desirous of that ancient beloved.

۱۵

حالیست مرا که طرفه باغی دارم

در ظلمت شام خود چراغی دارم

این باغ و چراغم از کجا حاصل شد

از هر که بجز دوست فراغی دارم

15

Mine is a state in which I have a wonderful garden.

I have light in the dark of the night.

How did I obtain this garden and light?

I am free from all except the friend.

۱۶

حالیست مرا که جمع مستان دانند

حلاج وشان و می پرستان دانند

از آمدگان و رفتگانش تو مپرس

عشق است چنین حالت و هستان دانند

16

Mine is a state which the crowd of drunkards know.

Persons like Hallaj and wine-worshippers know.

Ask not about this state of those who come and go.

Such a state is love, which those who exist know.

۱۷

حالیست مرا که از خدا خواسته ام

خود را ز هر آنچه غیر او کاسته ام

زین خواهش و کاهشم چه حاصل افتاد

خوش جامهٔ عشق بر تن آراسته ام

17

Mine is a state which I had asked of God.

I have lessened myself of anything except Him.

What have I gained from this asking and lessening?

I have decorated myself with the fine garment of love.

۱۸

حالیست مرا که حافظش خوش میداشت
رومی از آن جهان به چرخش میداشت
سعدی خوش از آن آب بر آتش میزد
منصور از آن سینه پر آتش میداشت

18

Mine is a state which kept Hafez rejoicing,
Which made Rumi keep the world turning.
Sa'di, happy in this state, kept pouring water on fire,
And Mansur kept his breast replete with fire.

۱۹

حالیست مرا که قید عالم زده ام
پا بر سر درد و رنج و ماتم زده ام
این شادی و این نشاط و سورم ز کجاست
با حضرت دوست لحظه ای دم زده ام

19

Mine is a state in which I have cut the fetters of the world.
I have stepped over the head of pain, suffering, and grief.
Whence is this joy, pleasure, and celerbration?
I have breathed for a moment in the presence of the friend.

علی اکبر دهخدا

(۱۳۳۴ هجری شمسی)

۱

گمنامی آدمی ز بدنامی به

ناکامی ما باز ز خودکامی به

بر گاه سخن سوخته و گشته هبا

صد بار ز ناپختگی و خامی به

Ali Akbar Dehkhodâ
(d. 1956 C.E.)

1

Anonymity is better than infamy.
Ungratification is better than self-gratification.
Being burned and destroyed at the time of speaking is
A hundred times better than being raw and inexperienced.

۲

تا چند ز بیداد به بیداد شوی

ای مرغ درین قفس بفریاد شوی

این قصه گذار قصهٔ خود را باش

آزاد شو از غیر که آزاد شوی

2

How long shall you go from one cruelty to another?
How long shall you cry out in this cage, O bird?
Let this story go. Mind your own story.
Become free from others, so that you free yourself.

آصف
(۱۳۳۲هجری شمسی)

۱

آن باده که عارفان حق‌گو گویند
و آن باده که صادقان حق جو جویند
آن جذبهٔ عشق وحدت ربانی است
وندر دل شب چون گل شب بو بویند

Âsaf
(d. 1954 C.E.)

1

The wine meant by the truth-telling ârefs,
And the wine sought by the honest truth-seekers,
Is the attraction of the love of divine unity,
Which they smell like a wallflower in the heart of the night.

۲

محبوب منی و یار دلجوی منی
هر سو که روم تو نیز در سوی منی
با چشم یقین نه با جهان بین گمان
هر جا نگرم مقابل روی منی

2

You are my beloved and my affable friend.
Any direction I go, you are in my direction.
With the eye of certainty, not with that of illusion,
Wherever I look, you are in front of me.

٣

ای در همه عمر زندگانیم از تو
وی در همه بزم شادمانیم از تو
فخر است مرا عشق تو در دل به جهان
ای فخر جهان فخر جهانیم از تو

3
O you, to whom I owe my whole life
And from whom I have my joy in every feast,
Your love in my heart is my honor in the world.
O honor of the world, my honor in the world in from you.

قیصر امین پور

١

برخیز به خون دل وضویی بکنیم
در آب ترانه شستشویی بکنیم
عمر اندک و فرصت خموشی بسیار
تلخ است سکوت گفتگویی بکنیم

Qaysar Aminpur

1
Get up and let us do ablutions with our hearts' blood,
And wash ourselves in the water of song.
Life is short and the time for silence long.
Silence is bitter. Let us have a chat.

٢

چون نی بنوای خسته خوانیم نماز
افتاده ز پا نشسته خوانیم نماز
دور از وطن اصلی خویشیم و رواست
در حال سفر شکسته خوانیم نماز

2

Like a reed, we say our prayers in a weary tune.
Having collapsed, we say our prayers sitting.
We are far from our original homeland.
So it is all right to do our prayers short.

٣

آن سان که تویی هیچکس آگه بتو نیست
راهی ز فراز عقل کوته بتو نیست
هر چند ترا هزار ره باشد لیک
جز راه دل از هیچ رهیٰ ره بتو نیست

3

No one knows you as you are.
No path to you is short from the peak of reason.
Although there are a thousand paths toward you,
Except the path of heart, no path actually leads to you.

جواد نوربخش

١

ساقی بده آن باده که هستی ببرد

اندیشهٔ هر چه خود پرستی ببرد

یا کور کند دیدهٔ پندار مرا

یا باز کند چشمم و مستی ببرد

Javâd Nurbakhsh

1

Sâqi, give me the wine that takes existence away,
That takes the thought of any selfishness away.
Let this wine either blind the eye of my illusion
Or open my eyes and take drunkenness away.

٢

با اهل صفا جز به صفا نتوان بود

با بی من و ما با من و ما نتوان بود

هر چند قلندران ز خود بی خبرند

هم صحبت آنان به ریا نتوان بود

2

With the men of sincerity, one cannot but sincere be.
With those without *I* and *we*, one cannot with *I* and *we* be.
Although the calenders are unconscious of themselves,
One cannot with them in hypocritical conversation be.

۳

بی عشق اگرچه زنده ای مرداری
بی عشق اگر عزیز باشی خواری
بی عشق اگر شهنشهی مسکینی
با عشق اگرچه عاجزی سرداری

3

Without love, though alive, a carrion are you.
Without love, though dear, despicable are you.
Without love, though king of kings, a pauper are you.
With love, though wretched, a commander are you.

۴

تا در رهٔ عشق پاکبازی نکنی
بر خوان صفا دست درازی نکنی
راهت ندهند در خرابات فنا
تا ترک من و مای مجازی نکنی

4

Unless you lose all in the way of love,
You will have no access to the table of purity.
Unless you renounce this false *I* and *we*,
You will not be admitted to the tavern of nonexistence.

۵

تا در پی آنی که نکویت دانند
شایسته و پاک و نیکخویت دانند
در پیش قلندران دم از بحر مزن
زی خویش رهت دهند و جویت دانند

5

If you wish to be known
As good, deserving, pious, and virtuous,
Do not claim of being an ocean before the calenders.
They will lead you to yourself and know you are a stream.

Glossary

Adham, Ibrâhim, one of the early Sufis of Iran.

Alast, Day of, Primordial Day. The day when God called on Adam's family, *alasto berabbekom* am I not your Lord?

Anqâ, Simorgh. *lit.* thirty birds. name of a legendary bird.

Âsaf, Solomon's Vizier.

Azrâ, beloved woman of Vâmaq.

Balkh, Bactria. an ancient country in N.E. Afghanistan.

Bu Said, Abusaid Abulkhayr, name of an Iranian Sufi.

faqr, poverty. in Sufic expression, being needy of God and needless of worldly possessions.

Farhâd, name of a legendary lover who was madly in love with a princess called Shirin.

ghâlia, fragrant substance made of musk and ambergris.

Hâji, a pilgrim to Mecca.

Hajj, pilgrimage to Mecca.

Hallâj, see under Mansur.

Hâtam Tâi, a 6th c. Arab nobleman, known for his generosity.

homâ, a legendary bird, like an eagle, which is believed to bring good luck to anyone on whom it casts its shade.

Jamshid, one of the ancient kings of Iran.

jinn, (plural of **jinni**) in Moslem belief, invisible beings with supernatural powers.

Ka'ba, the House of God in Mecca.

Kâwus, Kay, one of the ancient kings of Iran.

kebla, kiblah, or **qebla**, the direction of the Ka'ba: Moslems face the kebla when they do their daily prayers.

Kermân, a province in S.E. Iran.

kesmat, kismat, kismet, or **qesmat**, fate, appointed lot. predetermined fortune.

Khâja, master. nobleman. Hâfez was called Khâja Hâfez.

khalvat, solitude, privacy, retreat.

khatt, freshly grown hair on a young man's face. writing.

kherqa, a patched cloak a Sufi receives from his master during a ceremony.

Khezr, Elias, he was believed to have reached the fountain of youth (the water of life) in a dark place. in Sufism, he is the leader of the Path, who leads the seekers of the Truth to eternal life.

Khosrow, Kay, one of the ancient kings of Iran.

Khotan, ancient name of East Turkistan, which was famous for its musk and musk-deer.

Kosar, name of a stream in paradise.

Lâ ilâha illa Allah, there is no god but Allah.

Layla, Leili, or **Leili**, beloved lady of Majnun. Layli and Majnun were madly in love with each other.

lo kushef(a), if discovered. in rubái 44, Bidel probably refers to a Koranic verse which includes these words.

Majnun, Layla's lover. *lit*. mad. lunatic.

Mansur Hallâj, name of an Islamic mystic who was hanged in Baghdad for his unorthodox claim of divinity (922 C.E.)

mehrâb, a niche in a mosque to indicate the qebla.

Noruz, Nowruz, Nowrooz, Iranian New Year which begins the first day of spring. *lit*. new day.

orphan pearl, a large pearl found singly in an oyster-shell.

pâluda, sweet beverage made of ice and starch fibers.

Parviz, one of the ancient kings of Iran.

Qadr, Night of, the night when the Qur'an was revealed to Mohammad.

qebla, see under kebla.

qesmat, see under **kesmat**

Qobâd, Kay, father of Kay Kâwus, legendary king of Iran.

Qur'ân, Korân, holy book of Islam.

rend, in Sufism, a *rend* is a person who is heedless to his appearance and to all social formalities and standards but has a pious inner self.

rubáiyát, rubâiyyât, plural of **rubái**, quatrain. A Persian poem composed of four lines, in which the first, second, fourth, (and sometimes even the third) rhyme together.

samâ', music. singing and dancing.

Shâhed, witness. manifestation. a beautiful young person. a perfect man.

Takbir, to say *Allâh-o-Akbar* (God is great). **Chahâr takbir**, or **châr takbir**, four takbirs which are pronounced by Moslems in their prayers for the dead. to say *chahar takbir* means to give up, to renounce completely.

Tus, city in N.E. Iran.

Va in yakâd, a Qur'ânic verse, often recited for protection against an evil eye.

Vâmaq, lover of Azrâ.

ruzi, daily provision determined by God.

Sâqi, cupbearer. wine-server. a handsome youth who served wine in a tavern or in a drinking assembly. in the Sufic symbolism, a spiritual master.

shabestân, harem. dormitory. part of a mosque designed for sleeping or nocturnal prayers.

sharia, religious law.

Shemshâd, a kind of box-tree in Iran.
Shirin, beloved of Farhâd. sweet.
zekr, praise of God. invocation. repeating names of God.

Index of Poets

In **A THOUSAND YEARS OF PERSIAN RUBÁIYÁT**, Reza Saberi translates over 1,500 quatrains from more than a hundred Iranian poets from the beginning of written Persian poetry to the present. In addition to the quatrains of better known poets such as Hâfez, Sa'di, Rumi and Khayyâm, the poems of many poets less-known in the West have been rendered into English for the first time.

A *rubá'i* is a poem in four lines, which is complete in itself and expresses a single feeling or thought in a very concise and elegant language. Their subjects of rubáiyát include divine love, the ecstasy of love, mystical knowledge, and the nature of life and existence. The tradition of sufism, the Irano-Islamic mysticism that advocates the oneness and wholeness of all things and the unity of existence (*vahdate vjud*), is conveyed in the majority of the poems.

Reza Saberi has tried to be as faithful to the original text as is possible in English. His translation can be of special interest for speakers of Persian who try to communicate the sense of beauty of their poetry in the English language. The bilingual format of the book is also very useful for students of Persian language and literature.

REZA SABERI is a linguist, author, translator, educator, lecturer, and philosopher. He was born and raised in Iran. He is the author of six other books including *The Poems of Hafez*. Though he has degrees in English from Iran and United States, he has been in love with Persian poetry throughout his life. He has been living in the United States since 1973 and presently makes his home in Fargo, North Dakota.

هزار سال رباعی فارسی

ترجمهٔ انگلیسی

رضا صابری

چاپ پاژن